STORYTELLING IN OPERA AND MUSICAL THEATER

MUSICAL MEANING AND INTERPRETATION

Robert S. Hatten, *editor*

STORYTELLING IN OPERA AND MUSICAL THEATER

Nina Penner

INDIANA UNIVERSITY PRESS

This book is a publication of

Indiana University Press
Office of Scholarly Publishing
Herman B Wells Library 350
1320 East 10th Street
Bloomington, Indiana 47405 USA

iupress.org

© 2020 by Nina Penner

All rights reserved
No part of this book may be reproduced or utilized in any form or by any means, electronic or mechanical, including photocopying and recording, or by any information storage and retrieval system, without permission in writing from the publisher. The paper used in this publication meets the minimum requirements of the American National Standard for Information Sciences—Permanence of Paper for Printed Library Materials, ANSI Z39.48-1992.

Manufactured in the United States of America

Library of Congress Cataloging-in-Publication Data

Names: Penner, Nina, author.
Title: Storytelling in opera and musical theater / Nina Penner.
Other titles: Musical meaning and interpretation.
Description: Bloomington : Indiana University Press, 2020. | Series: Musical meaning and interpretation | Includes bibliographical references and index.
Identifiers: LCCN 2020010918 (print) | LCCN 2020010919 (ebook) | ISBN 9780253049971 (paperback) | ISBN 9780253049964 (hardback) | ISBN 9780253049988 (ebook)
Subjects: LCSH: Opera. | Musical theater. | Storytelling.
Classification: LCC ML1700 .P426 2020 (print) | LCC ML1700 (ebook) | DDC 782.1—dc23
LC record available at https://lccn.loc.gov/2020010918
LC ebook record available at https://lccn.loc.gov/2020010919

1 2 3 4 5   25 24 23 22 21 20

For Kevin

CONTENTS

Acknowledgments ix

Overture xv

1 What Is a Narrative? 1

2 Telling, Operatically 23

3 Character-Narrators 40

4 Orchestral Narration and Authorial Commentary 89

5 Character-Focused Narration 110

6 Works and Performances 161

7 Performances of Works 184

8 Performances as Works 216

   Finale 243

Bibliography 249

Index 273

ACKNOWLEDGMENTS

I AM MUCH BETTER SUITED TO TALKING ABOUT narratives than telling them. Nevertheless, the only orderly way I can conceive of recognizing the many individuals who have shaped the ideas in this book and have made its publication possible is as a story. It begins with a clarinetist in the pit of the MacMillan Theatre at the University of Toronto. As my husband is fond of relating, he could always pick me out as the one whose head was firmly turned toward the stage whenever I was not required to play. When I decided that I needed to see more of that world, I discovered that the University of Toronto was also home to a large and lively community of opera scholars. The courses I took in my first term of graduate studies in musicology—Linda Hutcheon and Caryl Clark's interdisciplinary opera class and Sherry Lee's aesthetics seminar—anticipate many of the aims and preoccupations of this book. Linda, Caryl, Sherry, and the other members of the Operatics working group provided me with a model of collaborative, interdisciplinary scholarship.

In Trevor Ponech's cinematic narrative seminar at McGill University, I discovered that many of the questions philosophers were asking of cinema had not been given serious attention in opera studies. More than providing me with the topic and methodology for this book, Trevor's class opened up an entire branch of scholarship that was virtually unknown in musicology. There I found my scholarly calling to make work in analytic philosophy better known in my field. I am grateful for Trevor's unwavering belief in my work and continual encouragement to think bigger in terms of its import. In revising my early work on this book, his advice—"be shorter, sharper, and more shocking"—has served me well.

These ideas may never have reached a musicological audience without the mentorship of Lloyd Whitesell. Even when he was less than convinced by some of them, he helped me make the best possible case for their utility to the musicological reader. There have been many times that I have submitted something to him, believing that to be my final version, only to be told that I could do better. Although I can't say that I always appreciated this advice at the time, those extra rounds of revision have often made the difference between a verdict of "revise and resubmit" and an outright rejection.

Edmund Goehring is another scholar who has helped me find a place in musicology. Ed assured me that the discipline could benefit from what I had to say and that there were kindred spirits who would listen. He has been one of my most important interlocutors and incisive critics. His good influence has encouraged me to read more widely, think more broadly, and heed that old narratological adage to "show," whenever possible, rather than "tell."

McGill proved to be an equally fertile intellectual and creative environment in which to develop the ideas for this study. I benefitted from countless conversations with and suggestions from Lloyd Whitesell, Trevor Ponech, Steven Huebner, David Davies, Lars Lih, and Allan Hepburn. David Davies suggested that the ingredients model may have more applicability to opera performance than I had initially assumed, a suggestion that led me to rethink the theoretical foundations of the latter portion of this book.

My tremendously talented peers at McGill and elsewhere provided invaluable intellectual and moral support. Zoey M. Cochran has taught me a tremendous amount about Italian opera and also how to become my own refuge from life's disappointments. The singer-cum-director Russell Wustenberg's belief that these ideas would be of interest to performers has encouraged me to expand my coverage of performance in this book. I am grateful to Harry Thorrington for improving my taste in literature and for sharing his insatiable appetite for life; Alyssa Michaud for discussions about opera and new media and for Sunday *Star Trek*, a highlight of my week; Kristin Franseen for conversations about British literature and queer culture over beers at Benelux; Kyle Kaplan for being a lively interlocutor on any subject; and Margaret Frainier for being the first scholar to apply the ideas in this book and, in so doing, expanding my knowledge of Russian opera. My regular Skype chats with Amanda Hsieh, no matter where in the world we happen to be, have kept me feeling connected and supported.

I finished drafting this book during a postdoctoral fellowship at Duke University, funded by the Social Sciences and Humanities Research Council of Canada. Philip Rupprecht and Cathy Shuman made me feel welcome at Duke and in Durham. Phil helped me navigate the tricky transition from student to scholar through many long conversations at Whole Foods and careful readings of drafts of several chapters of this book. I benefited from conversations with many members of the music faculty, staff, and students, particularly Bryan Gilliam and Karen Messina.

This book's inclusion of more popular forms of musical theater is a product of the seminars I taught at Duke. I am especially grateful to the students of Adaptation and Musical Theatre for reading an early draft of chapter 3 and for suggesting examples for the section on ambiguous cases. That this book contains any musicals from the twenty-first century is largely due to conversations I had with Adam Beskind, Alexus Wells, Chandler Richards,

Brennan Zook, C. J. Cruz, and other dedicated members of my classes and Duke's student-run musical theater company Hoof 'n' Horn.

My arguments have matured through sharing this work with audiences at McGill, Duke, the University of Western Ontario, the College of Charleston Aesthetic Work Group, the Royal Musical Association Music and Philosophy Study Group, the Canadian University Music Society, the Modern Language Association, and the American Society for Aesthetics. Tomas McAuley's tireless stewardship of the RMA MPSG has done much to facilitate productive exchanges between musicology and analytic philosophy.

When I attended my first ASA in 2018, I was overwhelmed by the welcome I received and impressed by the society's commitment to diversity and inclusivity. I thank James Hamilton for his formal response to my paper and for our conversations during the course of the conference. At the business luncheon, I had the good fortune of sitting next to Andrew Kania, who was generous enough to read the entire manuscript. His comments and our exchanges over email have helped me to clarify my arguments, particularly on ontological matters.

One of the challenges of studying a live performance medium is that one is typically able to experience works only a single time. My ability to comment in detail on many of the works I discuss has been made possible by the composers, librettists, and directors who have shared unpublished materials with me. Joel Ivany and Aria Umezawa shared their libretti to *A Little Too Cozy* and *The Barber of Cowtown*. Kevin March generously provided me with the score and an archival video recording of his and Michel Marc Bouchard's *Les feluettes*, granted me permission to reproduce musical examples in this book, and caught several mistakes in chapter 3.

I am grateful to Robert Hatten for understanding what this study is about and for suggesting that, like any good story, it needs an ending. Thanks are also due to my editors at Indiana University Press, Janice Frisch and Allison Chaplin, to the two anonymous reviewers for their thoughtful comments and suggestions, and to Jennifer Crane for her careful copyediting.

The completion of this book has also depended on the support of many people outside of the academy, particularly my parents, Alvin Penner and Ewa Franks, and my partner in opera appreciation and in life, Kevin Bragg. The difference they have made is as great as it is difficult to enumerate. Kevin has spent more time than anyone else discussing the ideas in this book with me. Thank you for the post-opera postmortems and for teaching me that there is more to life than work. I look forward to bringing this story to a close and to starting a new one very soon.

Excerpts from the following works are reprinted by permission of the copyright holders:

"Another National Anthem" and "The Ballad of Booth (Part 1)" from *Assassins*
Words and Music by Stephen Sondheim
© 1991 RILTING MUSIC, INC.
This arrangement © 2019 RILTING MUSIC, INC.
All Rights Administered by WC MUSIC CORP.
All Rights Reserved. Used by Permission.
Reprinted by permission of Hal Leonard LLC.

"Opening" from *Assassins*
Words and Music by Stephen Sondheim
© 1990, 1992 RILTING MUSIC, INC.
This arrangement © 2019 RILTING MUSIC, INC.
All Rights Administered by WC MUSIC CORP.
All Rights Reserved. Used by Permission.
Reprinted by permission of Hal Leonard LLC.

"Scene 16" from *Assassins*
Words and Music by Stephen Sondheim
© 1990 RILTING MUSIC, INC.
This arrangement © 2019 RILTING MUSIC, INC.
All Rights Administered by WC MUSIC CORP.
All Rights Reserved. Used by Permission.
Reprinted by permission of Hal Leonard LLC.

Billy Budd by Benjamin Britten
© 1951, 1952 by Hawkes & Son (London) Ltd.
International Copyright Secured. Reprinted by Permission. All Rights Reserved.

Les feluettes
© 2016 by Kevin March and Michel Marc Bouchard

Gloriana by Benjamin Britten
© 1954 by Hawkes & Son (London) Ltd
International Copyright Secured. Reprinted by Permission. All Rights Reserved.

Owen Wingrave
Music by Benjamin Britten
Libretto by Myfanwy Piper
© 1970, 1995 Faber Music Ltd
Reproduced by permission of the publishers.
All Rights Reserved.

The Rape of Lucretia by Benjamin Britten
© 1946, 1947 by Hawkes & Son (London) Ltd.
International Copyright Secured. Reprinted by Permission. All Rights Reserved.

"No Place Like London," "Poor Thing," and "Epiphany" from *Sweeney Todd*
Words and Music by Stephen Sondheim
© 1978 RILTING MUSIC, INC.
This arrangement © 2019 RILTING MUSIC, INC.
All Rights Administered by WC MUSIC CORP.
All Rights Reserved. Used by Permission.
Reprinted by permission of Hal Leonard LLC.

The Turn of the Screw by Benjamin Britten
© 1955 by Hawkes & Son (London) Ltd
International Copyright Secured. Reprinted by Permission. All Rights Reserved.

"Tonight" from *West Side Story* by Leonard Bernstein and Stephen Sondheim
© 1956, 1957, 1958, 1959 by Amberson Holdings LLCV and Stephen Sondheim.
Copyright Renewed.
Leonard Bernstein Music Publishing Company LLC, Publisher. Boosey & Hawkes, Agent for Rental. International Copyright Secured. Reprinted by Permission. All Rights Reserved.

OVERTURE

Most operas and musicals convey stories. The question of who is doing the telling has not been of particular concern to musicologists, and perhaps understandably so, as most operas lack fictional narrators. For this reason, many scholars have doubted that they ought to be considered narratives. Yet some works of sung drama do have narrators. Even in those that do not, the orchestra often seems to take on a narrator-like role, providing access to characters' inner thoughts and feelings, even suggesting which of them are most deserving of our sympathies.

An example of an opera with especially self-conscious narrative framing is Benjamin Britten and Myfanwy Piper's *The Turn of the Screw* (1954). It begins with a man addressing the audience directly. "It is a curious story," he tells us. "I have it written in faded ink—a woman's hand, governess to two children—long ago."[1] After providing some backstory, he exits the stage and we see the Governess on her way to her new post at Bly. The prologue implies that the rest of the opera is a representation of the Governess's written account. If so, she would be its narrator. Yet her role in the opera is not entirely analogous to that of her counterpart in Henry James's novella. Readers' access to the happenings at Bly are entirely mediated by the Governess in James's story. There are no interjections from an external observer to provide evidence for or against the Governess's assertions that the estate is haunted. In the opera, by contrast, Britten's music draws connections that exceed the protagonist's level of self-awareness. Most troubling are the musical similarities between the Governess's interactions with the children and those of the (real or imagined) ghost Quint. The question of who is telling the story is not trivial in this case. The prologue suggests that it is the Governess, but it is not reasonable to imagine that she is drawing comparisons between herself and her ghostly opponent. Rather, this musical commentary seems to stem from an external source, whether a fictional commentator or the real or implied Benjamin Britten.

The issue of narrative agency becomes even more tangled when one considers performances that depart from the stage directions. In Tom Diamond's production for Opera McGill (2011), the tenor did not exit the stage at the end of the prologue but turned to greet the Governess. After taking a seat on a divan, she proceeded to relive her experiences at Bly with him, her therapist, as part of her "talking cure." Clearly our potential list of tellers ought to also include directors and performers.

Storytelling in Opera and Musical Theater explores how sung forms of drama convey stories. The reader may reasonably wonder at the impulse to revisit this topic in the second decade of the twenty-first century, long after the heyday of music and narrative studies in the 1990s and early 2000s. Musicology's narrative turn roughly corresponded to the emergence of New Musicology, which sought to reorient the discipline away from philology and formalism and toward history and hermeneutics. However, deriving meaning from works of purely instrumental music is not as straightforward as it is with novels or plays. Pioneers in narrative-based approaches to instrumental music, such as Fred Maus and Anthony Newcomb, drew on methods from structuralist narratology (e.g., those of Vladimir Propp, Tzvetan Todorov, and Gérard Genette) regarding musical themes, instruments, and pitches as the agents of their narratives.[2]

In opera studies, one of the most influential contributions has been Carolyn Abbate's *Unsung Voices* (1991). Although predominantly concerned with Wagner, Abbate also criticized initial forays into narrative-based analyses of instrumental music. She argued that narratives consist of more than agents and events; they require tellers and listeners. Yet she rejected Edward T. Cone's suggestion, in *The Composer's Voice* (1974), that the teller may be regarded as the composer. The "voices" of which she speaks are also not those of real-life performers but, rather, consist of elements of the music itself, personified into fictional narrating agents.[3]

Philip Rupprecht's *Britten's Musical Language* (2001) brought narrative and speech-act theory to bear on the work of a twentieth-century composer. His investigation of the ways in which Britten used his orchestra both to comment on the characters and to express their points of view was an inspiration for this study.

Over the past three decades, there have been many applications of narrative theory to the interpretation of individual works. What we lack is a theory of storytelling in the musical theater comparable to Byron Almén's *A Theory of Musical Narrative* (2008), concerning instrumental music, or the dozens of theories of narration in the novel or the cinema. What a theoretically focused study offers that the collection of close readings does not is a more critical and rigorous investigation of concepts such as narrative and point of view. By exploring their application to a wider range of repertoire, I develop terms and approaches that can illuminate works not examined in this study.

I revisit some topics that have been addressed by the first wave of music and narrative studies, offering, for example, a different answer to the question of what a narrative is. I also ask some new questions concerning performance. More recently, musicology has shifted attention from composers and their works to performers and performances.[4] Most prior studies of narrative in opera and musical theater confine their inquiry to the contents of the score and libretto, overlooking the realities of what happens to these texts in the rehearsal room.[5] *Storytelling in Opera and Musical Theater* offers the first sustained meditation on how the performers' choices affect not only who is telling the story but what story is being told.

Another reason to revisit the topic of opera and narrative is to respond to the rich body of scholarship on narrative and fiction that has emerged in Anglo-American philosophy in the last fifteen years.[6] This work remains virtually unknown in musicology in spite of the discipline's increasing engagement with philosophy during this same period. That music is largely absent from existing philosophical discussions of narrative is surely one reason. Another lies in wider disciplinary allegiances within the academy.

Two discernable traditions emerged within Western philosophy during the twentieth century. Anglophone musicology has developed robust connections with the *continental* tradition while remaining rather separate from work in anglophone philosophy, most of which is in the *analytic* tradition.[7] The typical approach to differentiating these traditions is through methodological contrasts. For instance, Stephen Davies has characterized continental philosophy as "subjectively focused," involving "the creation of all-encompassing, elaborate metaphysical systems, or . . . elucidating and comparing the theories of the 'great men' of the tradition." By contrast, he describes analytic philosophy as committed to "objective, clear argument and to an interpersonal, empirically oriented approach," one that "eschews grand theories in favor of treating specific philosophical issues and problems in a piecemeal or cumulative fashion."[8]

Today, many philosophers on both sides of this divide are working toward a reconciliation. As David Davies has observed, focusing on methodological differences hinders a productive exchange of ideas between these traditions.[9] He recommends parsing the distinction between continental and analytic philosophy in terms of the body of work with which scholars are predominantly engaging. For continental philosophy, that body of work includes writings by Edmund Husserl, Martin Heidegger, Henri Bergson, Maurice Merleau-Ponty, Walter Benjamin, Theodor W. Adorno, Michel Foucault, Jacques Derrida, and Gilles Deleuze. Accordingly, continental philosophy has focused on phenomenological questions about the experience of music, music and identity, and music's relationship to politics.

The analytic tradition descends from work in the philosophy of language by Gottlob Frege, Bertrand Russell, G. E. Moore, Ludwig Wittgenstein, Willard Van Orman Quine, and Saul Kripke. With the exception of Wittgenstein, none of these thinkers had much interest in art. It was only in the latter half of the twentieth century that aesthetics became a significant concern for analytic philosophers. Peter Kivy (1934–2017) was one of the first philosophers in this tradition to write predominantly about music. Other analytic philosophers who have made substantial contributions to the philosophy of music include Jerrold Levinson, Roger Scruton, Jenefer Robinson, Stephen Davies, David Davies, and Theodore Gracyk. Central concerns of these philosophers have included the nature of musical works and their relationship to performances, musical expression and meaning, and music's relationship to the emotions.

Storytelling in Opera and Musical Theater illustrates what musicology stands to gain from taking a greater interest in analytic philosophy. I show how recent work on narrative, the nature of musical works, and musical and theatrical performance can help us understand how operas and musicals tell stories. More unusually, this book also shows how philosophy could benefit from musicology. Historically, work in the area of music and philosophy by music scholars has proceeded in two directions. There are many studies about the historical influence of philosophers on composers and vice versa. For example, much has been written about Schopenhauer's influence on Wagner, particularly on *Tristan und Isolde* (1865), and on Wagner's influence on Nietzsche's early writings, such as *The Birth of Tragedy* (1872).[10] There are also many studies that use philosophical theories to interpret a work or corpus, where the theory may not have influenced the production of the works under consideration. A recent example in this vein is J. P. E. Harper-Scott's use of Alain Badiou's concept of an *event* in *Ideology in Britten's Operas* (2018).

Storytelling in Opera and Musical Theater takes a different approach. I survey existing theories of narrative and performance that have been developed to describe other art forms (literature, cinema, spoken theater, instrumental music) and examine how well these theories describe opera and musical theater. When I encounter incongruities, I propose revisions to existing models or explore alternatives. This study, thus, involves two kinds of analysis employed in tandem. The first is the kind of analysis for which analytic philosophy is named: the analysis of concepts such as narrative, point of view, work, and performance. The second is the sort of analysis more familiar to music scholarship: the analysis of operas, musicals, and performances thereof.

The influence of analytic philosophy also extends to the book's structure. As an argument-driven book, it will be most accessible if read in sequence. Arguments build from uncontroversial observations, developing complexity and nuance gradually through the consideration of counterexamples. My choice and use of examples mirrors philosophical or theoretical studies more closely than it does historical or hermeneutic ones by musicologists. Rather than focusing on a few closely related case studies, I illustrate my theory of operatic storytelling with illustrations from works from many different periods, styles, and genres. In most cases, I have included multiple shorter examples of a single phenomenon rather than one lengthier one, to make the book accessible to readers with diverse areas of interest and expertise.

The writing style has also been influenced by current work in analytic philosophy, which aims at clarity and precision without resorting to jargon. I have consciously avoided the pseudo-Greek neologisms and mysterious diagrams that plagued narratology of the 1970s and 1980s. Gregory Currie's *Narratives and Narrators* (2010) demonstrated that something substantive could be said about narrative that is also a pleasure to read. This book is my attempt to offer something analogous about opera and musical theater that would be accessible to scholars and practitioners without backgrounds in narrative theory or philosophy.

As its title suggests, this study bridges another gap between two discourses that have, historically, had little to do with one another. The separation of opera and musical theater may be sensible in some domains, such as the economics and logistics of how performances are produced. Yet in terms of the materials that librettists, composers, and directors are working with, operas and musicals are broadly comparable. The main differences in medium stem from the different types of voices required to perform them. Since live performances of opera still proceed largely without the assistance of electronic amplification, singers require some degree of classical training to be heard over a full orchestra. By contrast, most roles in musicals are accessible to a wider range of vocal techniques and abilities.[11] These differences in personnel often translate into differences in musical idiom, with operas drawing more heavily on European high art traditions and musicals being more closely aligned with the popular music of the period.[12]

Spoken dialogue plays a more important role in musical theater than it does in opera, but there are many exceptions. *Singspiel* (e.g., *Die Zauberflöte* [1791]) and *opéra comique* (e.g., *Carmen* [1875]) are genres of opera that contain spoken dialogue instead of recitative, and in the past few decades, an increasing number of musical-theater composers have opted for through-composed formats. Most *rock operas* (e.g., *Rent* [1996]) and *megamusicals* (e.g., *Les Misérables* [1980]) contain a minimum of spoken dialogue, as does the hip-hop sensation *Hamilton* (2015). Dance also plays a more important role in musicals than it does in operas, though *Carmen* (and, indeed, much French opera) provides an exception to this rule as well. In light of such exceptions, my initial attempts to define what separates operatic storytelling from other forms that involve singing (chap. 2) were unable to differentiate operas from musicals. Initially regarding this as a problem, I eventually decided to consider it as an opportunity to explore what might be gained from studying these art forms side by side.

In the performance-focused chapters, I discuss productions that I have seen live and those I have experienced only through video recordings. I also mention a few film adaptations of operas and musicals, works that were shot in a film studio or on location, without a live audience, typically with the actors lip-synching to a recording of themselves or their voice doubles. Although opera began as a medium for live performance, twenty-first-century enthusiasts are just as likely to engage with this art form in the cinema or on their televisions or computer screens. Concerns about the fundamental differences between the experience of live versus mediated forms of opera can be addressed through a sensitivity to the medium-specific features of these various ways of presenting and consuming sung drama.[13] Furthermore, limiting myself to performances that I have seen live would have hindered my ability to place the productions I discuss in a performing tradition. Another advantage of recordings is the potential for repeat engagement, essential to detailed analysis. Discussing productions that are available on DVD or for online streaming also allows readers the ability to view these works themselves and thus to evaluate my assertions against their own experiences.

In the first wave of writings on music and narrative, there was a tendency to apply existing theories of narrative to music without considering the ways in which those theories have been shaped by the author's target medium.[14] For instance, the relative ubiquity of narrators in literary narratives led some scholars to doubt that works of theater, including operas and musicals, are properly understood as narratives. I dispel such doubts in chapter 1, which argues that narratives are utterances intentionally made to convey a story, whether through telling or through showing. In considering what a story is, I focus on the limit case of instrumental music.

Readers uninterested in whether the category of *narrative* includes Beethoven's Fifth Symphony may wish to proceed directly to chapter 2, where

I explore the medium-specific features of opera and musical theater through comparisons with other narrative art forms that involve singing, such as songs, oratorios, and cantatas. To differentiate sung drama from spoken plays and nonmusical films, I argue that singing is a normal mode of communication and expression in the fictional worlds of operas and musicals. In so doing, I argue against Abbate's suggestion that if one entered the world of an opera, one would predominantly hear speech, not song.[15]

Although fictional narrators are not essential to narration, as I define it, some works of sung drama do have such narrators. Chapter 3 concerns the roles character-narrators play in operas and musicals, defining several common storytelling situations. Another important medium-specific feature of musical theater emerges from this discussion: Whereas novels often invite readers to imagine that there is a fictional source for the entire text we are reading, few works of sung drama support analogous imaginings. Even in operas that have character-narrators, such as *The Turn of the Screw*, one is not encouraged to regard those characters as being responsible for the orchestral music. Indeed, the orchestra often seems to know more than any character in the story.

For this reason, the orchestra's role is often likened to that of a narrator. Despite the prevalence of these sorts of comparisons, the concept of the *orchestral narrator* has been subject to little theoretical investigation. How far should we take comparisons to literary narrators? Is it appropriate to imagine that the orchestra is responsible for presenting the opera to us, or is its role more akin to that of the chorus of ancient Greek tragedy, which merely comments on the action and guides the audience's attention? Does the orchestra always function in a narrator-like capacity, or does it do so only at certain moments? Chapter 4 addresses these and other questions concerning orchestral commentary in operas and musicals. Although most scholars view the orchestral narrator as a fictional entity, I argue that at least some acts of orchestral narration are more coherently understood as authorial commentary.

The orchestra can also be used to express characters' points of view. Chapter 5 exposes several commonplace but faulty assumptions about point of view: the tendency to conflate the focal character with the narrator; the assumption that character-focused narration invariably leads to identification, sympathy, or empathy; and the suspicion that harboring such feelings for characters who commit morally reprehensible acts has a deleterious effect on one's moral character.

In chapter 6, my focus shifts from the work of librettists and composers to that of directors, conductors, and singers. Readers with more practical concerns may wish to begin the book at this point. Since my interest is in productions that depart significantly from the score and libretto, operatic examples outweigh those from musical theater. Such departures are more common in the opera house, which relies more heavily on historical repertory. The impulse to rework an opera's libretto or score arises not only from concerns of monotony but, in many of the examples I discuss, from a need to rectify aspects of the work—sexism, racism, colonialist attitudes—that may be offensive to audiences today. Many musicals are plagued by similar problems, but until recently, few directors working in commercial musical theater have attempted more than minor revisions to address them.[16] However, given that Broadway and the West End are increasingly relying on revivals of musicals from the so-called Golden Age (from roughly *Show Boat* [1927] to the end of 1950s), and audiences are expecting these shows to reflect current attitudes about race, gender, and sexuality, it is reasonable to expect more revisionist approaches in the future.

Chapter 6 identifies some problems with the prevailing way of understanding the work-performance relationship in opera studies, the *two-text model*. This account is unable to explain how seeing a performance of an opera is to see the opera itself. It also has difficulty explaining the motivations behind productions that deviate from the score or libretto. Such productions also constitute exceptions to the standard philosophical account of performance in the Western art music tradition, the *classical paradigm*. I argue that the philosopher James Hamilton's *ingredients model*, developed for spoken theater, does a better job of describing productions containing substantial revisions to the score or libretto or that use these texts to tell different stories or convey different artistic or political points.[17]

Yet Hamilton's suggestion that theater performances are *never* performances of preexisting works is untrue of opera and musical theater. Amid recent experiments at revising the score and adding new ingredients, many directors are still guided by the ideology of *Werktreue* (fidelity to the work). I propose that there are two paradigms of opera and musical theater performance today. Some productions can be understood according to the classical paradigm: The production is primarily intended to offer perceptual experiences of a preexisting work. Accordingly, the performers pursue a high degree of fidelity to its score and libretto. Other productions are better understood along the lines Hamilton proposes: The performers regard libretti and scores as merely optional ingredients. Rather than focusing on conveying the artistic statements of the composer and librettist, the performers are primarily concerned with making a statement of their own.

Throughout this book, I use the classical paradigm and ingredients model as the primary means of categorizing opera and musical-theater productions.

Although these categories may seem analogous to the more familiar opposition between traditional or Werktreue productions and radical or *Regieoper* ones, they are not precisely equivalent. There are several reasons why I have appropriated these terms from philosophy rather than employing the ones common to opera criticism. First, the term *Regieoper* (director's opera) implies that this directorial approach is primarily found in German-speaking countries, which is no longer the case. It is also predominantly used by critics in a pejorative or honorific sense (depending on the critic's predilections), rather than as a means of identifying productions that are guided by a coherent set of artistic practices. To the extent that there is anything in common among productions that are commonly classified as Regieoper, it is their "look" (non-naturalistic, set in the "wrong" period), as opposed to their "sound," which is usually indistinguishable from more "traditional" productions. By contrast, the classical paradigm and the ingredients model describe the performance's visual and sonic components.

The final two chapters explore what happens to an opera or musical's narrative when the performers decide not to follow the performing directions. The examples in chapter 7 involve deviations from the stage directions that are designed to bring spectators to a deeper understanding of the work being performed. Through his use of lighting and placement of musicians, Peter Sellars enhanced Wagner's musical strategies of character-focused narration in his production of *Tristan und Isolde* (Opéra national de Paris, 2006). Tim Albery's *Billy Budd* (English National Opera, 1988) and Tom Diamond's *Turn of the Screw* drew attention to the narrative framing of these works and the way their frames raise questions of narrative reliability. All of these productions involved research into the historical influences on the creation of the work being performed and helped bring these influences to the attention of their audiences.

Chapter 8 considers directors whose work is motivated less by concerns of fidelity than by a desire to present performances that accord with the interests and concerns of their audience. I discuss productions that remove character-narrators and insert new ones as well as those that reframe a portion of the dramatic action as a character's dream or hallucination, such as Joachim Herz's 1964 film adaptation of Wagner's *Der fliegende Holländer*. Another way of contending with the offensive political content of many of Wagner's works is to alter his recommended lines of sympathy. Inspired by an essay by the philosopher Ernst Bloch, Katharina Wagner's production of *Die Meistersinger von Nürnberg* (Bayreuth, 2007) upheld Beckmesser as the true artist of the future while linking Sachs's and Walther's increasing artistic conservatism with the rise of fascism. Finally, I consider the issue of how to attract new audiences to opera and musical theater by examining Deaf West Theatre's success at bringing musical theater to a community commonly assumed to be excluded from the appreciation of this art form.

Storytelling in Opera and Musical Theater offers the first systematic exploration of how sung forms of drama tell stories in comparison to novels, plays, and films. I expose problematic assumptions underlying prevailing accounts of narrative and point of view in music scholarship and develop alternatives. I also make fine-grained distinctions between types of narrators and the roles of the orchestra and introduce terminology with which to talk about them.

By considering two art forms that have, historically, been ignored in theories of narrative, this book also contributes to philosophy and literary theory. Bringing opera and musical theater to debates about the necessity of narrators reveals additional exceptions to the claim that all narratives have fictional narrators. This book also offers the first detailed examination of musical means of aligning spectators with characters' points of view.

Debates about the nature of musical works and musical performance have also proceeded without a serious consideration of opera and musical theater. Drawing attention both to historical practices, such as aria substitution, and to more recent directorial interventions, I show how opera and musical theater constitute exceptions to the prevailing philosophical account of performance in the Western art music tradition.

I also consider problems singers and directors confront on a daily basis, such as what to do about Wagner's Jewish caricatures or the racism of Orientalist operas. More generally, I reflect on how centuries-old works remain meaningful to contemporary audiences and have the power to attract new, more diverse audiences to opera and musical theater. By exploring how practitioners past and present have addressed these issues, I offer suggestions for how opera and musical theater can continue to entertain and enrich the lives of audiences in the twenty-first century.

Notes

1. Myfanwy Piper, *The Turn of the Screw* (libretto), in *The Operas of Benjamin Britten: The Complete Librettos*, ed. David Herbert (New York: Columbia University Press, 1979), 233.

2. Fred E. Maus, "Music as Narrative," *Indiana Theory Review* 12 (1991): 1–41; Anthony Newcomb, "Narrative Archetypes and Mahler's Ninth Symphony," in *Music and Text: Critical Inquiries*, ed. Steven Paul Scher (Cambridge: Cambridge University Press, 1992), 118–36.

3. Carolyn Abbate, *Unsung Voices: Opera and Musical Narrative in the Nineteenth Century* (Princeton: Princeton University Press, 1991), 28, 13.

4. In opera studies, much of this work has been on historical singers: Suzanne Aspden, *The Rival Sirens: Performance and Identity on Handel's Operatic Stage* (Cambridge: Cambridge University Press, 2013); Martha Feldman, *The Castrato: Reflections on Natures and Kinds* (Berkeley: University of California Press, 2015); Roger Freitas, *Portrait of a Castrato: Politics, Patronage, and Music in the Life of Atto Melani* (Cambridge: Cambridge University Press, 2009); Karen Henson, *Opera Acts: Singers and Performance in the Late Nineteenth Century* (Cambridge: Cambridge University Press, 2015); Patricia Howard, *The Modern Castrato: Gaetano Guadagni and the Coming of a New Operatic Age* (New York: Oxford University Press, 2014); Hilary Poriss, *Changing the Score: Arias, Prima Donnas, and the Authority of Performance* (Oxford: Oxford University Press, 2009); Susan Rutherford, *The Prima Donna and Opera, 1815–1930* (Cambridge: Cambridge University Press, 2006); Susan Rutherford, *Verdi Opera, Women* (Cambridge: Cambridge University Press, 2013); Kimberly White, *Female Singers on the French Stage, 1830–1848* (Cambridge: Cambridge University Press, 2018). Most treatments of opera staging focus on continental Europe: Evan Baker, *From the Score to the Stage: An Illustrated History of Continental Opera Production and Staging* (Chicago: University of Chicago Press, 2013); Patrick Carnegy, *Wagner and the Art of the Theatre* (New Haven: Yale University Press, 2006); Gundula Kreuzer, *Curtain, Gong, Steam: Wagnerian Technologies of Nineteenth-Century Opera* (Berkeley: University of California Press, 2018); David J. Levin, *Unsettling Opera: Staging Mozart, Verdi, Wagner, and Zemlinsky* (Chicago: University of Chicago Press, 2007); John A. Rice, *Mozart on the Stage* (Cambridge: Cambridge University Press, 2009).

5. Exceptions include Mauro Calcagno, *From Madrigal to Opera: Monteverdi's Staging of the Self* (Berkeley: University of California Press, 2012); Yayoi Uno Everett, *Reconfiguring Myth and Narrative in Contemporary Opera: Osvaldo Golijov, Kaija Saariaho, John Adams, and Tan Dun* (Bloomington: Indiana University Press, 2015).

6. See, for example, Gregory Currie, *Narratives and Narrators: A Philosophy of Stories* (Oxford: Oxford University Press, 2010); Berys Gaut, *A Philosophy of Cinematic Art* (Cambridge: Cambridge University Press, 2010), ch. 5; Andrew Kania, "Against the Ubiquity of Fictional Narrators," *Journal of Aesthetics and Art Criticism* 63, no. 1 (2005): 47–54; Derek Matravers, *Fiction and Narrative* (Oxford: Oxford University Press, 2014); George M. Wilson, *Seeing Fictions in Film: The Epistemology of Movies* (Oxford: Oxford University Press, 2011).

7. Music is not alone: A similar tale may be told about theater studies and cinema studies prior to the 1980s. On theater studies, refer to David Z. Saltz, "Why Performance Theory Needs Philosophy," *Journal of Dramatic Theory and Criticism* 16, no. 1 (2001): 149–54.

8. Stephen Davies, "Analytic Philosophy and Music," in *Routledge Companion to Philosophy and Music*, ed. Theodore Gracyk and Andrew Kania (London: Routledge, 2011), 294–95.

9. David Davies, "Analytic Philosophy of Music," in *Oxford Handbook of Western Music and Philosophy*, ed. Tomas McAuley, Jerrold Levinson, and Nanette Nielsen (Oxford: Oxford University Press, forthcoming).

10. On Schopenhauer's influence on Wagner, see Eric Chafe, *The Tragic and the Ecstatic: The Musical Revolution of Wagner's Tristan und Isolde* (New York: Oxford University Press, 2005). On Wagner's influence on Nietzsche, see Katherine Fry, "Nietzsche, *Tristan und Isolde*, and the Analysis of Wagnerian Rhythm," *Opera Quarterly* 29, no. 3–4 (2014): 253–76.

11. Some roles in musicals do require classical technique; for example, the high tessitura and elaborate coloratura of Cunégonde's "Glitter and Be Gay" from *Candide* (1956) and Johanna's "Green Finch and Linnet Bird" from *Sweeney Todd* (1979). However, most of the other roles in these works were intended for singers who are not classically trained.

12. Derek B. Scott, "Musical Theater(s)," in *Oxford Handbook of Opera*, ed. Helen M. Greenwald (New York: Oxford University Press, 2014), 53–72, discusses stylistic differences between opera and musical theater in more depth.

13. Opera scholars who have expressed concerns about the reliance on recordings include Carolyn Abbate, "Music—Drastic or Gnostic?" *Critical Inquiry* 30, no. 3 (2004): 505–36; James Treadwell, "Reading and Staging Again," *Cambridge Opera Journal* 10, no. 2 (1998): 205, 209. Like Nicholas Cook, *Beyond the Score: Music as Performance* (New York: Oxford University Press, 2013), 327–29, I see at least as many benefits as drawbacks.

14. Byron Almén, *A Theory of Musical Narrative* (Bloomington: Indiana University Press, 2008), 11–13, makes a similar point.

15. Abbate, *Unsung Voices*, 123. This line of thinking has also influenced writing on the musical; for example, Scott McMillin, *The Musical as Drama* (Princeton: Princeton University Press, 2006), 126.

16. Exceptions include Diane Paulus's deceptively titled *The Gershwins' Porgy and Bess* (American Repertory Theater, 2011), which attempted to rectify the work's racial stereotypes through textual revisions by Suzan-Lori Parks and a new musical arrangement by Diedre L. Murray. Sam Mendes's *Cabaret* (Donmar Warehouse, 1993), pulled Cliff out of the closet by revising the script and adding the songs Kander and Ebb composed for Bob Fosse's 1972 film adaptation. James Leve, *Kander and Ebb* (New Haven: Yale University Press, 2009), 72–76.

17. The first application of the two-text model to opera was Levin, *Unsettling Opera*, 11. David Davies coined the term *classical paradigm* in his *Philosophy of the Performing Arts* (Malden: Wiley-Blackwell, 2011). James Hamilton presented the ingredients model in *The Art of Theater* (Malden: Wiley-Blackwell, 2007), 31–33.

STORYTELLING IN OPERA AND MUSICAL THEATER

1

WHAT IS A NARRATIVE?

ALTHOUGH MUSIC SCHOLARS HAVE PUT NARRATIVE THEORY TO many innovative uses, when it comes to defining what a narrative is, we have largely left the task to our colleagues in literary theory. Based on their stipulations about the necessary components of narratives, some, such as Carolyn Abbate, have even come to doubt that the category has much applicability to music. Others, such as Byron Almén, have resisted the hegemony of literature in narratology, proposing new ways of conceptualizing narrative that include not only operas and musicals but also most works of instrumental music. Despite their differences, both camps understand narratives as merely the products of composers' labors (sound structures, in the case of instrumental works). Thus, narrative status depends primarily on the structural features of those products, such as contrast and discontinuity. In this chapter, I argue that works are better conceived as processes than as products alone, and I explore the consequences of this view for our definition of narrative.

Narrative in Music Scholarship

The first wave of work on narrative in music scholarship largely took their definitions from structuralist narratology, particularly Gérard Genette's *Narrative Discourse* (1983; 1972 in the original French) and Seymour Chatman's *Story and Discourse* (1978). Genette and Chatman argue that a narrative is not a mere sequence of events; it requires a narrator and the ability to distinguish the work's *story*, the events of which it is comprised, from its *discourse*, the way in which the events are told by the narrator.

Applying this definition to music in *Unsung Voices* (1991), Carolyn Abbate observes the difficulty of making a similar sort of distinction, even in an opera. Most operas convey stories, but in few cases are we invited to imagine that there is a fictional entity responsible for presenting the entire story to us. Abbate concludes that operas are not narratives, but they may contain "moments of narration" where the story-discourse distinction can be perceived through discontinuities within the score or between the score and the libretto.[1] The narrator of musical narratives remains unclear in Abbate's account, however. As she repeatedly informs her readers, the voices of which she speaks are not those of the historical persons who created the work, nor the implied author, nor even the singers who make the work perceptually accessible.[2] Through a process of elimination, these voices must refer to features of the work's structure.

This suspicion is borne out in the evidence Abbate presents for or against a work being a narrative. Her argument that the epilogue to Paul Dukas's symphonic poem *L'apprenti sorcier* (1897) constitutes a moment of narration rests on the appearance of the main theme in rhythmic augmentation. Abbate argues that the epilogue serves an analogous function to the quotation marks encasing the sorcerer's words at the end of the poem on which Dukas's work is based, Goethe's *Der Zauberlehrling* (1797). Both imply the presence of a "third person narrator" who recounts the events to us.[3] This storyteller is internal to the work's structure. Absent from Abbate's discussion is any consideration of the *work's* context of performance: what its storyteller (Dukas) was attempting to accomplish with *L'apprenti sorcier*, whether he was successful, and how his audiences interpreted his work. Did they imagine an apprentice sorcerer's futile attempts to put a stop to his spell, or did they regard the work as a purely abstract composition?

In the wake of *Unsung Voices* and other high-profile rejections of the possibility that musical works could constitute narratives, music scholars treaded more cautiously with regard to the narrative-definitional question, typically avoiding it altogether.[4] An exception is Byron Almén, a music theorist who is not merely content to say that musical works are *like* narratives or that we may gain insights about them by regarding them as such. In *A Theory of Musical Narrative* (2008), he argues that musical works *are* narratives and presents a new "medium-independent" definition to support this claim. For Almén, a narrative consists of a hierarchy, established within a system of signs, that is subject to change over time—change that a listener interprets as a change in a cultural hierarchy of some sort.[5]

Almén outlines a method for interpreting virtually any musical work as a narrative. The first step is to identify the salient features of the music (pitches, keys, themes, instruments) that are brought into conflict. One observes the hierarchy in which they are found at the beginning and tracks changes to that hierarchy throughout the composition. Next, one classifies one's findings according to the narrative archetypes that the literary theorist Northrop Frye proposed in his *Anatomy of Criticism* (1957): romance, tragedy, comedy, and irony (resulting from the permutations of order/transgression and victory/defeat). Finally, the analyst interprets these musical conflicts as representing conflicts taking place within a single agent, between agents or groups thereof, or between an individual and a group.

To highlight how his theory builds on existing practices in music theory and musicology, Almén illustrates it with discussions of preexisting analyses representing a variety of interpretive approaches. One such example is Susan McClary's interpretation of the first movement of Bach's Brandenburg Concerto no. 5 (1721). McClary focuses on the relationship between the harpsichord and the rest of the players (the *ripieno*, or large ensemble, as well as the other soloists). Bach's concerto initially appears to be for flute and violin, with the harpsichord performing its customary "service role" as part of the continuo. Before long, the harpsichord begins to assert itself beyond its station, eventually "hijacking" the piece by inserting an inordinately long solo capriccio in which it "unleashes elements of chaos, irrationality, and noise until finally it blurs almost entirely the sense of key, meter, and form upon which eighteenth-century style depends."[6] Only then does it deign to allow the ripieno to reenter and restore order with its performance of the final ritornello.

McClary interprets the conflict between the harpsichord and the rest of the instrumentalists as representing the conflict between the growing individualism of the bourgeoisie in Bach's time and European society, which was still largely under absolute rule. As Almén observes, a more typical concerto from this period would represent individualism and social stability as corealizable through either "the appropriate submission of individual aspiration for the good of society" or "the reconciliation of the apparently contradictory aims of the individual and society."[7] Bach's concerto, McClary argues, represents individualism that exceeds social acceptability. That the harpsichord eventually yields to the ripieno may appear to represent the individual submitting to the greater good of society, as in Almén's first scenario. Nevertheless, McClary observes that "the subversive elements of the piece seem far too powerful to be contained in so conventional a manner."[8]

Since the narrative resulting from Almén's method is largely the listener's confection, many different narratives may result from the same conflict. "Another analyst," he speculates, "might have viewed the intrusive harpsichord music as a threat that is ultimately excised by the final ritornello—a romance narrative of the successful quest, if you will, rather than a comic narrative of a blocked society renewed or an ironic narrative of a fractured society."[9]

Almén's stipulation that the work must establish a hierarchy that undergoes change specifies some structural features the music must possess in order to be considered a narrative. But unlike Abbate's definition, Almén's may not be solely dependent on the work's structure. Although he rejects Abbate's requirement of a storyteller, he affirms the importance of a listener who interprets the work as a narrative.[10] Precisely what role listeners play in determining a work's narrative status remains unclear, however. It may be that McClary, by interpreting Brandenburg Concerto no. 5 in the way she did, makes it a narrative. If that is correct, the work is a narrative for McClary, but it would not have been a narrative for Peter Kivy, who rejected the validity of such interpretations.[11] Alternatively, Almén may be arguing that the Fifth Brandenburg Concerto is a narrative, even if certain listeners refuse to regard it as such, because it is a work to which it is appropriate to adopt a method like the one he outlines. Given Almén's lack of interest in authorial intentions or historical practices of music listening, what makes this approach appropriate appears to be structural features capable of supporting such interpretations.

Texts and Works

To understand what separates the foregoing definitions from the one I will put forth in the following section, it will be necessary to expose some of the assumptions about the nature of musical works underlying these definitions. Inspired by French literary theory, particularly the work of Roland Barthes, New Musicologists such as Abbate and McClary moved away from regarding their subjects of study as *works* and began to think of them as *texts*. This is not to say that opera scholars abandoned the study of scores and focused instead on libretti. What Barthes seems to have meant by the work-text opposition was the difference between interpreting what one is reading or listening to in light of the historical circumstances of its production and approaching it as a mere sequence of words or sounds, which could be interpreted in any way one pleased.[12]

Another way of understanding the opposition between texts and works is through the contrast between products and processes. As a text or product, a work of instrumental music is merely a sound structure.[13] As a process, by contrast, it also includes all factors that contributed to its production, such as the performers, instruments, and performing circumstances for which it was written, and influences both artistic and nonartistic (e.g., religious or philosophical beliefs or events in the composer's private life).

Barthes preferred texts to works because of his interest in maximizing interpretive freedom. Reducing works to mere texts licensed musicologists to put forth interpretations that were implausible accounts of composers' intentions. It is unlikely that Bach's compositional choices were guided by the values of freedom and individualism underpinning McClary's interpretation of Brandenburg Concerto no. 5.[14] For those interested in understanding works in light of the actual historical circumstances of their creation, one is better off regarding them as processes—or at least as contextualized products—rather than as mere texts.[15] If a work is a process, determining whether it is a narrative involves not only analyzing its structural features but also investigating how and why it was created, including whether its author intended it to tell or present a story.

The relevance of the composer's intentions to interpretation remains a contentious topic in musicology and music theory. One of the larger aims of this study is to rehabilitate the figure of the author in music scholarship; depending on the object of appreciation, that may be the composer, librettist, director, or performer. As I have argued in more depth elsewhere, commitments to the "intentional fallacy" and the "death of the author" fostered the kind of interpretive freedom musicologists of the 1980s and 1990s were seeking but failed to align with the discipline's renewed interest in history in the past two decades.[16]

One of the reasons for this incongruity between theory and practice is a lack of awareness of more sophisticated forms of intentionalism that have been proposed in response to the criticisms of Barthes and the authors of "The Intentional Fallacy," William K. Wimsatt and Monroe C. Beardsley. The most robust of these accounts have come from philosophers working in the analytic philosophical tradition. Paisley Livingston's *Art and Intention* (2005) provides a clear and comprehensive discussion of what intentions are and the roles they play in the creation and interpretation of art. He defines an intention as an attitude one takes toward a plan of action. In contrast to desiring or wanting, intending involves being "settled upon executing that plan, or upon trying to execute it."[17] Even so, it is possible to be unaware of or mistaken about some of the intentions motivating one's actions. As action plans rather than actions themselves, intentions are subject to revision. Even when we decide to act, we may be unsuccessful in realizing our intentions.

The possibility of author failure is a serious problem for forms of intentionalism that equate the content and meaning of a work with authorial intentions (*absolute* or *extreme intentionalism*).[18] One response to this problem is to eschew reference to the real author in favor of an *implied author*, an entity that is constructed by the reader or listener through his or her engagement with the work. The concept of the implied author originates from *The Rhetoric of*

Fiction (1961) by the literary critic Wayne C. Booth. In philosophy, this interpretive approach is commonly referred to as *hypothetical intentionalism*, a term coined by Jerrold Levinson.[19] Hypothetical intentionalism may serve the purposes of some philosophers and theorists but is unable to explain the attention music historians pay to authors' sketches, notebooks, letters, and interviews. Such sources inform us about the actual author's intentions and actions, not those of the implied author. Throughout this study, the intentions to which I will be referring are those of the actual persons responsible for creating the works under consideration.[20]

Other philosophers, such as Livingston, have responded to the author fallibility problem by defining more moderate forms of real-author intentionalism. According to *moderate actual intentionalism*, authorial intentions determine meaning only in cases where they are successfully realized in the artistic product. Success is determined by assessing whether the intention and the features of the product "mesh." Not only does meshing entail a degree of consistency, "but [it] also carries the implication of a stronger condition involving relevance and integration: if there is a sense in which an extraneous hypothesis is consistent with data, but bears no meaningful, integrative relation with them, we would say that the two do not mesh."[21]

Another common objection to intentionalism is the putative impossibility of knowing another's intentions, particularly if one's subject died hundreds of years ago. In some cases, all we may have is a score. We may not even know who its author was. That there are limits to what may be known does not justify abandoning the search for what can be known. Inquiring into the artist's intentions does not require mind-reading abilities but merely the sorts of activities musicologists routinely engage in: studying the finished product, evidence about how it was produced, and the various influences on its production, with an aim to understanding how and why it possesses the features it does.

One may also be concerned that a commitment to real-author intentionalism unduly restricts the creativity of the interpreter. If one's primary aim in engaging with a work is to display one's creativity or to maximize one's enjoyment, one may wish to heed Barthes's call to regard that work as a product rather than as a process. But if one wishes to understand the historical influences on its creation, inquiring into the actual author's intentions ought to be a component of the interpretive process. Even so, not all questions about art require intentionalist explanations. One question that does, I argue, is the question of whether a work is a narrative, as this is a question of the work's "category of art."[22]

A Moderate Intentionalist Definition of Narrative

What separates Jane Austen's *Pride and Prejudice* (1813) from Almén's *A Theory of Musical Narrative*, Alfred Hitchcock's *Vertigo* (1958) from Stan Brakhage's *Mothlight* (1963), John Adams and Peter Sellars's *Doctor Atomic* (2005) from Philip Glass and Robert Wilson's *Einstein on the Beach* (1976), Richard Strauss's *Don Quixote* (1898) from Igor Stravinsky's Octet (1923), a recounting of my failed attempts to make a Sachertorte from a recipe for this delicious but formidable dessert? Without much thought or deliberation, someone sufficiently knowledgeable about the above items will tend to categorize the former but not the latter in the class of narratives. One of the factors motivating such determinations is that the former items were intentionally made to communicate stories (and succeed in doing so), whereas the latter were not.[23] Obviously, I have not gotten very far in determining what a narrative is. I have merely replaced the question "what is a narrative?" with "what is a story?"

Before addressing this question, it is worth interrogating the validity of the intuitive view that the former of each pair of items is a narrative. Not all narratologists agree. Genette, for instance, defines a narrative as an "oral or written discourse that undertakes to tell of an event or series of events," a definition that would include *Pride and Prejudice* and, potentially, my story about my attempt to make a Sachertorte but exclude the cases in between.[24] Theorists who have brought narratology to bear on cinema and theater have expanded the means of conveying story content to include showing by means of images and sounds. However, like Abbate, many have assumed that since fictional narrators are seemingly ubiquitous to literary narratives, they must be a component of narration in other media as well.[25] A more complete response to such claims will need to wait until chapter 3, where I explore the role of narrators in opera and musical theater. For now, I will simply state my agreement with Abbate that narratives require storytellers, not mere sequences of events. The point on which we disagree is her insistence that these tellers be fictional. There is no fictional agent responsible for presenting the entirety of *Vertigo*, *Doctor Atomic*, *Don Quixote*, or my story about my culinary disaster. Nevertheless, these utterances have authors who, in authoring their utterance, also narrate it.[26]

Although there are many differences between telling a story and presenting one (e.g., through a theatrical performance), everyday use of the term *narrative* cuts across this divide.[27] With regard to the question of whether a work is a narrative, I do not care how the story is conveyed, merely that the work was created to convey a story and that it succeeds in doing so. Thus, I will use *narrate* to describe any act of communicating narrative content and *narrator* to refer to any agent, fictional or real, engaged in such an act, regardless of whether it is conducted through language, music, sounds, gestures, pictures, or moving images.

Having clarified my position on the range of acceptable storytelling media, I now turn to the question of what a story is. Since most discussions in music scholarship focus on instrumental music, I will take as my central case studies the aforementioned pair of instrumental compositions, Strauss's tone poem *Don Quixote* and Stravinsky's Octet.

As Strauss's title advertises, his work is modeled on the characters and events of Cervantes's novel. Strauss begins with a character sketch of the protagonist (ex. 1.1). One of the more striking features of the first dozen measures is their unusual harmonic plan. Strauss establishes the key of D major with a cadence in measure 4, but only four bars later, he is tonicizing A♭ major, a tritone away, subsequently returning to D major by measure 12. Even in the context of late-Romantic harmonic practice, the establishment of tritone key relations within such a compressed time span is unorthodox. Yet the passage is stylistically unperturbed. The lilting rhythms and graceful, if exaggeratedly Romantic, swooping gestures in the strings create a sense of complacency, minimizing the effect of the unstable harmonic terrain being traversed. In just these twelve measures, Strauss has communicated a great deal about his protagonist, depicting him to be a romantic of questionable psychological stability, but whose eccentricities remain largely hidden at this point. Many may be fooled into thinking Don Quixote entirely normal, just as he does himself. This belief becomes increasingly unsustainable, however, as Strauss's harmonies become even more outlandish later on in the introduction.

Strauss then introduces Don Quixote's sidekick, Sancho Panza (ex. 1.2). The ungainly leaps in the tenor tuba and bass clarinet parts—so unidiomatic as to be impossible to execute with grace—are appropriate to his humble occupation as a farmer. Suddenly, a viola enters with a jittery, oscillating figure. After the first motive is repeated, the viola takes over, imitating, if wanly, the flamboyancy of Don Quixote's musical gestures and the noble heroism he espouses (rehearsal numbers 15 and 16, respectively). Strauss presents Sancho Panza as a country bumpkin, initially reticent of his friend's proposal (hence the oscillation between the bumbling-farmer and quasi-heroic-viola motives and the nervousness of the latter), who quickly becomes intoxicated by delusions of grandeur and agrees to play along.

Example 1.1. The harmonic eccentricity of Don Quixote, opening of Strauss's tone poem

Example 1.2. Character sketch of Sancho Panza

Example 1.2. *(Continued)*

Having introduced his characters, Strauss proceeds to represent them undertaking purposeful actions. They combat windmills Don Quixote believes to be giants (variation 1) and sheep he mistakes for an army (variation 2). In variation 4, they attempt to halt a procession of penitents with a portrait of the Virgin Mary, believed to be a damsel in distress. To provide comfort to his friend and perhaps some personal amusement, Sancho Panza attempts to pass off a peasant as Don Quixote's beloved Dulcinea (variation 6). They take an imaginary trip through the air (variation 7), followed by a real voyage by boat, which concludes with the capsizing of their vessel (variation 8). In variation 9, they attack a group of monks believed to be evil magicians. Finally, Don Quixote stakes his knighthood against the Knight of the Shining Moon and loses, which causes him to come to his senses and return home, where he dies (variation 10).

Although one may accept that my description of Strauss's *Don Quixote* is a narrative, one may still doubt that Strauss's music is responsible for conveying this story. Without Strauss's title and program, I would have had no hope of divining what his music was intended to represent. Jean-Jacques Nattiez has verified this hypothesis with an experiment involving playing *L'apprenti sorcier* to hosts of Montréal schoolchildren who had never heard it before and who were not provided with its program. They were merely told that the music conveys a story and were instructed to write down what they thought the story was. Nattiez received all sorts of responses—stories about battles, revolutions, animals, mountain climbing, espionage, medieval chivalry, even the life of Beethoven—but none even remotely resembling a story about a wizard in training with a procreating-broom problem.[28]

That is not to say that music is incapable of representation without extramusical aids. If one's target is an aural phenomenon, one could certainly expect more success. Nevertheless, the intended referent of even the most infamously onomatopoeic passages of *Don Quixote* (e.g., the sheep's distressed bleating in variation 2, represented by winds and brass performing dissonant chords while flutter-tonguing) are difficult to determine without extramusical cues. But although extramusical, Strauss's title and program are part of his work.[29] Accordingly, it is appropriate that I relied on them in my discussion.

A more serious objection is that my description went beyond the skimpy details Strauss provided in his score and program. I also relied on knowledge of Cervantes's novel. Unlike the novel, Strauss's tone poem does not bring into existence the characters Don Quixote and Sancho Panza. Rather, it is designed to put listeners who already have knowledge of the novel in mind of its characters and their adventures. Some narrative theorists may wish to place more stringent demands on the act of telling or presenting a story, claiming that simply pointing to a preexisting narrative is insufficient.[30] I suggest that such inclinations are predicated on too narrow a focus on linguistic narratives. In this regard, I agree with Almén that a consideration of musical works has something to teach us about narratives more generally.

In my discussion of *Don Quixote*, I have focused on Strauss's representation of agents and their goal-directed activities, both of which I take to be essential components of stories, at least within the context of humanist discourse.[31] These agents may not be human, but they must be represented as at least humanlike in their sentience, possession of beliefs and desires, and ability to perform self-impelled actions. But if representing an agent capable of action were sufficient, Strauss's opening character sketch of Don Quixote would be just as much a narrative as the ensuing representation of his and Sancho Panza's adventures. To exclude mere character sketches, the agent not only must be capable of action but also must exercise that ability.

The importance of agents to narratives is confirmed by the methodologies that have been employed in narrative-based analyses of instrumental music.[32] What is required to understand musical events as constituting a narrative is to regard them as representing one or more agents and their actions. The first step is to identify some salient musical features (themes, motives, keys, instruments, pitches) and anthropomorphize them, regarding them as agents, fleshing out their characteristics, and attributing to them beliefs and desires that serve to motivate their actions. As illustration, I will perform an analysis of this type on the beginning of variation B of the second movement of Stravinsky's Octet (ex. 1.3).

I take as the agents of my narrative the instrumental parts trumpet 2 and trombone 2. Trumpet 2 performs a solo march accompanied by the bassoons and trombones, which I interpret as a fictional act of marching, one that is curtailed by the crass glissando trombone 2 performs two measures before rehearsal 29. So far, I have some agents performing some actions. Almén may be inclined to regard my description as a narrative. Others may harbor doubts on this score. The problem, I suggest, is that neither trumpet 2 nor trombone 2 scores very high on the scale of particularity. Who are they? Why is trumpet 2 performing a march, and why does trombone 2 interrupt it? Narratives in other media provide answers to such questions.

Suppose I were to provide some. Since the musical topic of this passage is a march, a military setting seems apropos. The homophonic texture and regular pulse of the accompaniment suggest a scenario of a platoon going on a march with trumpet 2 as its leader—the corporal, let's imagine. Based on the

Example 1.3. Stravinsky, Octet, movement II, variation B

brisk tempo and dry accompaniment, the rigid dotted rhythms of trumpet 2's part and its relative loudness, and even Stravinsky's very choice of instrument, I could attribute to my corporal the character traits of seriousness, formality, arrogance, a need for control, and a desire to be the center of attention. The measure of triple meter (which would derail any attempt to march to this music) suggests that trumpet 2 is not as competent a leader as he thinks he is. Within the context of Stravinsky's rhythmic practice, however, the metric abnormality is slight (compare the march at the Allegro moderato of the first movement). Perhaps it is not appropriate to think of the corporal as entirely incompetent, merely inexperienced and overconfident.

Within this framework, trombone 2 may be cast in the role of a private with a chip on his shoulder. Fed up with taking orders, he cracks a rude joke. The vulgar sound of his glissando might even suggest the target of his joke: the corporal's sexual potency. Noticing the ensuing behavior exhibited by the other members of the platoon—the circus-like bassoon ostinato accompanying the flute, who lackadaisically mocks trumpet 2's dotted rhythms—we may conclude that the private's prank succeeded in putting a halt to the march, undermining the corporal's authority and causing a ruckus.

By now, my remarks on the Octet do constitute a narrative, based on my earlier stipulations, but a narrative of my making, not Stravinsky's.[33] One might argue that the same is true of my description of *Don Quixote*, but that would be to elide crucial differences between these two cases. Although my discussion of Strauss's work did involve creative extrapolations on my part, these were invited by Strauss and guided by features of his work—namely, its title and program.

Stravinsky's work may be an apt prop for imaginings that constitute narratives, but there is no indication that Stravinsky invited such imaginings. Its title as well as the titles of individual movements (Sinfonia, Tema con variazioni, Finale) do not recommend extramusical associations. Stravinsky's statements about his work provide further evidence that he did not intend it to present a story. The first sentence of an article he published shortly after the work's premiere is "My Octuor is a musical object." He elaborates that it "is not an 'emotive' work but a musical composition based on objective elements which are sufficient in themselves."[34] In his ghostwritten autobiography, Stravinsky sanctioned Walter Nouvel to publish the following aesthetic credo on his behalf: "I consider that music is, by its very nature, essentially powerless to *express* anything at all, whether a feeling, an attitude of mind, a psychological mood, a phenomenon of nature, etc. . . . *Expression* has never been an inherent property of music."[35] Such a claim is, of course, dubious in the extreme, as it is not even supported by the composer's own works, including the passage under consideration. Nevertheless, it does suggest that Stravinsky did not intend the Octet to represent a story.

At this point, one might object that I have chosen decidedly cut-and-dried examples. A more challenging case would be Mahler's *Todtenfeier*, which originated as a symphonic poem but eventually became the first movement of the composer's Second Symphony (1895). Adam Mickiewicz's verse drama *Dziady* (*Todtenfeier* in Siegfried Lipiner's 1887 German translation) served as inspiration for Mahler's compositional activities, but, unlike Strauss, he never made this fact public.

There were two actions Strauss performed that contributed to *Don Quixote* being a narrative. First, he modeled his composition on the characters and events of Cervantes's novel such that appropriately informed listeners could hear those characters and events in his work. Second, he took steps to ensure that listeners would be appropriately informed by gesturing to Cervantes's work in his title and indications in his score and by sanctioning Arthur Hahn to publish a more detailed program in his guidebook to the symphony.[36]

Mahler's decision not to publicize the story on which his *Todtenfeier* was based suggests that he did not intend it to be taken as a representation of Mickiewicz's story. Due to the substantial formal changes that occurred during the compositional process, there is also reason to doubt that Mahler's compositional activities were guided by an intention to achieve a high degree of correspondence between the musical form of his composition and the plot of *Dziady*.[37]

Even if Mahler did not intend for listeners to think about *Dziady* while listening to his *Todtenfeier*, one could still argue that he intended them to invent their own stories while listening to his work. Such an argument would find support in Mahler's decision to categorize his *Todtenfeier* as a symphonic poem, a genre of program music often used to tell stories. Furthermore, the musical features of the work all but demand extramusical explanations, and narrative listening was a part of the culture of music listening and criticism in Mahler's sociocultural context. Nevertheless, for my purposes, I will reserve the category of narrative to works that tell or present *particular* stories.[38] Since particularity admits of degrees, the question of the requisite degree of particularity arises. As sketchy as Strauss's musical representations are in comparison with Cervantes's novel, I suggest that they are sufficiently particular to qualify as a narrative. But to preserve a distinction between Strauss's *Don Quixote* and Stravinsky's Octet, I am disinclined to lower the bar such that any work that is conducive to narrative imaginings is able to clear it.

What about works that fall in between these two extremes, such as Beethoven's Fifth Symphony? In a famous scene from E. M. Forster's novel *Howard's End* (1910), the Schlegel siblings attend a performance of the symphony. While Margaret and Tibby concern themselves with the "music itself," Helen imagines "a goblin walking quietly over the universe" who is dispelled in the final movement with "gusts of splendour, gods and demigods contending with vast swords, colour and fragrance broadcast on the field of battle, magnificent victory, magnificent death!" Her more sober siblings dismiss the legitimacy of her response to the symphony. In Margaret's words, "she labels it with meanings from start to finish; turns it into literature. I wonder if the day will ever return when music will be treated as music."[39]

In response to the interpretive flights of fancy that characterized much music criticism of the Romantic era, many twentieth-century critics harbored similar doubts about the appropriateness of responses like Helen's. In philosophy, Peter Kivy has been one of the most outspoken opponents of narrative-based interpretations of instrumental music.[40] I take a more moderate view. The struggle-to-victory narrative Helen and many nonfictional interpreters have heard in Beethoven's Fifth Symphony is insufficiently particular to ground it as a narrative, in my view. Who is struggling? What is the nature of his struggle? With *Don Quixote*, there are answers to such questions. With Beethoven's Fifth, there are not.

Yet, like Forster himself, I am disinclined to agree with Margaret that her sister failed to treat Beethoven's music "as music."[41] The impulse to imagine fictional scenarios while listening to music is a natural one, born of our tendency to anthropomorphize objects and make sense of events in our lives with narratives. Narrative listening is not merely a way to make works of instrumental music accessible to children or members of the laity but can also benefit musicians and music scholars. Narrative-based analysis can be a powerful tool for understanding music because it draws attention to conflicts and discontinuities that may be overlooked by other analytical methods.

Almén is right to be skeptical of many of the stipulations about the necessary ingredients of narratives put forth by literary theorists. However, if they can be faulted for their failure to consider dramatic or musical narratives, an analogous complaint can be laid at Almén's feet, since his definition is plausible only in the context of instrumental music. Music scholars concerned that our field is a perennial outsider within broader discourses in the humanities ought to consider whether idiosyncratic definitions of shared concepts are apt to bring us closer to or further away from colleagues tackling similar questions in other fields. My motive for proposing a more circumscribed definition of narrative is to facilitate dialogues between music and other disciplines and between music scholars, performers, and members of the general public.

If works are more akin to processes than products alone, determining whether a work is a narrative involves more than merely studying its structural features. One must also consider the way it was made (was it modeled on a preexisting or composer-authored story?), its intended mode of reception (did its composer intend for listeners to hear this story's characters and events in the work?), and whether the composer was successful in achieving the desired response (are listeners able to hear the music as presenting this story?). Thus, I propose that a narrative is an utterance intentionally made to convey a story.

In defining what a story is, I have taken an agent-oriented approach, rather than one focused on the representation of events, because it directs our attention to one of the chief reasons for our interest in narratives: the agents at their center. These agents need not be human, but they do need to perform intentional actions. Comparing Strauss's *Don Quixote* to Stravinsky's Octet, I argued that narratives concern particular agents performing particular actions. As such, themes, pitches, and instrumental parts are not strong candidates to be the agents of narratives, but they may be rendered more particular if listeners use their imaginations. Composers of works of instrumental music express their intention that their work presents a story by inviting listeners to imagine that musical features, such as themes or instruments, represent agents. In most cases, this invitation is made through extramusical means, such as the work's title and accompanying program or pictures, which serve to guide listeners' imaginative escapades.[42]

Putting it all together, I propose the following definition: A narrative is an utterance intended to communicate a story, which necessarily involves representing particular agents exercising their agency through particular intentional actions. Due to music's lack of semantic specificity in comparison with literature or theater, successfully conveying a story in a work of instrumental music typically involves a suggestive title and a program that clarifies what the music is intended to represent. Thus, the category of *narrative music* overlaps with that of *program music*—music intended to represent or evoke extramusical phenomena—but not precisely. Debussy's *La mer* (1905) and Honegger's *Pacific 231* (1923) both fall into the latter category but not the former. Although both are representational and, furthermore, represent a change in state—of the sea and of a train gradually picking up speed, respectively—they do not represent any sentient beings and thus are not narratives under the proposed definition.[43]

In the next chapter, my focus shifts from instrumental music to opera and musical theater, exploring what is involved in conveying a story in a musical drama.

Notes

1. Carolyn Abbate, *Unsung Voices: Opera and Musical Narrative in the Nineteenth Century* (Princeton: Princeton University Press, 1991), ch. 1, 48–56.
2. Ibid., x, xii–xiii, 11–13.
3. Ibid., 57–60.
4. Another scholar who is dismissive of music's narrational abilities is Jean-Jacques Nattiez, "Can One Speak of Narrative Music?" *Journal of the Royal Musical Association* 115, no. 2 (1990): 240–57.
5. Byron Almén, *A Theory of Musical Narrative* (Bloomington: Indiana University Press, 2008), 40. Almén's definition is based on James Jakób Liszka, *The Semiotic of Myth: A Critical Study of the Symbol* (Bloomington: Indiana University Press, 1989).
6. Susan McClary, "The Blasphemy of Talking Politics during a Bach Year," in *Music and Society: The Politics of Composition, Performance, and Reception*, ed. Susan McClary and Richard Leppert (Cambridge: Cambridge University Press, 1987), 25, 28, 36.
7. Almén, *Theory of Musical Narrative*, 25.
8. McClary, "Talking Politics," 40.
9. Almén, *Theory of Musical Narrative*, 39.
10. Ibid., 32–35, 41.
11. Peter Kivy, "Action and Agency," in *Antithetical Arts: On the Ancient Quarrel between Literature and Music* (Oxford: Clarendon Press, 2009), 119–56.
12. Roland Barthes, "From Work to Text," in *Image—Music—Text*, ed. and trans. Stephen Heath (New York: Hill and Wang, 1977), 155–64.
13. Some music scholars treat the score as the composer's product (e.g., Michael Talbot, "Introduction," in *The Musical Work: Reality or Invention?* ed. Michael Talbot [Liverpool: Liverpool University Press 2000], 6), but if that were true, music appreciation would bear greater similarity to the appreciation of literature than it does.
14. For an interpretation that is more firmly grounded in the historical influences on Bach's work, see Michael Marissen, *The Social and Religious Designs of J. S. Bach's Brandenburg Concertos* (Princeton: Princeton University Press, 1995), ch. 3. I contrast McClary's and Marissen's interpretations in Nina Penner, "Intentions in Theory and Practice," *Music & Letters* 99, no. 3 (2018): 452–53.
15. David Davies defends a process-based understanding of works in *Art as Performance* (Malden: Blackwell, 2004), which focuses on visual art. There are other accounts that recognize aspects of a work's context as integral to work identity. Concerning music, the most influential of these was proposed by Jerrold Levinson, "What a Musical Work Is," in *Music, Art, and Metaphysics: Essays in Philosophical Aesthetics* (Oxford: Oxford University Press, 2011 [1980]), 63–88, who includes the composer's identity and the date of composition as part of work identity. I share Davies's concern that Levinson's account does not import enough contextual information into work identity. For a proposed synthesis of Davies's and Levinson's views, refer to Andrew Kania, Review of *Art as Performance* by David Davies, *Mind* 114, no. 453 (2005): 140–41. Jean-Jacques Nattiez, *Music and Discourse: Toward a Semiology of Music*, trans. Carolyn

Abbate (Princeton: Princeton University Press, 1990) has been influential in encouraging music scholars to consider the process of composition (what he calls *poiesis*), not merely the finished the product (the *trace* or *neutral level*). Nattiez's inclusion of the process of reception (*esthesis*) as part of work identity is one major difference between his position and the foregoing philosophical ones.

16. Penner, "Intentions in Theory and Practice." The quotations refer to William K. Wimsatt and Monroe C. Beardsley, "The Intentional Fallacy," *Sewanee Review* 54, no. 3 (1946): 468–88; Roland Barthes, "The Death of the Author," in *Image—Music—Text*, ed. and trans. Stephen Heath (New York: Hill and Wang, 1977), 142–48. Another recent musicological critique of anti-intentionalism is Edmund J. Goehring, *Coming to Terms with Our Musical Past: An Essay on Mozart and Modernist Aesthetics* (Rochester: University of Rochester Press, 2018), ch. 3.

17. Paisley Livingston, *Art and Intention: A Philosophical Study* (Oxford: Clarendon Press, 2005), 7. Livingston's account is based on Alfred R. Mele, "Deciding to Act," *Philosophical Studies* 100, no. 1 (2000): 81–108; Alfred R. Mele, *Springs of Action: Understanding Intentional Behaviour* (Oxford: Oxford University Press, 1992).

18. Absolute intentionalists include E. D. Hirsch, *Validity in Interpretation* (New Haven: Yale University Press, 1967); William Irwin, *Intentionalist Interpretation: A Philosophical Explanation and Defense* (Westport: Greenwood Press, 1999); William Irwin, "Authorial Declaration and Extreme Actual Intentionalism: Is Dumbledore Gay?" *Journal of Aesthetics and Art Criticism* 73, no. 2 (2015): 141–47; P. D. Juhl, *Interpretation: An Essay in the Philosophy of Literary Criticism* (Princeton: Princeton University Press, 1980); Steven Knapp and Walter Benn Michaels, "Against Theory," *Critical Inquiry* 8, no. 4 (1982): 723–42; Steven Knapp and Walter Benn Michaels, "Against Theory 2: Hermeneutics and Deconstruction," *Critical Inquiry* 14, no. 1 (1987): 49–68. Kathleen Stock, *Only Imagine: Fiction, Interpretation, and Imagination* (Oxford: Oxford University Press, 2017), defends extreme intentionalism but only with respect to fictional content (what one ought to imagine is true in the story).

19. Wayne C. Booth, *The Rhetoric of Fiction*, 2nd ed. (Chicago: University of Chicago Press, 1983), 70–71; Jerrold Levinson, "Intention and Interpretation in Literature," in *The Pleasures of Aesthetics: Philosophical Essays* (Ithaca: Cornell University Press, 1996), 175–213. Although Edward T. Cone does not use the term *implied composer* in *The Composer's Voice* (Berkeley: University of California Press, 1974), he has acknowledged that his concept of the "complete" or "implicit musical persona" is "something very like Booth's implied author." Fred E. Maus et al., "Edward T. Cone's *The Composer's Voice*: Elaborations and Departures," *College Music Symposium* 29 (1989): 77. The implied composer is often invoked by music semioticians; for example, Eero Terasti, *Signs of Music: A Guide to Musical Semiotics* (Berlin: Mouton, 2002), 73–76. See also Seth Monahan's discussion of the "fictional composer" in "Action and Agency Revisited," *Journal of Music Theory* 57, no. 2 (2013): 239–32. I discuss some differences between the foregoing accounts in "Intentions in Theory and Practice," 455–58.

20. In chapter 4, I will return to the concept of the implied author, addressing concerns that it is required to appreciate multiauthored works and cases where there is a disjuncture between the person who appears to have authored the work and facts about its actual author.

21. Livingston, *Art and Intention*, 142–43, quotation from 199. For a more extended discussion of moderate intentionalism and its congruence with current musicology, refer to Penner, "Intentions in Theory and Practice," 458–64.

22. Here I am referring to Kendall L. Walton, "Categories of Art," *Philosophical Review* 79, no. 3 (1970): 334–67. Even philosophers who are opposed to intentionalism as a general account of interpretation agree on the relevance of intentions to categorization. See, for example, David Davies, *Art as Performance*, 84–89; Levinson, "Intention and Interpretation," 188–89.

23. Gregory Currie, *Narratives and Narrators: A Philosophy of Stories* (Oxford: Oxford University Press, 2010), 5, also begins from this premise.

24. Gérard Genette, *Narrative Discourse: An Essay in Method*, trans. Jane E. Lewin (Ithaca: Cornell University Press, 1983), 25.

25. For arguments that films invariably have narrators, see Seymour Chatman, *Coming to Terms: The Rhetoric of Narrative in Fiction and Film* (Ithaca: Cornell University Press, 1990), 115–16; Jerrold Levinson, "Film Music and Narrative Agency," in *Contemplating Art: Essays in Aesthetics* (Oxford: Oxford University Press, 2006), 149–50. On theater, see Manfred Jahn, "Narrative Voice and Agency in Drama: Aspects of a Narratology of Drama," *New Literary History* 32, no. 3 (2001): 674.

26. Currie, *Narratives and Narrators*, 65, puts forth an argument to this effect.

27. Others who have made similar observations include ibid., 28n3; Brian Boyd, *On the Origin of Stories: Evolution, Cognition, and Fiction* (Cambridge, MA: Belknap Press, 2009), 177; Monika Fludernik, *Towards a 'Natural' Narratology* (London: Routledge, 1996), 349–51; James R. Hamilton, "Mimesis and Showing," in *Mimesis: Metaphysics, Cognition, Pragmatics*, ed. Gregory Currie, Petr Kotatko, and Martin Pokorny (London: College Publications, 2012), 355.

28. Jean-Jacques Nattiez, "Y a-t-il une diégèse musicale?" in *Musik und Verstehen*, ed. Peter Faltin and Hans-Peter Reinecke (Cologne: Arno Volk Verlag, 1973), 247–57. An English summary of this study may be found in Nattiez, "Narrative Music?" 246–48.

29. For arguments in favor of treating titles as part of the work, refer to Hazard Adams, "Titles, Titling, and Entitlement To," *Journal of Aesthetics and Art Criticism* 46, no. 1 (1987): 7–21; Jerrold Levinson, "Titles," in *Music, Art, and Metaphysics: Essays in Philosophical Aesthetics* (Oxford: Oxford University Press, 2011), 159–78. I see no reason why the same logic could not be applied to programs and pictures intended to accompany musical works.

30. I am grateful to Trevor Ponech for raising this objection.

31. Others who make similar claims include Aristotle, *Poetics*, ed. and trans. Stephen Halliwell (Cambridge, MA: Harvard University Press, 1995), 48–53; Roland Barthes, "Introduction to the Structural Analysis of Narratives," in *Image—Music—Text*, ed. and trans. Stephen Heath (New York: Hill and Wang, 1977), 105; Noël Carroll, "On the Narrative Connection," in *Beyond Aesthetics* (New York: Cambridge University Press, 2001), 126; Dorrit Cohn, *The Distinction of Fiction* (Baltimore: Johns Hopkins University Press, 1999), 12; Jerry R. Hobbs, *Literature and Cognition* (Stanford: Centre for the Study of Language and Information, 1990), 39–40; Trevor Ponech, *What Is Non-Fiction Cinema? On the Very Idea of Motion Picture Communication* (Boulder: Westview Press, 1999), 128; Murray Smith, *Engaging Characters: Fiction, Emotion, and the Cinema* (Oxford: Clarendon Press, 1995), ch. 1; Paul Woodruff, *The Necessity of Theatre: The Art of Watching and Being Watched* (Oxford: Oxford University Press, 2008), 68–72.

32. See, for example, Almén, *Theory of Musical Narrative*, ch. 4; Cone, *Composer's Voice*, ch. 5; Marion A. Guck, "Rehabilitating the Incorrigible," in *Theory, Analysis and Meaning in Music*, ed. Anthony Pople (Cambridge: Cambridge University Press, 1994), 57–73; Robert S. Hatten, *A Theory of Virtual Agency for Western Music* (Bloomington: Indiana University Press, 2018), 32–34, ch. 7, 287–88; Gregory Karl, "Structuralism and the Musical Plot," *Music Theory Spectrum* 19, no. 1 (1997): 13–34; Fred E. Maus, "Music as Narrative," *Indiana Theory Review* 12 (1991): 1–41; Fred E. Maus, "Music as Drama," in *Music and Meaning*, ed. Jenefer Robinson (Ithaca: Cornell University Press, 1998), 105–30; McClary, "Talking Politics"; Monahan, "Action and Agency Revisited"; Anthony Newcomb, "Action and Agency in Mahler's Ninth Symphony, Second Movement," in *Music and Meaning*, ed. Jenefer Robinson (Ithaca: Cornell University Press, 1997), 131–53; Philip Rupprecht, "Agency Effects in the Instrumental Drama of Musgrave

and Birtwistle," in *Music and Narrative since 1900*, ed. Michael L. Klein and Nicholas Reyland (Bloomington: Indiana University Press, 2012), 189–215.

33. Jerrold Levinson, "Music as Narrative and Music as Drama," in *Contemplating Art: Essays in Aesthetics* (Oxford: Oxford University Press, 2006), 134n6, also makes this distinction.

34. Igor Stravinsky, "Some Ideas about My Octuor," in *Stravinsky: The Composer and His Works*, 2nd ed., by Eric Walter White (Berkeley: University of California Press, 1979), 574, 575. Stravinsky's essay was originally published in *The Arts* in January 1924.

35. Walter Nouvel, *Igor Stravinsky: An Autobiography* (New York: Simon and Schuster, 1936), 83 (ellipsis in the original).

36. Walter Werbeck, *Die Tondichtungen von Richard Strauss* (Tutzing: Hans Schneider, 1996), 147–56, 543–44; James Hepokoski, Review of *Die Tondichtungen von Richard Strauss* by Walter Werbeck, *Journal of the American Musicological Society* 51, no. 3 (1998): 608–9.

37. Stephen E. Hefling, "Mahler's *Todtenfeier* and the Problem of Program Music," *19th-Century Music* 12, no. 1 (1988): 43. In a letter to Max Marschalk after the premiere of his Second Symphony, Mahler stated that he "was never concerned with the detailed description of an *event*, but to the highest degree with that of a *feeling*." Quoted in ibid., 41.

38. Particularity is also stressed by Currie, *Narratives and Narrators*, 11; Woodruff, *Necessity of Theatre*, 98–101.

39. E. M. Forster, *Howard's End* (London: Edward Arnold, 1973), 30, 31, 36. I thank Linda Hutcheon for recommending this example.

40. Kivy, "Action and Agency."

41. Michelle Fillion, *Difficult Rhythm: Music and the Word in E. M. Forster* (Urbana: University of Illinois Press, 2010), 83, notes that Margaret's and Helen's responses dramatize the two modes of listening Forster juxtaposes in his 1939 essay "Not Listening to Music": "music itself" and "music that reminds me of something." Although Forster cautions that the latter approach may lead to "inattention," he also states that "only a purist would condemn all visual parallels, all emotional labellings, all programmes." E. M. Forster, "Not Listening to Music," in *Two Cheers for Democracy*, ed. Oliver Stallybrass (London: Edward Arnold, 1972), 122, 123.

42. A musical work with accompanying pictures is Biber's "Mystery" Sonatas (1676).

43. If Honegger had represented an athlete running a race, it is possible that this hypothetical work would be a narrative. The train, however, does not have desires or aims.

2

TELLING, OPERATICALLY

In the past few decades, operatic programming has become ever more varied, including not only a wider range of repertoire from the seventeenth and eighteenth centuries but also an increasing number of works not generally considered to be operas, such as Handel oratorios and Broadway musicals. The Komische Oper Berlin has even staged a production of Mozart's Requiem. In response to the increasing diversity of items attracting operatic billing, Monika Hennemann has remarked that "there seem to be no limits to what falls under that category."[1]

In light of this trend, an attempt to define what differentiates operatic storytelling from that in related forms such as dramatic songs, oratorios, and cantatas may seem like a futile endeavor. In opera studies, there is a long history of skepticism that there is anything particular about the way operas tell stories, from Edward T. Cone's suggestion that "every song is to a certain extent a little opera, every opera is no less an expanded song" to Hennemann's more recent questioning of the distinction between opera and oratorio.[2] While recognizing the many connections among operas, songs, cantatas, and oratorios as well as the potential to stage many works in the latter categories as operas, this chapter also points to some key differences between these art forms. One distinction my account of operatic storytelling will not make is that between operas and musicals (for reasons given in the overture). In what follows, references to *opera* and *operatic storytelling* should be understood to encompass musicals.

My philosophical readers may harbor skepticism of a different sort, arising from the still controversial concept of medium specificity. Following David Davies and Berys Gaut, I understand medium in art as referring not merely to the *materials* (physical or otherwise) with which artists work but also to the *practices* governing how they use these materials.[3] Skeptics of medium specificity, such as Noël Carroll, target an extreme version of the thesis, by which each medium is believed to possess properties that are unique to it and artists are instructed to exploit *only* those unique properties.[4] My aim is merely to identify some features that differentiate opera from related media, such as song and oratorio, not to suggest that composers and librettists ought to focus their attention on only these features.

I also reject some of the evaluative claims endorsed by other moderate supporters of medium specificity. Gaut, for instance, suggests that the effective exploitation of the medium-specific features of cinema makes visual extravaganzas such as *Cloud Atlas* (2012)—chock-full of montage sequences and special effects—cinematically better than static, dialogue-driven films such as *My Dinner with André* (1981).[5] Although commonsensical, such a position would seem to limit the possibilities that are legitimate to pursue in any given medium, a situation I am keen to avoid. In my view, successfully exploiting the properties particular to opera may or may not generate operatic works that are superior in any respect to those that are less characteristically operatic. Nevertheless, knowing what medium the artists were working in, and its particular strengths and weaknesses, plays an important role in explaining and evaluating works of art. For example, understanding the challenges of conveying on the stage the kind of deep psychological investigations at which novels excel renders Britten and Myfanwy Piper's success at doing so in their 1973 operatic adaptation of Thomas Mann's *Der Tod in Venedig* (1912) all the more virtuosic.

As I did in my exploration of narrative in the previous chapter, I will begin by stating the obvious and then venture to more adventurous propositions. Operas require music, specifically song. Jerrold Levinson has defined "paradigm song" as "a melodically and rhythmically distinctive arch of fully-fledged tones of definite pitch, produced in the form of vocables coalescing into words and sentences, and typically with support, primarily harmonic, from some cohort of instruments."[6] Given that this definition would seem to exclude many commonplace components of opera—recitative, vocalise, *Sprechstimme*, and unaccompanied singing—I am inclined to be more generous. However, that is not to suggest that anything goes. Take, for instance, the Montréal-based composer Luna Pearl Woolf's "voiceless opera" *Mélange à trois* (2014) for violin, cello, and percussion. In this work, the performers do not merely play music; they also use their bodies to act out characters in a fictional narrative.[7] But at no point do they generate sounds with their vocal cords. Their "singing" is made up solely of the sounds they create with their instruments. As such, I regard this work as less an opera than a work of instrumental theater that is inspired by opera, particularly its penchant for melodramatic plots.

Another work that calls into question the nature of singing is Christine Sun Kim's *Face Opera II* (2013) for nine prelingually deaf performers. Although it concludes with the performers generating vocal utterances, it is primarily their facial expressions (from the American Sign Language lexicon) that Sun Kim is inviting her audiences to regard as singing.[8]

While acknowledging recent explorations of the limits of song and, accordingly, of opera in contemporary music and performance art, this study concerns opera of a more traditional sort. As such, I will be using the verb *to sing* in its more conventional or literal sense to refer to utterances produced by the performers' own vocal apparatus that possess a discernable pitch or pitches with at least enough sustainment to allow for pitch discernment. Given that I will be discussing modernist operas and works of musical theater, the bar on tunefulness will need to be sufficiently low to include not only Sprechstimme but also Rex Harrison–esque "talking on pitch," immortalized in the film musical *My Fair Lady* (1964).

Many genres of music tell stories through song. In this chapter, I isolate the medium-specific features of operatic storytelling by comparing it first to narrative songs; then to cantatas, oratorios, and serenatas; and finally to plays and films that contain songs but are not generally considered to be musical dramas.[9]

Operas versus Narrative Songs

One of the remarkable features of opera, in contrast to most other musical genres, is its practitioners' commitment to storytelling. Since its origins around 1600, opera has been understood as a medium for presenting stories. By far the most common generic label applied to the first operas was *favola in musica*, story presented through music. And so it has remained, even throughout the aesthetic upheavals of the previous century. While practitioners in virtually all other art forms in the West were abandoning narrative, even representation, librettists and composers kept on representing stories through their works. There are nonnarrative operas, such as *Einstein on the Beach* (1976), but these are few and far between, and they remain on the periphery of the opera canon, in part because of their denial of our expectation for storytelling. Significantly, we are not similarly disturbed by nonnarrative songs or cantatas. With oratorios and serenatas, the expectation of a story is higher. Notably both were used as opera substitutes during Lent and papal bans. But nonnarrative examples exist, including the most famous oratorio of all, Handel's *Messiah* (1742).

It would appear that operatic storytelling can be distinguished from that in songs through Plato's distinction between *mimesis* and *diegesis* or, in the terminology I will employ, *enacting* character and *telling about* character.[10] Operatic storytelling involves singers enacting characters: singers' utterances represent characters' utterances, and singers' actions represent characters' actions. In most songs, by contrast, the singer takes on the role of a narrator who summarizes or paraphrases characters' speeches and merely describes their activities.

As Cone has noted, there is not always a clear distinction between enacting a character and telling about a character. Schubert's *Lied* "Der Erlkönig" begins and ends with a narrator telling about the characters, but in the internal stanzas, the singer impersonates the utterances of the father, son, and elf king, thereby vocally enacting these characters.[11] Furthermore, many operas contain scenes of narration (a situation that I will discuss in more depth in the following chapter). From this evidence, Cone suggests that the difference between song and opera is primarily a matter of duration.

Cone is too hasty in his conclusions. One key difference between operas and songs is that one-to-one mapping between singers and characters is standard in the former but not in the latter. In an opera, typically all of the utterances made by a given singer are to be understood as representing the fictional utterances of the character the singer is playing. The less this is true, the more challenging it will be to perform the work as an opera.

Suppose one were tasked with producing an operatic staging of Stravinsky's *Renard* (1922). Richard Taruskin summarizes its intended mode of performance as follows: "a troupe of 'buffoons, ballet dancers, or acrobats'... act the story out in pantomime on a trestle-stage, which they never leave, while the singers remain seated with the instrumentalists in the rear, their voices disembodied after the fashion of Diaghilev's *Coq d'or*."[12] The first step would be to discard the dancers and acrobats and to mobilize the singers to enact the characters: Cock, Fox, Cat, and Ram. This effort would be rather challenging, as Stravinsky often uses multiple singers' voices to represent the voice of a single character. For this reason, the vocal parts are not designated by the characters' names, as they are in an opera, but as tenor 1, tenor 2, bass 1, and bass 2. Not all vocal music can support singers enacting characters. It requires approximately one-to-one mapping of singers to characters.

One commonplace exception is works that involve characters at different stages of life. In adapting Alison Bechdel's autobiographical graphic novel *Fun Home* (2006) into a musical (2013, music by Jeanine Tesori), the librettist

Lisa Kron decided to split the central character into Small Alison (age nine), Middle Alison (age nineteen), and (Adult) Alison (age forty-three). Even if the work does not prescribe a character to be divided into multiple roles, a director may decide to divide it between multiple performers. Hans-Jürgen Syberberg's opera film *Parsifal* (1982) distributed the singing and acting to different performers, most radically in the case of Parsifal, who was sung by the *Heldentenor* Reiner Goldberg but acted by a boy (Michael Kutter) and, after Kundry's kiss, a woman (Karen Krick). Deaf West Theatre's production of *Spring Awakening* (2014) involved character doubling of a different sort. Deaf actors were paired with hearing doubles who performed most of their vocal utterances. Wendla's and Melchior's singer doubles also appeared onstage for much of the show, often interacting with their signing counterparts (chap. 8 contains a more detailed discussion).

Narration scenes also pose no obstacle to distinguishing between operas and narrative songs. In the course of enacting a character in an opera, a performer may also tell about character, as when a soprano enacts Lakmé in Delibes's 1883 opera and in so doing tells the legend of the pariah's daughter. Scenes of narration do not collapse the distinction between enacting character and telling about character because the singer's act of telling about the pariah's daughter is embedded within her act of enacting the character Lakmé.

Operas versus Oratorios and Cantatas

Opera is not, of course, the only genre of vocal music capable of presenting stories by means of singers enacting characters. Some examples, incidentally all by Handel, include the oratorios *Il trionfo del Tempo e del Disinganno* (1707) and *Esther* (1732), the serenata *Aci, Galatea e Polifemo* (1708), and the cantatas *La Lucrezia* (1709) and *Clori, Tirsi e Fileno* (1707). The difference between these genres and opera hinges on how they are intended to be performed: theatrical performances involving sets, costumes, and singers enacting characters in the case of operas, and concerts involving singers performing in modern dress, standing in place, without backdrops or props in the case of oratorios, cantatas, and serenatas. Determining the intended mode of performance is not always a simple matter. Some composers endorsed both theatrical and concert performances.[13] Even if the composer has a definite opinion on the staging of his or her work, performers may decide to pursue an alternative approach. In what follows, I will be speaking about performances that comply with the author's intentions with regard to performance means. But any work that supports storytelling by means of singers enacting characters could theoretically be staged as an opera, and my account of operatic storytelling would be equally applicable to such performances.

Perhaps surprisingly for those who regard opera as a primarily musical art form, what makes a musical performance with singing an operatic performance, as opposed to a concert, turns on the function of its extramusical components. In operatic performances, what singers look like, what they are wearing, and the movements they perform typically make things true about the characters they play: what they look like and how they move. With dramatic songs, cantatas, oratorios, and serenatas, by contrast, the singers' appearance and movements do not typically generate facts about the appearance and behavior of the characters they play. It would be highly idiosyncratic for a singer performing *La Lucrezia* to appear in Roman garb and to pretend to commit suicide at the end. More commonly, the singer will appear in modern formal attire. The inappropriateness of her dress, in the context of the world of the story, does not disturb listeners, since her apparel is not intended to represent that of the character she plays.

To better understand this distinction, Gregory Currie's category of *visual fictions* will be useful. "Visual fictions are distinguished from non-visual ones by *how content is determined*. With a visual fiction, content is determined, in part, by what we see. We see, on stage or screen, a man who moves in a certain way. That man plays a character, and his visible movements determine as part of the content of the play or movie that the character moves in that way."[14] Although Currie is describing cinema, his description also holds true for operatic performances. However, since sound is necessary to opera, while it is not in the case of cinema and other forms of theater, I propose a new category for operas called *audiovisual fictions*.[15] If operas are audiovisual fictions, then songs, oratorios, cantatas, and serenatas (in addition to instrumental works such as Strauss's *Don Quixote* [1898]) are *aural fictions*: their content is determined primarily by what one hears.

The connoisseur of song recitals may protest that I am too hasty in dismissing the importance of seeing to appreciating such performances, asserting that watching their favorite singers contort their faces and gesticulate is an important part of their appreciation of vocal recitals. Indeed, most singers school their facial expressions and body language to be appropriate to the content of the songs they sing. These actions may be similar, even identical to those they might perform in an opera.

Empirical research in the psychology of music perception has shown that even musically trained listeners' evaluations of the expressivity of instrumental music depend not only on aural information but also on visual information, such as the performers' gestures and facial expressions.[16] In performances of narrative vocal music, gestures and facial expressions may make certain story facts more salient. Take, for example, "Ich grolle nicht" from Schumann's song cycle *Dichterliebe* (1840). The speaker has been jilted in love but declares, repeatedly, that he bears no grudge. If a singer were to perform this song with an angry facial expression and a clenched fist, one would be less likely to take his words at face value. Admittedly, the turgid pounding of the piano ought to prompt the astute listener to come to this conclusion even without these visual cues. But I can imagine another scenario in which a singer, through facial expressions and body language alone, marks an utterance as ironic that would not otherwise be interpreted as such. An example, albeit from an opera performance, is Dmitri Tcherniakov's staging of "Ah, chi mi dice mai" from *Don Giovanni* (Aix-en-Provence, 2010).

Mozart and Da Ponte intended Elvira's aria to be a sincere, if exaggerated, expression of the anger and hurt she feels after being betrayed by Don Giovanni. The asides performed by the Don and Leporello contribute levity to this moment for the audience. However, they remain unseen and unheard by Elvira until the end of her aria. In Tcherniakov's production, all of the characters are part of an extended mafia-like family. Elvira is Don Giovanni's wife, not a forgotten fling, and she sings this aria as an ironic performance for her wayward husband. The target of her ridicule is the kind of woman Don Giovanni perceives her to be, the kind of woman portrayed in most performances of this aria: one whose entire self-worth is tied up with her ability to attract and retain a man. Since the music and text of the aria have been unchanged, it is primarily through the visual elements of the performance—the singer's posture, gestures, and facial expressions as well as other staging choices in this aria and the preceding dramatic action—that the character's ironic intent is conveyed.

Watching singers' gestures and facial expressions is important to the full appreciation of song performances, even more so than piano recitals, I suspect, because of the rich representational content of vocal music. This observation does not, however, suggest that songs and oratorios ought to fall into the category of audiovisual fictions. One must be precise about the nature of the information gleaned from spectators' visual experiences in nonoperatic performances of song. In my hypothetical example of the angry-looking singer performing "Ich grolle nicht," the story fact generated by the singer's facial expression is better glossed as "the character is angry" as opposed to "the character is grimacing." Similarly, if the singer has a beard, that does not make it appropriate to imagine that the character does. Notice the disparity with opera performance, in which a bearded, grimacing singer playing the role of Otello makes it true in the story that Otello has a beard and is currently grimacing. In an opera performance, what singers look like and the actions they perform typically generate story content about the characters they play. Likewise, the visual appearance of the stage typically generates facts about their environment.

At this point, one might raise the objection that my account describes only naturalistic approaches to stage direction. Even "traditional" productions can pose difficulties due to color-blind casting. In the Metropolitan Opera's 1989 video recording of Otto Schenk's production of *Die Walküre*, the African American soprano Jessye Norman and the white Heldentenor Gary Lakes appear as the Wälsung twins, Siegmund and Sieglinde.[17] Clearly, when Sieglinde comments that she sees in Siegmund's face a likeness of her own (Act I, Scene 3), we are not to imagine that she is lying or deceived.

The casting of Lin-Manuel Miranda's musical *Hamilton* (2015) also complicates the present account, though for different reasons. It too features nonwhite singers playing white characters, but while the Met's decision to cast Norman was made irrespective of her race, singers' racial identities were taken into consideration by the casting directors of *Hamilton*. As a result, *Hamilton*'s casting policy is more accurately described as *color conscious*.[18] Singers were chosen specifically because their race differed from that of their characters. These disjunctures were integral to the work's point. In the words of the director Thomas Kail, *Hamilton* is "a story about America then, told by America now."[19] By casting predominantly African American and Latinx actors as America's founding fathers, Miranda and Kail draw attention to the diversity of contemporary America and, by contrast, the lack of diversity of most of what one sees on Broadway. Daveed Diggs, who created the roles of the Marquis de Lafayette and Thomas Jefferson, describes "walk[ing] out of the show with a sense of ownership over American history. Part of it is seeing brown bodies play these people."[20] Casting Diggs as Jefferson, or Norman as Sieglinde, did not make their characters black. Yet if one were to ignore Diggs's race, as one is encouraged to do in Norman's case, one would miss one of the show's key artistic and political points.

To be clear, I have no intent to discourage color-blind or color-conscious casting or to endorse discrimination against singers whose bodies do not correspond to the conventional body image of their characters.[21] Rather, my point is that spectators don't automatically assume that everything they see on stage represents contents or occurrences in the fictional world. A concern for equal opportunity for all singers, regardless of race or body type, should trump any mild discomforts that might arise from casting singers of color in "white" roles. After all, we tolerate design and direction choices that create even more blatant conflicts with the libretto and score readily enough, even when they lack the kind of ethical motivations behind color-blind and color-conscious casting.

A case in point is Martin Kušej's *Don Giovanni* for the Salzburg Festival (2002). By presenting audiences with an entirely white set, frequently populated by a dozen or so women underwear models, Kušej is not inviting us to imagine that Don Giovanni's world is literally devoid of color or that the women in this world stand about like living mannequins in nothing but their underclothes. Even though these features of the set and costuming do not represent what Don Giovanni's world looks like, they still play a role in our understanding of the opera's story. One way of interpreting these features is as representations of Don Giovanni's experience of the world. The bare, colorless set could be understood as conveying his boredom and loneliness.[22] The underwear models may indicate that Don Giovanni perceives women as sex objects or that this is an attitude generally held in his society.

There are also cases where the visual elements of the performance generate no story facts but merely express the director's attitude about the work or other topics. Another way of interpreting the underwear models in Kušej's production is to regard them as representing the director's belief that *Don Giovanni* represents women as sex objects. Even under such an interpretation, the visual features of the performance still help determine its content. And the expectation that what one sees will indicate something about the visual appearance of the characters and their fictional world remains appropriate, even when the expectation is denied.

Operas versus Plays and Films

So far, everything I have said about opera also holds true of plays and films containing singing, such as Shakespeare's *Othello* (1603) and the film *Casablanca* (1942). Despite Desdemona's "Willow Song" and Sam's rendition of "As Time Goes By," neither Shakespeare's *Othello* nor *Casablanca* is an opera. The difference between Shakespeare's *Othello* and Verdi and Boito's *Otello* (1887) is not merely a quantitative difference in the amount of music. It also amounts to a difference in kind, specifically one concerning the role music plays in presenting the story. Saying that an opera's story is told through its songs and other musical numbers is a truism. In this final section, I will attempt to be more specific about what this truism might mean.

It may be tempting to claim that what differentiates songs in operas and musicals from those in nonmusical plays and films is that the former advance the plot whereas the latter are incidental to it. However, a song may be integral the plot of a play or a film (as "As Time Goes By" is to *Casablanca*), and many songs in operas merely provide additional insights into what a character is feeling at a given moment, without a noticeable advancement toward or away from that character's goals.[23]

Perhaps songs in operas generate new story facts, whether or not these facts advance the plot. The litmus test would be whether omitting the song would result in a noticeable gap in the story. However, many songs don't even deepen our understanding of the characters. Many merely involve characters expounding on the current situation or feelings we already know them to have, and to opera enthusiasts, such songs are no worse off for their putative superfluity.[24] Furthermore, the requirement that songs generate new story facts is hardly exclusive to opera. When Ophelia sings her mad songs in Shakespeare's *Hamlet*, her performances make several things true in the story, including the crucial fact that she is mad.

I suggest that one difference between operas and nonmusical plays is that song is one of the main ways characters communicate in operatic fictional worlds.[25] As such, operatic worlds are strikingly nonnaturalistic, at least in this respect. When watching a play, one expects there to be a reason for a character to break into song—the character is a professional singer, for instance, or she is insane. In an opera, such explanations are not required. Songs happen anywhere at any time, even in the most unlikely scenarios, such as when one is dying of consumption!

Readers unaware of current discourses on the nature of operatic communication may find this proposal uncontroversial, even banal. However, within opera studies, the proposal that the characters are singing and, generally, hearing the music they and others make is highly contentious, or has been since the publication of Carolyn Abbate's *Unsung Voices* (1991). Abbate floats two different positions on this issue. First, she states that opera characters "often suffer from deafness; they do not *hear* the music that is the ambient fluid of their music-drowned world." Further along in the same paragraph, however, Abbate puts forth the more radical idea that the "music is not produced by or within the stage-world." Developing this second proposition, she invites readers to entertain the following thought experiment: "Suppose that while attending a performance of *Tosca* you are suddenly transformed, given the musical ears of an operatic character. You are struck deaf to most of the singing; everyone merely speaks—except at certain moments, during the offstage cantata in Act II, when you are able to hear the phenomenal performance."[26] According to Abbate's initial proposal, the characters are singing, but they do not hear the music. According to the subsequent more radical one, the characters sing only during the realistic instances of music-making; otherwise, they communicate as we do: by speaking. The latter position is also taken for granted by the philosophers Kendall Walton and Gregory Currie.[27]

One advantage of regarding opera characters as singing and as hearing the music is that it renders opera plots more coherent. Opera characters often fall in love at first sight and undergo other drastic changes to their beliefs and desires within a highly compressed time frame. A case in point is the duet between Violetta and Germont *père* in the second act of Verdi and Piave's *La traviata* (1853). Violetta is a courtesan who has fallen in love with a bourgeois man named Alfredo. By Act II, the couple has fled Paris for an idyllic life in the country—idyllic, that is, until the bills begin to pile up. In secret, Violetta has been selling off the accoutrements of her prior life to support herself and Alfredo. After discovering this fact, Alfredo returns to the city to cash in his inheritance and take control over the situation. While Alfredo is away, his father pays Violetta a visit to convince her to put an end to their affair before the scandal ruins not only the possibility of Alfredo's return to respectable society but also his sister's hope of marrying the man she loves.

There is little incentive for Violetta to capitulate to Germont's demands. His appeal to bourgeois morality holds little sway for someone who lives outside of that social sphere. Aside from Alfredo, Violetta has no family or friends who bear any genuine concern for her well-being. Furthermore, she knows that she is ill and, reasonably, wants to spend her remaining time with the man she loves. Yet by the end of the scene, she willingly sacrifices her only remaining opportunity for happiness.

Although Violetta's choice is the focus of this scene, Germont's trajectory is just as surprising. Initially affording Violetta little respect, he weeps for her in the end. Ostensibly, his "Piangi, piangi" represents him giving her the license to weep, but it is his vocal line, not hers, that mimics crying.[28] Finally, when the courtesan who has nearly ruined his family asks him to embrace her as he would his daughter, he consents without hesitation.

These radical changes to the characters' beliefs and desires may be unrealistic in our world, but they are not unrealistic for opera, I suggest, because such exchanges are conducted through song. The different capabilities of speech and song have been most thoroughly explored in forms of opera and musical theater that involve characters shifting between these modes of discourse. Raymond Knapp and Mitchell Morris observe that, while singing, characters in musicals are "more honest than normal, more intensely present, more capable of interpersonal connection, more empowered, more empower*ing*, and generally better to effect transformative change."[29] Successfully singing a duet involves a high degree of mutual attention, responsiveness, and support for each other's actions. Imagining that Violetta and Germont's conversation is conducted through music helps explain how they are able to form an emotional connection and harmonize their points of view in such a short amount of time.

Supposing that the characters are either not singing or that they fail to hear much of the music creates problems when one attempts to explain how the characters know the things that they do. Real-life opera spectators learn about opera characters not merely from the words they say but also from the music they make. The same is true of opera characters, I have argued elsewhere.[30]

The dominant view of operatic communication also limits the possible ways of explaining instances when characters have a musical-stylistic influence over one another.[31] The ostensible plot of the musical *My Fair Lady* (1956) revolves around Eliza learning to speak "proper English" from Professor Higgins. By the end, however, it is clear that Higgins has learned just as much from Eliza about being a character in a musical. Higgins is initially incapable of conforming his songs to conventional song forms. Furthermore, the role was created by the nonsinging actor Rex Harrison, who performed most of his songs in a kind of Sprechstimme. His final song, "I've Grown Accustomed to Her Face," displays much more formal coherence than his earlier songs "Why Can't the English?" and "A Hymn to Him" and, in the 1964 film adaptation, shows Higgins at his most lyrical.

If the characters do not hear the music, we cannot explain Higgins's transformation as resulting from him hearing Eliza's music and being influenced by its greater lyricism and formal coherence (an *internal* explanation). Rather, we are forced to regard his increasing musicality as part of the composer Frederick Loewe's attempts to demonstrate his growing attraction to and suitability for Eliza (an *external* explanation).[32] Regarding the characters as singing and as hearing each other's music allows for both types of explanation. It opens up the possibility that Eliza chooses to sing in a particular way and that Higgins models his subsequent songs on hers. Internal explanations, which elucidate the features of a narrative in terms of the actions and intentions of its characters, rather than merely those of its real-life author(s), endow characters with more agency. In light of the importance of agency to compelling characters, and thus compelling narratives, regarding opera characters as singing and as hearing the music may increase one's appreciation of the stories operas tell.[33]

There are cases where it is not reasonable to regard the characters as intending or perceiving all of the meanings their performances may have for us. This is especially true of the orchestral music in Wagner, a situation that I will return to in chapter 4. However, hearing need not entail understanding, and utterances, in opera as in everyday life, may possess meanings that are not intended by their authors. External explanations—for instance, viewing the music as authorial commentary—are still available to interpreters who regard opera characters as hearing the music and as singing intentionally.

By suggesting that the default position in opera is that characters hear the music, even when they fail to explicitly acknowledge its presence, I may appear to be undercutting a distinction that has become central to opera studies: the distinction between *phenomenal* and *noumenal* music, in Abbate's terminology, and *diegetic* and *nondiegetic* music, in terminology borrowed from film studies. In opera and musical-theater studies, phenomenal or diegetic music refers to music that takes place in realistic performance contexts or that is explicitly acknowledged as music by the fictional characters, such as the cantata in *Tosca* (1900) or Cherubino's aria "Voi che sapete" from *Le nozze di Figaro* (1786). Cherubino reveals that he is the composer of this song, and the Countess convinces him to perform it for her with guitar accompaniment provided by Susanna. Since the character does not profess to have authored his other aria, "Non so più cosa son, cosa faccio," nor is it acknowledged as a performance of song, it is typically regarded as noumenal or nondiegetic music.

Distinguishing between these two types of music can be important to understanding composers' musical-stylistic choices. Opera composers frequently take care to differentiate these two types of performance. Diegetic or phenomenal music is more likely to conform to conventional song forms. It may also be more simplistic or less skillful than the noumenal or nondiegetic music, particularly if its actual composer wishes us to regard its fictional composer as possessing only modest talents. Furthermore, if the opera is set in the past or in a foreign land, the diegetic music is likely to take on characteristics of the music of its fictional setting, whereas the nondiegetic music is likely to remain unmarked.

My concern is with the terms that have been chosen to describe this difference. Abbate's phenomenal-noumenal distinction suggests that the noumenal music is not part of the opera's fictional world. Additionally, current use of the diegetic-nondiegetic distinction in opera and musical-theater studies is at odds with the use of these terms in film studies. Film scholars use the adjective *diegetic* to refer to features of the audiovisual display that represent contents or occurrences in the fictional world of the film. This definition leads to logical problems when combined with opera scholars' equation of diegetic music with realistic music.[34] Regarding all of the unrealistic instances of music-making in an opera as nondiegetic is untenable, since many such songs are integral to the work's plot. In keeping with my aim to avoid jargon, I will refer to so-called phenomenal or diegetic performances as *embedded* or *nested* musical performances.

There are many reasons to attend the opera: for the opportunity to hear one's favorite singer, for the extravagant sets and costumes, for the jokes, or for its purely musical delights. Before Wagner dimmed the lights in the auditorium, it was also possible to go for the people watching, gambling, and other diversions. Another reason to attend the opera is for the stories operas tell. If that is one's interest, regarding opera characters as singing and as hearing each other's songs is a distinct advantage. It alleviates concerns about the implausibility of many opera plots. Violetta's choice to sacrifice her future with Alfredo may seem undermotivated if it were to happen in our world or even the world of a spoken play or film. Regarding her exchange with Alfredo's father as a duet renders it more plausible, as the act of singing together is capable of forging emotional bonds more effectively than spoken discourse. Understanding the characters as singing and as hearing the music also allows for explanations of characters' behavior that are grounded in the characters' intentions and actions, as opposed to merely those of the work's authors.

The foregoing investigation into the nature of operatic storytelling has revealed the following medium-specific features. In contrast to songs, operas present stories by means of singers enacting characters. Unlike nonoperatic performances of other genres of vocal music in which character enactment is possible, operas are audiovisual fictions. Content is determined not only by what we hear but also by what we see. Finally, opera may be differentiated from nonmusical theater and film by the fact that singing is one of main ways opera characters communicate.

The following chapter continues exploring the medium-specific features of storytelling in the musical theater by defining several common types of character-narrators and discussing the ways in which they differ from the kinds of narrators audiences encounter in literary and cinematic works.

Notes

1. Monika Hennemann, "Operatorio?" in *Oxford Handbook of Opera*, ed. Helen M. Greenwald (New York: Oxford University Press, 2014), 77. Hennemann is responding to the Komische Oper's production of Mozart's Requiem, directed by Sebastian Baumgarten (2008).
2. Edward T. Cone, *The Composer's Voice* (Berkeley: University of California Press, 1974), 21.
3. David Davies, "Medium," in *Routledge Companion to Philosophy and Music*, ed. Theodore Gracyk and Andrew Kania (London: Routledge, 2011), 48–49; Berys Gaut, *A Philosophy of Cinematic Art* (Cambridge: Cambridge University Press, 2010), 288–89.
4. Noël Carroll, "Forget the Medium!" in *Engaging the Moving Image* (New Haven: Yale University Press, 2003), 1–9.
5. Gaut, *Philosophy of Cinematic Art*, 294–95.
6. Jerrold Levinson, "Song and Music Drama," in *The Pleasures of Aesthetics: Philosophical Essays* (Ithaca: Cornell University Press, 1996), 44.
7. Since these characters are defined by the player, not by the instrument, *Mélange à trois* is a good illustration of Philip Rupprecht's concept of the *player-agent*. Philip Rupprecht, "Agency Effects in the Instrumental Drama of Musgrave and Birtwistle," in *Music and Narrative since 1900*, ed. Michael L. Klein and Nicholas Reyland (Bloomington: Indiana University Press, 2012), 190.
8. Jessica A. Holmes, "Singing beyond Hearing," *Journal of the American Musicological Society* 69, no. 2 (2016): 546. A video recording of *Face Opera II* may be streamed from vimeo.com/68027393.
9. A serenata is a large-scale dramatic cantata—dramatic in the sense of singers' utterances representing characters' utterances, not in the sense of singers wearing costumes and participating in a fully staged theatrical performance.
10. Plato, *The Republic*, ed. G. R. F. Ferrari, trans. Tom Griffith (Cambridge: Cambridge University Press, 2000), bk. 3, 392d–394c. In this translation, *mimesis* is rendered as *imitation* and *diegesis* as *narrative*.
11. Cone, *Composer's Voice*, 15–16.
12. Richard Taruskin, *Stravinsky and the Russian Traditions: A Biography of the Works through Mavra*, vol. 2 (Berkeley: University of California Press, 1996), 1237. Rimsky-Korsakov's opera *Le coq d'or* (1909) was intended to be staged with singers enacting characters, including the dancing the characters perform. When Diaghilev staged the work with the Ballet Russes in 1914, he separated the singing and dancing components as Taruskin describes.
13. For example, Handel's first English oratorio, *Esther*, was first given a staged performance at the Crown and Anchor Tavern in 1732. Handel investigated the possibility of mounting another staged performance at the King's Theatre but was unsuccessful due to the ban on theatrical performances of biblical stories in public (the previous performance was considered private). Accordingly, he turned his attentions to concert performances. Howard E. Smither, "Oratorio," *Grove Music Online*, last modified 2001, http://www.oxfordmusiconline.com/subscriber/article/grove/music/20397. For other examples of oratorios that have been staged as operas, refer to Hennemann, "Operatorio?"
14. Gregory Currie, "Visual Fictions," *Philosophical Quarterly* 41, no. 163 (1991): 140.
15. That is not to say that the aural properties of films and theatrical performances are unimportant but merely that there are silent films and theater performances. There are no silent operas.
16. For a summary of work in this area, refer to Vincent Bergeron and Dominic McIver Lopes, "Hearing and Seeing Musical Expression," *Philosophy and Phenomenological Research* 78, no. 1 (2009): 1–16.

17. I thank Udayan Sen for mentioning this example.

18. Chinua Thelwell, "Who Tells Your Story? *Hamilton*, Future Aesthetics, and Haiti," in *Theater and Cultural Politics for a New World*, ed. Chinua Thelwell (London: Routledge, 2017), 112. For an argument that color-conscious casting is preferable to color-blind casting, refer to Aria Umezawa, "Met's *Otello* Casting Begs the Question: Is Whitewash Better than Blackface?" *Globe and Mail*, August 7, 2015, last modified March 25, 2018, https://www.theglobeandmail.com/opinion/mets-otello-casting-begs-the-question-is-whitewash-better-than-blackface/article25879634/?arc404=true.

19. Thomas Kail, quoted in Lin-Manuel Miranda and Jeremy McCarter, *Hamilton: The Revolution* (New York: Grand Central Publishing, 2016), 33.

20. Daveed Diggs, quoted in Branden Janese, "*Hamilton* Roles Are This Rapper's Delight," *Wall Street Journal*, last modified July 7, 2015, https://www.wsj.com/articles/hamilton-roles-are-this-rappers-delight-1436303922; Leslie Odom Jr. expressed similar sentiments in Kathryn Lurie's "Playing the Man Who Shot Hamilton," *Wall Street Journal*, last modified August 6, 2015, https://www.wsj.com/articles/playing-the-man-who-shot-hamilton-1438896589.

21. I am grateful to an audience member at the 2014 Royal Musical Association Music and Philosophy Study Group conference for noting that my argument could be used to support the "fat shaming" of Tara Erraught as Octavian in Glyndebourne's 2014 *Rosenkavalier*. For a summary of the discourse surrounding Erraught's casting in this production, refer to Norman Lebrecht, "Singers in Uproar over Critical Body Insults at Glyndebourne," Slipped Disc, last modified May 19, 2014, https://slippedisc.com/2014/05/singers-in-uproar-at-critical-body-insults-at-glyndebourne/.

22. The interviews with Martin Kušej and Thomas Hampson (who performed the role of Don Giovanni) confirm that both intended to portray Don Giovanni as psychologically troubled, his sex addiction a vain attempt to alleviate his loneliness. Included in Martin Kušej, dir., *Don Giovanni* (Decca, 2006), DVD.

23. For an argument that "As Time Goes By" is "an essential part of the plot" to *Casablanca*, refer to Peter Kivy, "Realistic Song in the Movies," *Journal of Aesthetics and Art Criticism* 71, no. 1 (2013): 77.

24. John Mueller, "Fred Astaire and the Integrated Musical," *Cinema Journal* 24, no. 1 (1984): 28–30.

25. Singing is the primary means of communication in most operas, but in opéra comique, Singspiel, and most musicals, speaking is another. In many musicals and some operas (e.g., Auber's *La muette de Portici* [1828]), dance also plays an important role.

26. Carolyn Abbate, *Unsung Voices: Opera and Musical Narrative in the Nineteenth Century* (Princeton: Princeton University Press, 1991), 119, 123. Following Abbate, Scott McMillin, *The Musical as Drama* (Princeton: Princeton University Press, 2006), 126, contends that characters in musicals do not hear the orchestra unless a fictional source is identified (e.g., the onstage band in *Cabaret* [1966]). His stance on whether characters hear the so-called nondiegetic vocal music is unclear.

27. Kendall L. Walton, *Mimesis as Make-Believe: On the Foundations of the Representational Arts* (Cambridge, MA: Harvard University Press, 1990), 182; Gregory Currie, *Narratives and Narrators: A Philosophy of Stories* (Oxford: Oxford University Press, 2010), 59.

28. Mary Ann Smart, *Mimomania: Music and Gesture in Nineteenth-Century Opera* (Berkeley: University of California Press, 2004), 7; Roger Parker, "Verdi and *La traviata*: Two Routes to Realism," in *La traviata*, ed. Gary Kahn (London: Overture Publishing, 2013), 32.

29. Raymond Knapp and Mitchell Morris, "The Filmed Musical," in *The Oxford Handbook of the American Musical*, ed. Raymond Knapp, Mitchell Morris, and Stacy Wolf (Oxford: Oxford University Press, 2011), 143.

30. Nina Penner, "Opera Singing and Fictional Truth," *Journal of Aesthetics and Art Criticism* 71, no. 1 (2013): 85–86.

31. For a fuller exposition of this argument, see Nina Penner, "Rethinking the Diegetic/Nondiegetic Distinction in the Film Musical," *Music and the Moving Image* 10, no. 3 (2017): 9–12.

32. On the contrast between internal and external perspectives, refer to Currie, *Narratives and Narrators*, 49. For an example of an external explanation of the changes to Higgins's music, see McMillin, *Musical as Drama*, 67–68.

33. Paul Woodruff, *The Necessity of Theater: The Art of Watching and Being Watched* (Oxford: Oxford University Press, 2008), 94–95.

34. Penner, "Diegetic/Nondiegetic Distinction," 7.

3

CHARACTER-NARRATORS

Midway through the second act of Stephen Sondheim and James Lapine's *Into the Woods* (1987), the characters encounter a giant seeking vengeance from the boy who killed her husband by chopping down the beanstalk. Unwilling to give Jack up but unsure of how else to placate the giantess, the characters quarrel over the most appropriate course of action. Meanwhile, the Narrator pontificates on the morality of their decision. For the first time, the characters notice him and move in:

> NARRATOR: (*to the group*) Sorry, I tell the story, I'm not part of it.
>
> LITTLE RED RIDING HOOD: That's right. (*pulls out knife*)
>
> WITCH: Not one of us.
>
> BAKER: Always on the outside.
>
> *Baker grabs the Narrator and the group beings to pull him slowly towards the giant.*
>
> NARRATOR (*nervous*): That's my role. You must understand, there must always be someone on the outside.
>
> STEWARD: You're going to be on the inside now.
>
> NARRATOR (*frantic*): You're making a big mistake.
>
> STEPMOTHER: Nonsense.
>
> NARRATOR: You need an objective observer to pass the story along.
>
> WITCH: Some of us don't like the way you've been telling it.
>
> *They pull him further.*
>
> NARRATOR: If you drag me into this mess, you'll never know how your story ends. You'll be lost![1]

At the Narrator's threat, the Baker and Wife desist. Just as he begins to calm down, the Witch thrusts him at the Giant. Seeing that he is not the lad she is looking for, she tosses him away like an unwanted toy. As the Witch suspected, the story does indeed go on without the Narrator's guidance.

The moral most commonly drawn from the Narrator's unfortunate end is that such figures do not belong in the theater. Many scholars have suggested that his sacrifice is necessary, either so that the characters can assert their own agency or because his drawing attention to "the machinery that drives the story . . . is an even bigger problem than a vengeful giant."[2] I draw a different moral from this amusing episode: such narrators are indeed unnecessary, but neither are they uncommon nor are they inherently problematic. As I will explore in this chapter, narrators play a variety of roles in opera and musical theater.

At the outset, it will be advisable to identify the animal I'm hunting and to make some distinctions between different breeds within this species. I understand a narrator to be an agent who tells or presents a story to an audience. I employ the term *agent*, as opposed to *person* or *character*, to allow for storytellers that are nonhuman, such as the insertion aria that narrates its memoirs in the short story "Memoir of a Song" (1849), and those that are nonfictional, such as the story's real-life author.[3]

Among fictional narrators, a few more distinctions may be made. The first concerns the narrator's degree of characterization. Reading Nabokov's *Lolita* (1955), readers learn a great deal—for some, perhaps too much—about Humbert Humbert's personality and proclivities. In other cases, such as Ernest Hemingway's short story "The Killers" (1927) or Graham Greene's *The Heart of the Matter* (1948), it may be difficult to discern much of anything about the narrator's identity. Those who speak of the cinema camera or opera orchestra as narrating agents invoke narrators that are even more effaced or elusive, whose abilities bear little resemblance to those of any beings currently known to man.

Some acts of narration are directed toward a fictional audience, whereas others are directed solely at the work's actual audience. I will use the internal-external distinction to differentiate these two scenarios.[4] In Act I of *Into the Woods*, the Narrator summarizes characters' backstories for the benefit of the real-life audience, but his pleas in the quoted scene are directed at the other fictional characters, contradicting his claims to be an external observer. Narrators that better fit the Narrator's self-description include the Male Chorus and Female Chorus (played by individual singers) in Britten's *The Rape of Lucretia* (1946). Their references to the birth of Christ indicate that they occupy a different fictional world than Lucretia and Tarquinius. Although they possess knowledge about and even the power to influence these characters, imagining the reverse is incoherent. While it is possible for an internal narrator to break through the proverbial fourth wall and perform a direct address, external narrators can address *only* the work's real-life audience.

Finally, some narratives invite us to imagine that the text we are reading or the movie or performance we are watching has been produced by a fictional character or group thereof. Jo Walton's *Thessaly* trilogy (2015–16) prescribes that readers imagine that they are reading various characters' diaries, which have been compiled by the god Apollo. I will refer to narrators of this type as *authorial narrators* or *author figures*. In other cases, it is true in the story that the text, movie, or performance reports or presents a character's telling, but we are not invited to imagine that the character is responsible for creating and disseminating/presenting that text, movie, or performance.[5]

Most cinematic narrators are not authorial narrators. At the beginning of *All about Eve* (1950), Addison DeWitt provides voice-over commentary on Eve's award ceremony, appearing to direct the camera to each personage as he introduces them, to put the diegetic sound on mute because he finds the wizened actor's speech tedious and irrelevant, and to institute freeze-frame when Eve receives her award, allowing himself more time to pontificate. Despite DeWitt's apparent control over the cinematic apparatus, it is not true in the story that he has shot a documentary film about Eve's rise to stardom.[6] Only in exceptional cases such as *This Is Spinal Tap* (1984) and *The Blair Witch Project* (1999) is it true in the story that an entity in the fictional world of the film produces the entire film we are watching.

Perhaps due to narratology's traditional focus on literary narratives, it is uncommon for this last distinction to be distinguished from that of narrative level.[7] Whereas external literary narrators are usually also authorial narrators, that is not the case with cinematic and theatrical works.[8] The choruses of *Lucretia* are external to Lucretia's world and address an external audience, but there is nothing in the libretto or score to suggest that they are the authors of the performance we are watching.

With the foregoing distinctions in hand, it is now possible to critically evaluate leading arguments that all narratives require fictional narrators. Many literary theorists have argued that if one knows that a work is a narrative, one can conclude that it has a fictional narrator without even examining its particular features. The following is Seymour Chatman's argument to this effect, as parsed by the philosopher Katherine Thomson-Jones:

1. Narration is the activity of telling or showing a story.
2. Every activity has an agent.

> 3. The agent of fiction narration is the [fictional] narrator.
>
> So 4. All narrative fictions, including all narrative fiction films, have [fictional] narrators.[9]

As Thomson-Jones's digest makes clear, we are looking for a narrator who is the fictional author or presenter of the text, movie, or performance. Cases like Walton's *Thessaly* trilogy, in which the fictional authors are explicitly identified and robustly characterized, are uncontroversial. The contentious issue is whether one ought to posit a fictional narrating agency for narratives that lack such explicit evidence.

Premises one and two of Chatman's argument expose the incoherence of speaking about the narration itself performing actions like suppressing information.[10] Problems arise with premise three, which assumes that the agent responsible for these actions is fictional. Why can't the work's author(s) fulfill this function?[11] Although Chatman does not provide an answer to this question, Jerrold Levinson has. His argument runs as follows:

> 1. It is reasonable to expect an answer to the question of how we gain access to the fictional world of a narrative.
> 2. There exists an ontological gap between the fictional world and the real world.
> 3. The agent responsible for providing us access to the fictional world must be on the same side of the gap as the characters and events of which he or she narrates.
> 4. Authors, either real or implied, are on the other side of the gap.
>
> Thus 5. The narrating agent must be fictional.
>
> So 6. All fictional narratives have fictional narrators.[12]

Even if premise one were correct and premise two were to pose an obstacle to story comprehension (neither of which is established by Levinson's discussion), premise three does not solve the problem of the ontological gap. If a gap exists that prevents the author from telling or showing the fictional, it is unclear how a fictional agent would have any easier time traversing the gap. As the philosopher Andrew Kania has argued, it makes more sense that the author would be able to do so, since works of fiction are part of our world but our world is not part of all fictional worlds.[13]

George Wilson has taken a different approach to demonstrating the necessity of fictional narrators, one grounded in the phenomenology of cinema spectatorship. He argues that the normative mode of engaging with fiction films is to imagine seeing naturally iconic images of fictional characters and events.[14] Since our access to the fictional world is mediated, there must be a corresponding act of fictional showing performed by some entity or mechanism in the world of the story. Whether cinema spectators typically entertain such imaginings is an empirical question, but Wilson offers no empirical evidence to support it.[15] The number of scholars and critics who have taken issue with Wilson's proposed phenomenology raises doubts on this score.

So far, no one has provided any logical reasons why all acts of fictional storytelling require a fictional teller or presenter or effectively demonstrated that it is normative to imagine such an entity when engaging with fictional stories. Whether a given narrative has such a narrator must be decided on a case-by-case basis, not on general truths about narration *tout court* or narration in any particular medium.[16] To decide whether operas and works of musical theater have such narrators, we must look at some cases. Numerous taxonomies of types of narrators have been put forth for literature, cinema, and even spoken theater.[17] Since the terrain for musical theater is uncharted, the remainder of this chapter will outline some of the most common storytelling situations by fictional characters while the following chapter will begin exploring the orchestra's role as a narrating agent.

Before proceeding, it will be important to recall that the study of the performing arts may be directed toward two different objects: works for performance and particular performances. Works for performance possess fewer properties than any of their performances, a situation that allows a single work to give rise to many different but equally legitimate performances. Accordingly, it is possible that a work that lacks a fictional narrator may be given a performance that has such a narrator and vice versa. These and other possibilities will be explored in the final two chapters. Unless otherwise noted, the categorizations put forth in this chapter are based on the properties of works for performance, as outlined by their scores and libretti, and on performances that follow these directions, not on performances that depart from them.

Internal Narrators

Oral Storytelling

By far the most common storytelling situation in opera is oral storytelling by one character to another. Such stories are typically told as fact for the purpose of apprising other characters of past events and thus constitute nonfictional stories from the characters' perspective. Wagner had a particular penchant for backstory narrations. His most notorious work in this respect is his *Ring* cycle (1876). It is understandable that a story of such epic scope would require considerable narrative exposition, not only to inform spectators about events that could not be represented onstage for reasons of time or the practicalities of staging but also to remind them of the relationships between a large cast of characters. Historical operas foregrounding complex political intrigues, such as Modest Musorgsky's *Boris Godunov* (1874), also tend to contain a large number of narration scenes.

What is puzzling about the number of narration scenes in the *Ring* is that their presence conflicts with Wagner's explanations of the work's genesis. One of his stated motivations in expanding his initial idea for the *Ring*, *Siegfrieds Tod*, into a tetralogy was to replace the scenes of narration with enactments of those events. As Wagner explains in *Opera and Drama* (1851), he regarded enactment as a superior mode of presentation because of its immediacy, its ability to engage spectators "at the level of the senses rather than the intellect."[18] Nevertheless, the plan Wagner actually executed involved the addition rather than the subtraction of scenes of narration, and not just in the so-called "prelude" opera, *Das Rheingold*. *Götterdämmerung* contains the most expository scenes of them all. Its egregiousness has been memorably recounted by George Bernard Shaw:

> Siegfried inherits from Wotan a mania for autobiography which leads him to inflict on everyone he meets the story of Mime and the dragon, although the audience have spent a whole evening witnessing the events he is narrating. Hagen tells the story to Gunther; and the same night Alberich's ghost tells it over again to Hagen, who knows it already as well as the audience. Siegfried tells the Rhine maidens as much of it as they will listen to, and then keeps telling it to his hunting companions until they kill him. Wotan's autobiography on the second evening [*Die Walküre*] becomes his biography in the mouths of the Norns on the fourth [*Götterdämmerung*]. The little that the Norns add to it is repeated an hour later by Waltraute.[19]

Unlike Musorgsky, who uses narration to inform spectators about events that they have not witnessed, Wagner presents dozens of rehashings of scenes that spectators who are appreciating the work in the intended manner (that is, sequentially, as a cycle) will have already seen. Some events are even narrated multiple times.

Many explanations for these seemingly superfluous narration scenes have been offered. Carolyn Abbate suggests that Wagner was urging "listeners to complete gaps and form our own supplementary stretches of libretto" while James Treadwell proposes that Wagner was cultivating an audience "capable of interpretation, one that generates the meanings the work itself cannot supply."[20] As appealing as these explanations may be to critics raised on the theories of Roland Barthes and Mikhail Bakhtin, neither is a plausible account of the intentions guiding Wagner's creative choices. As David Levin has remarked, "it is hard to think of an artist . . . more single-minded in his determination to close off the meaning of his librettos and reserve to himself the right to adjudicate that meaning."[21]

Levin's theory is that Wagner included these acts of narration in order to demonstrate their inferiority to enactment. Although more consistent with Wagner's aesthetic theories and artistic aims, Levin's proposal is able to explain only the presence of unreliable narration (e.g., Mime's stories about how he raised Siegfried) and instances where telling stories leads to a character's unfortunate end (e.g., Siegfried's death in *Götterdämmerung*). He is unable to explain the far more numerous instances of oral storytelling by characters with whom Wagner intended audiences to sympathize, such as the Wälsung twins and Wotan, and which have no negative consequences for those characters. Both in the *Ring* cycle and in Wagner's theoretical writings, not all narration is suspect.[22]

The presence of multiple accounts of the same events suggests Wagner's interest in the subjectivity of narration. Since the content is familiar, one's attention is drawn to the manner of its telling and what that illuminates about its teller.[23] Wagner was not alone in such interests. Verdi and Salvadore Cammarano's *Il trovatore* (1853) is another opera unusually preoccupied with the past. The title character, Azucena, saw her mother burned at the stake for suspicions of malevolent sorcery against one of Count di Luna's infant sons. On the day of her mother's execution, Azucena went with her own child to exact vengeance on the Count's family by throwing the supposedly cursed child into the embers of her mother's pyre. Disoriented by visions of her mother's final cry, she threw the wrong baby into the fire. The opera's action begins decades later. Azucena has raised the infant she intended to murder as her son, named Manrico, and his brother has succeeded his father as count.

Verdi and Cammarano juxtapose two accounts of these events. In the first scene, Ferrando, a captain in the Count's army, enlivens the night watch with a tale about the "sorcerer" who cursed the Count's brother and the daughter who murdered him. While Ferrando relates these events as a ghost story, complete with trembling staccato figuration and grace notes, Azucena recounts them to Manrico as family history in Act II, Scene 1, her performance inviting sympathy for a mother falsely accused and a daughter driven to drastic measures by her mother's cry for vengeance.

Opera characters may also entertain their companions with fictional stories. Often such stories are mere divertissements for both external and internal audiences. In the Tchaikovsky brothers' *Queen of Spades* (1890), however, Tomsky's story about the Countess's secret to gambling success serves as a catalyst for the rest of the drama. Although Tomsky tells the story as a mere legend, his friend Herman believes it, and his quest to know the three winning cards eventually drives him insane.

As Abbate has remarked, fictional stories often mirror the story of the opera in which they are a part.²⁴ Examples include Pedrillo's *Romanze* in Mozart's *Die Entführung aus dem Serail* (1782), Senta's ballad in Wagner's *Der fliegende Holländer* (1843), Lakmé's Bell Song in Delibes's 1883 opera of the same title, and Brooke's courting song from Mark Adamo's *Little Women* (1998). In the lattermost work, Meg teaches her suitor a family game called Truth or Fabrication, in which the first participant begins a story but stops at the most exciting part, leaving the next to take it up. Lacking the creativity of Meg's sister Jo, an aspiring novelist, Brooke tells a story about a knight in a similar predicament to his own: wishing to court a maiden but lacking anything to offer her but love. Despite his hackneyed attempt at storytelling, Brooke's song brings his and Meg's story to the desired conclusion.

Another conventional nonfictional storytelling situation is the *Mauerschau* (literally: wall-show), in which a character, perched on a literal or proverbial wall, describes events that are concurrently happening on the side not visible to the audience. That it is most often employed as a solution to staging problems, such as how to represent gods on flying horses (*Die Walküre*, Act III, Scene 1), should not blind one to its potential to create particular dramatic effects. Hagen's narration of Siegfried's approach to the Gibichungs' court (*Götterdämmerung*, Act I, Scene 1), together with the sounding of the Curse motive in the orchestra, creates a feeling of inevitability, as if Hagen has conjured Siegfried at will. It can also be used to align spectators with characters' points of view. Having the torture of Cavaradossi (*Tosca*, Act II) take place offstage places spectators in a similar perceptual and epistemic position as his lover, Tosca. Like her, we are reliant solely on Scarpia and his henchmen's accounts of Cavaradossi's condition and his intermittent cries of pain.²⁵

Letter-reading and -writing scenes are another common storytelling situation, particularly in nineteenth-century opera. In Verdi and Arrigo Boito's *Falstaff* (1893), Act II, Scene 2, Alice and Meg read each other's love letters from Falstaff aloud, discovering them to be identical. There are also cases where the oral reading or writing does not have a fictional audience, as in Tatyana's feverish declaration of love to Onegin (Tchaikovsky's *Eugene Onegin*, Act II, Scene 2) or Violetta's spoken recitation of a letter from Germont père (*La traviata*, Act III, Scene 4).

A related phenomenon is the backstory narration conveyed as an interior monologue as in "Helpless" and "Satisfied" from *Hamilton* (2015). From the impact of a predominantly minority cast presenting a story about America's founding fathers to the refrain of its finale, "Who Lives, Who Dies, Who Tells Your Story," *Hamilton* explores the influence of the storyteller on the story told. In one of the show's few deviations from a chronological presentation, "Helpless" and "Satisfied" both dramatize the same series of events—the Schuyler sisters meeting Hamilton and his and Eliza's courtship—from Eliza's and Angelica's perspectives.

Modeled on R&B-rapper duets, such as Beyoncé and Jay Z's "Crazy in Love" (2003), "Helpless" juxtaposes Eliza's R&B-based narration and private effusions of giddy infatuation with spoken or rapped enactments of her first conversation with Hamilton and his confession of his penniless state.[26] "Satisfied" takes up where the previous song ends—Eliza and Hamilton's wedding—but in the middle of Angelica's toast, she turns to the real-life audience and reveals her role in engineering this outcome: her thrill at matching wits with an intellectual equal, realization both that Hamilton's interest in her lies primarily in the possibility of social advancement and that Eliza has also fallen for him, and decision to sacrifice her happiness for that of her sister. Like "Helpless," "Satisfied" alternates Angelica's narration with enactments of scenes from the Winter's Ball. But Angelica's narration is a virtuosic rap, Hamilton's medium of choice. Miranda's musical demonstration of their compatibility suggests that Angelica's closing remarks are prescient: neither she nor Hamilton will be satisfied by his marriage.

For critics who insist that all narratives require narrators, the presence of these kinds of narrators is not going to ground the foregoing works as narratives. None are posited as the fictional presenters of the show or even all aspects of their narration scenes. Only in exceptional cases is one invited to imagine that internal oral narrators are the authors of their accompaniments. Abbate has made such a case for Wotan's monologue in *Die Walküre*, Act II, Scene 2. Pointing to the supposedly uncharacteristic tautologies in the orchestral music, she argues that "the music comes from Wotan. There is no untainted or external musical narrator."[27]

I suggest that we ought to distinguish between cases where it is appropriate to imagine that a character is responsible for performing or otherwise authoring the accompaniment and others where the orchestral music assists in the character's act of storytelling but where it is fictionally indeterminate how it does so and who its author is. Although the following are not scenes of narration, examples of the former situation would include the mandolin or guitar accompaniments to Cherubino's "Voi che sapete" from *Le nozze di Figaro* (1786) and Aldonza's "It's All the Same" from Mitch Leigh, Joe Darion, and Dale Wasserman's *Man of La Mancha* (1965); the harp accompaniment in Olympia's aria from Offenbach and Jules Barbier's *Les contes d'Hoffmann* (1881); the harpsichord in Antonia's romance and her duet with Hoffmann (*Hoffmann*, Act III, Scenes 1 and 8); and the onstage band in the portions of Kander and Ebb's *Cabaret* (1966) that take place at the Kit Kat Klub. The invitation to imagine that characters are responsible for the accompaniment is made not only by stage directions indicating that characters play (or pretend to play) instruments but also by the orchestration, which either employs the instrument(s) in question or otherwise mimics their sound (e.g., Offenbach substitutes harp for harpsichord in *Hoffmann*).

Although the orchestral accompaniment to Wotan's monologue corroborates his story, there is no indication that we ought to regard him as its author. His relationship to the orchestral music is, thus, analogous to that of Addison DeWitt to the audio-visual display at the beginning of *All about Eve*. It is necessary to imagine some other narrating agent who is responsible for generating an appropriate accompaniment to Wotan's narration.

Theatrical Storytelling

What theorists who insist on the necessity of fictional narrators need is a character or, more likely, fictional production team who are responsible for putting on the show we are watching: words, music, and staging. Thus, a more likely source would seem to be operas about putting on an opera where the characters' opera is not merely described but made perceptually accessible to the work's real-life audience through a nested performance for a fictional audience.[28]

Man of La Mancha is an archetypal example. The musical opens with Cervantes in jail. While awaiting his hearing at the Spanish Inquisition, his fellow inmates subject him to their own trial. His charges include "being an idealist, a bad poet, and an honest man." As his defense, he presents a musical-theatrical adaptation of the manuscript in his possession, which is, of course, *Don Quixote*. In the verse of his first number, "Man of La Mancha," we watch him put on his makeup, transforming himself from playwright to knight-errant. When he and Sancho Panza (played by his manservant) arrive at an inn, Cervantes momentarily steps out of character to do some stage managing, enlisting members of his fictional audience to play the roles of innkeeper, muleteers, and the waitress/prostitute Aldonza (evidently it is a mixed-gender prison). He also plays the role of music director. The stage directions before "Little Bird" describe him "entering with the Muleteers, prompting them in the next song they are to sing," and remaining until he is "satisfied that they are singing it properly."²⁹ The other inmates are no mere servants to Cervantes's will, however. After he enacts Don Quixote's disillusionment and resumption of his life as Alonso Quijano, Cervantes declares the story finished. The jury is unimpressed. But before they can make their ruling, he improvises a new ending in which Aldonza returns in search of the first man who treated her with respect. By reciting the words of the songs he had sung, she rekindles the old man's belief in his fantasy, and he dies during his reprise of "Man of La Mancha."

In this case, a fictional musical nests another fictional musical, but fiction can also nest nonfiction.³⁰ Although the idea of a nonfiction opera might seem bizarre in our world, there is nothing implausible about characters in an opera, who live in a musical world, mounting a nonfiction opera. That is precisely what happens in *Les feluettes* (2016), with music by Kevin March to a libretto by Michel Marc Bouchard, based on the latter's play of the same title.³¹ Coincidentally, the framing action also takes place in a jail, this time in Québec in 1952. The function of the prisoners' performance is not, however, to plead their case but, as in *Hamlet*, to elicit a confession from their audience, a visiting bishop. Bishop Bilodeau thinks that he will be hearing the last confession of a man he knew in his youth named Simon, but instead Simon and the other prisoners force Bilodeau to watch their own operatic dramatization of the events leading up to Simon's incarceration forty years earlier.

Through the embedded opera, we discover that Bilodeau was the odd man out of a love triangle between Simon and Vallier. After suffering a brutal whipping from his father for kissing another man, Simon decides that he must "think about girls" and proceeds to court a visiting Parisian aristocrat named Lydie-Anne. After Simon's cover becomes threadbare and other events transpire that prevent a future for him and Vallier in their hometown of Roberval, Bilodeau proposes that the three of them run away to a logging camp. But since Bilodeau has subjected the lovers to nothing but ridicule thus far, Simon refuses, and the lovers commit suicide by setting fire to their school. At the conclusion of the prisoners' performance, the bishop confesses that he rescued the man he loved, Simon, but, out of spite, left Vallier to die.

March and Bouchard went to great lengths to put forth the prisoners as the fictional authors of the embedded opera. Unlike *Man of La Mancha*, *Les feluettes* was written for an all-male cast. Lydie-Anne is to be played by a countertenor, and Vallier's slightly unhinged mother, the Countess Marie-Laure de Tilly, is a baritone role. The score specifies that the prisoners effect (or at least appear to effect) their own set changes. Serge Denoncourt, director of the original production, even went as far as to place the orchestra onstage and in costume.³² And like the intended staging of *Man of La Mancha*, the costumes and props were made from materials that one would find in a prison, if not perhaps the tools and skills with which to make them.

Even March's musical-stylistic choices contributed to the plausibility of the prisoners being its fictional composers. While the music of the framing prison scenes is largely atonal, somewhat aleatoric, and employing extended performing techniques, the stylistic influences over the embedded drama stick more closely to those likely to be familiar to a Québécois man who had been incarcerated since 1912.

The score to the embedded performance contains a remarkable number of borrowings and allusions, most obviously to Debussy's and Gabrielle D'Annunzio's *Le Martyre de saint Sébastien* (1911), a cross between oratorio, melodrama, and ballet. The first scene of the embedded performance involves Simon and Vallier rehearsing this work at their school. Thus, there is an additional layer of nesting: March and Bouchard's fictional opera *Les feluettes* embeds the prisoners' nonfictional enactment of events from 1912, which in turn embeds excerpts from Debussy and D'Annunzio's *Le Martyre*.

The instrumental prélude to the first act of *Le Martyre* underscores old-Simon's introduction of the dramatis personae of the embedded performance, sung to newly composed vocal lines (ex. 3.1).³³ With the changes largely confined to orchestration, necessitated by March's more modest woodwind section, this is the most literal quotation from Debussy. Once the scene is set, March jumps to the prélude to Act IV, the scene the students are rehearsing. In Bouchard's play, unspecified sections of Debussy's music were to be played as underscoring to the young men's dramatic reading of D'Annunzio's narrator's (spoken) lines from Act IV. March set these lines to newly composed music, transforming the scene into a lyric drama (ex. 3.2). In an effort to represent the meager resources of a school in rural Québec, March took more liberties with the orchestration, giving the English horn solo to the fiddle. Initially accompanied by the accordion and wooden spoons, other more exotic instruments gradually join in.³⁴ March also reshapes Debussy's form to suit his new dramatic ends. After borrowing measures 3 through 12 of Debussy's Act IV prélude, March inserts the undulating chromatic scales from measures 24 and 25 before returning to the horn solo beginning in measure 12, used to underscore Simon's/Sébastien's reply.

The other scene that contains extended quotations from *Le Martyre* is episode 4, Simon and Lydie-Anne's engagement party, which Vallier derails by performing a portion of the play the men were previously rehearsing. Although the text is not in fact D'Annunzio's, March borrows Debussy's

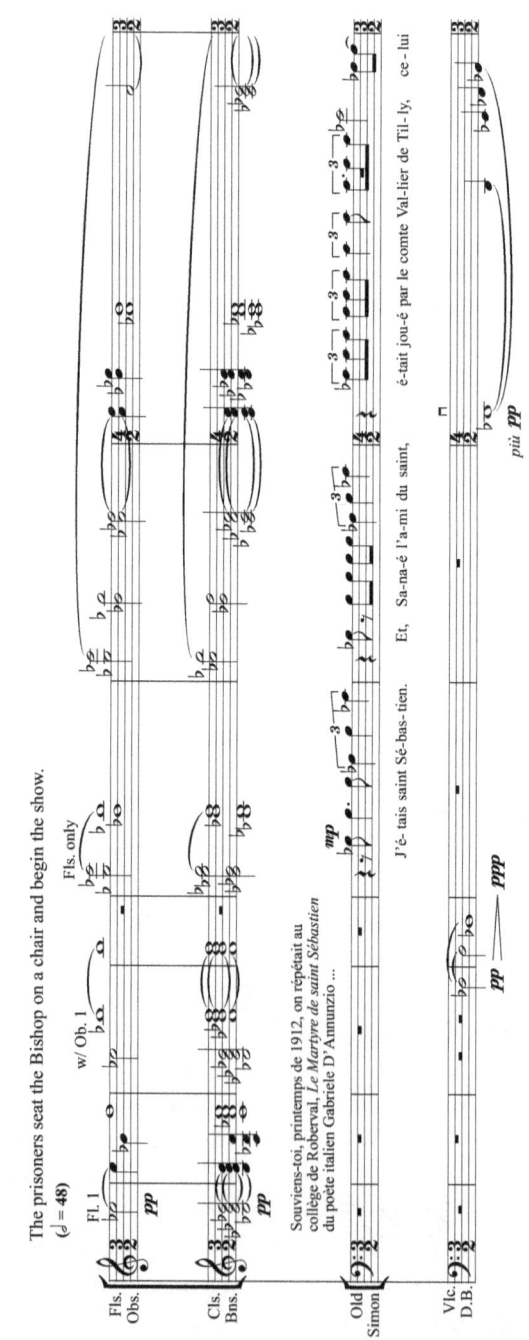

Example 3.1. Quotation of the Act I prélude of Debussy's *Le Martyre* in the prologue of *Les feluettes* by Kevin March and Michel Marc Bouchard. Used by permission of the authors.

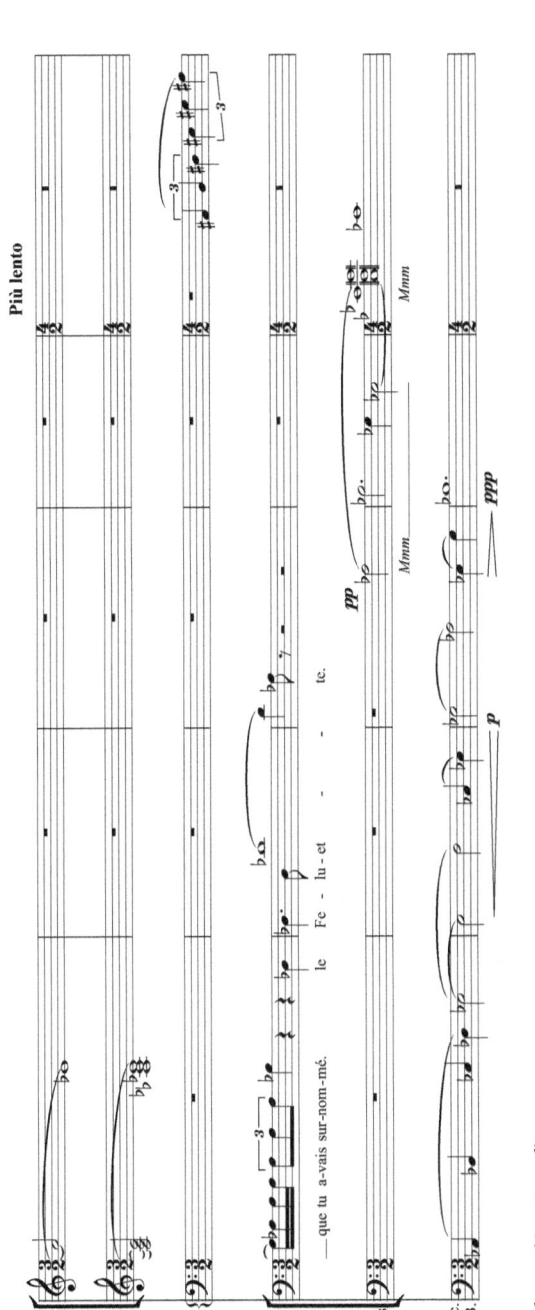

Example 3.1. (Continued)

EPISODE 1

Theatre of the college of Roberval. A cobbled-together setting of the production *St. Sebastian*. A backdrop, a landscape of Roman antiquity; the façade of a temple, some hills. In front of the canvas, a puny tree. Some manuscript pages lie around. The young Simon, playing St. Sebastian, is near Vallier, playing Sanae, friend of the saint, who threatens him with a drawn bow and arrow. They play with conviction but take full measure of what they say. In the darkness, we make out the silhouette of a prisoner playing Father Saint-Michel, the director of the play, script in hand. This first scene is light and youthful.

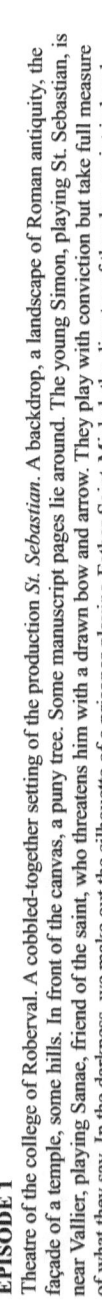

Example 3.2. Quotation of the Act IV prélude of *Le Martyre* in *Les feluettes*, episode 1

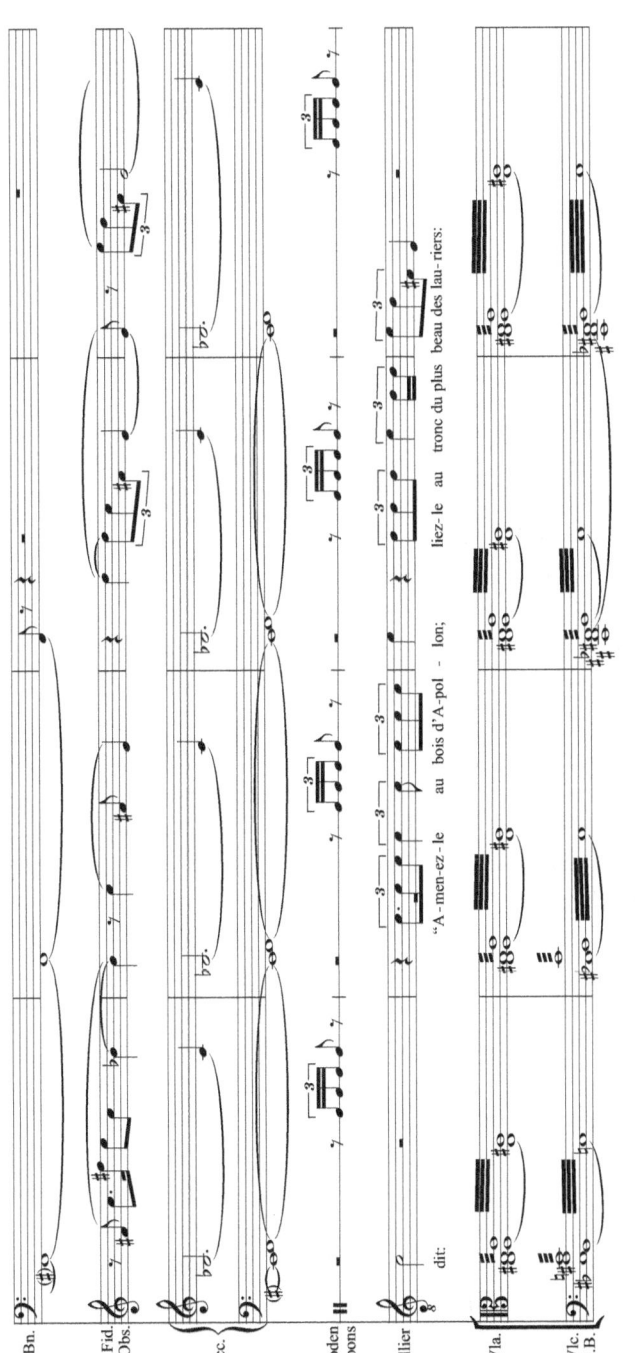

Example 3.2. (Continued)

Example 3.3. Love-Death motive, *Les feluettes*, episode 1

pseudo-Roman fanfare from the Act III prélude for Vallier's entrance as Caesar. Aside from the chorus's exultant cries of "Sébastien," borrowed from the final chorus of Act V, the ensuing duet between the lovers is newly composed, though still in the style of Debussy.

There are also quotations from *Le Martyre* in scenes not framed as performances of the work. When the director of the school play, Father Saint-Michel, explains why Sébastien longs for death, the orchestra plays the violin melody at the beginning of the second part of Act IV (ex. 3.3). Although it opens the ensuing rehearsal scene, it also appears during the love duet Simon and Vallier perform out of character, after they believe everyone else has departed. It goes on to become one of the most pervasive musical motives associated with their love.

Perhaps inspired by the close relationship between love and death in the libretto, the influence of Wagner can also be heard in the score. Most conspicuously, March borrows the Magic Fire music from the *Ring* when Father Saint-Michel laments that most clergymen are interested only in stories about saints who are burned at the stake (ex. 3.4).

The song associated with Lydie-Anne's hot-air balloon is in the style of a turn-of-the-century cabaret song, "possibly with a Satie-esque twist to it."[35] Similarly to the beginning of episode 1, the scene on the hotel terrasse begins with traditional Québécois instrumentation, with less realistic instruments entering later (ex. 3.5 begins after the orchestration has filled out).

Since Bouchard's Roberval includes not only members of the French aristocracy but also working-class Québécois, March drew from more popular sources as well. Lydie-Anne's first appearance is marked by a quotation of Scott Joplin's rag-waltz "Pleasant Moments," which runs in counterpoint to the chorus's restatement of the Balloon Song (ex. 3.6). Lydie-Anne is a master confectioner of pleasant moments, even if it involves a certain amount of

Example 3.4. Quotation of Wagner's Magic Fire motive in *Les feluettes*, episode 1

Example 3.5. Balloon Song, *Les feluettes*, episode 2

Example 3.6. Quotation of Scott Joplin's "Pleasant Moments" in *Les feluettes*, episode 2

* "Pleasant Moments" (1909) by Scott Joplin

Example 3.6. (Continued)

pretense. In addition to the periodic instances of local color in the orchestration, March launches the engagement party with the "Reel du perdu," a Québéçois fiddle tune that was a fixture at nuptial ceremonies around the turn of the previous century.

The way March begins the embedded opera with literal quotations and then transitions to looser borrowings and stylistic allusions suggests a fictional authorship scenario for the embedded opera's music. The prisoners began by piecing together the score out of familiar works and songs. But since only fragments could be recalled, and perhaps some of these were only half remembered, they also had to come up with new music. In some cases, as in the Love-Death motive, they mined the borrowed material for leitmotivs. In others, they composed new music in the style of their favorite composers. Yet not all of the embedded opera's music is stylistically appropriate for its ostensible setting. At moments of anger or violence, the modernist cluster chords and motoric accompaniments of the prison scenes encroach on the embedded performance.

A more ambiguous meta-operatic example is Richard Strauss and Hugo von Hofmannsthal's *Ariadne auf Naxos* (1916). The work opens with the Composer's anxious preparations for the premiere of his first opera, "Ariadne auf Naxos." Without his knowledge and to his considerable dismay, his patron has also engaged a *commedia dell'arte* troupe who plan to perform "The Faithless Zerbinetta and Her Four Lovers." Despite the money the patron has spent on these operatic entertainments, he demands that the two works be performed simultaneously so that they will conclude in time for the fireworks. The prologue quickly degenerates into a dramatization of what Paisley Livingston has termed a traffic-jam authorship scenario, one in which sabotage and coercion prevent anyone from exercising sufficient control to be considered the author of the resulting monstrosity.[36] The Prima Donna and Tenor both attempt to convince the Music Master that the requisite cuts be taken from each other's roles. Only the can-do leader of the comedy troupe, Zerbinetta, manages to keep a level head, proposing solutions to the problem of integrating the two plotlines and employing her beauty and acting abilities to manipulate the Composer. But as the Composer witnesses the singers getting into place, he regrets his decision to allow the show to go on and runs away in despair.

Act I opens in the fictional world of Ariadne on Naxos. The libretto does not indicate the presence of either the Composer or a fictional audience, though many productions involve the former conducting or otherwise supervising Act I. From the score and libretto, however, it is unclear what we ought to imagine Act I represents. As some productions suggest, it could represent the performance for the patron. But given the Composer's disavowal of the performance, it is also plausible to imagine that he stopped the travesty from taking place and that Act I merely represents the hypothetical result of the authorship scenario dramatized in the prologue.[37] In chapter 6, I discuss a production directed by Katharina Thoma that pursues yet another possibility.

The prisoners of *Man of La Mancha* and *Les feluettes* may appear to perform an analogous role to the various diarists in Walton's *Thessaly* trilogy. However, they are only the fictional presenters of the embedded performances. It is still necessary to invoke some other narrating agent to understand the features of the framing prison scenes.

External Narrators

Choral Narrators

Some operatic narrators direct their stories to the real-life audience of the performance. The most time-honored form of external operatic narrator is the Greek chorus. Choral narrators not only exist in a different fictional world than the other characters, but they are often in a position of greater knowledge and power. The *testo* of Monteverdi's *Il combattimento di Tancredi e Clorinda* (1624), for example, has access to the characters' unexpressed thoughts, beliefs, and desires.[38] Choral narrators made a resurgence in the modern era not only as a consequence of a renewed interest in ancient Greek drama but also because of the influence of Asian theater—particularly Japanese Noh and Kabuki—on Brecht, Stravinsky, Britten, and Sondheim.[39]

For their ability to provide background information and subjective access to characters, choral narrators are especially useful in historical operas about societies distinct from the target audience either temporally or culturally. *The Rape of Lucretia* begins with the choruses reading and recounting extracts from Etruscan history. Inspired by the use of narrators in Kabuki theater, Sondheim and John Weidman included a Reciter in *Pacific Overtures* (1976), who functions as a "teacher/guide," explaining to their American audience pertinent aspects of Japanese culture and history.[40] Although he is clearly of the audience's time, looking back on the events being presented on stage, he is not American. Robert K. McLaughlin observes that "when he says 'we,' 'us,' or 'our,' he means the Japanese, and is counting himself as part of that group. When he refers to the Americans, he calls them 'Westerners,' 'they,' or 'them.'" As a result, Sondheim and Weidman place "an American audience in the position of the Other" and invite them to view these events from a Japanese perspective.[41]

Choral narrators can also alleviate staging difficulties by relating events that could not be represented onstage. These events could be coextensive with the other stage action, as in a Mauerschau (e.g., Tarquinius's ride to Lucretia's house), or be from the past or future. Sometimes they even serve a sportscasting-like function, providing play-by-play commentary on events as they are being enacted. Although Tasso did not intend *Gerusalemme liberata* (1581) to be staged as theater, Monteverdi did intend his *Combattimento* to involve Tancredi and Clorinda enacting the events described by the testo. In *Lucretia*, once Tarquinius arrives at Lucretia's home, the choruses describe her and her servants greeting him as spectators watch the scene being enacted. In so doing, the librettist Ronald Duncan highlighted the disjuncture between thought and speech in this scene, affording spectators access to the desires and fears that could not, for the sake of politeness and propriety, be spoken by the characters.

Choral narrators can also serve more didactic purposes, attempting to school audience responses; recommending what events ought to arouse sympathy, pity, or fear; or privileging one interpretation over another. Infamously, the choruses of *Lucretia* downplay the role of Lucretia's death in the founding of Rome and instead encourage spectators to equate her suicide with Christ's crucifixion.

The choral trio in Bernstein's *Trouble in Tahiti* (1952) extols the virtues of suburban life, oblivious to the strife of the couple in the story: Sam and Dinah. Bernstein represents this disjuncture musically with the trio singing in the sweet-jazz-inspired style of 1950s radio commercials while the couple, particularly Dinah, employ a more modernist idiom.[42] Through the devastating irony of many of the juxtapositions—between Sam and Dinah's mutual recognition that they are now practically strangers (Scene 4) to the trio's equation of an "up-to-date kitchen" with a "wonderful life" (interlude), for example—Bernstein encourages spectators to take a critical attitude toward the promises made in American advertising and the value of escapist entertainments, such as the film *Trouble in Tahiti*, which Dinah attends to evade her troubles.

Some choral narrators have more knowledge and power than others. At one extreme lie the choruses of André Obey's play *Le viol de Lucrèce* (1931), the source of Britten's opera. Not only are they no more apprised of future events than the other characters but they are less successful than most spectators in grasping characters' motivations. When Tarquinius decides to go to Rome, Obey's male narrator expresses fear and confusion about Tarquinius's actions. Finally realizing his intended destination, the Male Chorus is unpleasantly surprised: "My God! He resumes galloping! He's going to Rome! He just shouted it while whipping his exhausted horse. To Rome! To Rome! It's senseless! Is he deserting? . . . Is he conspiring? . . . Is he betraying? . . . Is someone waiting for him? . . . Will he surprise? . . . Tarquinius in Rome like last night! But all alone tonight! . . . And why tonight?"[43] When he finally divines Tarquinius's intended course of action, he attempts, unsuccessfully, to persuade him against it.

Although the opera's choruses purport to be mere observers, Britten and Duncan portray the Male Chorus as instigating Tarquinius's decision to visit Lucretia in Rome. Junius is the first to taunt Tarquinius, but Tarquinius does not take the bait until the Male Chorus applies more pressure after Junius has retired for the evening:

> Tarquinius does not dare,
> When Tarquinius does not desire;
> But I am the Prince of Rome
> And Lucretia's eyes my Empire.
> It is not far to Rome . . .
> Oh, go to bed, Tarquinius . . .
> The lights of Rome are beckoning . . .
> The city sleeps. Collatinus sleeps.
> Lucretia! Lucretia![44]

With the first two lines, the Male Chorus comments on Tarquinius's nature, but with lines three and four, he gives voice to Tarquinius's thoughts and desires. After this point, it is ambiguous which of the two functions the Male Chorus is performing. Indeed, he may be performing both if we think of him as planting thoughts in Tarquinius's mind.

Britten's musical treatment of these lines—particularly the alluring manner in which he set Lucretia's name—supports such an interpretation. Earlier in the scene, Britten associated Lucretia's name with a quintuplet motive (ex. 3.7). Initially, it performs an ornamental function, but it quickly pervades the musical texture like sonic wallpaper, representing Tarquinius's growing obsession with Collatinus's wife. The rhythmic augmentation to which Britten subjects the motive brings out its melodic qualities and, in so doing, exploits its slinky chromaticism and contour (ex. 3.8). Seemingly in response to the Male Chorus's seductive strains, Tarquinius calls for his horse and "goes off with sudden resolution." Despite his power to influence Tarquinius, the Male Chorus still occupies a different plane of existence. Britten articulates this distance musically with a tonal disjuncture between the Male Chorus's D minor and Tarquinius's E♭ major.

Example 3.7. First appearance of Lucretia's motive

Example 3.8. The Male Chorus's seductive strains

The Female Chorus possesses less power in comparison. The empathy she evidently feels for Lucretia makes it clear that she would intervene if she could, but unlike the Male Chorus, her words seem to have no power to change the course of history.

Another choral narrator with unusual powers is the Reciter in *Pacific Overtures*. In accordance with Kabuki conventions, he is able to speak for certain characters and even periodically act out their parts.[45] Yet his knowledge is limited. Given the lack of a Japanese account of the first diplomatic meeting with America, he is unable to amplify the decidedly uninformative testimonies offered in "Someone in a Tree."

Despite the power some choral narrators possess to influence characters and direct the course of fictional events, in none of these cases are we invited to imagine that the chorus is responsible for presenting the opera, or even a part of it, to us.

Frame Narrators

A more likely candidate for this kind of narrator may be the frame narrator, which began gracing operatic stages in the nineteenth century as composers and librettists increasingly looked to novels and short stories for their sources. This type of narrator appears at the beginning and end of the opera, which represent the commencement and conclusion of an extended act of storytelling or private reminiscence. Spectators are invited to imagine that the middle portion is a representation of the narrator's story, whether told orally, written down, or internally recalled. Examples of oral autobiography include *Les contes d'Hoffmann* and Zoltán Kodály and Béla Paulini's *Háry János* (1926). The former is an adaptation of three short stories by E. T. A. Hoffmann.[46] A fictional version of Hoffmann regales patrons of a tavern with tales of three prior love affairs. Spectators are invited to imagine that Acts II through IV are operatic representations of the stories Hoffmann tells.

Whereas János and Hoffmann intend their audiences to believe the stories they tell, other frame narrators present fictional tales. The prologue of Vaughan Williams's *Pilgrim's Progress* (1951) depicts John Bunyan in prison writing down the final words to his Christian allegory. Once he finishes, he begins reading the story from the beginning. As he does so, his protagonist, the Pilgrim, appears and begins to enact the story, and Bunyan fades into the background. Acts II through IV represent the Pilgrim's journey to the Celestial City. In the epilogue, we return to Bunyan, who offers us the book from which he has been reading.

If Wagner takes home the award for the most backstory narrations, Britten would almost certainly win the category for most frame narrators. Britten's partner, Peter Pears, made his debut as a professional opera singer in the title role of *Hoffmann*.[47] Britten went on to compose several more frame-narrator roles for him, including the Narrator (doubling as the ghost Quint) in *The Turn of the Screw* (1954) and Captain Vere in *Billy Budd* (1951). In the prologue to *The Turn of the Screw*, the Narrator tells us that he is in possession of a governess's account of a haunting and invites us to imagine that we are going to watch a dramatization of that account. The interior portion of *Billy Budd*, by contrast, represents Vere's memories of the events of 1797, when he was captain of the *Indomitable*.

Although most operas that have frame narrators are adaptations of works of literature, not all operatic adaptations of literature contain frame narrators. More commonly, librettists discard such framing devices in the adaptation process. Thus, one question that arises from the foregoing examples is why one would wish to retain the frame (or, in the case of *Billy Budd*, impose one). One aim suggested by *Les contes d'Hoffmann* and *Pilgrim's Progress* is a desire to draw attention to one's source—in other words, to ensure spectators appreciate the opera as an adaptation.

Another suggested by *The Turn of the Screw* is a desire to imbue the opera with ambiguity by raising the possibility of unreliable narration. Its source, Henry James's novella of 1898, is one of the most famous instances of unreliable narration in English literature. The protagonist is a young woman who assumes a post as governess of two children, Miles and Flora, in a country house called Bly. The Governess becomes convinced that the house is haunted by the ghosts of her predecessor, Miss Jessel, and Peter Quint, a valet suspected of having an inappropriate relationship with Miles. She attempts to protect the children against the corrupting influence she believes the ghosts to represent, but the story ends with Miles dying in her arms of an indeterminate cause.

At the time of the opera's composition, the question of whether James's novella was a ghost story or one about female sexual repression resulting in psychosis was hotly debated by scholars of literature.[48] Chief contributor to the story's ambiguity is the elaborate way in which it was framed. First, there is an unidentified narrator who tells readers that he was present at an oral reading of a real woman's account of a haunting. The narrator on this occasion was a man by the name of Douglas, who later bequeathed to the unidentified narrator the Governess's written account on which his oral narration was based. Readers are told that the text they are reading (excluding the initial framing chapter) is an "exact transcript" the narrator made of the account Douglas gave him.[49] Despite the narrator's attempts to demonstrate its legitimacy, the number of hands through which the Governess's account has passed raises doubts about whether readers enjoy unadulterated access to that account, doubts that are further exacerbated by Douglas's insinuation of a former romantic relationship between himself and the Governess. In the first chapter of his story, James expended considerable effort building not only anticipation but also the possibility for unreliable narration. At the other end, however, he cut off the narrative at the death of Miles, leaving the frame incomplete and many questions unanswered.

The opera's frame is, thankfully, less byzantine, as it contains one fewer layer of narration:

James's Novella	Britten and Piper's Opera
An unnamed narrator introduces a transcript of the Governess's story once read to him and others by Douglas.	An unnamed narrator is in possession of the Governess's story.

It begins with a prologue in which an unnamed Narrator tells us that he is in possession of a "curious story ... written in faded ink—a woman's hand, governess to two children—long ago."[50] Vis-à-vis the Governess's account, the Narrator is in a similar position as James's Douglas. Britten musically sets the frame apart from the remainder of the opera by scoring it for voice and piano alone, a gesture that harkens back to the days when scenes of narration would have been performed as *secco* recitative (with continuo accompaniment only);

Example 3.9. The Screw theme

for example, the Count's account of finding Cherubino in Barbarina's house in the Act I trio of *Le nozze di Figaro*.[51] The orchestra enters surreptitiously under the Narrator's last line, which relays the Governess's marriage-like vow to the Guardian.

Many commentators have argued that the opera is less ambiguous than the novella on account of Britten's stipulation to his librettist, Myfanwy Piper, that the ghosts sing semantically meaningful utterances and appear onstage, even when the Governess is not present (Act I, Scene 8 and Act II, Scene 1).[52] If, as the prologue implies, the Governess is the source of everything we are seeing and hearing in the rest of the opera, it is possible that what we are seeing and hearing represents her imaginings, even hallucinations, which could very well include private conversations between the ghosts.

The question is whether the prologue's recommendation is consistent with the features of the rest of the opera. The opera's meticulous yet unconventional formal design suggests the presence of a storyteller. When the orchestra enters, it presents a theme, commonly referred to as the Screw theme, comprising an aggregate of all twelve pitch classes (ex. 3.9). In interludes between the opera's scenes, Britten subjects this theme to variations, each with a different pitch class as its tonal center (the tonal centers also form a twelve-tone aggregate). Not only does the Screw theme permeate the interludes but it constitutes the primordial soup from which most of the other themes evolve, thus pervading the entire score.[53]

Other aspects of the score are less congruent with the prologue's suggestion that the Governess is its source. Unlike previous commentators, I propose that the problem lies less in Piper's libretto and stage directions than in other features of Britten's musical setting. Narration involves not only conveying what happened but also expressing attitudes about the story's characters and events. The attitudes the music expresses are difficult to attribute to the Governess. Most problematic are the comparisons Britten draws between the Governess's and Quint's behavior toward the children. To quote Patricia Howard, "The governess expresses her intention to *protect* the children in notes almost identical to those Quint uses to *corrupt* them."[54]

The Governess and Quint share the most recognizable motive of the score (a derivative of the Screw theme). Example 3.10 represents its first occurrence

Example 3.10. The Governess expresses her doubts

in the Governess's vocal line as she expresses her doubts about coming to Bly. We hear the motive during her first meeting with the children (Act I, rehearsal [hereafter "reh."] 9^{+3}) and whenever she performs pivotal actions or inactions regarding their well-being: deciding not to respond to Miles's dismissal from school (Act I, reh. 15), vowing to protect the children against the ghosts without the help of the Guardian (Act II, reh. 44; Act I, reh. 46^{+5}; Act II, reh. 39^{-3}), attempting to force Flora to confess to seeing Miss Jessel (Act II, reh. 113), and pledging to save Miles in a mode of discourse more appropriate to the address of a lover (Act II, reh. 121).[55]

In Quint's employ, the motive is a siren song to Miles (Act I, reh. 72^{-7}, represented in ex. 3.11; Act II, reh. 125).[56] Although more blatantly erotic than the Governess's final outpouring of sentiment, the music suggests that the motivations behind these utterances are not substantially different. Given that the Governess views herself as occupying a role antithetical to that of the ghosts—as a combatant against the threat she believes them to pose, not as a threat herself—it is implausible to imagine that she is the one drawing such comparisons. Like the choral narrator examples, we need to invoke some other agent to explain these portions of the music.

While the prologue was an eleventh-hour addition to *The Turn of the Screw*, the frame of *Billy Budd* was one of the first elements Britten and his librettists E. M. Forster and Eric Crozier discussed.[57] Their decision to frame the drama as old-Vere's recollections is all the more surprising given that it was not clearly motivated by the narration of Melville's novel. Vere is captain of a British naval ship during the French Revolutionary Wars. His master-at-arms Claggart wrongfully accuses new recruit Billy of planning a mutiny. Billy's speech impediment prevents him from speaking out against Claggart's groundless claim. He expresses himself in the only way he is able: striking Claggart, accidentally killing him. Vere is faced with the moral dilemma of following the rule of law and sentencing Billy to death or doing what he feels to be right, which would be to pardon Billy, whom he knows to be the best and most loyal of his men. Billy is condemned to death, and, rather improbably, his last act is to bless the man responsible for this verdict.

Example 3.11. Quint's siren song

Vere is not the narrator of Melville's novel, nor does he even live to be the age at which he appears in the opera's framing scenes. But that is not to say that there is nothing in the novel that may have served as inspiration for the opera's frame. Melville goes out of his way to draw attention to the gaps in his narrator's knowledge and the extent to which his narration is based on mere speculation. At a crucial point in the narrative, Vere's private interview with Billy, the narrator confesses the limits of his knowledge: "Beyond the communication of the sentence, what took place at this interview was never known." Nevertheless, he continues, "some conjectures may be ventured," and he proceeds to offer many indeed.[58] Britten and his collaborators may have employed a frame narrator to raise similar epistemological questions, but that still does not explain why they chose Vere to be the narrator.

Potentially suggestive is Crozier's explanation that this decision was a "natural development" from their decision to cast Pears as Vere.[59] Although Crozier did not elaborate on why he saw a relation between these seemingly independent decisions, it does not take much to fill in the gaps in logic. From

Britten's perspective, making Pears the narrator would focus the audience's attention on his character and encourage feelings of empathy, even identification. The frame also played a crucial role in Forster's attempt to "rescue Vere from Melville" by bringing the story in line with the narrative archetypes of Forster's other prose works (for more on this topic, see chap. 7).[60]

In comparison with *The Turn of the Screw*, there is more agreement among scholars that Vere is the source of everything we see and hear in the interior portion of *Billy Budd*.[61] Yet similar obstacles face such a proposal. Again, the problems lie less in the presence of scenes that Vere did not witness than in Britten's music, specifically the convergence of Vere's and Claggart's musical personae. As early as their first appearances in the opera, Britten forges a connection between them via a motive of falling fourths followed by a stepwise ascent (cf. exx. 3.12 and 3.13). Claggart's vocal lines are saturated with fourths. Vere's accompaniments contain similar features, but these features do not infiltrate his vocal part until after Claggart's death. In his "Scylla and Charybdis" and "verdict" arias, he even quotes an entire line (music and lyrics) from Claggart's vow to take down Billy, commonly referred to as his "Credo" aria (cf. ex. 3.14 with exx. 3.15 and 3.16). Disconcertingly, Vere never heard Claggart sing this music. Thus, the citation cannot be construed as intentional on Vere's part. As Donald Mitchell has remarked, Vere's unintentional echoes of Claggart's music suggest that we ought to regard Vere as completing "Claggart's task for him, despite—or rather . . . because of—the latter's death."[62] Even though Vere's guilt over his decision to sentence Billy to death haunts him into old age in the opera, it is difficult to imagine his viewing himself as having anything in common with Claggart. To explain why Vere's and Claggart's musical personae converge, we need to invoke another narrating agent.

How an opera is staged can enhance or undermine the presence and authority of narrators like the Governess and Vere. In chapter 7, I will discuss productions that do a better job at putting forth these characters as the sources of the interior portions of their operas than productions that follow the stage directions. Yet only extensive revisions to the music would remove the foregoing obstacles to understanding them as performing an analogous function to literary narrators. Even if Britten had composed music that better accorded with the attitudes of his characters, there would still be an asymmetry between the function of frame narrators in opera and literature. Literary frame narrators are usually implied to be the fictional authors of the text we are reading, either in whole or in part. In none of the foregoing operatic examples were we invited to imagine that the narrator was responsible for presenting the performance or even a portion thereof.

Example 3.12. Introduction of Vere in the prologue of *Billy Budd*

Example 3.13. Introduction of Claggart

Example 3.14. Claggart's "Credo" aria

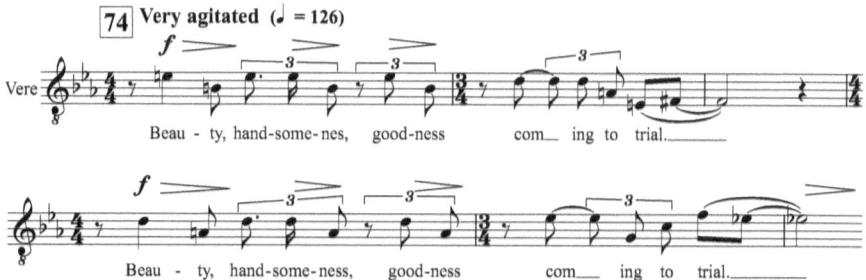

Example 3.15. Vere's "Scylla and Charybdis" aria

Example 3.16. Vere's "verdict" aria

Author Figures

That is not to suggest that there are no external operatic narrators who are put forth as the fictional presenters of the performance we are watching. Many of the first operas contain prologues that imply that gods or allegorical figures are the fictional authors of the performance. In the prologue to Jacopo Peri and Ottavio Rinuccini's *Euridice* (1600), Tragedy proclaims that she will present a musical drama about the consummate musician Orpheus. Monteverdi and Alessandro Striggio's *Orfeo* (1607) contains a similar speech by Music.[63] Some operas are even more explicit in their invitation to treat such figures as fictional surrogates for the actual author of the opera or its source text. Rinuccini's libretto to *Dafne* (1598, music by Jacopo Peri) begins with a direct address by Ovid, and his *Narciso* (never set to music) contains a prologue by Giulio Romano (a.k.a. the composer Giulio Caccini, who was presumably expected to set the libretto).[64]

Prologues in the French tradition perform similar invitations. In Lully and Quinault's *Atys* (1676), Melpomène dismisses the pastoral goddess Flore to "give way to the magnificent trappings of the tragic Muse and her solemn spectacles." In Lully and Corneille's *Bellérophon* (1679), Apollo orders his entourage to "leave off [their] trivial songs. We must through more noble means honor today the hero of France [Louis XIV]. Let us now transform ourselves, and in a charming spectacle celebrate before his eyes the fortunate event that in former times gave birth to Parnassus. For this great king, come, redouble your efforts; prepare your sweetest music."[65] Rameau and Pierre-Joseph Bernard's *Castor et Pollux* (1737) contains a similar implication: in celebration of the end of the War of the Polish Succession, Minerva entreats Venus to subdue Mars with the power of love, after which she announces "un spectacle nouveau." Even in cases where there is no explicit reference to the prologue figures staging a performance, there is often an implicit invitation to imagine them as the opera's presenters.

With the decline of the prologue (late seventeenth century in Italy; mid-eighteenth century in France), the figure of the authorial presenter also largely disappeared until the early twentieth century. Stravinsky's *Oedipus Rex* (1927) opens with the Speaker announcing to the real-life audience that they are about to hear the story of Oedipus. Appearing in modern evening attire, he presents himself as a lecturer or tour guide, whose apparent role is to help us understand this relic of the past.[66] Since the action is conducted in Latin and is considerably compressed, most spectators need as much help as they can get. Unfortunately, the Speaker fails to make good on his promise to "spare [us] all effort of ear and memory" by "recall[ing] Sophocles's drama as we go along."[67] Although he does recall snippets of Sophocles, his intrusions are frequently ill-timed and insufficient to offer much by way of clarity. For this reason, Stephen Walsh has suggested that the Speaker is less a "comprehension aid" than a "structural device both for articulating the musical *tableaux vivants* of the Latin setting and for emphasising their monumentality and artificiality."[68]

Oedipus Rex was influential on later modernist theater.[69] Poulenc begins *Les mamelles de Tirésias* (1947) with a direct address by Le Directeur, also appearing in evening dress, but unlike Stravinsky's Speaker, he delivers his commentary as a song and does not reappear. Instead, the Zanzibar chorus provides the moral of the story: "faites des enfants!"

In a less whimsical but equally didactic vein, Britten and William Plomer's church parables *Curlew River* (1964), *The Burning Fiery Furnace* (1966), and *The Prodigal Son* (1968) were influenced by Japanese Noh and the European mystery play tradition.[70] The stage directions of the first of these state that the setting is "a church by a Fenland river in early medieval times."[71] Even the instrumentalists are in costume. As the monks process through the church, they sing the plainsong hymn *Te lucis ante terminum*. The Abbot comes forward and tells us that they are going to perform a mystery. We watch the monks put on their costumes as the orchestra plays a Japanese translation of the plainchant melody, now treated heterophonically (multiple players perform the same basic melody but do so somewhat asynchronously and with different ornamentation) and featuring flute and drums.[72] At the end of their performance, we see them get out of costume for the Abbot's delivery of the moral of the story. Britten and Plomer's church parables differ from the previous modernist examples in that the presenters are not from our time. Rather, we are invited to join theirs, imagining ourselves as the medieval congregation they appear to be addressing.[73]

Ambiguous Cases

In making the foregoing distinctions (summarized in fig. 3.1), I do not wish to suggest that a narrator's function is invariably static. One commonplace shift is for the presenter of an authorial preface to play a character in the ensuing show. In Ruggero Leoncavallo's *Pagliacci* (1892), Tonio assumes the role of an author figure in the prologue, but once Act I begins, he is in no superior a position than the other characters to avert the disaster of Act II. The Astrologer in Rimsky-Korsakov and Vladimir Nikolayevich Belsky's *Le coq d'or* (1909) undergoes a similar transition but retains the magical powers to which he alludes in his prologue.

Both of these works begin with direct addresses, but conspiratorial turns to the audience can also occur in the middle of the drama. When such moments are isolated occurrences (e.g., Angelica's "Satisfied"), there is little incentive to regard the character as performing a narrator-like role for the show as a whole. But when asides to the audience are peppered throughout, the sense of that character as guiding the narrative, or at least our reception of it, is much stronger. For this reason, many regard Mark as the narrator of Jonathan Larson's *Rent* (1996).[74] If so, he is a narrator unlike any I have surveyed so far.

The show begins with Mark turning to the audience and setting the scene: "We begin on Christmas Eve with me, Mark, and my roommate Roger. We

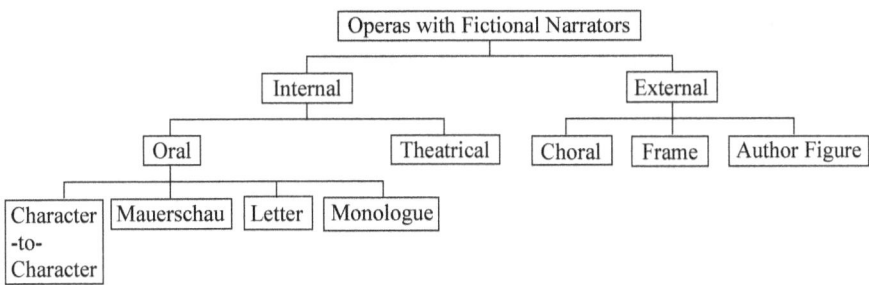

Figure 3.1. Types of narrators in opera and musical theater

live in an industrial loft on the corner of 11th Street and Avenue B." The awkwardness of a character announcing what ought to be obvious to his fictional fellows is typically alleviated by the conceit that such remarks bypass the notice of the rest of the characters and are for the audience's ears alone. In this case, Mark's scene-setting is naturalized as voice-over narration for the movie he is making about the AIDS crisis (portions of which are screened in the final scene). Most other asides to the audience are made with camera in hand: "zoom in on the answering machine," "close-up: our ex-roommate Benjamin Coffin III," "pan to the padlocked door."[75] Mark introduces the dramatis personae, announces transitions to new locations, places events temporally, and summarizes plot developments in the intervening time. The latter two functions are especially important in Act II, which telescopes an entire year.

Mark performs a similar structural and functional role to that of a choral narrator: through multiple periodic asides to the audience, he facilitates their comprehension of the story. But unlike the other external examples previously discussed, he exists in the same fictional world as the other characters at the same period in time. He is an integral part of the story. Other characters in musicals whose numerous asides suggest a narrator-like role include the Emcee of *Cabaret* and Johnny in *American Idiot* (2010), based on Green Day's album of the same title.[76]

Confusions of narrative level are especially common in comedy, as the opening example from *Into the Woods* illustrates. In this case, the Narrator initially presents himself as a choral narrator, providing background information on the characters without intervening in their affairs. However, as spectators eventually discover, he has been playing puppet master in the guise of the Mysterious Man. As belated compensation for being an absentee father to the Baker, he has been helping him and his friends fulfill their wishes. Despite the fact that he knows more than many of the other characters, the limits to his knowledge are demonstrated by the Witch's ability to surprise him at several points in the story, most disastrously in the scene with the giantess. Yet this is not the end for the Narrator/Mysterious Man. In the latter guise, he participates in the show's finale.

Although such ontological confusions are often assumed to be the exclusive preoccupation of postmodern dramatists, they are present in operas of earlier periods. In the prologue to Lully and Quinault's *Amadis* (1684), the magicians Alquif and Urgande declare that they will bring the titular hero back to life for the delight of the "new hero" (Louis XIV). Although they are the implied presenters of Acts I through V, they are also participants in the drama, rescuing Amadis from the evil sorcerers Arcalaüs and Arcabonne.[77]

Prokofiev's *L'amour des trois oranges* (1921) opens with an argument between the advocates of tragedy, comedy, lyric drama, and farce about which form of drama is superior. Les Ridicules burst on the scene, announcing that they are going to put on a show called "L'amour pour trois oranges" and enlisting the other factions as their audience. But almost immediately after establishing this meta-operatic scenario, doubts arise about their status as the opera's presenters, due to the limits of their knowledge and eventual intervention in the plot (rescuing Princess Ninette on two separate occasions).[78]

The Balladeer in Sondheim and John Weidman's *Assassins* (1990) suffers a similar demotion to his counterpart in *Into the Woods*, but the result is far from comedic. He too initially performs a chorus-like role, but unlike *Into the Woods*, the characters are aware of his presence from the outset. After suggesting that the first assassin, the actor John Wilkes Booth, was motivated less by a disagreement with Lincoln's political policies than "a slew of bad reviews," Booth orders him to shut up. But when Booth finds himself surrounded by union soldiers, he entrusts his diary to the Balladeer, urging him to "pass on the truth."[79] The Balladeer proceeds to turn its contents into a song. By Scene 15, the assassins have become dissatisfied with the way he has been telling their stories and force him off the stage before breaking out into "Another National Anthem." Unlike the Narrator of *Into the Woods*, the Balladeer does not return.[80]

In interpreting the significance of the Balladeer and his overthrow, it is important to note that he is defined as a singer. Although the Narrator of *Into the Woods* does sing occasionally, he was modeled on an intellectual, specifically Bruno Bettelheim, whose *The Uses of Enchantment: The Meaning and Importance of Fairy Tales* (1976) was a source for the musical.[81] By contrast, the libretto to *Assassins* describes the Balladeer as a "Woody Guthrie/Pete Seeger-style folk singer."[82] Throughout the musical, he articulates an unflaggingly cheery outlook on the nation through a simple, folk-inspired musical idiom. The conflict between the Balladeer's optimism and the disillusionment

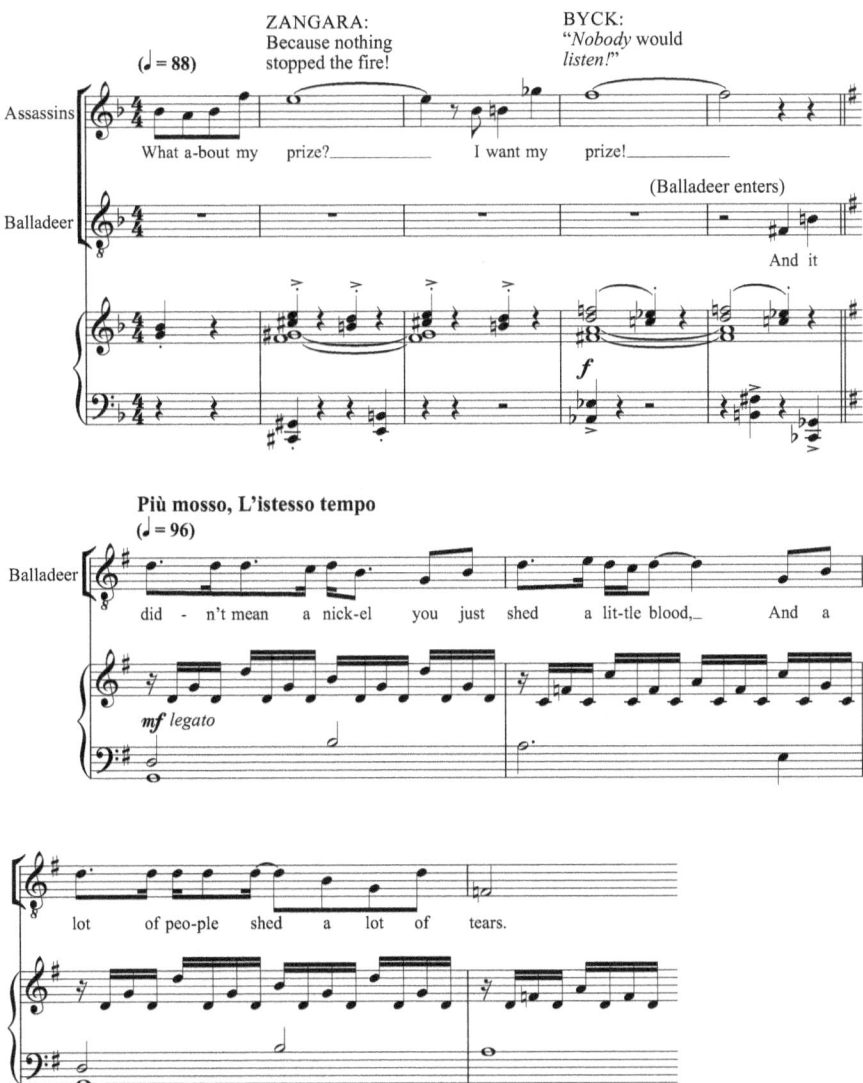

Example 3.17. Juxtaposition of the assassins and the Balladeer in "Another National Anthem"

of the assassins comes to a head in "Another National Anthem." The Balladeer's suggestions that a mailman could win the lottery or become the president are countered by the assassins' harsh doses of reality. The juxtaposition between the Balladeer's and assassins' respective music becomes increasingly jarring as the Balladeer persists with a simple, consistently consonant harmonic language while the assassins' music becomes increasingly dissonant (ex. 3.17).

Sondheim has described the role of the Balladeer as means of dramatizing the way history is disseminated through stories and songs.[83] In particular, he notes how the complex acts and motivations of historical persons are simplified as the heroes are separated from the villains. To counteract this effect, the show illuminates the circumstances and motivations that led these men and women to commit their crimes. Comparing the resulting picture from the potted accounts spouted by the Balladeer in "The Ballad of Booth," spectators are encouraged to contemplate the morality of storytelling through songs. Both *Assassins* and *Into the Woods* invite us to critically examine the stories we tell and the songs we sing. "Children may not obey, but children will listen."[84]

Robustly characterized fictional narrators have played, and continue to play, a variety of roles in operatic storytelling. In the Baroque era, most were of the external variety. Prologues introduced gods or allegorical figures, implied to be the fictional presenters of the entire drama we are watching. Addressing the performance's actual patrons as surrogates for the work's actual authors, they acquainted them with the conventions of the new art form.[85] For operas commissioned by a member of the aristocracy or royal court, they could also perform the role of a panegyric or "performed dedication," glorifying the person or persons who made this extravagant spectacle possible.[86] As Mauro Calcagno has observed, such prologues not only indicated that the patron authorized the work being performed but that the composer authorized the musicians' performance as the vehicle by which that work was delivered.[87] Some prologues, such as that to Rinuccini's *Dafne*, also acknowledge the author of the opera's source text. In later public operas, prologues remained an opportunity to highlight the work's central theme or moral conflict, as in the contest between Love, Virtue, and Fortune dramatized in the prologue to Monteverdi and Giovanni Francesco Busenello's *L'incoronazione di Poppea* (1643). Delivered by a figure able to mediate between real and fictional worlds, prologues could also draw connections to current events, as in *Castor et Pollux*.

By the middle of the eighteenth century, prologues and their attendant external narrators had been largely abandoned with opera's other Baroque accoutrements. Most narrators in Classical and Romantic opera are internal: characters telling each other the stories of their lives, reading or writing letters, or entertaining their friends with fictional confections. With the rise of the novel as a source for opera plots, the frame narrator emerged on the operatic stage in the nineteenth century and only increased in prominence in the twentieth as a means of drawing attention to the opera's literary origins, calling into question the veracity of what we are seeing and hearing, or focusing the audience's attention on a particular character's point of view. The latter half of the nineteenth century saw an increased interest in the subjectivity of narration, demonstrated by the tendency for librettists to juxtapose multiple accounts of the same event.

Narration became a positive obsession in the twentieth century. In addition to the persistence of internal narrators of various types, there was a resurgence of author figures and choral narrators, now used to different ends than their Baroque predecessors. While Brecht and Stravinsky employed them as distancing devices, Britten and Plomer used them to encourage spectators to imagine themselves as medieval parishioners taking part in a mystery play. In the hands of Bernstein (*Trouble in Tahiti*) and Sondheim and Weidman (*Pacific Overtures*), they were also used for social critique.

New preoccupations emerged in the modern era, including meta-operas ranging from *Ariadne*'s frothy parody of operatic conventions and personnel (egocentric prima donnas, temperamental tenors, "l'art pour l'art" composers) to *Les feluettes*' gestures to opera's long history of cross-dressing and association with gay culture. Modernist librettists and composers also experimented with narrators having fluid, even paradoxical roles, such as the purported presenters of *L'amour des trois oranges* who are surprised by the twists and turns of their own show. While such paradoxes can be a source of comedy, *Assassins* shows that they can also raise moral questions about the nature of storytelling through song.

Despite the number and diversity of character-narrators in opera, few perform the role Chatman, Levinson, and Wilson assume to be necessary to narratives. Only author figures are the imagined source for the entirety of the performance we are watching, and examples of this type are rare, at least post-1750. Thus, there is an asymmetry between opera and literature with respect to the prevalence of such narrators. In this respect, opera is more akin to cinema. As a multimedia spectacle, the demands on omnipotence are higher than they are with literature. In particular, the opera orchestra often provides a perspective that diverges from that of even external narrators. As a result, many opera theorists have proposed that the orchestra be regarded as a narrative agent, a suggestion I investigate in more depth in the next chapter.

Notes

1. Stephen Sondheim and James Lapine, *Into the Woods* (libretto) (New York: Theatre Communications Group, 1987), 102.
2. Alexandra Grabarchuk, "The Finality of Stories Such as These: Exploring Narrative and Concept in Stephen Sondheim's *Into the Woods*," in *From Stage to Screen: Musical Films in*

Europe and United States (1927–1961), ed. Massimiliano Sala (Turnhout: Brepols, 2012), 118. See also Jim Lovensheimer, "Stephen Sondheim and the Musical of the Outsider," in *Cambridge Companion to the Musical*, ed. William A. Everett (Cambridge: Cambridge University Press, 2002), 188–89; Scott McMillin, *The Musical as Drama* (Princeton: Princeton University Press, 2006), 152.

3. "Memoir of a Song" was published anonymously in the London-based periodical *Fraser's Magazine* in 1849 and is reprinted in Hilary Poriss, *Changing the Score: Arias, Prima Donnas, and the Authority of Performance* (Oxford: Oxford University Press, 2009), 189–203. Although narratology has traditionally defended a strict separation between narrators and authors, I side with Gregory Currie, *Narratives and Narrators: A Philosophy of Stories* (Oxford: Oxford University Press, 2010), 65, who contends that "there is no distinction that should or can be made between authors and narrators, for there is no distinction to be made between narrative-making and narrative-telling."

4. My use of this distinction diverges from Currie's in *Narratives and Narrators*, 67–69, where it differentiates narrators that are internal to the work (for fictional stories, these would be fictional narrators) and those that are external (i.e., the work's real-life authors). My use is more similar to Avrom Fleischman, *Narrated Films: Storytelling Situations in Cinema History* (Baltimore: Johns Hopkins University Press, 1992), 22–25.

5. I take this distinction from Gregory Currie, *Image and Mind: Film, Philosophy, and Cognitive Science* (Cambridge: Cambridge University Press, 1995), 265–66, but diverge from his terminology (*controlling* versus *embedded*) because it confuses the question of fictional authorship with that of narrative level. Some internal narrators may be the authors of a portion of the narrative, and, especially with opera, not all external narrators are controlling narrators in Currie's sense. Theater scholars who distinguish authorial narrators from other types of external narrators include Nancy Anne Cluck, "Showing or Telling: Narrators in the Drama of Tennessee Williams," *American Literature* 51, no. 1 (1979): 86–88; Walter F. Eggers Jr., "Shakespeare's Gower and the Role of the Authorial Presenter," *Philological Quarterly* 54, no. 2 (1975): 434; Manfred Pfister, *The Theory and Analysis of Drama*, trans. John Halliday (Cambridge: Cambridge University Press, 1988), 74–76; Brian Richardson, "Point of View in Drama: Diegetic Monologue, Unreliable Narrators, and the Author's Voice on Stage," *Comparative Drama* 22, no. 3 (1988): 197; Brian Richardson, "Voice and Narration in Postmodern Drama," *New Literary History* 32, no. 3 (2001): 685–86.

6. Scholars arguing that DeWitt ought to be construed as the fictional presenter of at least this opening sequence include Berys Gaut, *A Philosophy of Cinematic Art* (Cambridge: Cambridge University Press, 2010), 210–11; Sarah Kozloff, *Invisible Storytellers: Voice-Over Narration in American Fiction Film* (Berkeley: University of California Press, 1988), 65–69. However, Kozloff later admits the existence of some other presenter, which she terms the "image-maker." Ibid., 71. Mario Slugan, "Some Thoughts on Controlling Fictional Narrators in Fiction Film," *American Society for Aesthetics Graduate E-Journal* 6, no. 2 (2014): 4–5, argues against regarding DeWitt as the film's fictional presenter.

7. Gérard Genette, *Narrative Discourse: An Essay in Method*, trans. Jane E. Lewin (Ithaca: Cornell University Press, 1983), 227–31, conflates these issues. Roland Barthes, "Introduction to the Structural Analysis of Narratives," in *Image—Music—Text*, ed. and trans. Stephen Heath (New York: Hill and Wang, 1977), 116; Bertil Romberg, *Studies in the Narrative Technique of the First-Person Novel*, trans. Michael Taylor and Harold H. Borland (Stockholm: Almqvist and Wiksell, 1962), 9, remark that most literary narrators are the fictional authors of the text we are reading.

8. On the asymmetry between literature and cinema, refer to Currie, *Image and Mind*, 266–68; Kozloff, *Invisible Storytellers*, 43–44, 52–53.

9. Katherine Thomson-Jones, "The Literary Origins of the Cinematic Narrator," *British Journal of Aesthetics* 47, no. 1 (2007): 83, summarizes Seymour Chatman, *Coming to Terms: The Rhetoric of Narrative in Fiction and Film* (Ithaca: Cornell University Press, 1990), 115–16. Barthes, "Structural Analysis of Narratives," 109, 111, advances a similar argument to Chatman's.

10. See, for example, David Bordwell, *Narration in the Fiction Film* (Madison: University of Wisconsin Press, 1985), 62.

11. My references to "the author" refer to the actual person(s) who created the work, not to an implied author. An explanation of my preference for the real author over an implied author may be found in chapter 1.

12. This is my own summary of Jerrold Levinson, "Film Music and Narrative Agency," in *Contemplating Art: Essays in Aesthetics* (Oxford: Oxford University Press, 2006), 149–50. Similar arguments have been made by Félix Martínez Bonati, *Fictive Discourse and the Structures of Literature: A Phenomenological Approach* (Ithaca: Cornell University Press, 1981), 85; Tamar Yacobi, "Narrative Structure and Fictional Mediation," *Poetics Today* 8, no. 2 (2007): 335. Andrew Kania, "Against the Ubiquity of Fictional Narrators," *Journal of Aesthetics and Art Criticism* 63, no. 1 (2005): 48, coined the term *ontological gap* to describe this type of argument.

13. Kania, "Against the Ubiquity of Fictional Narrators," 51.

14. George M. Wilson, *Seeing Fictions in Film: The Epistemology of Movies* (Oxford: Oxford University Press, 2011), ch. 6. The qualifier *naturally iconic* specifies that the images possess *natural counterfactual dependence*, which is to say that their properties do not depend on anyone's intentions, beliefs, or desires. Unaltered photographically produced images qualify; paintings do not. Wilson uses the term *images* instead of *motion-picture shots* because he wants to avoid the stipulation that the images were produced with a motion-picture camera.

15. A point made by Robert Stecker, "Film Narration, Imaginative Seeing, and Seeing-In," *Projections* 7, no. 1 (2013): 153.

16. Other scholars who have taken such a stance include Currie, *Narratives and Narrators*, 68–69; David Davies, "Eluding Wilson's 'Elusive Narrators,'" *Philosophical Studies* 147, no. 3 (2010): 393; Kania, "Against the Ubiquity of Fictional Narrators," 52; Tilmann Köppe and Jan Stühring, "Against Pan-Narrator Theories," *Journal of Literary Semantics* 40, no. 1 (2011): 74; Thomson-Jones, "Literary Origins of the Cinematic Narrator," 93–94.

17. For literature, see Genette, *Narrative Discourse*, ch. 5; Romberg, *Narrative Technique of the First-Person Novel*, ch. 2. For cinema, see Fleischman, *Narrated Films*, 21, 71–72; Kozloff, *Invisible Storytellers*, chs. 3–4. For theater, see Hugo Bowles, *Storytelling and Drama: Exploring Narrative Episodes in Plays* (Amsterdam: John Benjamins, 2010), 172–76; Pfister, *Theory and Analysis of Drama*, 71–83; Richardson, "Point of View in Drama." Carolyn Abbate, *Unsung Voices: Opera and Musical Narrative in the Nineteenth Century* (Princeton: Princeton University Press, 1991), ch. 3, is the most extensive treatment of character-narrators in opera, but she limits her discussion to oral storytelling, particularly *mise-en-abyme* songs.

18. Daniel H. Foster, *Wagner's Ring Cycle and the Greeks* (Cambridge: Cambridge University Press, 2010), 59. Richard Wagner, *Opera and Drama*, trans. William Ashton Ellis (Lincoln: University of Nebraska Press, 1995), 119, criticizes narration for "appealing to the imagination and not the senses."

19. George Bernard Shaw, *The Perfect Wagnerite: A Commentary on the Niblung's Ring* (New York: Dover, 1967 [1898]), 109. I have normalized Shaw's spelling of proper names.

20. Abbate, *Unsung Voices*, 161; James Treadwell, "The *Ring* and the Conditions of Interpretation: Wagner's Writing, 1848 to 1852," *Cambridge Opera Journal* 7, no. 3 (1995): 231.

21. David J. Levin, *Richard Wagner, Fritz Lang, and the Nibelungen: The Dramaturgy of Disavowal* (Princeton: Princeton University Press, 1998), 39.

22. Ibid., 83; Foster, *Wagner's Ring Cycle and the Greeks*, 60.

23. Similar arguments have been made by the director Keith Warner in Barry Millington, "'A Theatre of Generosity': Interview with Keith Warner," *Wagner Journal* 1, no. 3 (2007): 73; Alain Badiou, *Five Lessons on Wagner*, trans. Susan Spitzer (London: Verso, 2010), 117.

24. Abbate, *Unsung Voices*, ch. 3.

25. I thank Karen Messina for recommending this example.

26. Lin-Manuel Miranda and Jeremy McCarter, *Hamilton: The Revolution* (New York: Grand Central Publishing, 2016), 68–69.

27. Abbate, *Unsung Voices*, 201. Edward T. Cone, "The World of Opera and Its Inhabitants," in *Music, a View from Delft: Selected Essays*, ed. Robert P. Morgan (Chicago: University of Chicago Press, 1989), 136–37; Peter Kivy, "Opera Talk: A Philosophical 'Phantasie,'" *Cambridge Opera Journal* 3, no. 1 (1991): 73–77, have argued that opera characters typically author their accompaniments. I have argued against this position in Nina Penner, "Opera Singing and Fictional Truth," *Journal of Aesthetics and Art Criticism* 71, no. 1 (2013): 84–85.

28. I am using the concept of *nesting* in the sense defined by Paisley Livingston, "Nested Art," *Journal of Aesthetics and Art Criticism* 61, no. 3 (2003): 233.

29. Joe Darion and Dale Wasserman, *Man of La Mancha: A Musical Play* (libretto) (New York: Random House, 1966), 9, 36.

30. Since the singing is largely confined to the embedded performance (unlike *Kiss Me, Kate* [1948]), one might argue that a play nests a musical. The stage directions (Darion and Wasserman, *Man of La Mancha* [libretto], 3) even encourage such an interpretation. But if the prisoners' world were entirely realistic, they would produce less musically polished performances than they do. Furthermore, when Cervantes is taken away for his actual trial, the woman who played the role of Aldonza begins to sing "The Impossible Dream," which is taken up by the rest of the prisoners as an anthem.

31. *Feluette*, Vallier's nickname, is a historical Québécois slang term for a homosexual man.

32. The score specifies the use of an onstage band consisting of only fiddle, accordion, and wooden spoons. As of spring 2019, the score has not been published. I am grateful to Kevin March for providing me access to it and for answering my questions about the work.

33. The corresponding passage in *Le Martyre* begins at rehearsal 1, though March takes his opening rhythm from the beginning of Debussy's work. The change from horn to harp at the end of example 3.1 is the one nonpragmatic change.

34. In cinema studies, this phenomenon is referred to as an *audio dissolve*. Rick Altman, *The American Film Musical* (Bloomington: Indiana University Press, 1987), 62–74, claims that it is unique to film musicals, but this example suggests otherwise.

35. Kevin March, email to author, January 23, 2017.

36. Paisley Livingston, "Cinematic Authorship," in *Film Theory and Philosophy*, ed. Richard Allen and Murray Smith (Oxford: Clarendon Press, 1997), 138–40.

37. I am grateful to Bryan Gilliam for suggesting this possibility.

38. Although Monteverdi's *Combattimento* is not an opera, the composer's preface (Claudio Monteverdi, *Claudio Monteverdi Madrigals*, bk. 8, ed. Francesco Malipiero, trans. Stanley Appelbaum [New York: Dover, 1991], xvii) states that it was "intended to be performed with dramatic action" and describes the warriors wearing armor. Thus, the definition of operatic storytelling advanced in chapter 2 would include Monteverdi's *Combattimento*.

39. W. Anthony Sheppard, *Revealing Masks: Exotic Influences and Ritualized Performance in Modernist Music Theater* (Berkeley: University of California Press, 2001), 84–87 (Brecht), 67–71 (Stravinsky), ch. 9 (Britten).

40. Stephen Sondheim, *Finishing the Hat: Collected Lyrics (1954–1981)* (New York: Knopf, 2010), 306.

41. Robert L. McLaughlin, *Stephen Sondheim and the Reinvention of the American Musical* (Jackson: University Press of Mississippi, 2016), 108. For a more detailed discussion of the Reciter's role, refer to Barbara Means Fraser, "Revisiting Greece: The Sondheim Chorus," in *Stephen Sondheim: A Casebook*, ed. Joanne Gordon (New York: Garland, 1997), 234–336.

42. Bernstein refers to the trio as "a Greek chorus born of the radio commercial." Leonard Bernstein, *Trouble in Tahiti: An Opera in Seven Scenes* (vocal score) (New York: Boosey & Hawkes, 2000), cast of characters page.

43. André Obey, *Le viol de Lucrèce* (Paris: Nouvelles éditions latines, 1931), 26 (ellipses in the original; author's translation).

44. Ronald Duncan, *The Rape of Lucretia* (libretto), in *The Operas of Benjamin Britten: The Complete Librettos*, ed. David Herbert (New York: Columbia University Press, 1979), 120 (ellipses in the original).

45. The Reciter supplies the voices of Manjiro (Act I, Scene 1) and the Emperor (Act II, Scene 6) and the sobbing of Kayama (Act I, Scene 6); reads the journal of Commodore Matthew Perry (Act I, Scene 9) and the letter from Kayama to the Shogun (Act II, Scene 4); and acts out the part of the Shogun in "Chrysanthemum Tea."

46. Acts II through IV were based on "Der Sandmann" (1816), "Rat Krespel" (1818), and "Das verlorene Spiegelbild" (1814). Hoffmann's "Chanson de Kleinzach" is based on "Klein Zaches, genannt Zinnober" (1819).

47. Christopher Headington, *Peter Pears: A Biography* (London: Faber, 1992), 116–17. Britten praised Pears's appearance in *Hoffmann* in a letter to Beata Mayer from May 17, 1942. Mervyn Cooke, Donald Mitchell, and Philip Reed, eds., *Letters from a Life: The Selected Letters of Benjamin Britten, 1913–1976*, 6 vols. (Woodbridge: Boydell, 1991–2012), 2:1052.

48. Edna Kenton's 1934 essay, "Henry James to the Ruminant Reader: *The Turn of the Screw*," in *A Casebook on Henry James's The Turn of the Screw*, ed. Gerald Willen (New York: Thomas Y. Crowell Company, 1960), 102–14, was first to call the Governess's sanity into question. The most frequently cited Freudian interpretation is Edmund Wilson's 1934 essay, "The Ambiguity of Henry James," in *A Casebook on Henry James's The Turn of the Screw*, ed. Gerald Willen (New York: Thomas Y. Crowell Company, 1960), 115–53. Myfanwy Piper, "Writing for Britten," in *The Operas of Benjamin Britten: The Complete Librettos*, ed. David Herbert (New York: Columbia University Press, 1979), 12, indicates her awareness of this critical tradition.

49. Henry James, *The Turn of the Screw: Authoritative Text, Contexts, Criticism*, ed. Deborah Esch and Jonathan Warren (New York: Norton, 1999), 4.

50. Myfanwy Piper, *The Turn of the Screw* (libretto), in *The Operas of Benjamin Britten: The Complete Librettos*, ed. David Herbert (New York: Columbia University Press, 1979), 233.

51. Britten also imitates recitative in the opening of *The Rape of Lucretia*.

52. Piper, "Writing for Britten," 9. Arguments that Britten's stipulations removed the ambiguity from the opera include David Clippinger, "The Hidden Life: Benjamin Britten's Homoerotic Reading of Henry James's *The Turn of the Screw*," in *Literature and Musical Adaptation*, ed. Michael J. Meyer (Amsterdam: Rodopi, 2002), 137; Michelle Deutsch, "Ceremonies of Innocence: Men, Boys and Women in *The Turn of the Screw*," in *Henry James on Stage and Screen*, ed. John R. Bradley (New York: Palgrave, 2000), 82; Patricia Howard, "Myfanwy Piper's *The Turn of the Screw*: Libretto and Synopsis," in *Benjamin Britten: The Turn of the Screw*, ed. Patricia Howard (Cambridge: Cambridge University Press, 1985), 23–24; Gary Tomlinson, *Metaphysical Song: An Essay on Opera* (Princeton: Princeton University Press, 1999), 155–56. Scholars who argue that the opera is as ambiguous as the novella, though for different reasons, include Philip Rupprecht, *Britten's Musical Language* (New York: Cambridge University Press, 2001), 180–81; Linda Hutcheon, *A Theory of Adaptation* (New York: Routledge, 2006), 69.

53. Patricia Howard, "Structures: An Overall View," in *Benjamin Britten: The Turn of the Screw*, ed. Patricia Howard (Cambridge: Cambridge University Press, 1985), 71–90.

54. Ibid., 72–73.

55. The numbers in superscript indicate the number of measures before or after the rehearsal number, not including the measure in which the number appears.

56. For a discussion of the erotic overtones of this moment, see Lloyd Whitesell, "Britten's Dubious Trysts," *Journal of the American Musicological Society* 56, no. 3 (2003): 647, 658–59.

57. Britten broached the subject to Piper in a letter from April 12, 1954, after he had started composing. His stated motivation for adding a prologue was fear that the work would be too short. Britten finished his short-score draft in July. In a letter to Piper from August 1, Britten rejected her second attempt, a dramatization of James's ghost-story-party scene. By August 15, he reported that "rehearsals are in *full* swing," but the prologue was still not finished, even though the premiere was only a month away. Cooke, Mitchell, and Reed, eds., *Letters from a Life*, 4:236, 261, 266. The decision to impose a frame on *Billy Budd* was made during the collaborators' meeting in January 1949, during which they produced the first synopsis. By January 27, Forster wrote to Britten with a first draft of the prologue. Philip Reed, "From First Thoughts to First Night: A *Billy Budd* Chronology," in *Benjamin Britten: Billy Budd*, ed. Mervyn Cooke and Philip Reed (Cambridge: Cambridge University Press, 1993), 47–49.

58. Herman Melville, *Billy Budd, Sailor: An Inside Narrative* (Chicago: Chicago University Press, 1962), 114–15.

59. Eric Crozier, "The Writing of *Billy Budd*," *Opera Quarterly* 4, no. 3 (1986): 13.

60. Letter from E. M. Forster to William Plomer, March 17, 1949, quoted in Hanna Rochlitz, *Sea-Changes: Melville—Forster—Britten* (Göttingen: Universitätsverlag Göttingen, 2012), 499n669.

61. See, for example, Stephen Arthur Allen, "*Billy Budd*: Temporary Salvation and the Faustian Pact," *Journal of Musicological Research* 25, no. 1 (2006): 46; Michelle Fillion, *Difficult Rhythm: Music and the Word in E. M. Forster* (Urbana: University of Illinois Press, 2010), 135; Michael Halliwell, "Narrative Elements in Opera," in *Word and Music Studies: Defining the Field*, ed. Walter Bernhart, Steven Paul Scher, and Werner Wolf (Amsterdam: Rodopi, 1999), 138; Joe K. Law, "'We Have Ventured to Tidy Up Vere': The Adapters' Dialogue in *Billy Budd*," *Twentieth-Century Literature* 31, no. 2–3 (1985): 298, 300, 301; Joe K. Law, "The Dialogics of Operatic Adaptation: Reading Benjamin Britten," *A Yearbook of Interdisciplinary Studies in the Fine Arts* 1 (1989): 419; Robert K. Martin, "Saving Captain Vere: *Billy Budd* from Melville's Novella to Britten's Opera," *Studies in Short Fiction* 23, no. 1 (1986): 51; Shannon McKellar, "Re-Visioning the 'Missing' Scene: Critical and Tonal Trajectories in Britten's *Billy Budd*," *Journal of the Royal Musical Association* 122, no. 2 (1997): 261; Andrew Porter, "Britten's *Billy Budd*," *Music & Letters* 33, no. 2 (1952): 112; Claire Seymour, *The Operas of Benjamin Britten: Expression and Evasion* (Woodbridge: Boydell, 2004), 136; Erwin Stein, "*Billy Budd*," in *Benjamin Britten: A Commentary on His Work from a Group of Specialists*, ed. Donald Mitchell and Hans Keller (London: Rockliff, 1952), 198; Arnold Whittall, "*Billy Budd*," Grove Music Online, last modified 2002, https://www.oxfordmusiconline.com/subscriber/article/grove/music/O009276. Scholars opposing this view include Rochlitz, *Sea-Changes*, 114–17, 122–23; Rupprecht, *Britten's Musical Language*, ch. 3.

62. Donald Mitchell, "A *Billy Budd* Notebook (1979–1991)," in *Benjamin Britten: Billy Budd*, ed. Mervyn Cooke and Philip Reed (Cambridge: Cambridge University Press, 1993), 128, was the first to comment on the Vere-Claggart convergence. Rupprecht, *Britten's Musical Language*, 122–23, has extended this line of inquiry.

63. For literal English translations of these prologues, refer to Jette Barnholdt Hansen, "From Invention to Interpretation: The Prologues of the First Court Operas Where Oral

and Written Cultures Meet," *Journal of Musicology* 20, no. 4 (2003): 581–82, 590–91. Other scholars who regard Music as the fictional presenter of *Orfeo* include Mauro Calcagno, *From Madrigal to Opera: Monteverdi's Staging of the Self* (Berkeley: University of California Press, 2012), 38; Ilias Chrissochoidis, "An Emblem of Modern Music," *Early Music* 39, no. 4 (2011): 519.

64. *Narciso* was written for the marriage of Duke Vincenzo's second son, but once the wedding was postponed, another work was chosen. Barbara Russano Hanning, "Apologia pro Ottavio Rinuccini," *Journal of the American Musicological Society* 26, no. 2 (1973): 255n53.

65. Rebecca Harris-Warrick, *Dance and Drama in French Baroque Opera: A History* (Cambridge: Cambridge University Press, 2016), 143, 142. Other Lully-Quinault operas containing invitations to regard the prologue characters as the opera's presenters include *Alceste* (1674), *Thésée* (1675), and *Isis* (1677).

66. Stravinsky describes the Speaker as wearing "a black suit. . . . He expresses himself like a conferencier, presenting the story with a detached voice." Igor Stravinsky, *Oedipus Rex* (full score) (London: Boosey & Hawkes, 1949), staging notes. The tour-guide comparison comes from Stephen Walsh, *Stravinsky: Oedipus Rex* (Cambridge: Cambridge University Press, 1993), 30.

67. A complete libretto, translated by Stephen Walsh and e. e. cummings, is included in Walsh, *Stravinsky: Oedipus Rex*, 79.

68. Ibid., 17.

69. Susan C. Cook, "*Der Zar lässt sich photographieren*: Weill and Comic Opera," in *A New Orpheus: Essays on Kurt Weill*, ed. Kim H. Kowalke (New Haven: Yale University Press, 1986), 90–92, 94–95, argues that Weill's *Der Zar lässt sich photographieren* (1928) was influenced by *Oedipus Rex*.

70. Beginning in the fourteenth century, theatrical performances of Bible stories became part of Corpus Christi celebrations in Europe. Although suppressed in England during the Reformation, the practice was revived in the 1950s. Sheppard, *Revealing Masks*, 118–20.

71. William Plomer, *Curlew River* (libretto), in *The Operas of Benjamin Britten: The Complete Librettos*, ed. David Herbert (New York: Columbia University Press, 1979), 283.

72. The music of this passage was influenced by the *nanoribue* (entrance music) of the *Sumidagawa*, *Curlew River*'s Japanese source. Heterophony is not employed in Noh drama but is a component of other Japanese music, such as *gagaku*. For a fuller discussion of the Japanese influences over this passage, refer to J. P. E. Harper-Scott, *Ideology in Britten's Operas* (Cambridge: Cambridge University Press, 2018), 245–46.

73. Donald Mitchell, quoted in Michael Kennedy, *Britten*, rev. ed. (Oxford: Oxford University Press, 2001), 220; Sheppard, *Revealing Masks*, 117.

74. C. J. Cruz brought this interpretation of Mark's role to my attention in an assignment for Adaptation and Musical Theatre (Duke University, 2018). Published arguments to this effect include Ian Nisbet, "Transposition in Jonathan Larson's *Rent*," *Studies in Musical Theatre* 5, no. 3 (2011): 227; Judith Sebesta, "Of Fire, Death, and Desire: Transgression and Carnival in Jonathan Larson's *Rent*," *Contemporary Theatre Review* 16, no. 4 (2006): 428.

75. Jonathan Larson, *Rent* (libretto), in *The New American Musical: An Anthology from the End of the Century*, ed. Wiley Hausam (New York: Theatre Communications Group, 2003), 109, 111, 131, 180.

76. I am grateful to the students of Adaptation and Musical Theatre for supplying these and other examples of musical-theater narrators that do not fit in any of the above categories.

77. *Amadis* is the only Lully-Quinault opera in which a prologue character appears in the following acts. There are more examples from Rameau, including *Dardanus* (1739) and *Platée* (1745). The first Venetian opera to have a prologue character that reappears is Benedetto Ferrari's *L'Armida* (1639). Robin A. Miller, "The Prologue in the Seventeenth-Century Venetian Operatic

Libretto: Its Dramatic Purpose and the Function of Its Characters" (PhD diss., University of North Texas, 1998), 100.

78. Richard Taruskin, "From Fairy Tale to Opera in Four Moves," in *On Russian Music* (Berkeley: University of California Press, 2009), 220, notes that the expanded role of the narrators is one of the major changes Prokofiev made to Carlo Gozzi's play *L'amore delle tre melarance* (1761).

79. Stephen Sondheim and John Weidman, *Assassins* (libretto) (New York: Theatre Communications Group, 1991), 18, 19. Steven Swayne, *How Sondheim Found His Sound* (Ann Arbor: University of Michigan Press, 2005), 178, discusses the singularity of moments in Sondheim's works when characters "talk back to the narrator," linking them to the narrative style of the French New Wave.

80. Often the singer also performs the role of Lee Harvey Oswald.

81. James Lapine, quoted in Nina Mankin, "The *PAJ* Casebook #2: *Into the Woods*," *Performing Arts Journal* 11, no. 1 (1988): 55.

82. Sondheim and Weidman, *Assassins* (libretto), 4.

83. Stephen Sondheim in Roger Englander, dir., *Assassins: A Conversation Piece* (New York: Music Theatre International, 1991), accessed March 5, 2020, http://www.youtube.com/watch?v=29P7x4z6NXU, beginning at 5:00.

84. Sondheim and Lapine, *Into the Woods* (libretto), 136.

85. The prologue's function as an authorial manifesto reemerged in later periods with the introduction of new subgenres and artistic approaches. The prologue to *Pagliacci*, for example, explains the premise of *verismo*.

86. Geoffrey Burgess, "Revisiting *Atys*: Reflections on Les Arts Florissants' Production," *Early Music* 34, no. 3 (2006): 466.

87. Calcagno, *Monteverdi's Staging of the Self*, 25, 34–35.

4

ORCHESTRAL NARRATION AND AUTHORIAL COMMENTARY

The previous chapter explored the roles robustly characterized fictional narrators play in opera and musical theater. In few cases are we invited to imagine that such narrators are the source of the entire performance we are watching. The orchestra, in particular, often communicates facts about the story that exceed the levels of awareness of the characters therein. In response to the prevalence of such moments in Wagner as well as his remarks on his use of the orchestra in his prose writings, critics began to regard the orchestra as performing a role analogous to that of a literary narrator. Today, references to the "orchestral narrator" are as commonplace in opera and musical theater studies as invocations of the "cinematic narrator" are in cinema studies. Unlike the cinematic narrator, however, the orchestral narrator has been subject to virtually no theoretical investigation.

In this chapter, I explore how this entity has been used by composers and critics, beginning with Wagner's theoretical writings and examples from his works. The tendency to regard the orchestra as a narrating agent can also be found in discourse on musical theater, including criticism of Bernstein and Sondheim's *West Side Story* (1957) and Sondheim and Hugh Wheeler's *Sweeney Todd* (1979). Although the orchestral narrator is most commonly invoked in leitmotivic scores, I show how music-text conflicts can also create a sense of the orchestra as commenting on the action with an aria from Gluck and Nicholas-François Guillard's *Iphigénie en Tauride* (1779). Most critics understand instances of orchestral commentary as issuing from a fictional agent. Through an example from Wagner's *Die Meistersinger von Nürnberg* (1868), I illustrate some pitfalls of this approach and suggest an alternative: regarding the orchestra as a tool the work's real-life authors use to comment on the narrative. I conclude with a discussion of who the authors of operas and operatic performances are.

Theories of the Orchestra's Narrational Role

Wagner was pivotal in changing the way we think about the opera orchestra. Not only do his later music dramas (*Tristan und Isolde* [1865], *Die Meistersinger*, the *Ring* cycle [1876], and *Parsifal* [1882]) offer some of the most compelling illustrations of the orchestra's narrator-like capacity, but his prose writings were some of the first attempts to theorize this capacity. Given that Wagner conceived of his ideal form of opera as a reimagining of Greek tragedy, he gravitated toward comparisons with the choruses of such works. In "Music of the Future" (1860), he derides contemporary Italian composers for treating the orchestra as nothing more than a "huge guitar for accompanying the aria." In his operas, by contrast,

> the orchestra's relation to the dramatic action will be roughly similar to that of the chorus in Greek tragedy. This latter was constantly in attendance, watching the motivation of the action unfold before its eyes and seeking to fathom the meaning of those motives in order thereby to form an opinion concerning the action. But this interest on the part of the chorus was essentially reflective in nature; the chorus itself stood apart from the action and from its motives. The modern symphony orchestra, by contrast, will be so intimately involved in the motivation of the action that, just as, on the one hand, it is uniquely able, as harmony incarnate, to invest the melody with a specific expression, it will, on the other hand, maintain that melody in a state of uninterrupted flux, and thus convey the motives to the audience's feelings with the most forceful conviction.[1]

What, precisely, this involvement entails becomes clearer in "Prologue to a Reading of *Götterdämmerung* before a Select Audience in Berlin" (1873), where Wagner describes the music as "revealing the innermost motivation of the action in its widest ramifications" and "allowing us to sympathize with those motives."[2] In other words, the orchestra does not motivate the drama in the sense of influencing its outcome but rather in terms of revealing the motives that are driving the characters' actions. Expressed in terms I will define more precisely in the following chapter, the orchestra affords spectators access to characters' points of view. From these quotations, it would appear that Wagner conceived of his orchestra as a guide to the action, one that aids in our comprehension of the characters' motivations and suggests which characters deserve our sympathies.

However, in this same essay on *Götterdämmerung*, Wagner puts forth another rather different conception of the orchestra's role in operatic storytelling. Continuing his comparison with Greek tragedy, Wagner observes that the Greek chorus performed only an intermittent role. "Whereas antique tragedy had to insert the dramatic dialogue between the choruses, dividing it off from them," the opera orchestra "is no longer divorced from the dialogue" but rather "constantly accompanies the action, and may be said, in a profounder sense, to embrace the motives of the entire action as though in its mother's womb."³ With this maternal metaphor, Wagner seems to suggest that the orchestra is no mere guide to the drama but, rather, its author.

Given the flowery nature of Wagner's prose, it might be tempting to take his mixed metaphors with a grain of salt. One reason not to is that Wagner returned repeatedly to maternal metaphors when describing the orchestra's role. In his essay "On the Name 'Music Drama'" (1872), he refers to the music as "the mother's womb of drama. Yet in this higher calling it must stand neither before nor behind the drama: it is not drama's rival but its mother."⁴ In his explanation of Bayreuth's hidden orchestra pit in "The Festival-Playhouse at Bayreuth" (1873), he describes "the spectral music, rising up from the 'mystic abyss' like vapours wafting up from the sacred primeval womb of Gaia beneath the Pythia's seat, transports [the spectator] into that inspired state of clairvoyance in which the scenic picture becomes the truest reflection of life itself."⁵

Subsequent critics and scholars have favored Wagner's less mystic idea of the orchestra as guide. One notable exception is Michael Halliwell, who has proposed that "just as the characters in [literary] fiction are the direct result of a narrative act performed by a narrator (of whatever kind), so too are the operatic characters the result of an act of narration by the orchestra-narrator."⁶ Halliwell would seem to be suggesting that the orchestra be regarded as the fictional mechanism by which we gain access to the story. As such, it presumably performs this role not only in Wagner but in every opera.

The view more prevalent today is that the orchestra is an accompaniment to the story, not its source. Although nearly always in attendance, only occasionally does it perform a commentative role. Despite Wagner's focus on the orchestra's capacity to provide access to characters' points of view, that is not the function present-day scholars and critics predominantly attribute to the orchestral narrator. More typically, it is evoked to explain music that *cannot* be understood as expressing any character's point of view. The comparison Britten's music draws between Vere and Claggart in *Billy Budd* (1951) is an example from the previous chapter. In this chapter, I will provide some additional examples from both leitmotivic and non-leitmotivic scores. To be clear, my aim in this section is merely to give a sense of the kinds of situations in which contemporary scholars invoke the orchestral narrator, not to suggest that this is the only or even the preferable way of understanding these moments.

Example 4.1. Alberich's curse

Example 4.2. The Curse motive after Fasolt's death

In opera prior to Wagner, the vast majority of the orchestra's contributions to conveying the opera's story could be understood as expressions of characters' points of view or as representations of aspects of their environments. In the *Ring*, by contrast, much of what the orchestra communicates is beyond the understanding of the characters, or in blatant contradiction with their thoughts and feelings. The orchestra foreshadows events no character foresees, recalls events no character has witnessed, reveals information no character knows, and draws connections between characters and ideas that exceed the characters' levels of understanding.

Some of the most heavy-handed instances of foreshadowing are the occurrences of the Curse motive in *Götterdämmerung*. In the first installment of the cycle, *Das Rheingold*, Alberich loses the ring to Wotan and curses it (ex. 4.1), proclaiming that it will deal death to its wearers. Those who possess it shall never experience joy, and those who do not will be ravaged by envy. At the first casualty of Alberich's curse, Fasolt's death at the hands of his brother Fafner, the trombones ominously reprise the melody of Alberich's curse (ex. 4.2). Henceforth, this instrumental version of the motive resounds each time death or misfortune attends those who covet the ring: Wotan's obligations to kill his son Siegfried and punish his daughter Brünnhilde, Fafner's death at the hands of Siegfried, Alberich's death at the hands of his son Hagen, and Hagen's suicidal dive into the Rhine in pursuit of the ring at the end of the cycle. These iterations of the Curse motive recall this pivotal event and suggest that listeners regard these subsequent events as causally linked to it.

In *Götterdämmerung*, Wagner uses the Curse motive to foreshadow the numerous ring-related deaths that take place during the opera. Its first appearance occurs when Hagen and the Gibichungs are concocting a plan to manipulate Siegfried to enhance their wealth, power, and renown. When

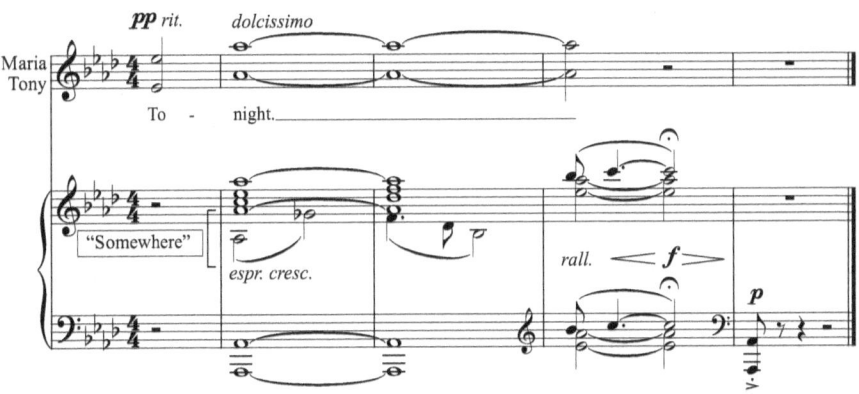

Example 4.3. Foreshadowing at the end of "Tonight" from *West Side Story*

Gunther wonders how they will find Siegfried, the orchestra answers him with the Curse motive. It foretells that Siegfried will fall into their trap and suggests that he will do so because of Alberich's curse and Siegfried's possession of the ring. Rather pedantically, Wagner repeats the motive at every step Siegfried takes toward his demise: his appearance at the Gibichungs' court, his confusion about how they know his name, his taking of the magic potion, his swearing of an oath of blood-brotherhood with Gunther, and finally his capture of Brünnhilde as Gunther's bride.

Such uses of the orchestra are by no means confined to Wagner or even to opera. Scholars of musical theater also invoke the orchestral narrator to explain musical foreshadowing, such as Bernstein's anticipation of motives from *West Side Story*'s Act II dream ballet "Somewhere" at the end of Tony and Maria's Act I love duet "Tonight" (ex. 4.3). Geoffrey Block remarks, "As in Wagner's music dramas, the orchestra gives an alert audience classified information to which the principals are not privy. At the conclusion of 'Tonight' the idealistic lovers show their oneness by singing in unison and the celestial heights of youthful optimistic love by singing and holding high A♭'s. Meanwhile, back on earth, the omniscient orchestra warns audiences of their imminent doom."[7] Unlike Wagner, Bernstein does not have the luxury of drawing on a catalog of motives from three previous operas. Accordingly, only the repeat listener who remembers the orchestra's mournful reprise of these motives after Tony's death is likely to regard the final measures of "Tonight" as ominous.

Another way the orchestra can express a perspective that is close to omniscience is by revealing aspects of characters' identities of which they are not aware. Before Siegmund and Sieglinde discover that they are descendants of the gods, Wagner reminds spectators of this fact with the motive associated with the gods' home, Valhalla (ex. 4.8 [reproduced later in the chapter], beginning at Scene 2). When their son Siegfried ponders his own origins in the subsequent opera, Wagner reprises the motive associated with his parents.

Similar examples may be found in more popular forms of musical theater. Sondheim drops a clue as to the identity of the Beggar Woman in *Sweeney Todd* during Mrs. Lovett's "Poor Thing," an example of internal, character-to-character storytelling. Mrs. Lovett recounts the story of the barber's wife who used to live above her shop, ostensibly for Todd's benefit but largely for the real-life audience's. (At this point in the story, Todd has not identified himself as the barber. Mrs. Lovett knows who he is but pretends to be meeting him for the first time.)

The minuet representing the background music at the party at which Todd's wife, Lucy, was raped is a slowed-down and heavily ornamented version of the music the Beggar Woman previously sang as she propositioned Todd and the young sailor Anthony in "No Place Like London" (cf. exx. 4.4 and 4.5).[8] In true melodramatic fashion, Todd does not discover that the Beggar Woman is his long-lost wife until after he has murdered her in the final scene. Although the orchestra is generally aligned with Todd's perspective, this is one demonstration of its greater knowledge.[9] A character who does know the identity of the Beggar Woman is Mrs. Lovett, and given that this is her song, one could also interpret the orchestral music as expressing her point of view.

There are times when the orchestra expresses a point of view no character in the narrative holds. An example from the *Ring* is the connection Wagner makes between the ring and Valhalla through their musical motives. The former is initially sung by the Rheinmaiden Wellgunde as she explains the power of the Rheingold (ex. 4.6). Wagner uses the Ring motive not only in connection with the ring Alberich forges with the gold but also with the corrupting influence of wealth and power more generally. In the interlude between Scenes 1 and 2, as Wagner's music transports the listener from the bowels of the Rhine to Wotan's glittering new castle, we hear the Ring motive gradually transform into the Valhalla motive. From the compound meter ($\frac{9}{8}$) associated with the Rheinmaidens' music, the Ring motive is squared off into a simple meter ($\frac{4}{4}$) (ex. 4.7). Timbrally, it passes from the voice and winds to just winds, then horns, and finally to the Valhalla motive's characteristic Wagner tubas (ex. 4.8). At this final stage, Wagner resolves the Ring motive's tonal ambiguity in favor of E♭ major and fills out the harmony from parallel thirds to full triads, appropriate to representing the grandeur and scale of Wotan's new abode.

Example 4.4. The Beggar Woman's proposition in "No Place Like London" from *Sweeney Todd*

Example 4.5. The Beggar Woman's music as minuet in "Poor Thing"

96 | *Storytelling in Opera and Musical Theater*

Example 4.6. First appearance of the Ring motive

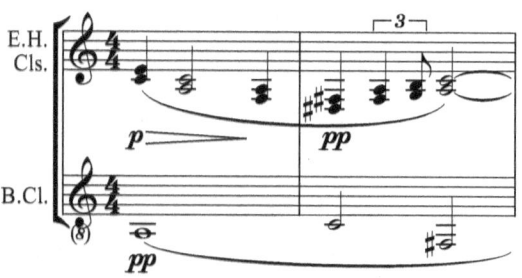

Example 4.7. The Ring motive in winds in $\frac{4}{4}$

This gradual transformation of motivic material not only provides continuity between scenes but also contributes to the astute listener's understanding of the narrative, forging a connection between the two objects the motives represent, their respective owners, and what these characters sacrificed in order to attain them.[10] In both cases, it was love. Alberich renounces love in order to forge the ring, and Wotan barters his sister-in-law Freia, goddess of love, in order to pay the giants for building this physical representation of his power. The implicit critique of Wotan's most recent accomplishment at the moment of its unveiling cannot be understood as expressing the perspective of any character at this point in the story. Even more strongly than the previous example from *Sweeney Todd*, understanding what the orchestra is communicating here involves looking beyond the characters in the story to some external agent.

So far, all of my examples of orchestral commentary involve leitmotivs, but thematic reprises are not the only way the orchestra can comment on the drama. Another situation in which critics commonly invoke the orchestral narrator is when the music contradicts a character's words. Describing Orestes's aria "Le calme rentre dans mon coeur" from the original production of *Iphigénie en Tauride* in 1779, an anonymous reviewer observed that while

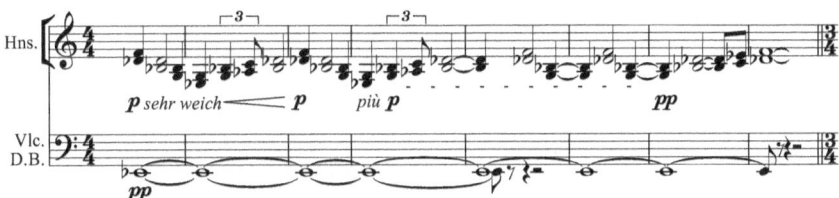

SCENE 2

An open space on a mountain summit. In the growing light of the dawning day a castle with glittering battlements can be seen standing on a rocky summit in the background; between it and the front of the stage a deep valley must be imagined, with the Rhine River flowing through it. Wotan and Fricka are asleep.

Example 4.8. The Ring motive transforms into the Valhalla motive

Orestes professes his calm state of being, if one "listen[s] to the instruments; they will tell you that this is exhaustion, not repose. They will tell you that Orestes has lost not the awareness of his troubles, but the strength to give them voice. Indeed, his melody is more admirable, the more true, in that it extends over a very small range of harmonies, and has no periodic phrasing; his melody is accompanied by the violas, which lash the subdued, remorseful voice, which the violins express a profound agitation, mingled with sighs and tears."[11] Berlioz had a similar reaction to this scene when he saw the work performed in 1821: "And the orchestra! It's all in the orchestra. If you could only hear how every situation is depicted in it, above all when Orestes appears to have grown calm—well, the violins hold a long note, very soft, which

Example 4.9. Orestes is not calm: "Le calme rentre dans mon coeur" from *Iphigénie en Tauride*

suggests tranquility; but below it you hear the cellos murmuring, like the remorse which despite his apparent calm still sounds in the depths of the parricide's heart."[12]

Most immediately noticeable, and exceptional for its time, is the syncopation in the violas (ex. 4.9). Gluck's careful dynamic markings, particularly the sfzorzandos, also contribute to the skittish effect. The "agitation, mingled with sighs and tears" comes from the violin parts, specifically their articulation markings. When Gluck's musicians attempted to soften their performance so that it better accorded with Orestes's words, the composer irritably exclaimed: "Don't listen to Orestes: He says he is calm but he is lying."[13] That Orestes' vocal line proceeds almost entirely by step lends credence to the anonymous reviewer's mention of exhaustion. The harmony is static, featuring a pedal A, the key of the aria, but notice the F♮ in the voice, which brings about modal mixture. It is as if Orestes lacks the energy to reach the F♯. The music presents a rather different perspective on Orestes's state than that which he professes through his words.

Most contemporary scholarship on operas and musicals treats the orchestra as a guide to the narrative, not its source. Scholars regard this commentative role as one the orchestra performs only occasionally, typically through leitmotivic reprises and music-text conflicts. Although Wagner did not pioneer the narratorial use of the orchestra, his works, particularly the *Ring*, contain a much higher proportion of potential examples than previous forms of opera. His prose writings also helped to popularize the view of the orchestra as a narrative agent.

Authors as Narrators

Today most scholars understand the orchestral narrator as a fictional agent that is distinct from the work's implied and actual authors. As such, it bears some similarity to the cinematic narrator. This connection is especially strong if one follows Halliwell in regarding the orchestra as the fictional source for the entire drama. But even in a more circumscribed role, imagining how a fictional agent is responsible for the instances of commentary described in the previous section leads to a plethora of silly questions concerning what kind of being this is and how it possesses the knowledge it does.[14] It is certainly possible that an opera may invite us to ascribe some or all of the orchestra's music to a fictional entity. However, in general, I suggest that instances of orchestral commentary are more coherently understood as issuing from the work's real-life author.[15]

A particularly compelling example is Wagner's quotations and allusions to *Tristan* in his subsequent opera *Die Meistersinger*. The most blatant occurrence is in Act III, Scene 4, when Sachs renounces his claim on Eva's heart and tells her to marry young Walther instead. As he explains, this is no self-sacrificial gesture; he has no interest in playing the part of King Marke to their Tristan and Isolde. He knows how that story ends. Whereas earlier evocations of *Tristan* were confined to instances of the eponymous chord (often in different voicings) and musical-stylistic allusions, Wagner underscores Sachs's explicit verbal reference with a quotation from the prelude, including not only its characteristic motivic material but also its orchestration, with oboe and then clarinet providing the ascending chromatic line (ex. 4.10).[16]

Given the opera's intended setting, mid-sixteenth-century Nuremberg, it is to be expected than an educated man such as Sachs would be aware of the legend of Tristan and Isolde. What is not reasonable to imagine is that Wagner's operatic adaptation of 1865 is part of the fictional world. If the orchestral narrator is a fictional agent internal to the world of *Die Meistersinger*, it is difficult to explain how this agent would be able to quote from Wagner's

100 | *Storytelling in Opera and Musical Theater*

Example 4.10. Quotation of *Tristan* in *Die Meistersinger*

previous opera. One possible response would be to claim that the narrator resides in a different fictional world than the other characters, a world in which Wagner's *Tristan* exists. By now, this narrator is beginning to sound suspiciously like the work's actual author.

The temptation to collapse the distinction between narrator and author is especially strong in this case, and not just because of Wagner's self-quotations.[17] The orchestra's opinions on who is worthy of the title of Mastersinger matches Wagner's own aesthetic principles and political agenda. As illustration of this point, one has only to compare the orchestral accompaniments of Walther's and Beckmesser's performances on the Festival Meadow.[18] Then there is the blatantly autobiographical nature of the opera's plot. Eduard Hanslick's and other conservative critics' dismissals of Wagner's innovations are mirrored in Beckmesser's and the other masters' pedantic criticisms of Walther. Significantly, Wagner originally intended Walther's nemesis to be named Hanslich.[19] And, as many critics have noted, Wagner's portrayal of Sachs's relationship with Eva was colored by his love for and ultimate renunciation of Mathilde Wesendonck, the wife of one of his patrons.[20]

Just because it is tempting to conflate the orchestral narrator and Wagner in this case does not, however, make it justified. What reasons are there to resist this temptation? In the previous chapter, I examined the argument that every narrative is told or presented by an agent in the fictional world. Even if this were to be a logical necessity, the orchestral narrator (as it is typically understood) does not fulfil the right role, as it is not the fictional source of everything we are seeing and hearing. Until better arguments are put forth in favor of conceiving of the orchestral narrator as a fictional agent, I suggest that there is no reason to resist the tendency to collapse orchestral commentary into authorial commentary. In cases where knowledge of the composer's actual life and convictions are less important to comprehending why the work possesses the features it does, this temptation is likely to be less strong. Yet if there is no logical reason why the orchestra ought to be regarded as a fictional entity, why complicate matters unnecessarily?

One commonly cited reason to maintain a separation between narrator and author is to allow for cases when the narration expresses a point of view that cannot be attributed to its author. Imagine that Wagner decided, against his own inclinations, to have the orchestra root for Beckmesser instead of Walther. The entity commonly invoked to contend with such cases is not, however, a fictional narrator but an implied author.[21] In chapter 1, I argued that relying on the implied author runs contrary to an interest in historical understandings of musical works and that moderate real-author intentionalism is able to contend with situations in which authors fail to realize their intentions. Now I will consider arguments that the implied author is necessary to certain interpretive situations, beginning with cases of duplicitous self-presentation.

In justification of the concept of the implied author, Wayne C. Booth observed that it is common for writers to confect an authorial persona tailored to the particular aims of the work in question, which may differ from those projected in other works or in everyday life.[22] A canonical example is Thomas Mann's novella *Der Tod in Venedig* (1912). A reader approaching this work without any knowledge of Mann's life and attitudes is likely to assume that he was a highly judgmental individual with no sympathy for the protagonist, Gustav von Aschenbach. In reality, Mann based much of the story on personal experience and had considerable sympathy for Aschenbach's struggles with homosexual desire.[23]

In everyday life, we have no difficulty understanding how our manner of communication, and thus the image of ourselves that may be gleaned from our correspondence, can change depending on the addressee, context, and purpose of the message. We accept that some of our utterances reveal our personalities and beliefs more fully and faithfully than others without having to invoke the implied author.[24] I suggest that we can apply a similar approach to understanding Mann's narration of *Der Tod in Venedig*: Mann told the story according to a point of view he did not himself hold.

There are many reasons why an author may wish to do this. In the case of *Der Tod in Venedig*, Philip Kitcher has proposed that the narrator's judgments serve "as protective covering for the author's own leanings" by allowing "committed homophobes" to regard the story as a "defense of rectitude and decency." However, readers without such prejudices can interpret the novel as "a depiction of the deformation of a once-vulnerable youth who has been compelled, throughout his life, to confine and deny central elements of his character."[25] Mann may also have decided to pretend to narrate Aschenbach's story from a critical perspective in order to point out the flaws in such a conservative worldview and to arouse sympathy for Aschenbach and his plight.

Another commonly cited use for the implied author is to contend with cases of "problematic authorship," a category James Phelan and Peter J. Rabinowitz use to encompass not only "ghostwritten, anonymous, and fraudulent texts" but also those that are "collaboratively written."[26] They and other literary theorists have argued that interpreting a work produced by multiple authors requires us to imagine that it was produced by a single agent—namely, the implied author. Here is another instance of literary scholars imposing their norms on the study of other art forms. Single authorship may be the norm for novels, but it is not for operas and musicals. Even if the collaborative nature of these arts were to pose a "problem," literature scholars' proposed "solution" is more apt to hinder than aid attempts to understand how and why such works possess the features they do.[27]

It is common to speak of "Britten's *Billy Budd*" rather than "Britten, E. M. Forster, and Eric Crozier's *Billy Budd*" or "Tim Albery's *Billy Budd*" as opposed to "*Billy Budd*, staged by Tim Albery, Antony McDonald, and Tom Cairns, featuring Philip Langridge, Sir Thomas Allen, Richard van Allen. . . ." However, it would be wrong to regard this tendency as more than mere convenience or shorthand.[28] Taking it to indicate that an interpretation of *Billy Budd* need only consider Britten's actions and intentions, for example, is apt to lead one astray, particularly when grappling with the music-text conflicts in the epilogue. As I will discuss in more detail in chapter 7, Forster's text answers the questions he posed at the opera's beginning and represents Vere taking comfort in the remembrance of Billy's blessing. Britten's music, by contrast, fails to resolve its ambiguities and is decidedly more equivocal about Vere's ability to move on from past trauma. Imagining that this work was created by a single individual makes it difficult to explain these divergences of expressive effect, if one notices them at all.[29]

Opera Authorship

Given the important role authors play in operatic storytelling, according to this account, the question of who the authors are becomes crucial. This is another question that is not commonly asked by opera scholars, either due to skepticism about the relevance of the real author to music criticism or because the answer is taken to be self-evident. In early writings about opera, music scholars assumed the answer was "the composer."[30] In the 1990s, an increasing number of scholars of literature became involved in opera and musical-theater studies. In large part due to these new voices in the field, the answer one is more likely to receive today is "the composer and librettist."[31] The tendency to regard the director as the primary author of an opera *production* remains strong. However, recent scholarly work on historical singers has raised the question of whether at least some singers ought to be regarded as authors, if not of the work being performed then of the performances they give, particularly in cases where improvisation is involved.[32]

Operas and musicals admit a greater diversity of authorship scenarios than is generally acknowledged.[33] In the previous chapter, I argued that the question of whether a given work has a fictional narrator must be decided on a case-by-case basis. Similarly, the authors of a work can be determined only by examining its particular process of making. Obviously, to count as an author, one needs to contribute to this process, but not all contributions are equal. Copyists and stagehands contribute to the processes of completing the score and putting on a successful opera performance, but they are not likely to be regarded as the authors of these artistic achievements. Without their contributions, these processes may have taken longer or been less smooth. Nevertheless, they are not the authors of the resulting artistic products because they did not make an *artistic* contribution to their creation.

According to Berys Gaut, intentionally making an artistic contribution to the work is all that is required.[34] As a result, just about everyone who works on a film (save the caterers, personal assistants, grips, and the like) would count among its authors. In assessing the merits of Gaut's proposal, it is useful to reflect on the roles authors play in art appreciation by those with an interest in achieving historical understandings of art. Such appreciators look to the work's author(s), and the various influences over their endeavors, when puzzling over why and how the work possesses the features it does or finding in it something worthy of praise or of blame. For most critics, the anachronistic Christian commentary to *The Rape of Lucretia* (1946) is a regrettable feature of the work. Since it is principally found in the libretto, one may be tempted to blame the librettist, Ronald Duncan. In actuality, Britten was responsible for generating much of this material, to the dismay of his ostensible librettist.[35] Critics interested in knowing what these bits of moralizing are doing in this pre-Christian story need to look to the actions and intentions of Britten, not Duncan, for enlightenment.

This example lends weight to Paisley Livingston's opposing view that authorship involves more than merely making an artistic contribution to the work; one must also exercise sufficient control over its final form.[36] It also illustrates the importance of distinguishing between multiple authorship and coauthorship. The latter involves not only the creative input of multiple persons but also a collaboration or co-laboring, involving a shared commitment to the project, mutual responsiveness and support for each other's actions and ideas, and efforts by all parties to coordinate their respective plans such that they could be co-realizable. Ingredients vitiating coauthorship include coercion, sabotage, and strongly hierarchical, nonegalitarian divisions of labor and decision-making processes.

Britten's disregard for Duncan's opinions prevented the librettist from being an author of *The Rape of Lucretia* to the same degree that Forster was for *Billy Budd*. Duncan has a firmer claim to authorship of the libretto, of course, but still not an exclusive one. To be clear, it is not Britten's contributions that vitiate Duncan's authorial claim. Rather, it is Duncan's disapproval of the final form the libretto took that prevents it from being unproblematically understood as his artistic statement. Just as Livingston argues that a film produced by many people may have only one author, I suggest that *The Rape of Lucretia* has only one author, Benjamin Britten, because he was responsible for the overall shape the work took.

However, in cases where the composer and librettist enjoyed a more egalitarian working relationship, the result may be said to be coauthored. Although Eric Crozier contributed to the libretto of *Billy Budd*, Hanna Rochlitz's detailed study of the creative process has revealed that Forster was the one guiding the libretto's production. Forster was responsible for reconceptualizing Vere's character and reshaping the story according to the archetypes of his previous prose works (for more information, see chap. 7). He also provided feedback on an early draft of the score, feedback that influenced its final form.[37] As such, I regard *Billy Budd* as an especially robust case of coauthorship.

Although close working relationships between composers and librettists are the norm today, in the seventeenth and eighteenth centuries, multiple authorship without collaboration was equally if not more common. Poets produced libretti as freestanding artistic products, which they hoped would be selected by a patron or impresario, who would commission a composer to set them to music, often without any contact with their authors. Popular libretti, such as those by Metastasio (1698–1782), were set dozens of times, even after the librettist's death. Often a local poet was engaged to tailor the libretto to particular singers or its new sociopolitical context, or to bring it up to date in terms of its scenic structure and favored forms of arias and ensembles. Although Mozart's *La clemenza di Tito* (1791) is ostensibly a setting of Metastasio, the changes Caterino Mazzolà made to bring this Baroque relic into the

1790s were so extensive that many Mozart scholars regard him as deserving of authorial credit.[38]

It is also possible that individuals other than the librettist and composer may perform an authorial role. An example of a singer taking on such a role is Peter Pears's contributions to *Peter Grimes* (1945). Pears's work on this project began on his and Britten's sea voyage back to Britain during World War II. Before they had even decided on a librettist (Montagu Slater), they had already made significant progress on transforming the title character from the sadist he is in George Crabbe's narrative poem *The Borough* (1810) to the poet and visionary of "The Great Bear and Pleiades" aria.[39] It is not the fact that Britten wrote the part for Pears or that Pears's performance was emulated by subsequent tenors that leads me to argue that he be considered an author of *Peter Grimes*. What makes this an especially convincing case of a singer authoring an opera as a work for performance (rather than simply a performance the singer appeared in) is Pears's role in developing the opera's central character, and thus the opera's story and overall artistic point, from initial conception to opening night. Similarly, a director involved in the conception of an opera from an early stage, as Robert Wilson was for Philip Glass's *Einstein on the Beach* (1976), may warrant him or her being regarded as one of the authors of the work for performance and not merely the original production.

An opera *production* is even more necessarily the product of many hands. The short list includes the director, possibly in collaboration with a dramaturg, choreographer, or fight director; set, costume, and lighting designers; and singers, conductor, and orchestra. Nevertheless, it is conventional to regard the director as the author of an opera production. Livingston's sufficient-control stipulation would seem to reinforce a focus on the director for the visual components and the conductor for the aural. Although some conductors are rightly regarded as having an authorial role on a production, there are a variety of practical reasons why this is not usually the case. As I will discuss in more depth in chapter 6, the institutions of opera and musical theater currently allow directors much more creative license than conductors.

An example of a conductor who was able to assert his own creative agenda is Nikolaus Harnoncourt on Claus Guth's 2006 staging of *Le nozze di Figaro*. Harnoncourt's wildly unconventional tempi and unscored dramatic pauses played an important role in articulating the artistic point of the production's initial run at the Salzburg Festival. When I saw the production in Toronto in 2016, Guth's artistic vision had changed little, but the Canadian Opera Company's music director Johannes Debus pursued a more conventional interpretation of Mozart's score. When productions transfer houses, the music staff is likely to be entirely different, and their work is typically unfettered by the artistic choices of their predecessors. It is for this reason that I refer to productions by their directors and single out other collaborators when appropriate.

Narratives are invariably inflected by the narrator's point of view. However, narrators may also choose to tell the story in ways that orient listeners to the point of view of a character in the story. The next chapter explores how the music of operas and musicals can be used for this purpose.

Notes

1. Richard Wagner, *Gesammelte Schriften*, 2nd ed., 10 vols. (Hildesheim: Olms, 1976), 7:130; translation from Dieter Borchmeyer, *Richard Wagner: Theory and Theatre*, trans. Stewart Spencer (Oxford: Clarendon Press, 1991), 165.
2. Wagner, *Gesammelte Schriften*, 9:309; translation from Borchmeyer, *Richard Wagner*, 167.
3. Ibid.
4. Wagner, *Gesammelte Schriften*, 9:305; translation from Jean-Jacques Nattiez, *Wagner Androgyne: A Study in Interpretation*, trans. Stewart Spencer (Princeton: Princeton University Press, 1993), 161. Wagner borrowed this metaphor from Nietzsche's *Birth of Tragedy*, which he read in 1872.
5. Wagner, *Gesammelte Schriften*, 9:338; translation from Borchmeyer, *Richard Wagner*, 71.
6. Michael Halliwell, *Opera and the Novel: The Case of Henry James* (Amsterdam: Rodopi, 2005), 68.
7. Geoffrey Block, *Enchanted Evenings: The Broadway Musical from Show Boat to Sondheim*, 2nd ed. (New York: Oxford University Press, 2009), 264.
8. Stephen Banfield, *Sondheim's Broadway Musicals* (Ann Arbor: University of Michigan Press, 1993), 294, 296; Raymond Knapp, *The American Musical and the Performance of Personal Identity* (Princeton: Princeton University Press, 2006), 333–34; Craig M. McGill, "'It Might Have Been Sophisticated Film Music': The Role of the Orchestra in Stage and Screen Versions of *Sweeney Todd, the Demon Barber of Fleet Street*," *Studies in Musical Theatre* 8, no. 1 (2014): 13. Knapp compares Sondheim's use of motives to Wagner while McGill links it to classical Hollywood film scores (also influenced by Wagner). For Sondheim's own remarks on this motivic relationship, refer to Stephen Sondheim, *Finishing the Hat: Collected Lyrics (1954–1981)* (New York: Knopf, 2010), 372–73; Craig Zadan, ed., *Sondheim & Co.* (New York: Harper & Row, 1986), 251–52.
9. This example provides an exception to Raymond Knapp's assertion that "the music of *Sweeney Todd* fuses with and expresses [Todd's] sense of the world above all else." Knapp, *Performance of Personal Identity*, 336.
10. Daniel H. Foster, *Wagner's Ring Cycle and the Greeks* (Cambridge: Cambridge University Press, 2010), 80–82.
11. *Mercure de France*, June 15, 1779; translation from Patricia Howard, *Gluck: An Eighteenth-Century Portrait in Letters and Documents* (Oxford: Clarendon Press, 1995), 199–200.

12. Letter from Berlioz to his sister Nanci, December 13, 1821; translation from David Cairns, *Berlioz*, vol. 1 (London: Deutsch, 1989), 111. Berlioz's remark about the cellos was surely intended to describe the violas.

13. This anecdote is relayed in Madame de Staël's *De l'Allemagne*, vol. 3 (Paris: Hachette, 1959 [1813]), 177 (author's translation).

14. These questions are silly in the sense that contemplating them would distract one from the task of appreciating the work. Kendall L. Walton, *Mimesis as Make-Believe: On the Foundations of the Representational Arts* (Cambridge, MA: Harvard University Press, 1990), 174–83.

15. Others who make similar claims include Karol Berger, "*Der Dichter spricht*: Self-Representation in *Parsifal*," in *Representation in Western Music*, ed. Joshua S. Walden (New York: Cambridge University Press, 2013), 200; Mauro Calcagno, *From Madrigal to Opera: Monteverdi's Staging of the Self* (Berkeley: University of California Press, 2012), 73; John Deathridge and Carl Dahlhaus, *The New Grove Wagner* (New York: Norton, 1984), 100–3; Foster, *Wagner's Ring Cycle and the Greeks*, 67; Scott McMillin, *The Musical as Drama* (Princeton: Princeton University Press, 2006), 127–28; Michael Tanner, "Richard Wagner and Hans Sachs," in *Richard Wagner: Die Meistersinger von Nürnberg*, ed. John Warrack (Cambridge: Cambridge University Press, 1994), 89.

16. The Tristan chord also appears when Walther asks Eva if she is betrothed (Act I, Scene 1) and during Walther's lesson with Sachs in Act III, Scene 2. Walther's Trial Song is also the style of Isolde's *Liebestod*. Steven Huebner, "Tristan's Traces," in *Richard Wagner: Tristan und Isolde*, ed. Arthur Groos (Cambridge: Cambridge University Press, 2011), 142–43; William Kinderman, "Hans Sachs's 'Cobbler's Song,' and the 'Bitter Cry of the Resigned Man,'" *Journal of Musicological Research* 13, no. 3–4 (1993): 172–81.

17. For a more comprehensive rumination on the conditions under which one is apt to conflate narrator and author, refer to Susan S. Lanser, "The 'I' of the Beholder: Equivocal Attachments and the Limits of Structuralist Narratology," in *A Companion to Narrative Theory*, ed. James Phelan and Peter J. Rabinowitz (Malden: Blackwell, 2005), 206–19.

18. Tanner, "Wagner and Hans Sachs," 89.

19. John Warrack, "The Sources and Genesis of the Text," in *Richard Wagner: Die Meistersinger von Nürnberg*, ed. John Warrack (Cambridge: Cambridge University Press, 1994), 12.

20. Lucy Beckett, "Sachs and Schopenhauer," in *Richard Wagner: Die Meistersinger von Nürnberg*, ed. John Warrack (Cambridge: Cambridge University Press, 1994), 72; Kinderman, "Hans Sachs's 'Cobbler's Song,'" 182–83; Eva Rieger, "'I Married Eva': Gender Construction and *Die Meistersinger*," trans. Nicholas Vazsonyi, in *Wagner's Meistersinger: Performance, History, Representation*, ed. Nicholas Vazsonyi (Rochester: University of Rochester Press, 2003), 215–17. That Wagner was conscious of this parallel is clear from his wishing the Wesendoncks "Viel Glück" for 1862 from "Hans Sachs." Richard Wagner, *Wagner to Mathilde Wesendonck*, trans. William Ashton Ellis (New York: Scribner's, 1905), 291.

21. See, for example, Seymour Chatman, *Coming to Terms: The Rhetoric of Narrative in Fiction and Film* (Ithaca: Cornell University Press, 1990), 90–97; Dorrit Cohn, *The Distinction of Fiction* (Baltimore: Johns Hopkins University Press, 1999), ch. 8 (employs the term *second author* instead of implied author); Gregory Currie, *Narratives and Narrators: A Philosophy of Stories* (Oxford: Oxford University Press, 2010), 70–71; Gérard Genette, *Narrative Discourse Revisited*, trans. Jane E. Lewin (Ithaca: Cornell University Press, 1988), 146–47; David Herman, James Phelan, Peter J. Rabinowitz, Brian Richardson, and Robyn Warhol, "Authors, Narrators, Narration," in *Narrative Theory: Core Concepts and Critical Debates*, ed. David Herman, James Phelan, Peter J. Rabinowitz, Brian Richardson, and Robyn Warhol (Columbus: Ohio State

University Press, 2012), 31–33; Peter J. Rabinowitz, "'The Absence of Her Voice from that Concord': The Value of the Implied Author," *Style* 45, no. 1 (2011): 102–5; Brian Richardson, "Introduction," *Style* 45, no. 1 (2011): 4–7.

22. Wayne C. Booth, *The Rhetoric of Fiction*, 2nd ed. (Chicago: University of Chicago Press, 1983), 70–71.

23. Mann revealed his thoughts on homosexuality in a letter to Carl Maria Weber from July 4, 1920. Thomas Mann, *Letters of Thomas Mann, 1889–1955*, trans. Richard Winston and Clara Winston (New York: Knopf, 1971), 102–6. For a more detailed discussion of *Der Tod in Venedig*, see Cohn, *Distinction of Fiction*, ch. 8.

24. Marie-Laure Ryan, "Meaning, Intent, and the Implied Author," *Style* 45, no. 1 (2011): 42, makes a similar point.

25. Philip Kitcher, *Deaths in Venice: The Cases of Gustav von Aschenbach* (New York: Columbia University Press, 2013), 39, 63.

26. Herman et al., "Authors, Narrators, Narration," 33.

27. A similar point has been made concerning cinema by Berys Gaut, *A Philosophy of Cinematic Art* (Cambridge: Cambridge University Press, 2010), 114–18; Paisley Livingston, "Cinematic Authorship," in *Film Theory and Philosophy*, ed. Richard Allen and Murray Smith (Oxford: Clarendon Press, 1997), 144–46; Ryan, "Meaning, Intent, and the Implied Author," 37–38.

28. Albery makes this very point in Max Loppert, "Tim Albery," *Opera* (November 1993): 1288.

29. In response to this criticism, some literary theorists have suggested the possibility of positing multiple implied authors. Isabell Klaiber, "Multiple Implied Authors: How Many Can a Single Text Have?" *Style* 45, no. 1 (2011): 138–52.

30. See, for example, Edward T. Cone, "The Old Man's Toys: Verdi's Last Operas," in *Music, a View from Delft: Selected Essays*, ed. Robert P. Morgan (Chicago: University of Chicago Press, 1989), 172; Joseph Kerman, *Opera as Drama*, rev. ed. (Berkeley: University of California Press, 1988 [1956]), xiii.

31. Linda Hutcheon and Michael Hutcheon, *Opera: Desire, Disease, Death* (Lincoln: University of Nebraska Press, 1996), xvi, were leaders in this shift.

32. Melina Esse, "Encountering the *improvvisatrice* in Italian Opera," *Journal of the American Musicological Society* 66, no. 3 (2013): 709–70; Jim Lovensheimer, "Texts and Authors," in *Oxford History of the American Musical*, ed. Raymond Knapp, Mitchell Morris, and Stacy Wolf (New York: Oxford University Press, 2011), 25.

33. Musical-theater scholars have given this topic more thought, which is unsurprising given that even a musical's score is typically produced by multiple hands. See, for example, Dominic McHugh, "'I'll Never Know Exactly Who Did What': Broadway Composes as Musical Collaborators," *Journal of the American Musicological Society* 68, no. 3 (2015): 605–52.

34. Gaut, *Philosophy of Cinematic Art*, ch. 3. Others who endorse similar views include Sondra Bacharach and Deborah Tollefsen, "*We Did It*: From Mere Contributors to Coauthors," *Journal of Aesthetics and Art Criticism* 68, no. 1 (2010): 23–32; Sondra Bacharach and Deborah Tollefsen, "We Did It Again: A Reply to Livingston," *Journal of Aesthetics and Art Criticism* 69, no. 2 (2011): 225–30; Darren Hudson Hick, "Authorship, Co-Authorship, and Multiple Authorship," *Journal of Aesthetics and Art Criticism* 72, no. 2 (2014): 147–56; C. Paul Sellors, "Collective Authorship in Film," *Journal of Aesthetics and Art Criticism* 65, no. 3 (2007): 263–71.

35. On the genesis of *The Rape of Lucretia*, refer to Claire Seymour, *The Operas of Benjamin Britten: Expression and Evasion* (Woodbridge: Boydell, 2004), ch. 4.

36. Livingston, "Cinematic Authorship," 136, 143–44; Paisley Livingston, *Art and Intention: A Philosophical Study* (Oxford: Clarendon Press, 2005), ch. 3; Paisley Livingston, *Cinema, Philosophy, Bergman: On Film as Philosophy* (Oxford: Oxford University Press, 2009), ch. 3.

37. Hanna Rochlitz, *Sea-Changes: Melville—Forster—Britten* (Göttingen: Universitätsverlag Göttingen, 2012), sec. III.3; Michelle Fillion, *Difficult Rhythm: Music and the Word in E. M. Forster* (Urbana: University of Illinois Press, 2010), ch. 8.

38. Don J. Neville, "*La clemenza di Tito*: Metastasio, Mazzolà, and Mozart," *Studies in Music from the University of Western Ontario* 1 (1976): 124–48; John A. Rice, "Mazzolà's Revision," in *W. A. Mozart: La clemenza di Tito* (Cambridge: Cambridge University Press, 1991), 31–44; M. Tessing Schneider, "From Metastasio to Mazzolà: Clemency and Pity in *La clemenza di Tito*," in *Mozart's La clemenza di Tito: A Reappraisal*, ed. M. Tessing Schneider and Ruth Tatlow (Stockholm: Stockholm University Press, 2018), 56–96.

39. Philip Brett, "'Fiery Visions' (and Revisions): *Peter Grimes* in Process," in *Benjamin Britten: Peter Grimes*, ed. Philip Brett (Cambridge: Cambridge University Press, 1983), 47–57, 61; Philip Brett, "*Peter Grimes*: The Growth of the Libretto," in *The Making of Peter Grimes*, ed. Paul Banks (Woodbridge: Boydell, 2000), 58–61.

5

CHARACTER-FOCUSED NARRATION

THE SECOND ACT OF *TRISTAN UND ISOLDE* (1865) opens with an argument between Isolde and her maid Brangäne about whether the horns of King Marke's hunting party are still audible, and thus whether Isolde should signal to Tristan that it is safe for him to come to her for their planned assignation. Wagner calls for two groups of horns. The larger one (six players) is located behind the painted backcloth (today, typically performing from the wings) while the other four horns remain in the pit and play with mutes.[1] As Brangäne listens, spectators hear the sounds of the unmuted group in close proximity to the singers, which adds credence to her pronouncement that the horns are still near. Isolde accuses Brangäne of being misled by fear into mistaking the sounds of the wind for those of her husband's hunting party. Indeed, as Isolde listens, string tremolos performed near the bridge imitate the sound of rustling leaves. The horns do appear, but they sound as if from a distance, due to the fact that they are muted and located under the stage. After a single strain of their call, their musical material transfers to the clarinets before dissipating into the nature sounds once more. The unmuted group returns when Brangäne professes to still hear the horns and declares that Isolde's senses have been clouded by desire. But when Isolde listens for one last time, the horns are nowhere to be heard, just as she professes.

Carolyn Abbate concludes her discussion of this exchange by stating that "we hear—with Isolde. The music emanating from the orchestra at this moment seems to be a trace of sound inside her mind, this sound pushed outward, sung to us. She is no longer deaf to the music that *we* can hear, for *she* has imagined it and created it, and in this is momentarily celebrated as the locus of authorial discourse."[2] Yet Wagner does not merely allow us to hear as Isolde does; he also gives us a sense of Brangäne's experiences. In fact, it is only through his juxtaposition of their differing perceptions that the particularity of each is made apparent to the audience. That is not to say that Abbate's focus on Isolde is unjustified, however. What we hear when Brangäne is listening is what anyone in their world with normally functioning hearing would hear if she or he were in Brangäne's position. Isolde's experience is, by contrast, idiosyncratic. In allowing us to hear what she hears, we are able to share in an experience that is particular to her. The passages representing her perceptual experiences are inflected by her subjectivity in ways that the corresponding moments for Brangäne are not.

From the observation that the orchestral music expresses Isolde's point of view, Abbate concludes that she is the author of this music. Much musicological writing about point of view in opera suffers from a similar sort of confusion that Gérard Genette has identified in writing about literature, "a confusion between the question *who is the character whose point of view orients the narrative perspective?* and the very different question *who is the narrator?*"[3]

Henry James was a master at *character-focused narration* or strategies of aligning readers with characters' points of view.[4] Most of James's novels are told by relatively effaced or elusive narrators whose few defining characteristics are closely modeled on their real-life author (hence my use of masculine pronouns). Their relative opacity was strategic, allowing them to better reflect the personalities of James's characters. For instance, *What Maisie Knew* (1897) is largely told according to the point of view of its eponymous protagonist, a six-year-old girl who becomes a pawn in a series of games between her divorced parents and their new romantic liaisons. Not only does the narrator confine his remarks to what Maisie observes but his interpretations are largely limited by the level of understanding she is able to achieve, reflecting, in particular, her lack of knowledge about the intricacies of Victorian-era protocols governing the interactions of unmarried men and women. When Maisie returns to her father's care after spending several months with her mother, she asks him about his relationship with her governess Miss Overmore. Mr. Farange's responses imply that they had continued to cohabitate, sending the governess into a horrified frenzy of denials for reasons Maisie cannot surmise but, one assumes, the narrator can. Nevertheless, he avoids divulging the cause of Miss Overmore's distress until Maisie is provided with an explanation.[5]

The narrator's descriptions also occasionally reflect a childlike sensibility, as when he describes "a lady with eyebrows arched like skipping-ropes."[6] But by and large the prose style is consistent with James's other writings, its intricacy and subtlety ill-suited to representing a child's account. That Maisie is not the narrator is also clear from the numerous occasions when the narrator abandons his focus on her to offer his own commentary on the behavior of the adults around her. Consider the following description of Maisie's mother, Mrs. Farange: "She was a person addicted to extremes—sometimes barely speaking to her child and sometimes pressing this tender shoot to a bosom cut, as Mrs Wix had also observed, remarkably low. She was always in a fearful hurry, and the lower the bosom was cut the more it was to be gathered she was wanted elsewhere."[7] This passage provides readers with the narrator's perspective on not only Mrs. Farange but also Mrs. Wix, another one of Maisie's governesses.

That Maisie's point of view often orients the narrative perspective does not make her the narrator. Similarly, that Wagner's orchestrations reflect Isolde's and Brangäne's differing perceptual experiences does not demonstrate that either is the narrator, much less the author, of the relevant passages.

Another commonplace assumption in opera studies worthy of more thorough interrogation is that music providing subjective access to characters inevitably arouses sympathy or empathy. This assumption motivated many of Wagner's artistic choices, as discussed in the previous chapter, and persists in much opera scholarship today. Alessandra Campana's description of Manon and Des Grieux's initial encounter in Puccini, Domenico Oliva, and Luigi Illica's *Manon Lescaut* (1893) is a case in point: "at the coach's arrival, Des Grieux is standing downstage, almost at the footlights, his back half turned to the audience. He is positioned as close as possible to the spectators and, by looking at the stage from their viewpoint, momentarily assumes their role. When he first raises his eyes and sees Manon, his gesture of amazement intercepts the audience's look, so that Manon is seen through the filter of his amazement and admiration. In other words, the audience is forcefully aligned with his eyes, their looking connoted by his emotions, entangled in the same desire."[8]

Campana is describing the staging of the work prescribed by its *disposizione scenica*, a manual created with the original production to assist future directors in remounting that particular realization. As the following chapter will explore in more depth, such manuals are of predominantly scholarly interest today. Present-day opera directors are unlikely to consult such sources as part of their working processes. Even in a performance that follows these instructions, the sense of sharing Des Grieux's visual perspective is weak in comparison with cinematic point-of-view shots, given that each spectator views the stage from a different perspective. Depending on where one is seated, one might not even perceive any similarity of visual perspective between oneself and Des Grieux. For those who do perceive such a connection, whether it arouses a similar desire for Manon depends on the spectator's personal preferences, which may or may not align with the character's.

This chapter begins by defining point of view and exploring how character-focused narration is accomplished in literary and cinematic works. Turning to operas and musicals, I focus on musical means of orienting audiences to characters' points of view, saving my discussion of visual means for the final two chapters. Through examples from Sondheim and Hugh Wheeler's *Sweeney Todd* (1979) and Britten and William Plomer's *Gloriana* (1953), I explore which facets of point of view (perception, knowledge, thought processes, emotional and psychological states) can be communicated musically and which take precedence in this medium. Turning to the relationship between character-focused narration, sympathy, and empathy, I take a more extended look at Britten and Myfanwy Piper's *Owen Wingrave* (1971). Finally, I discuss the moral consequences of our feelings about opera characters through two works that align spectators with murderers: Sondheim and John Weidman's *Assassins* (1990) and Shostakovich and Alexander Preys's *Lady Macbeth of the Mtsensk District* (1934).

Mechanics of Character-Focused Narration

Literature and Cinema

Genette's disentangling of the role of the narrator from that of the focal character has led to more sophisticated discussions of point of view in literature. However, his suggestions of how to answer his first question—"who is the character whose point of view orients the narrative perspective?"—are problematic, even when applied to literary narratives. Genette initially suggests that this question can be paraphrased as "who sees?"[9] Yet my determination that the narrator's description of Mrs. Farange reflected Mrs. Wix's perspective, not Maisie's, was dependent not on a difference in what these characters saw but in what occupied the focus of their attention and in the inferences they drew from their perceptions.

More promising is Genette's subsequent suggestion that narrating according to someone else's point of view involves limiting oneself to the knowledge the other possesses.[10] Equating point of view with knowledge goes further in explaining why this passage of *What Maisie Knew* reflects Mrs. Wix's perspective. However, the reason why it fails to reflect Maisie's point of view is not only her lack of knowledge of seductive sartorial strategies but also the implied moral censure of Mrs. Farange—her attire, its purpose, and her merely intermittent interest in the well-being of her child—which does not correspond with Maisie's attitude toward her mother at this point in the story.[11]

When applied to opera and musical theater, Genette's two methods of identifying the focal character are of even more limited use. These art forms possess few resources for aligning spectators with characters' visual perspectives. Although music can be used to provide us access to what characters know, a more salient difference between characters in an opera is their emotional responses to events in the story.

In everyday conversations, our use of "point of view" extends beyond the domain of visual perception, even sensory perception in any modality. Commonplace confessions like "I can't understand your point of view" use the phrase to refer to beliefs, values, and desires. Accordingly, I take a more inclusive view about what comprises an agent's point of view, following Gregory Currie's suggestion that "point of view arises from an agent's limitations of access to and capacity to act on the world."[12] Thus, it encompasses not only one's resources and habits of perceiving and knowing but also of thinking, feeling, and doing.

Narrators cannot help but tell their stories from their own point of view, but in addition, they may do so in ways that are expressive of a point of view of a character in the story. This is what Currie calls character-focused narration. In contrast to narrating *from* a point of view—which is non-optional and all or nothing—narrating *according to* a point of view is optional and admits of degrees. James contemplated telling Maisie's story from her point of view but ultimately found the idea of confining himself more completely to a child's perspective too limiting.[13] Narrating the story from the perspective of an adult allowed James to pick and choose what aspects of Maisie's point of view to represent and to abandon his focus on her if it did not serve his purposes.[14]

If *point of view* refers to a person's characteristic ways of responding to and engaging with the world then narrating according to that point of view involves telling the story in ways that are imitative or expressive of those characteristic modes of response. Currie's insistence that character-focused narration must involve subjective access to the focal character is a salient divergence from Genette's more familiar account of *focalization*. Genette's concept of focalization includes what he calls "externally focalized narratives," such as Hemingway's short story "The Killers" (1927), in which readers follow a character's trajectory through the narrative but do not have access to the character's unexpressed feelings and thoughts.[15]

How an author provides the audience with such access depends on their chosen medium. Since Currie's account of character-focused narration is directed at literary works, he focuses on the phenomenon of *free indirect discourse*, a technique by which the narrator imitates a character's speech or thought patterns but without providing direct quotations. As the philosopher Kathleen Stock observes, free indirect discourse not only provides readers with access to a character's thoughts but also gives them a sense of what it would be like to have that point of view, and thus invites "the reader to imagine the perspective of a character from the inside."[16]

One might assume that the point-of-view shot would be the primary means of achieving similar effects in film. Although some point-of-view shots do offer spectators access to the peculiarities of characters' perceptual experiences—a canted, out-of-focus shot representing drunkenness, for example—the majority of point-of-view shots represent what anyone would see if they were in the character's position.[17] Murray Smith has argued that reaction shots, particularly close-ups, are a more powerful device for orienting cinematic viewers to characters' points of view because they inform us about how the character is responding to what he or she is seeing, knowledge typical point-of-view shots fail to provide. Furthermore, through affective mimicry (the tendency for sad faces to make one feel sad), close-ups are apt to trigger empathic responses.[18]

The point-of-view shot is hardly the only type of shot that can be subjectively inflected, a point amply demonstrated by David Fincher's *Fight Club* (1999). The unnamed protagonist (played by Edward Norton) finds a cure for his chronic insomnia when he meets the charismatic soap salesman Tyler Durden (Brad Pitt), who orders him to hit him as hard as he can. Their impromptu fights in parking lots lead to the establishment of a series of Fight Clubs where young men beat their frustrations out on one another. Under Tyler's leadership, these clubs evolve into Project Mayhem, a militant organization that aims to bring down the American economy. When Norton's character attempts to put a stop to Tyler's activities, Fincher reveals that he and Tyler are one and the same person. Modeling how spectators ought to reinterpret Brad Pitt's appearances throughout the film, Fincher provides objective perspectives of scenes shown earlier in the film. Now we see Norton's character punching himself in the parking lot, and the protagonist outlining the rules of Fight Club instead of Tyler. Fincher aligns spectators with Norton's character by allowing us to share in his hallucinations of Tyler Durden and by obscuring the subjective inflection of these sequences until he discovers the truth about his identity. As George Wilson notes, Tyler's appearances are not confined to point-of-view shots from Norton's character's perspective.[19] In fact, most shots of Tyler also include the protagonist.

The visual qualities of shots can also provide access to characters' emotional and psychological states. Wilson has shown how features of the mise-en-scène and choice of camera angles and lenses express the teenagers' feelings of claustrophobia and imprisonment in Nicholas Ray's *Rebel without a Cause* (1955).[20] In *A Single Man* (2009), Tom Ford uses color to express both George's depression after the death of his lover and also what ultimately motivates him to abandon his plan to commit suicide. The generally desaturated color palette, dominated by grays and browns, "blooms" at moments when George is able to recognize beauty in the world—watching two young men playing tennis, for example—or to connect with another human being, such as the student who approaches him after class and the Spanish man he runs into while buying liquor.[21] These moments of subjective inflection are, again, not confined to point-of-view shots. In fact, their effect might be lessened if they were. Since we are able to look simultaneously *at* and *with* the character, we are able to see not only what the character is reacting to but also how it makes him or her feel.

Music is, of course, another powerful tool for expressing characters' points of view in films. It takes on an even more central role in opera and musical theater, given that most attendees of performances in conventional venues are seated too far away from the stage to discern much about the singers' facial expressions.

Opera and Musical Theater

Since each spectator views the stage from a distinct visual perspective and has the freedom to focus on any aspect of the performance, creating the sorts of alignments of visual perspective discussed in connection with cinema is difficult. Although live theater offers few resources with which to allow spectators to share a character's field of vision, the composer can musically express aspects of a character's gaze. For example, Philip Rupprecht has argued that Britten's exotic, gamelan-inspired music for Tadzio in *Death in Venice* (1973) expresses Aschenbach's erotic interest in the boy.[22] In so doing, Britten allows us to *hear* how Aschenbach *sees* Tadzio.

Opera and musical theater are better poised to allow spectators to share in characters' aural perceptions, as the opening example from *Tristan* illustrated. In the interest of gaining a better understanding of the differences between musical means of character-focused narration as compared with visual ones, it is worth noting the exceptional nature of this example. Wagner's ability to differentiate Isolde's and Brangäne's perceptions is dependent on the peculiar nature of Isolde's experiences. A more typical example is the penultimate scene from *Les Huguenots* (1836). In placing the chorus of Huguenot martyrs singing "Ein feste Burg" backstage, Meyerbeer aligns spectators with the characters onstage—Valentine, Raoul, and Marcel—who hear the singing from outside the church in which it is taking place. However, it is impossible to be more specific about whose aural perspective is being expressed in this example. Rather, Meyerbeer's music seems to express the aural perceptions of all three characters onstage. By contrast, visual point-of-view shots typically represent a single character's perspective. Due to human beings' vastly superior abilities at distinguishing between visual perspectives, as compared with aural ones, we tend to aim for greater precision in our representation of visual perspectives and how we talk about them.[23] With aural perception, it typically takes some kind of abnormality to set apart one character from others onstage.

A more reliable way of isolating a particular character in an opera and aligning spectators with his or her point of view is by using the music to provide access to the character's thoughts and emotions. The process of adapting a novel or a play into a musical drama is often described in terms of what is lost: typically, about half of a play's text, and much more in the case of a novel. Yet focusing solely on the reduction of words neglects what music can add in the hands of a composer like Sondheim or Britten.

Sondheim observed that the transition from Sweeney Todd "wanting to kill one man to wanting to kill all men" was a weak point in the play by Christopher Bond that inspired his musical *Sweeney Todd*.[24] Here is the relevant stretch of dialogue from Bond's *Sweeney Todd* (1973):

> TODD: A second chance may come. It must, it shall! Until it does, I'll pass the time in practice on less honoured throats.
>
> MRS LOVETT: I don't understand you. You let that Judge escape one minute, and the next you're on about slicing up any Tom, Dick or Harry. This revenge business don't half blow hot and cold, it don't.
>
> TODD: Revenge? Oh, no! The work's its own reward. For now I find I have a taste for blood, and all the world's my meat.[25]

Whereas Bond's barber simply announces the universality of his bloodlust, the equivalent moment in Sondheim's musical, Todd's "Epiphany," offers spectators a glimpse into the mind of a mass murderer in the making through radical shifts in poetic and musical style. In one of Sondheim's many recorded discussions of this number, he remarks on the alternation between "fixed, rhythmic, rhymed sections to represent Todd's organized determination to be a Sword of Justice ['There's a hole in the world . . .'], and free-flowing unrhymed passages to mirror his disorganized grief ['I'll never see Johanna . . .'], in the middle of which he could break the fourth wall and make

Example 5.1. Todd's murderous thoughts, "Epiphany" from *Sweeney Todd*

direct contact with the world outside the stage ['All right! You, sir . . .'], a truly mad gesture."[26]

The number's musical style is equally diverse and discontinuous. Sondheim expresses Todd's initial frustration at Anthony's unwitting interruption of his plan to murder the Judge through the ostinato associated with Todd's thoughts of revenge, derived from the *Dies irae* (mm. 1–2 of ex. 5.1). Mrs. Lovett attempts to calm him with a reprise of her earlier song "Wait." However, the accompaniment does not go along with her attempt at de-escalation but remains aligned with Todd's psychological states, turning even more murderous with stabbing tone clusters evocative of the shower scene from Hitchcock's *Psycho* (1960) (mm. 3–4 of ex. 5.1).[27] The strings return to the revenge ostinato—now performed double-time and marked *feroce* and double *forte*—for Todd's rant: "There's a hole in the world like a great black pit and it's filled with people who are filled with shit. . . ." At his proclamation "they all deserve to die!" the tempo suddenly decreases from Agitato to Meno mosso. The strings and brass pound out another series of dissonant tone clusters,

Meno mosso (♩ = 120)

Example 5.2. *Dies irae* in the inner voices

the inner voices of which beat out the *Dies irae* to an effect reminiscent of "The Dance of the Adolescents" from Stravinsky's *Le sacre du printemps* (1913) (ex. 5.2).

When Todd's mind turns to his wife and child, believed to be dead, the music suddenly shifts in meter, affect, and style (4/4 to 3/2 with expressive marking of *cantabile* and "keening"; mm. 1–4 of ex. 5.3). Todd's threnody lasts for only four measures before his thoughts turn back to vengeance (mm. 5–10 of ex. 5.3). While slashing his razor, he turns toward the real-life audience, inviting them to "visit [their] good friend Sweeney!" Todd's thoughts become even more scattered as he flits back and forth between the threnody theme—now sung to thoughts of mass murder, Lucy and Johanna temporarily forgotten (mm. 11–13 of ex. 5.3)—and entreaties to the audience to try out his chair. Finally, Todd reprises the threnody theme in its original association with his family, but as the music builds to a climax, his mind turns back to his "work," which leaves him feeling "alive" and "full of joy."[28]

The sceptic of music's ability to contribute much by way of psychological depth to characters of sung drama might admit that Sondheim's representation of Todd's psychotic break is more convincing than Bond's but contend that it is Sondheim's lyrics that account for this difference; his music merely mirrors or, at best, amplifies the insights conveyed by the text without adding any new content of its own.[29] In response to such a concern, I draw attention to the progress of the threnody theme throughout the number. Its initial association with Todd's daughter, Johanna, followed by vengeance and mass murder, illustrates the slippage in Todd's mind from grief for the loss of his family to a desire for vengeance against the man presumed responsible for that loss to a desire to kill all men. It is only through the interaction between

Example 5.3. Threnody from Johanna to vengeance

Sondheim's music and lyrics that this slippage is articulated. Neither the text nor the music alone provides this insight into Todd's psyche.

Another example of music providing insights into characters' emotional and psychological states, insights not conveyed through the libretto alone, is the reprise of the love theme in the epilogue of Britten and Plomer's *Gloriana*. Britten first introduced this theme during the tête-a-tête between Queen Elizabeth I and the Earl of Essex in Act I, Scene 2. The Queen bids her lord to take up the lute and transport her away from the "cares of state." Hoping to lift her spirits, Essex begins with a cheery tune. While he plays, the pedal tones, foreign to the key of his singing, and the repeated intrusions of the motive previously associated with the Queen's "cares," reveal that his song is not having the intended effect. Eventually, she cuts him off. "Too light, too gay: a song for careless hearts," she explains and urges him to "turn to the lute again, evoke some far-off place or time, a dream, a mood, an air to spirit us both away."[30]

Essex satisfies her desire with his second attempt, a melancholy song about a hermit living out his days with only "hips and haws and brambleberry" as company (ex. 5.4).[31] The text of the second lute song was written by the historical earl himself.[32] And if the music suddenly sounds more evocative of Tudor times, that is because it too is based on music of the period. Britten borrowed the melodic incipit from a madrigal by John Wilbye, "Happy, Oh Happy He," though, as Heather Wiebe notes, his treatment of it owes more to Henry Purcell's songwriting.[33] To ensure that performers and scholars would notice and appreciate his gesture of homage, Britten even included quotation marks in the score of the *tutti* first violin part, which, unlike the vocal line, is an exact quotation.

Strains of the second lute song are heard at pivotal moments in the Queen and Essex's relationship, such as their quarrel about Essex's failure to subdue the threat of the Irish rebels, and the Queen's signing of his death warrant in the epilogue. Essex's sister, Penelope Rich, expresses her horror and despair through a glissando of truly operatic proportions. The Queen, by contrast, can afford no outward manifestation of her grief. Nevertheless, Britten gives voice to it through the orchestra's reprise of Essex's song.

Britten planned this effect early on in the opera's genesis. In a letter to his librettist, he described his vision of the final scene as follows: "Signing of warrant. Take lights down except for a spot on Elizabeth. Then, so as to suggest her mind is on Essex, play an orchestral version of the 'Brambleberry' song, while people come & hand her documents to sign, consult her on matters—to which she replies automatically or not at all."[34] Britten's perfunctory description does not do justice to the expressive effect he achieved

Example 5.4. Second lute song from *Gloriana*, first two phrases

through the song's transformation (cf. exx. 5.4 and 5.5). No longer an intimate bardic tune, improvisatory in character, Britten has forced it into a bombastic march. The delicate flourishes of the original song—now performed exactly in time, *marcato*, and triple *forte* by a full complement of brass and winds— have become garish, even grotesque. The first phrase is virtually identical to its original appearance in terms of melody, harmony, and even key. Nevertheless, Britten achieves a complete transformation of affect from wistful rapture to anguished recollection through manipulations of orchestration, dynamics, articulation, and performance style.

Example 5.5. Reprise of the first phrase of the lute song

Example 5.5. *(Continued)*

Example 5.6. Reprise of the second phrase of the lute song

The remainder of the epilogue is a variation on Essex's song with spoken recitations acting as punctuation between the song's phrases. Since each phrase is treated in turn and only once, it is less a theme and variations than a modern resuscitation of Renaissance paraphrase technique. The imitative treatment to which some of the phrases are subjected also recommends such a comparison. In the section following the Queen's first spoken reflection, Britten uses the first four notes of the song's second poetic line as a point of imitation, reaching a climax with the Queen's entrance at the pitch level of the original song (ex. 5.6). Entries occur at irregular time and pitch intervals and create dissonance both against one another and against the walking bass line (e.g., the second entry [clarinets, bass clarinet, bassoons] generates a tritone with the first entry [flutes, oboes, English horn], and the third entry [trumpet] is a major second away from the bass [basses, contrabassoon, tuba]).

The song's reprise indicates that the Queen's thoughts turn to Essex, a fact that is already implied by the dramatic context, one could argue. However, Britten's deformations of the couple's song communicate something the libretto does not about the tortured nature of those thoughts and the grief she is unable to express before her courtiers. More than that, Britten's music allows spectators to experience those feelings in ways the libretto cannot.

The brutal military-march topic is less easily understood as an expression of the Queen's point of view and is better regarded as external commentary from the orchestral narrator or Britten himself on the steely will that led her to place the needs of her country over her personal desires. As seen in connection with *What Maisie Knew*, the question of whose point of view is being expressed at any given time can be a complex matter. Strategies of character-focused narration, both through words and through music, can combine with moments of narrational or authorial commentary.

Alignment and Allegiance

In shifting from the question of how character-focused narration works in sung drama to the consequences of such narrational strategies, it will be useful to explore a more extended example. I have chosen Britten and Piper's *Owen Wingrave*, an opera written for and premiered on television in 1971, but which also has a place in the repertory for the stage. Its source is a short story by Henry James, published in 1891 under the same title. Owen Wingrave is the last in a long line of military men. Despite his family history, Owen decides to abandon his studies at Mr. Coyle's military academy because of his pacifist convictions. Owen's aunt Miss Wingrave orders him to report to Paramore, the family estate, where she has assembled an army of his family and friends who attempt to shame him into submission. After their efforts prove ineffective, Owen is disowned. His fiancée, Kate, dares him to spend a night in a room thought to be haunted by two of Owen's ancestors, a boy who was struck by his father after backing down from a fight and the boy's father, whose body was found the following morning without a wound. Owen agrees to be locked in the haunted room and is found dead hours later under similarly mysterious circumstances.

James's story is told by one of his effaced or elusive narrators. From the foregoing summary, one might assume that the focal character would be the protagonist, Owen, but James chose his teacher, Mr. Coyle. However, similarly to *What Maisie Knew*, James also provides glimpses into the thoughts of the other characters as well as commentary on Coyle that exceeds his level of self-understanding.

When Britten was asked about his reasons for picking one of James's more obscure stories as the subject for his latest opera, he responded that "this bombshell which arrived in the middle of this family and the circle in which Owen Wingrave moved would give a marvelous opportunity to show each person's individual reactions to the bombshell."[35] Like James, Britten and Piper did not pay their characters equal attention. While James's focus was on Coyle's struggle to come to grips with the fact that his pupil is a pacifist, Britten and Piper decided to focus on Owen's attempt to break free from the yoke of family tradition and pursue his own path.

Piper's libretto dramatizes several parts of the story that were elided in James's telling. Due to James's choice of Coyle as his focal character, he does not describe Owen's arrival at Paramore or the browbeating he underwent at the hands of his family before the Coyles' arrival. Readers hear about the effects of their bullying only indirectly, from the narrator's descriptions of the Coyles' reactions, such as Mrs. Coyle's shock "that they should find their young charge looking five years older."[36] Spectators of the opera witness snatches of these conversations in the "How dare you!" ensemble of Act I, Scene 5. That this scene telescopes a week's worth of "attacks" was made clear in the original television production through multiple changes of setting.

Piper also provides Owen with more opportunities than any of the other characters to express his thoughts, beliefs, and desires. The most memorable of these moments is Owen's paean to peace in Act II. Notably, this aria has no basis in James's story and was included on Britten's suggestion. Piper explained that it gave him "a vehicle, an opportunity, for a great impassioned musical statement about his own views, as well as those of Owen himself."[37]

Piper's focus on Owen was intensified through Britten's setting of her words. Before delving into the first scene, however, it will be useful to spend

Example 5.7. Opening chords and reveille of *Owen Wingrave*

some time with the opera's prelude, which is the source of most of the score's musical motives. The work opens with three violently clangorous chords—two dominant sevenths and a dominant ninth—scored for timpani, side and tenor drums, xylophone, glockenspiel, harp, piano, and double basses (ex. 5.7, mm. 1–3). Together they form an aggregate of all twelve pitch classes. The voicing of the dominant sevenths, with diminished triads at the bottom, draws attention to a sonority that will play a prominent role in the rest of the score. A *reveille* ensues (ex 5.7, mm. 4–8), which features the expected complement of brass, but instead of the major triads of bugle calls, they outline diminished triads.

At the repetition of the martial chords, Britten's score specifies that spectators are to see the gallery at Paramore with a "series of military portraits" hanging on the walls. It appears to have been Piper's idea to represent the weight of tradition through a sequence of family portraits, with Owen appearing "like an eleventh portrait."[38] As each portrait is isolated in turn, we hear a cadenza for wind and/or brass instruments. The strings provide harmonic accompaniment in the form of a tremolo chord, to which one note is added as each personage is introduced. The D that is heard when Owen appears completes another aggregate of all twelve pitch classes (the fifth portrait is a double portrait of the father and son who are believed to haunt Paramore).

Owen's theme, played by the horn (ex. 5.8), is similar in melodic contour and rhythm to the reveille but otherwise could not be more contrasting to the

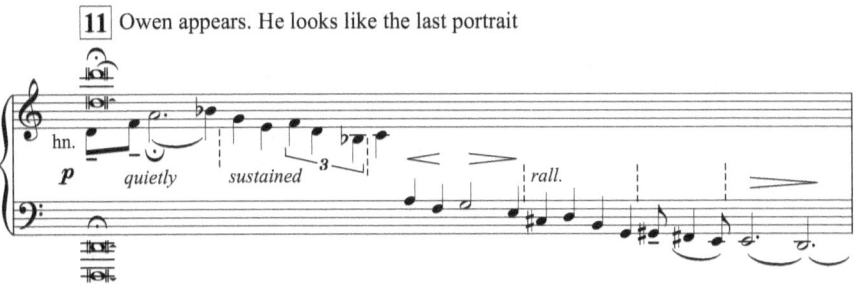

Example 5.8. Owen's theme

music that has come before.³⁹ It outlines major and minor triads, not diminished ones. For the first time in the work, a tonal center may be discerned. The theme remains entirely in D minor until the whole-tone descent at the end. Furthermore, the pedal A underscoring the preceding percussive chords provides something like a dominant preparation for the theme. After hearing Owen's father's motive (ex. 5.9), which contains a complete tone row and is scored in the manner of *Klangfarbenmelodie*, this emergence of tonality is unexpected, to say the least.⁴⁰ The rest of the score follows Owen's example more closely than that of his father. Britten evokes serial procedures in conjunction with Owen's family (the "How dare you!" ensemble is one of the more systemically serial passages), but most instances of tone rows occur in tonal contexts.

The association between the opening percussive chords and the Wingraves' tradition of military service is confirmed in the chords' subsequent appearances in the opera. Most suggestively, they provide recitative-like punctuations during Owen's litany of deaths resulting from military service in Act I, Scene 3 (beginning at reh. 94). Diminished triads and quasi-serial procedures come to represent the military more generally. For instance, when Coyle recognizes the irony that Owen is a fighter, the horn plays a distorted version of Owen's theme in diminished triads, after which Owen exclaims, "Ugh! We're tainted all!" (ex. 5.10).

With some background in the main themes and musical dichotomies of the score, I will now turn to the first scene of the opera proper, which takes place at Mr. Coyle's academy. Given James's focus on Coyle, his story begins with Coyle's reactions to Owen's decision to abandon his studies. To focus the opera on Owen's experience, Britten requested that Piper first establish the environment and ideals Owen will be fighting against before he reveals his plans to his teacher.⁴¹

The first scene begins in the middle of a lecture on the Battle of Austerlitz (Napoleonic Wars, 1805). Coyle's vocal line and the horn pedal seem to take a

Example 5.9. Owen's father's theme

Example 5.10. The horn plays Owen's theme in diminished triads

cue from the key signature of two sharps, but the ability for either D major or B minor to be unambiguously asserted is thwarted by persistent diminished triads in the strings (ex. 5.11). When Coyle details the casualties, the horn's sustained descending line is in the shape of Owen's theme from the prelude. Although Coyle is singing at the beginning of this scene, I suggest that Britten's music orients spectators to Owen's point of view. Specifically, the oppressive monotony of the diminished triads and their unpredictable pattern of repetition express his feelings of suffocating tedium and growing dismay at his teacher's seeming indifference to the lives lost in war.

We know that these feelings belong to Owen and are not shared by his friend Lechmere because of the students' contrasting reactions to Coyle's lecture. The energetic fourths and dotted rhythms of Lechmere's questions give us a taste of the sort of accompaniment Britten might have composed if he had wanted to predominantly express Lechmere's perspective on the lecture. Owen is slower to offer his reactions verbally, but spectators may be cued to them even before he speaks through the performer's gestures and facial expressions, features that are much more apparent when watching the work on television. Furthermore, at the beginning of Scene 1, Britten writes in his score, "First Owen is seen alone, then Coyle and Lechmere."[42] The original television production, which followed these directions, encourages spectators to focus on Owen's reactions. Although Benjamin Luxon's face is not particularly expressive in the first part of this scene, the camera focuses on him when the descending horn line plays and he stops taking notes. Coyle's suggestion that thousands of casualties amount to a "victory" is clearly giving Owen pause.

The following scene, intended to represent Owen and Miss Wingrave's contrasting reactions to an exercise of the horse guards in Hyde Park, provided

SCENE 1

The study at Mr Coyle's military establishment. First Owen is seen alone, then Coyle and Lechmere.

Example 5.11. Owen's reactions to Coyle's lecture

Britten with another opportunity to juxtapose two very different attitudes toward the military and align spectators with Owen's pacifist stance. Miss Wingrave, who watches the proceedings with Mr. Coyle from her Baker Street lodgings, expresses the glory she finds in the sight and the pride she feels. For Owen, seated on a bench in the park, the same maneuvers conjure an imaginary "scene of military carnage."[43]

Britten represents the physical separation of the characters musically by having each part proceed independently in terms of meter and tonality. Owen begins in a leisurely $\frac{6}{8}$ meter, gesturing to a pastoral topic, appropriate to his location in the park. The horse guards' music is also in a compound meter but proceeds at two or three times the speed of Owen's part. While Miss Wingrave obstinately sticks to cut time, the rhythmic freedom of Coyle's more measured replies expresses his more open-minded views.

Tonally, Owen's part begins in G minor, but Miss Wingrave and Coyle's conversation as well as the woodwind trills (but not the rocking accompaniment that persists from earlier in the scene) are notated in the parallel major. The brass fanfares associated with the horse guards constitute an independent atonal layer. When Owen imagines the scene degenerating into a "vision of battle, blood and death," the grotesque cries in the brass represent Owen's aural imaginings, providing spectators with a sample of his subjective experiences (ex. 5.12).[44]

Britten fails to marshal similar expressive effects on Miss Wingrave's behalf. We learn of her positive attitude toward the military from her words, and Britten's use of cut time expresses her orderly, if constricted, worldview.[45] In comparison with Owen, however, the music offers little sense of what it would be like to have that point of view.

James periodically uses free indirect discourse to provide readers glimpses into the thoughts and minds of Owen's family and Lechmere. These are less frequent and less sustained than the access he provides to Coyle or Owen, but they do give readers a sense of the perspectives of Owen's opponents. Britten and Piper offer their audiences few opportunities to experience the world from the side of the opposition. One exception is Owen's conversation with his grandfather, Sir Philip, which takes place behind closed doors in the fictional world (backstage in real life) while the rest of the characters (onstage) attempt to listen in. As in the horse-guards' scene, Britten represents the spatial separation between the two groups musically through independent metrical and tonal relations between the parts (ex. 5.13).

Britten aligns his real-life spectators with the fictional eavesdroppers by saddling both parties with imperfect access to the conversation. We can hear enough of Sir Philip's utterances to discern that he is invoking the weight of family tradition by singing a fantasia on the portrait themes.[46] Predictably, the fifth portrait (representing the boy who refused to fight and the father who killed him for it) makes the most prominent appearance, beginning with Sir Philip's "God save us all." The singer performing the role of Owen does not sing at all during this exchange. Owen's prior association with the horn and the way that the horn part seems to respond to Sir Philip's remarks in recitative-like repetitions of a single note suggest that it represents Owen's "voice" during this

Example 5.12. Owen's aural imaginings in Hyde Park

Example 5.12. *(Continued)*

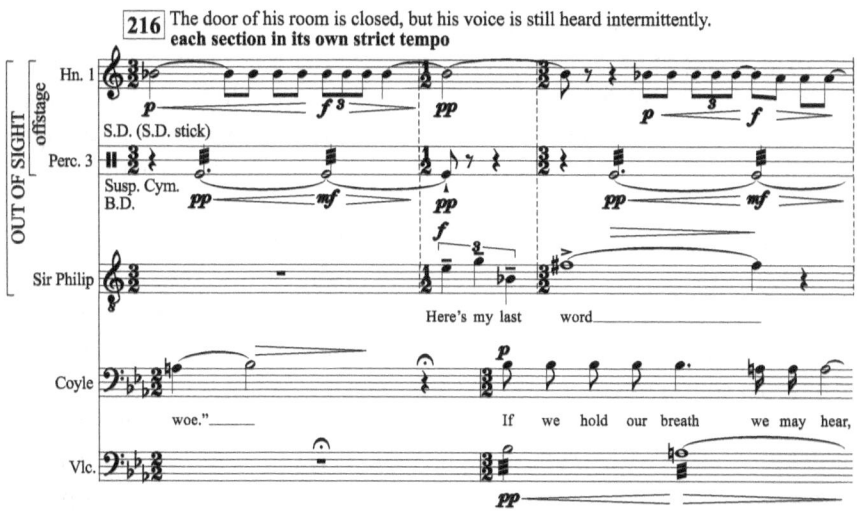

Example 5.13. Owen's family attempts to eavesdrop on Owen's conversation with Sir Philip. The horn supplies Owen's responses.

exchange. In assigning Owen's part to an instrument, Britten denies spectators access to the semantic content of his explanations. As a consequence, both spectators and eavesdroppers are barred access to keenly sought knowledge concerning what is prompting the older man's decision to disinherit his only heir. Britten's novel scoring aligns spectators with the eavesdroppers in terms of perception and knowledge. If Britten had also provided access to their affective states, they may have appeared more human and sympathetic.

Even when Piper gives the Paramore characters a chance to express their points of view, Britten's music often undercuts, even repudiates what they are saying. Two of the more systematic victims of Britten's caricature or parody techniques are Mrs. Julian (the mother of Owen's fiancée, Kate) and Lechmere.[47] Mrs. Julian's first appearance in Act I, Scene 4 is plagued by an absurd amount of textual repetition and a stuttering vocal line (note the punctuating rests and repeated hairpins in ex. 5.14). The jittery pizzicato accompaniment is a canon by inversion based on the opening chords.[48] Britten ensures a frantic, disjointed delivery by dividing the string parts such that the desks trade back and forth irregularly shaped shards of musical material.

Owen's foil, the enthusiastic young recruit Lechmere, is undoubtedly the most ridiculous character of the lot. At the end of Coyle's lecture, Lechmere bursts into strains of Thomas Moore's patriotic song "The Minstrel Boy" (ex. 5.15).[49] Owen joins him in canon, ironically observing how well war has worked out for the Wingraves, but Lechmere is too dense to pick up on the irony. Britten undercuts Lechmere's ruminations on the glory of a soldier's life by refusing to provide a suitable evocation of a military musical topic. Instead of the expected trumpets and drums, only a feeble band of winds supports Lechmere's assertions. Britten's decision not to provide more appropriate underscoring is especially striking given the imposing musical illustration of military might he presented in the prelude.

There is also something wrong with Lechmere's singing of "The Minstrel Boy." Britten distorted the song's traditional melody, the Irish air "The Moreen," by replacing the major chords it outlines with diminished ones (ex. 5.16). Lechmere's singing of "The Minstrel Boy" violates one of the norms of operatic communication discussed in chapter 2. When watching an opera, one typically proceeds from the assumption that the characters are responsible for the content of their utterances in both their verbal and musical components. In other words, we regard their vocalizations as expressing their points of view or, in the case of Owen's ironic responses, as intentional imitations of others' points of view. Lechmere's utterance cannot be understood in this fashion. It mocks Moore's song, but it is not reasonable to understand that to be Lechmere's intention. Everything we know about the character suggests

Example 5.14. Introduction of Mrs. Julian

Example 5.14. (Continued)

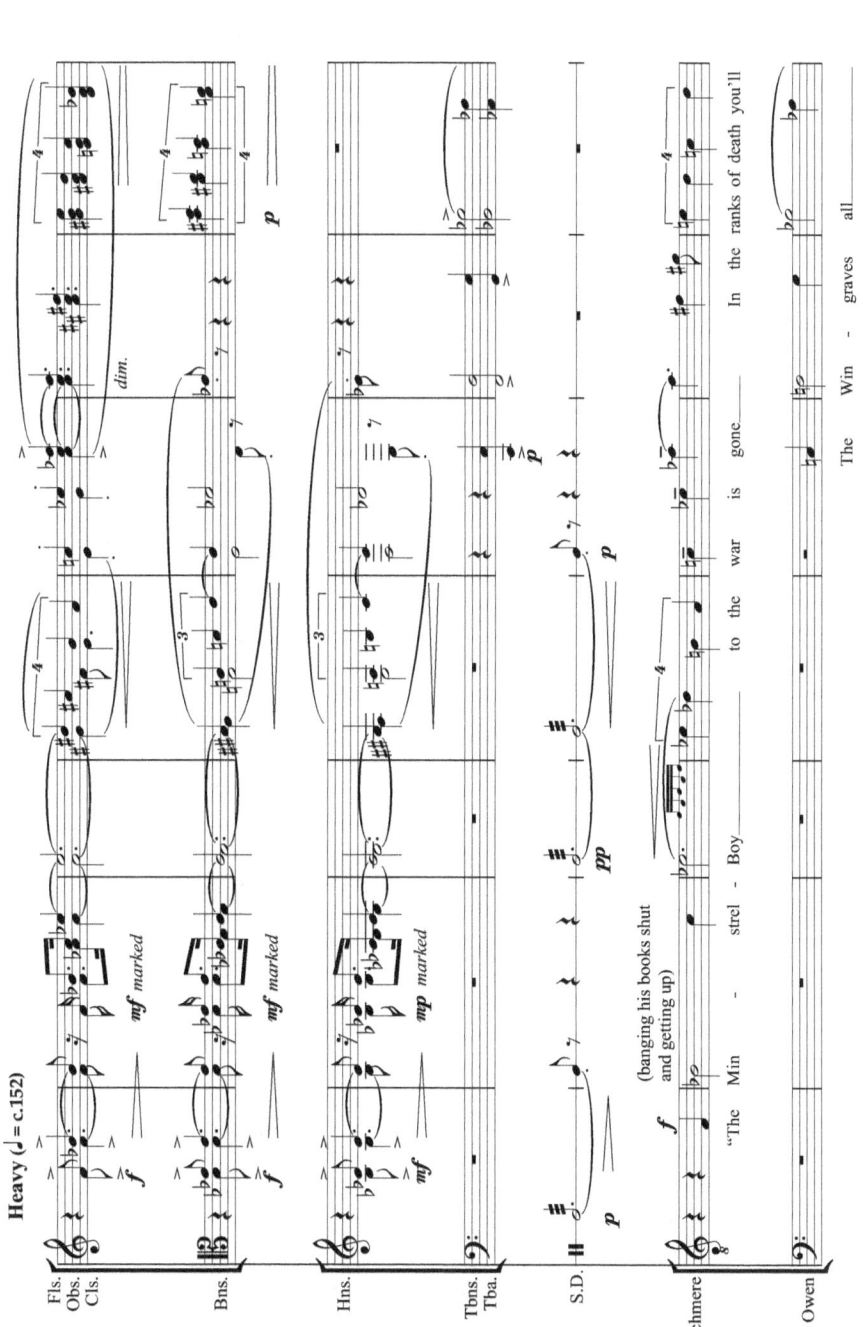

Example 5.15. "The Minstrel Boy" quotations

Example 5.15. (Continued)

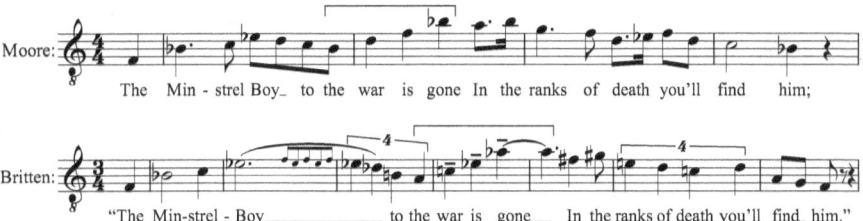

Example 5.16. Britten's distortion of Moore's song with diminished triads

that he would endorse the sentiments expressed in the song and would not wish to make a mockery of it. Thus, the point of view on war Lechmere expresses here is not his own.

Taking the perspective of someone in the fictional world—what Currie calls an *internal* perspective—there is no answer to the question of why Lechmere's utterance is a parody of Moore.[50] If spectators are interested in pursuing an answer to this question, they are forced to take an *external* perspective on the narrative, viewing it as the work of the real-life individuals Benjamin Britten and Myfanwy Piper. From this perspective, one could argue that Britten intended to mock "The Minstrel Boy" by distorting his musical setting of Moore's words in the ways he did. Given the congruence of Britten's attitudes on war with those of his protagonist, the distortions also reflect Owen's point of view on Lechmere's bellicosity.

By now I hope to have shown some of the ways in which Piper's libretto and Britten's music orient spectators to Owen's point of view and undermine the abilities of his opponents to express theirs. Now I wish to turn to the significance of such features. Another commonplace assumption in opera studies is that character-focused narration inevitably leads spectators to identify with the focal character. Recall Campana's assertion that "the audience is forcefully aligned with [Des Grieux's] eyes, their looking connoted by his emotions, entangled in the same desire."[51] A more nuanced argument to this effect is J. P. E. Harper-Scott's discussion of the consequences of Britten's strategies of aligning spectators with Aschenbach's perspective in *Death in Venice*: "If the opera works effectively on us, we begin to lose any sense of a distinction between Aschenbach and ourselves; his fascination with the boy and his loss of control become ours."[52] Harper-Scott's opening caveat "if the opera works effectively on us" is key, as it acknowledges the possibility that spectators will resist Britten's invitation to empathize with Aschenbach.[53] From my observations of audience reactions to a performance by the Canadian Opera Company in Toronto in 2010, nervous laughter, disgust, and even anger are also common responses.

Knowing about a character's point of view is necessary for sympathy and some forms of empathy, but it is clearly not sufficient to arouse such responses. Just as the characters of *Owen Wingrave* have diverse reactions to Owen's pacifist beliefs—some sympathetic (the Coyles, eventually), some dismissive (Sir Philip and Miss Wingrave), others uncomprehending (Lechmere)—real-life spectators are apt to have equally diverse reactions based on their own experiences, values, and beliefs. Yet narrative makers often attempt to guide their audiences toward a preferred set of "cognitive, evaluative, and emotional responses to the story."[54] Currie terms this set of intended responses a work's *framework* while Smith uses the term *allegiance* to refer to the process by which spectators evaluate and respond emotionally to fictional characters.[55]

Sympathizing with Owen and taking a critical view of his family is part of the framework of *Owen Wingrave*, I argue. Britten and Piper's greater attention to Owen's point of view already marks it as more important than those of the other characters, and the caricature techniques previously discussed serve to further devalue the points of view of the Paramore set. Britten's musical stylistic choices provide additional suggestions of how spectators ought to evaluate the relative merits of the two sides to this conflict. Britten's decision to represent the side of tradition with atonality while associating the progressive outsider Owen and, to a lesser extent, the Coyles with tonality is a striking inversion of expectations for modernist opera.[56] In determining what values are being put forth with Britten's compositional choices, it is insufficient merely to rely on general musical conventions. Schoenberg's *Moses und Aron* (abandoned, unfinished, in 1932) contains a similar opposition but to different ends. Moses speaks the word of God in twelve-tone Sprechstimme whereas Aron uses his Heldentenor voice to pander to the masses. It is only by considering the real Benjamin Britten's intentions that his compositional decisions have any meaning.

Britten was working on *Owen Wingrave* in the late 1960s, a time when he felt that his continued commitment to tonality was seen as backward-looking. Serialism, thus, carries a different evaluative valence in *Owen Wingrave*, as compared with *Moses und Aron*, and indeed as compared with other Britten operas.[57] Britten's association of Schoenberg's compositional methods with individuals who lack the capacity for independent thought and who make decisions by means of arbitrary rules not only announces where his sympathies lie with his fictional characters but also makes a pointed statement about contemporary trends in composition.[58]

Owen's grand pacifist statement in Act II is also set apart from the rest of the opera timbrally and texturally by its evocation of Balinese gamelan music (ex. 5.17). Much has been written about the significance of Britten's gamelan

Example 5.17. Britten's gamelan topic in Owen's peace aria

topic. In light of its association with homoeroticism in *The Turn of the Screw* (1954) and *Death in Venice*, Philip Brett and Stephen McClatchie have interpreted its use in *Owen Wingrave* as evidence that Owen is not an outsider merely because of his pacifist convictions but also because of his homosexuality, much like Britten himself.[59] Mervyn Cooke has interpreted it as representing the allure of peace but also its unattainability.[60] Notably, the gamelan layer is saturated with diminished triads and is accompanied by a series of major and minor triads whose roots form a tone row.[61] Musically, Owen is not quite as different from his ancestors as his words assert. Under both interpretations, the gamelan-like quality of the aria's accompaniment marks it as special, as worthy of attention, and as carrying a positive evaluative force, even if that force is not strong enough to break free from family tradition.

Now I wish to consider whether Britten and Piper's strategies of creating alignment and allegiance with Owen amount to merits or demerits of the work. In so doing, it will be useful to return to James's short story and reflect on the effect of his choice of Mr. Coyle as his focal character. Although Coyle is by no means a disinterested party, the fact that he is not part of Owen's family allows him to view the conflict at a remove. This distance, in addition to Coyle's open-mindedness, allows his point of view on Owen's pacifist beliefs to change. In fact, James's story is less about Owen's struggle against his family than about Coyle's journey from his initial state of incomprehension and outright rejection of Owen's point of view to his eventual respect for it, despite it being contradictory to his own. Seeing the Wingrave family from Owen's perspective may have rendered them too unsympathetic. The Paramore set is already thoroughly unappealing in James's hands, and Britten's music serves to further alienate his audiences from them.

Character-focused narration directed primarily or even exclusively toward a single character is not necessarily a flaw of a narrative. In one like *Death in Venice*, where the central conflict takes place within the protagonist's mind, Britten and Piper's exclusive focus on Aschenbach's experience is perhaps the work's greatest strength. It may be one of the keys to the mystery of how they were able to craft a successful opera out of such an unlikely source: a story almost devoid of event but rich in philosophical reflection.

In a story centering on a conflict between two points of view on an ethical question, providing subjective access to only one side of the debate is a problem, one further exacerbated by the work's framework, which leaves no doubt about which side the authors are on. Weighting the narrative in this way undermines its capacity to offer an ethical exploration of the topic at hand.[62] Thus, I am inclined to agree with Winton Dean's assessment that in caricaturing the Paramore characters, Britten does a disservice both to Owen and to his pacifist stance:

> James is not emotionally committed to one side or the other; he leaves us to judge.... Myfanwy Piper does not. In expanding the plot she retains the basic stance of the Coyles... but turns the Paramore contingent into cardboard devils who live on a different plane and repel not only belief but interest. When a moral issue is raised, as it is here, it is fatal to load the dice or indulge in the sort of parody appropriate to a comedy like *Albert Herring*, and counter-productive to disturb one of the coefficients by presenting the Wingraves and Julians as targets for scorn. They have a point of view, whether we like it or not.... By caricaturing them, the authors devalue their hero and his dilemma.[63]

One corrective is in order, however. The faults Dean finds in the opera are largely not the work of Piper. Although her libretto facilitated the opera's focus on Owen, it is Britten's musical setting that is responsible for reducing the Paramore characters to mere caricatures. In fact, Piper urged Britten to take a more compassionate view of Owen's opponents, most notably his fiancée, Kate. Piper recalled:

> One of the characters who was unsatisfactory and over whom I had a great deal of argument was Kate. Kate was treated by James in the same slightly larger than life way as the rest of the household at Paramore: bigoted, unimaginative and

unsympathetic, black against Owen's white, although he did allow her a certain brusque independence and strangeness, as well as an unconventional beauty. Britten took Mrs Coyle's view of her that she was an impossible and arrogant girl, not worthy of the thoughtful Owen. I felt that in spite of her insufferable behaviour she was as much a victim of her background as Owen, but lacked his opportunities to think again; that she must have had another side or he wouldn't have been attracted by her.[64]

Piper was responsible for inserting a moment of reminiscence for the couple during their final conversation, which adds considerable warmth to Kate's character.[65] Unfortunately, this new side of Kate appears too late in the story to fully redeem her, especially given her cruel flirting with Lechmere in the previous scene (inserted on Britten's request) and her childish insistence that Owen spend a night in the haunted room.[66] Had Britten been more receptive to Piper's ideas, the resulting opera might have avoided some of the aforementioned flaws in conception.

Because of Britten's bias toward Owen, many commentators have remarked that the work lacks the moral ambivalence that characterizes the composer's more celebrated operas *Peter Grimes* (1945) and *Billy Budd* (1951).[67] The question *why* has been answered by Philip Brett and John Evans through reference to the composer's lifelong pacifist convictions as well as historical events such as the Vietnam War and the Kent State University shootings.[68] What I hope to have contributed is a more detailed investigation of the question *how* as well as some thoughts about the consequences of character-focused narration. I continue the latter investigation in the next section, which considers works that invite us to sympathize with morally reprehensible characters.

Sympathy for the Devil

Narratives often allow us to get a sense of what it would be like to experience the world from points of view that are not our own.[69] The moral benefits of gaining a better grasp of the struggles of people of color and other minorities are obvious. But what if the point of view we are invited to share is that of a murderer?

Most ethical assessments of art are confined to the attitudes the work expresses and encourages in spectators, such as moral evaluations or feelings of disgust or admiration toward characters' actions. But if an artwork is not merely an object but more akin to an action or utterance (as proposed in chap. 1), ethical criticism ought to also extend to the work's generative process, such as the real author's behavior toward collaborators or intent for the work to cause offense or encourage moral deviance.[70] In this section, I consider two works that have been topics of ethical debate: Sondheim and Weidman's

Assassins and Shostakovich and Preys's *Lady Macbeth of the Mtsensk District*. My conclusions that the former is morally educative while the latter is morally suspect rest not only on differences in the works' content but also in the ways in which their creators approached the task of adapting these stories to the musical stage and their intentions concerning audience response.

Sondheim has done more than possibly anyone else to push the boundaries of what the American musical could sing about. None of his shows have raised more ethical questions than *Assassins*, a transhistorical revue about men and women who have assassinated or attempted to assassinate the president of the United States. In response to critics' ethical concerns about the show, Sondheim and Weidman have had quite a lot to say about why they approached the topic in the way that they did and how they intended audiences to respond. The following is a transcription of remarks Weidman made in a series of video interviews intended for those interested in performing the work:

> It's become easy to shove these people aside, to view them as a collection of freaks, un-American freaks, people outside our experience, who really have nothing to teach us and nothing to say to us.... What the show asks the audience to do is to spend some time with these people, perhaps to discover as the show goes along that their feelings about them are, at any rate, more complicated than the feelings that they had when they came into the theater. In a sense, what we ask the audience to do is to step back beyond the moment of assassination. In Hinckley's case, for example, to stop thinking of John Hinckley as John Hinckley, Assassin ... and to see him as the deeply disturbed, perhaps, person that he was, living at the edge of stability, a kid with terrific problems, which he was unable to resolve. That makes him somebody who may have more in common with other people which we encounter in everyday life than we perhaps would like to admit.[71]

One of the ways Weidman and Sondheim suggest to their audiences that the assassins are more like them than they may have initially assumed is by dramatizing the circumstances and motivations that led these men and women to commit (or attempt to commit) murder. Given their targets, surprisingly few of these acts were politically motivated (of those chosen, only John Wilkes Booth and Samuel Byck). Other motivations dramatized in the show include the pursuit of fame (Charles Guiteau and Giuseppe Zangara), disillusionment with the American dream (Zangara, Guiteau, and Leon Czolgosz), inequality or lack of acceptance in American society (Zangara and Czolgosz), and even love (Lynette Fromme and John Hinckley).[72] As Weidman remarks, these motivations are not extraordinary, even though the acts they precipitated are.

Sondheim and Weidman not only humanize the assassins, they also claim them as American citizens. In Weidman's words, "*Assassins* suggests that while these individuals are, to say the least, peculiar—taken as a group they are peculiarly *American*."[73] The musical explores why, in America's relatively young

Lights come up on a Shooting Gallery in a fairground. The targets are Presidential figures. Shelves of prizes. A Proprietor stands behind the counter, idly picking his teeth.

Example 5.18. "Hail to the Chief" as carnival waltz, opening of *Assassins*

life as a nation, so many of its citizens have attempted to kill their head of state. The opening and closing number, "Everybody's Got the Right," points both to the American dream and to the Declaration of Independence, which lists "the pursuit of happiness" as one of the "unalienable rights" of American citizens. "There is a difference between the right to *pursue* happiness and the right to *be* happy," Sondheim reflects in the same series of interviews. "The bleeding of the first thought into the second thought is part of what this show is about."[74]

The assassins' Americanness is also expressed through Sondheim's musical-stylistic choices. He describes the score as a "panorama of American music," its sources ranging from the second half of the nineteenth century to the time of composition.[75] The only direct quotations are "Hail to the Chief" and the Sousa marches "El Capitan" and "The Washington Post" (both used in "How I Saved Roosevelt"). The official presidential anthem is heard in various guises, initially as a melancholic carnival waltz (ex. 5.18), then in more familiar form at the beginning of "The Ballad of Booth," and also in the hemiola rhythm of *West Side Story*'s "America" as Byck dictates his message to Leonard Bernstein (Scene 9). The majority of references are more along the lines of stylistic allusions. The slow section of Booth's ballad was inspired by Stephen Foster.[76] Guiteau dances a cakewalk up to the scaffold. The Balladeer's portions of Booth's song evoke bluegrass. Czolgosz's ballad is a cumulative folk song (e.g., "The Twelve Days of Christmas"). The barbershop number "The Gun Song" and foxtrot "Everybody's Got the Right" both evoke the sound of Golden Era musical comedies. And for the contemporary figures, Fromme and Hinckley, Sondheim wrote a ballad in the style of The Carpenters ("Unworthy of Your Love"). He also drew on high-art forms of American music. The quartal harmonies that accompany the reprise of "Hail to the Chief" after the Kennedy assassination evoke Aaron Copland in his more bombastic and patriotic mode (ex. 5.19).

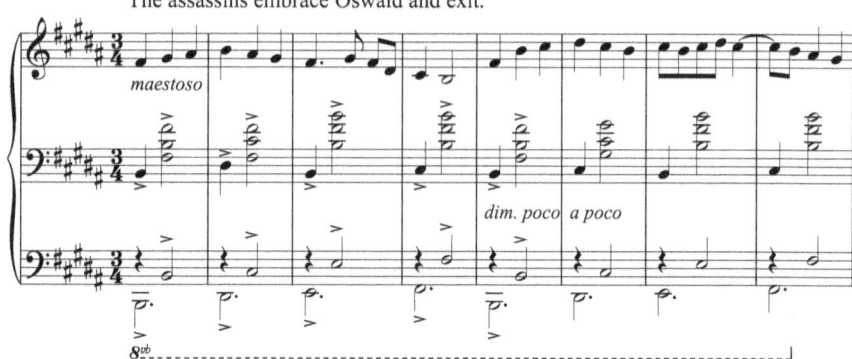

Example 5.19. Coplandesque "Hail to the Chief" after Kennedy assassination

For American audiences, the familiarity of the assassins' music has proved to be one of the more disturbing elements of the show. Steven Swayne has argued that the fact that the assassins "sing our songs" causes us to "identify with them." The assassins' singing may evoke various styles of American music, but as Raymond Knapp has noted, there are many subtle and not so subtle hints that they are not "just like us."[77] The aberrant nature of these individuals is clear from the first sounds one hears, the twisted triple-meter version of "Hail to the Chief" (ex. 5.18). The next song, "The Ballad of Booth," seems to be a standard bluegrass tune, accompanied by steady strumming on the banjo, but if one counts the beats or looks at the score, one discovers that the meter is constantly shifting without any apparent rhyme or reason (ex. 5.20).[78]

Even someone with no ear for music can discern that something is seriously askew in Fromme and Hinckley's "Unworthy of Your Love." First, they do not sing to or about one another, but each addresses an absent lover, a celebrity that does not even know that they exist. Second, Fromme's lyrics "take my blood and my body for your love. Let me feel fire, let me drink poison" are not likely to be airing on mainstream radio any time soon, as much as they may have pleased her addressee, Charles Manson.[79]

"The Gun Song" is reminiscent of barbershop numbers in musicals of yesteryear, such as "Lida Rose" from *The Music Man* (1957), but rather than singing about the love of another person, Guiteau, Moore, Booth, and Czolgosz all sing to their respective guns.[80] While singing in close harmony brings the men of *The Music Man* closer together, in *Assassins*, each character is just as self-absorbed by the end of the song as they were at the beginning. Sondheim expresses the assassins' increasing disaffection through increasing harmonic dissonance, especially in comparison with the Balladeer's music, in

Example 5.20. Shifting meters in "The Ballad of Booth"

"Another National Anthem" (chap. 3 contains a more substantial discussion of this number).

Sondheim's references to musical Americana claim these individuals as American, but his deviations from the conventions of the styles he invokes indicate that they are decidedly wayward citizens. Their problems—dead-end jobs, unrequited love, chronic pain—may be ordinary, but their solutions are not.

Sondheim and Weidman certainly *align* us with the assassins' points of view, but do they encourage us to *ally* ourselves with them?[81] Weidman claims that he and Sondheim "don't ask the audience to sympathize with these characters. We don't ask the audience even to empathize with them. We simply ask them to see them as more multi-dimensional and complicated than they are if we simply see them as a group of murderers."[82] Sondheim and Weidman do invite sympathy for at least some of the assassins, despite Weidman's protests to the contrary. As other critics have remarked, Czolgosz is a particularly sympathetic character.[83] He is forced to work in unsafe conditions because, as the son of Polish immigrants, he is unable to find better employment. It is easy to sympathize with Czolgosz not only because of the injustices he faced but also because of the way Sondheim and Weidman tell his story. His scene with the political activist Emma Goldman (Scene 5) is, in Weidman's description, "as close to a naturalistic scene as there is in the piece." Weidman characterizes it as "sentimental" and intended it to be "played very warmly."[84] By contrast, the following scene involving Fromme and Sara Jane Moore takes its inspiration from sitcoms like *I Love Lucy* (1951–57), inviting audiences to laugh at the characters' expense.

That the assassins' stories are largely communicated through song also facilitates a degree of emotional attunement or empathy with the characters. I feel anger on Czolgosz's behalf when I contemplate the prejudice he faced and how even contemporary America is far from its putative ideal as a land of equal opportunity. What I do not share, and what the work does not encourage me to share, is Czolgosz's conviction that shooting the president is a reasonable response to his situation or one that is likely to improve working conditions or the treatment of immigrants in American society. I take Weidman's denial that the work encourages sympathy or empathy as a denial that it encourages *unqualified* allegiance with the assassins. To the extent that the work encourages sympathy or empathy for them, it is not *because* they commit (or attempt to commit) murder but *in spite of* these actions and intentions.[85]

Even so, many American critics have accused Sondheim and Weidman of failing to offer a clear moral point of view. Knapp has argued that, with the removal of the Balladeer's "normalising reassurances" in "Another National Anthem," "the audience is left . . . virtually defenceless against the assassins' twisted perspective." Knapp assumes too passive a role for the audience. *Assassins* is not a show for nursery school children but one for adults, who are not likely to question their belief that murder is wrong without a "perspective of health with which [to] identify."[86]

Through its songs and sketches, *Assassins* explores the dark sides of the American dream, the power of advertising, the Second Amendment ("right of the people to keep and bear arms"), and America's fascination with celebrities. Sondheim and Weidman raise these topics more as questions to ponder and debate than as lessons to be learned. "The last song does not draw a conclusion, it mustn't," Sondheim advises future directors of the show. "Everything in the show is both arguable and controversial. The audience should be stimulated through having a good time to talk about what the show is about, and indeed perhaps to discuss or even argue it. That is why John [Weidman] and I decided not to make a moral point at the end of this."[87] Far from being a failing of the show, I suggest that Sondheim and Weidman's decision not to provide a pat moral lesson at the end is a moral and artistic virtue as it encourages audiences to actively participate in the ethical questions *Assassins* raises.

Shostakovich and Preys's *Lady Macbeth of the Mtsensk District* has aroused ethical concerns of a similar nature. After Stalin attended a performance in 1936, the work was denounced in *Pravda* and was not heard again in the Soviet Union for nearly thirty years, and even then, only with significant revisions. Some of the features that provoked Stalin's disapproval—for example, the score's progressive harmonic language and explicit representation of sexual acts—may not be of particular concern to critics today. However, Shostakovich's encouragement of feelings of admiration toward a murderer and indifference toward her victims' deaths remains morally problematic. Although declaring that Stalin's censure of the work "was for wrong and hateful reasons," Richard Taruskin admits that "if ever an opera deserved to be banned it was this one."[88]

Significantly, the opera's source, a short story of the same title by Nikolai Leskov (1865), has not aroused similar moral outrage, despite containing roughly the same characters and events: Katerina, a housewife trapped in a loveless marriage, has an affair and commits multiple murders in order to continue with the affair. Where the short story and opera differ is in the ways Leskov and Shostakovich approached their respective portrayals of Katerina and the attitudes they encourage readers/spectators to take toward her actions.

Leskov's story is told by an unnamed fictional resident of the Mtsensk district.[89] The Russian literature scholar Caryl Emerson describes it as a "coolly detached and amoral tale," remarking that the narrator "demonstrates little sympathy for (or even interest in) the heroine."[90] Yet readers follow Katerina's trajectory throughout the narrative, and most expository sections concern her past, providing context for her subsequent acts. Readers learn, for instance, that she was not given a choice about whom to marry; that she is under constant surveillance by her husband's family; and that they blame her for her husband's infertility. No one cares about her or the fact that she has no purpose in life.[91]

The sense of the narrator's detachment from his protagonist comes from Leskov's impartial tone and limited use of free indirect discourse. Taruskin has likened the narrational style to that of a procurator, "an impartial court officer whose job it is to prepare summaries of evidence for criminal cases."[92] The narrator generally refrains from passing moral judgment on Katerina's actions. However, consider his description of her murder of the child-heir Fedya. Readers are told that Katerina's lover, Sergei, has repeatedly bemoaned the complications caused by the discovery of an heir to her deceased husband's estate. As Katerina contemplates the child one evening, "suddenly it was as if demons came unleashed, and all her former thoughts descended on her of how much evil this boy had caused her and how good it would be if he were not there."[93] The sense of the narration shifting blame away from Katerina is intensified in Shostakovich and Preys's operatic adaptation.

In the program notes to the work's premiere in Leningrad, Shostakovich explained his attraction to the story: "There is no work of Russian literature that more vividly or expressively characterizes the position of women in the old prerevolutionary time." The problem, for the composer, was in Leskov's treatment of the story's protagonist. Shostakovich explains that his aim in adapting the work for the Soviet stage was "in every way to justify Katerina so that she would impress the audience as a positive character." To be clear, Shostakovich's Katerina still commits multiple murders in the course of the narrative. Although acknowledging her crimes, the composer regards them as "a protest against the tenor of the life she is forced to live, against the dark and suffocating atmosphere of the merchant class in the last century."[94]

The first step in his and Preys's rehabilitation of Katerina involved several minor but significant changes to the plot. They transformed Katerina's father-in-law, Boris (her first victim), from a judgmental old man to a sexual predator, of whose abuse Katerina lives in constant fear. The murder of the child Fedya was removed entirely and replaced with scenes exposing the corruption of those in positions of power: members of the clergy and the police. The operatic Katerina, furthermore, takes responsibility for her actions. In Leskov's short story, Katerina confesses only after Sergei does and pushes the blame in his direction. In the opera, she is the first to confess and, unlike Leskov's character, feels guilt (this is clear in Act IV when she describes a lake as "black like my conscience"). Not only did Shostakovich and Preys remove some of Katerina's more deplorable actions, they also added some morally laudable ones. Katerina stops the workers on her husband's estate from raping Aksinya in Act I, Scene 2 and delivers a proto-feminist speech.[95] However, as the composer himself admitted, "the real justification [of Katerina] is to be found in the musical material."[96]

Katerina's music is lyrical, sensual, and based on Russian folk melodies—features that carry a positive moral valence in Shostakovich's musical language. The orchestra is predominantly occupied with expressing her emotional and psychological states, even when she is not onstage (as in the many orchestral interludes).[97] Martin Kušej dramatizes the orchestra's alignment with Katerina in his production for the Dutch National Opera (2006). When the orchestra expresses her anguish and horror over Sergei leaving her for Sonyetka, Eva-Maria Westbroek opens her mouth in a silent scream, indicating that the orchestra represents her "voice" at this moment.

By contrast, virtually all of the other characters are reduced to caricatures even more grotesque than those in *Owen Wingrave*. But rather than serialism, Shostakovich's parodies target popular styles of music from the operetta, music hall, circus, and cinema.[98] As Boris surveils Katerina's nocturnal activities, he ponders how he would "alleviate her boredom" to an operetta-style waltz (Act II, Scene 4, reh. 209–12). Even when the other characters' vocal lines achieve a level of lyricism, they are undercut by the orchestra. Katerina's husband Zinovy's feeble farewell in the first scene is met with derisive, even lewd commentary from the trombone section (reh. 47–50). Shostakovich singled out this moment in his program notes: "When [Zinovy] tries to speak authoritatively as the master in his home, the music exposes him and we see a weak, pathetic, specimen of the merchant class."[99] Taruskin observes that Shostakovich's caricature techniques dehumanize her victims, effectively mitigating her crimes to "cruelty to animals."[100]

Unlike the characters of *Assassins*, the operatic Katerina is a good candidate for the category A. W. Eaton and Adriana Clavel-Vazquez term the *rough hero/heroine*.[101] Her moral flaws are grievous but are an integral part of her character. She commits her crimes knowing them to be evil. Although she shows signs of remorse after getting caught for the first two murders, that does not prevent her from murdering her rival Sonyetka. Shostakovich and Preys do attempt to contextualize Katerina's crimes and balance her vices with virtues, but these additional ingredients in their telling are not sufficient to outweigh the heinous nature of her actions. And unlike Sondheim in *Assassins*, Shostakovich intended spectators to sustain positive attitudes toward Katerina throughout the narrative and, through his musical-stylistic choices, took effective steps toward realizing this intention (even if some audience members resist the invitation to sympathize with Katerina). For these reasons, Taruskin speculates that the opera "could well be the most pernicious use to which music has ever been put."[102]

Shostakovich's encouragement of unqualified allegiance toward Katerina, and feelings of indifference, even satisfaction at the suffering of her victims, do constitute moral failings of the opera. Yet I suspect that *Lady Macbeth*'s place in the modernist opera canon is due, in part, to its transgressiveness, not only artistically but also morally.[103] Whether, as Taruskin seems to suggest, we ought to reconsider its place within the repertory is, however, more of a question for political philosophy. Addressing this question is likely to involve considering whether entertaining morally dubious imaginings has any effect on one's feelings and actions toward actual persons. That is a question that also warrants further study but is one that is more suited to the fields of psychology and sociology than either musicology or philosophy.

In this chapter, I have aimed to provide more nuance to discussions of point of view in opera by drawing attention to the following distinctions, frequently elided in opera scholarship. The first is Gérard Genette's distinction between imagining that the narration expresses a character's point of view and imagining that the character in question is the narrator or author. *What Maisie Knew* is largely told according to Maisie's point of view, but it is clear from the narrator's moral evaluations of her parents that an adult is ultimately responsible for telling her story. Similarly, the orchestral music of *Owen Wingrave* aligns spectators with Owen's perspective, but it is not appropriate to imagine that he composed or is otherwise responsible for generating this music.

The second is Murray Smith's distinction between the narration aligning spectators with a character's point of view and spectators responding to that character with sympathy or empathy. Some works, such as *Owen Wingrave*, encourage spectators to ally themselves with the character orienting the narrative perspective. In others, such as *Assassins*, these processes are decoupled. By allowing the assassins to tell their stories and to do so through song, Sondheim and Weidman align spectators with the assassins, but they do not encourage unqualified allegiance with them. Crucially, we are not encouraged to share in the assassins' conviction that murdering one's head of state will solve one's problems. In *Lady Macbeth*, Shostakovich does encourage allegiance with Katerina, but due to the severity of her moral failings, some spectators may resist the invitation to ally themselves with her. Finally, I have distinguished between works that merely represent immoral actions, such as *Assassins*, and those that are the product of flawed moral thinking, such as *Lady Macbeth*.

So far, my focus has been on the work of composers and librettists. Beginning in the following chapter, I explore what happens when the performers decide not to follow their instructions.

Notes

1. Concerning the onstage group, Wagner issues the following directions: "On the stage, behind the backcloth, becoming very gradually more distant. (When possible, this group of horns should be doubled, or increased in size even further.)" At the beginning, he directs them to play with their bells in the air, which would also increase their volume. Richard Wagner, *Richard Wagner Sämtliche Werke*, ed. Isolde Vetter and Egon Voss (Mainz: Schott, 1992), vol. 8, pt. 2, 9 (author's translation).

2. Carolyn Abbate, *Unsung Voices: Opera and Musical Narrative in the Nineteenth Century* (Princeton: Princeton University Press, 1991), 131.

3. Gérard Genette, *Narrative Discourse: An Essay in Method*, trans. Jane E. Lewin (Ithaca: Cornell University Press, 1983), 186.

4. I take the term *character-focused narration* from Gregory Currie, *Narratives and Narrators: A Philosophy of Stories* (Oxford: Oxford University Press, 2010), ch. 7. The term *alignment* is from Murray Smith, *Engaging Characters: Fiction, Emotion, and the Cinema* (Oxford: Clarendon Press, 1995), ch. 5. These concepts are similar but not equivalent to Genette's concept of *focalization*.

5. Henry James, *What Maisie Knew* (London: Penguin, 1985), 53.

6. Ibid., 50. Paul Theroux draws attention to this remark in his introduction to the 1985 Penguin edition. Ibid., 13.

7. Ibid., 88.

8. Alessandra Campana, *Opera and Modern Spectatorship in Late Nineteenth-Century Italy* (Cambridge: Cambridge University Press, 2014), 158, 160.

9. Genette, *Narrative Discourse*, 186.

10. Ibid., 189.

11. Currie, *Narratives and Narrators*, 127–29, also critiques Genette's suggestion that one's point of view can be equated with one's knowledge base.

12. Ibid., 89.

13. James discussed this possibility in the preface to the New York Edition (1909), reprinted in Henry James, *The Art of the Novel: Critical Prefaces* (New York: Scribner's, 1934), 145–46.

14. The distinction between narrating *from* and *according to* a point of view is another refinement introduced by Currie. Genette's account of focalization elides this distinction. He argues that a difference in narrator, without a difference in focal character, does not amount to a difference in point of view. In other words, he claims that there is no difference between the point of view from which the published version of *What Maisie Knew* is told and the point of view of a version in which Maisie is the narrator. Genette, *Narrative Discourse*, 186–87. Refer to Currie, *Narratives and Narrators*, 124–27, for Currie's critique.

15. Compare Currie, *Narratives and Narrators*, 130; Genette, *Narrative Discourse*, 190.

16. Kathleen Stock, "Free Indirect Style and Imagining from the Inside," in *Art, Mind, and Narrative: Themes from the Work of Peter Goldie*, ed. Julian Dodd (Oxford: Oxford University Press, 2016), 110. Although free indirect discourse is often understood as displacing the narrator, Daniel P. Gunn, "Free Indirect Discourse and Narrative Authority in *Emma*," *Narrative* 12, no. 1 (2004): 35–36, argues that this hypothesis is unsupported by literary practice. Instead, he characterizes it as "a kind of narratorial *mimicry*." See also Currie, *Narratives and Narrators*, 140–44.

17. George M. Wilson, *Seeing Fictions in Film: The Epistemology of Movies* (Oxford: Oxford University Press, 2011), 148–49.

18. Smith, *Engaging Characters*, 156–61; Murray Smith, *Film, Art, and the Third Culture: A Naturalized Aesthetics of Film* (Oxford: Oxford University Press, 2017), 145–46.

19. Wilson, *Seeing Fictions in Film*, 159–62.

20. George M. Wilson, *Narration in Light: Studies in Cinematic Point of View* (Baltimore: Johns Hopkins University Press, 1986), ch. 9.

21. Most of these effects were done digitally in postproduction. Kirsten Moana Thompson, "Falling in (to) Color," *Moving Image* 15, no. 1 (2015): 68.

22. Philip Rupprecht, *Britten's Musical Language* (New York: Cambridge University Press, 2001), 267–74.

23. Michel Chion, *Audio-Vision: Sound on Screen*, trans. Claudia Gorbman (New York: Columbia University Press, 1994), 90–91, makes a similar point.

24. Stephen Sondheim, quoted in Foster Hirsch, *Harold Prince and the American Musical Theatre* (New York: Applause, 2005), 125.

25. Christopher G. Bond, *Sweeney Todd: The Demon Barber of Fleet Street* (New York: Samuel French, 1974), 21.

26. Stephen Sondheim, *Finishing the Hat: Collected Lyrics (1954–1981)* (New York: Knopf, 2010), 355. See also Sondheim's remarks in Alan Benson, dir., *Sweeney Todd: Scenes from the Making of a Musical*, broadcast by the South Bank Show, London Weekend Television, July 11, 1980, accessed March 5, 2020, https://www.youtube.com/watch?v=o3OAf45IaUk, beginning at 4:20; Mark Eden Horowitz, ed., *Sondheim on Music: Minor Details and Major Decisions* (Lanham: Scarecrow, 2003), 140.

27. Sondheim described *Sweeney Todd* as his "homage to Bernard Herrmann." He was particularly inspired by *Psycho*: "What happens in *Psycho* in the orchestra is just as frightening as what happens on the screen. And not just the shrieking birds, but those unresolved chords that keep going on so that nothing ever reaches a cadence, and so you're constantly upset." Quoted in Horowitz, ed., *Sondheim on Music*, 72.

28. Stephen Sondheim and Hugh Wheeler, *Sweeney Todd: The Demon Barber of Fleet Street* (libretto) (New York: Dodd, Mead, & Co., 1979), 94–96.

29. I have in mind Kivy's remark on "the obvious inability of music to impart much in the way of fictional truths about the psychology of operatic characters." Peter Kivy, "How Did Mozart Do It? Living Conditions in the World of Opera," in *The Fine Art of Repetition: Essays in the Philosophy of Music* (Cambridge: Cambridge University Press, 1993), 166.

30. William Plomer, *Gloriana* (libretto), in *The Operas of Benjamin Britten: The Complete Librettos*, ed. David Herbert (New York: Columbia University Press, 1979), 213.

31. Ibid.

32. Plomer and Britten came upon it in Lytton Strachey, *Elizabeth and Essex: A Tragic History* (New York: Harcourt, 1928), 107–8, chief source for the opera. Only minor word substitutions were made, presumably in the interest of singability.

33. Heather Wiebe, *Britten's Unquiet Pasts: Sound and Memory in Postwar Reconstruction* (Cambridge: Cambridge University Press, 2012), 144. Comparative musical examples of Wilbye and Britten may be found in Antonia Malloy-Chirgwin, "*Gloriana*: Britten's 'Slighted Child,'" in *Cambridge Companion to Benjamin Britten*, ed. Mervyn Cooke (Cambridge: Cambridge University Press, 1999), 126–27.

34. Letter from Britten to Plomer, July 24, 1952. Mervyn Cooke, Donald Mitchell, and Philip Reed, eds., *Letters from a Life: The Selected Letters of Benjamin Britten, 1913–1976*, 6 vols. (Woodbridge: Boydell, 1991–2012), 4:76.

35. Benjamin Britten, interviewed by John Amis in 1970 for the BBC's "Music Now," included in Colin Graham, dir., *Owen Wingrave* (Decca, 2009), DVD.

36. Henry James, "Owen Wingrave," in *The Complete Tales of Henry James*, ed. Leon Edel (London: Rupert Hart-Davis, 1963), 30.

37. Myfanwy Piper, interviewed by Roderic Dunnett, "A Collaboration Recalled," *Opera* 46, no. 10 (1995): 1163.

38. Jennifer Barnes, *Television Opera: The Fall of Opera Commissioned for Television* (Woodbridge: Boydell, 2003), 65. The quotations are from Benjamin Britten, *Owen Wingrave* (study score) (London: Faber Music, 1995), 2–3; Myfanwy Piper, *Owen Wingrave* (libretto), in *The Operas of Benjamin Britten: The Complete Librettos*, ed. David Herbert (New York: Columbia University Press, 1979), 331.

39. Peter Evans, *The Music of Benjamin Britten* (London: J. M. Dent & Sons, 1979), 506–9; Stephen McClatchie, "Benjamin Britten, *Owen Wingrave* and the Politics of the Closet; Or, 'He Shall Be Straightened out at Paramore,'" *Cambridge Opera Journal* 8, no. 1 (1996): 66; Donald Mitchell, "*Owen Wingrave* and the Sense of the Past," in *Cradles of the New: Writings on Music, 1951–1991*, ed. Mervyn Cooke (London: Faber, 1995), 422–23; Arne Muus, "'The Minstrel Boy to the War Is Gone': Father Figures and Fighting Sons in Britten's *Owen Wingrave*," in *Benjamin Britten: New Perspectives on His Life and Work*, ed. Lucy Walker (Woodbridge: Boydell, 2009), 102.

40. Philip Brett, *Owen Wingrave* liner notes, 10, English Chamber Orchestra conducted by Benjamin Britten (London: Decca, 1993), CD.

41. Letter from Britten to Piper, April 29, 1969. Cooke, Mitchell, and Reed, eds., *Letters from a Life*, 6:273.

42. Britten, *Owen Wingrave* (study score), 9.

43. Piper, *Owen Wingrave* (libretto), 333. The BBC was not able to realize Britten and Piper's intentions for this scene. Finding no suitable stock footage, they were forced to stage the scene themselves, but due to budget restrictions, they were able to film only the realistic portion of the exercise, not Owen's imaginings. Furthermore, Miss Wingrave's responses were not precipitated by her viewing of the horse guards but by a painting of a cavalry charge. Barnes, *Television Opera*, 65–68.

44. Britten, *Owen Wingrave* (study score), 53.

45. I am grateful to Andrew Kania for making this point and for suggesting that the difference between the degree to which Britten's music aligns us with Owen and Miss Wingrave is better understood on a continuum rather than as an all-or-nothing matter.

46. P. Evans, *Music of Benjamin Britten*, 509–10; McClatchie, "Politics of the Closet," 68.

47. Many critics have remarked that Britten reduces Owen's opponents to mere caricatures by indulging in parody techniques he previously confined to comedies such as *Albert Herring* (1947). Winton Dean, Review of *Owen Wingrave* (Covent Garden premiere), *Musical Times* 114, no. 1565 (1973): 719; John Evans, "*Owen Wingrave*: A Case for Pacifism," in *The Britten Companion*, ed. Christopher Palmer (London: Faber, 1984), 231; Peter Heyworth, "Britten Tackles the Great Divide," *Observer*, May 16, 1971; Mitchell, "Sense of the Past," 426–27; John Warrack, "Box for the Opera," *Sunday Telegraph*, May 16, 1971. Even Piper admitted that "the Paramore characters *do* become caricatures." Dunnett, "A Collaboration Recalled," 1161.

48. Muus, "Father Figures and Fighting Songs," 112.

49. "The Minstrel Boy" is part of Thomas's Moore's *Irish Melodies* (1808–1834), a collection of poems set to preexisting tunes. Although listeners today may not recognize Lechmere's utterance as a quotation, many early critics did; for example, Brett, *Owen Wingrave*, liner notes, 10; J. Evans, "Case for Pacifism," 235; Peter Evans, "Britten's Television Opera," *Musical Times* 112, no. 1539 (1971): 427; Arnold Whittall, *The Music of Britten and Tippett: Studies in Themes and Techniques* (Cambridge: Cambridge University Press, 1982), 251. On the distortions, see Muus, "Father Figures and Fighting Sons," 99–100; J. P. E. Harper-Scott, *Ideology in Britten's Operas* (Cambridge: Cambridge University Press, 2018), 51–54.

50. On the distinction between internal and external perspectives, refer to Currie, *Narratives and Narrators*, 49, and my discussion of *My Fair Lady* in chapter 2.

51. Campana, *Opera and Modern Spectatorship*, 160.

52. J. P. E. Harper-Scott, "Made You Look! Children in *Salome* and *Death in Venice*," in *Benjamin Britten: New Perspectives on His Life and Work*, ed. Lucy Walker (Woodbridge: Boydell, 2009), 129.

53. There is a large body of work in philosophy on the phenomenon of *imaginative resistance*, one facet of which is the asymmetry between our ability or willingness to imagine the immoral as compared with the impossible. Tamar Szabó Gendler, "The Puzzle of Imaginative Resistance," *Journal of Philosophy* 97, no. 2 (2000): 55–81; Richard Moran, "The Expression of Feeling in Imagination," *Philosophical Review* 103, no. 1 (1994): 75–106; Kendall L. Walton and Michael Tanner, "Morals in Fiction and Fictional Morality," *Proceedings of the Aristotelian Society* 68 (1994): 27–66; Derek Matravers, "Fictional Assent and the (So-Called) 'Puzzle of Imaginative Resistance,'" in *Imagination, Philosophy, and the Arts*, ed. Matthew Kieran and Dominic McIver Lopes (London: Routledge, 2003), 91–106; Tamar Szabó Gendler, "Imaginative Resistance Revisited," in *The Architecture of the Imagination: New Essays on

Pretence, Possibility, and Fiction, ed. Shaun Nichols (Oxford: Clarendon Press, 2006), 149–74; Kendall L. Walton, "On the (So-Called) Puzzle of Imaginative Resistance," in *The Architecture of the Imagination: New Essays on Pretence, Possibility, and Fiction*, ed. Shaun Nichols (Oxford: Clarendon Press, 2006), 137–48; Currie, *Narratives and Narrators*, ch. 6; Kathleen Stock, *Only Imagine: Fiction, Interpretation, and Imagination* (Oxford: Oxford University Press, 2017), ch. 4. David Hume, "Of the Standard of Taste," in *Four Dissertations* (London: A. Millar, 1757), 203–40, is often cited as a forerunner of this discourse.

54. Currie, *Narratives and Narrators*, 86.

55. Smith, *Engaging Characters*, 188.

56. McClatchie, "Politics of the Closet," 67.

57. As Harper-Scott, *Ideology in Britten's Operas*, 58n55, notes, Britten's "association of serialism with violence in *Owen Wingrave* is . . . particular to this opera. In *Death in Venice*, serialism is associated with the rationality of Aschenbach's fantasy of himself; in *The Turn of the Screw* it is associated with the pressure of the eponymous 'screw', namely the pressure towards adult sexuality."

58. Britten expressed his thoughts on serialism in a 1963 interview with Murray Schafer: "It has simply never attracted me as a method. . . . I cannot feel that tonality is outworn, and find many serial 'rules' arbitrary. 'Socially' I am seriously disturbed by its limitations. I can see it taking no part in the music-lover's music-making. Its methods make writing *gratefully* for voices or instruments an impossibility, which inhibits amateurs and children." Murray Schafer, "British Composers in Interview: Benjamin Britten," in *Britten on Music*, ed. Paul Kildea (Oxford: Oxford University Press, 2008), 228–29.

59. Philip Brett, "Eros and Orientalism in Britten's Operas," in *Music and Sexuality in Britten: Selected Essays*, ed. George E. Haggerty (Berkeley: University of California Press, 2006), 148–49; McClatchie, "Politics of the Closet," 71–72.

60. Mervyn Cooke, *Britten and the Far East: Asian Influences in the Music of Benjamin Britten* (Woodbridge: Boydell, 1998), 227.

61. Arnold Whittall, "Britten's Lament: The World of *Owen Wingrave*," *Music Analysis* 19, no. 2 (2000): 154, provides a chart summarizing the relationship between the "gamelan" and "triad" layers. Donald Mitchell, "Violent Climates," in *Cambridge Companion to Benjamin Britten*, ed. Mervyn Cooke (Cambridge: Cambridge University Press, 1999), 195, argues that "the rotation of the triads represents by virtue of its totality of all twelve pitches the ideal of 'wholeness', of a world, not without contrast (major/minor) or inner tension, but one in which everything (everybody) is interrelated." Arnold Whittall takes a more pessimistic view in "Breaking the Balance," *Musical Times* 137, no. 1843 (1996): 5–6; Whittall, "Britten's Lament," 153–55.

62. I am grateful to Murray Smith for helping me to clarify the nature of the ethical flaws of *Owen Wingrave*.

63. Dean, Review of *Owen Wingrave*, 719.

64. Myfanwy Piper, "Writing for Britten," in *The Operas of Benjamin Britten: The Complete Librettos*, ed. David Herbert (New York: Columbia University Press, 1979), 14.

65. Frances Spalding, "Dramatic Invention in Myfanwy Piper's Libretto for *Owen Wingrave*," in *Benjamin Britten: New Perspectives on His Life and Work*, ed. Lucy Walker (Woodbridge: Boydell, 2009), 90.

66. Myfanwy Piper, interviewed by John Amis in 1970 for the BBC's *Music Now*, included in Graham, dir., *Owen Wingrave*, DVD. In James's story, Kate's flirting with Lechmere is recounted by the narrator but not as directly quoted speech. James, "Owen Wingrave," 36.

67. See the following reviews of the 1971 television broadcast: Heyworth, "Britten Tackles the Great Divide"; Stanley Sadie, "*Owen Wingrave*," *Musical Times* 112, no. 1541 (1971): 663, 665–66; Warrack, "Box for the Opera." Similar sentiments were expressed in reviews of its stage premiere at Covent Garden in 1973: Dean, Review of *Owen Wingrave*; Jeremy Noble, "Old Haunts," *Sunday*

Telegraph, May 13, 1973; Desmond Shawe-Taylor, "Haunted House," *Sunday Times*, May 13, 1973; Gilliam Widdicombe, Review of *Owen Wingrave, Financial Times*, May 11, 1973.

68. Philip Brett, "Pacifism, Political Action, and Artistic Endeavor," in *Music and Sexuality in Britten: Selected Essays*, ed. George E. Haggerty (Berkeley: University of California Press, 2006), 172–85; J. Evans, "Case for Pacifism," 229. Britten kept a newspaper cutting about the tragedy at Kent State University. Spalding, "Dramatic Invention," 94n4.

69. Noël Carroll, "Art and the Moral Realm," in *Blackwell Guide to Aesthetics*, ed. Peter Kivy (Malden: Blackwell, 2004), 132–33; Smith, *Third Culture*, 191–92.

70. Scholars who confine ethical criticism to the properties of the artistic product include Wayne C. Booth, *The Company We Keep: An Ethics of Fiction* (Berkeley: University of California Press, 1988); Mary Devereaux, "Moral Judgments and Works of Art: The Case of Narrative Literature," *Journal of Aesthetics and Art Criticism* 62, no. 1 (2004): 3–11; A. W. Eaton, "Robust Immoralism," *Journal of Aesthetics and Art Criticism* 70, no. 3 (2012): 282; Berys Gaut, *Art, Emotion and Ethics* (Oxford: Oxford University Press, 2007), 69. For an argument concerning the deficiency of this approach and the necessity of considering the real artist's actions and intentions, refer to Trevor Ponech, "Moral Agency, Artistic Immorality, and Critical Appreciation: Lars von Trier's *The Idiots*," in *Cine-Ethics: Ethical Dimensions of Film Theory, Practice, and Spectatorship*, ed. Jinhee Choi and Mattias Frey (New York: Routledge, 2013), 163–77. I thank Trevor Ponech and Andrew Kania for helping me to clarify my argument in this section.

71. John Weidman in Roger Englander, dir., *Assassins: A Conversation Piece* (New York: Music Theatre International, 1991), accessed March 5, 2020, http://www.youtube.com/watch?v=29P7x4z6NXU, beginning at 3:20.

72. To be clear, I am describing the motivations represented in the show, which may differ from the actual motivations of the historical individuals on which these characters are based.

73. John Weidman, quoted by André Bishop in his preface to Stephen Sondheim and John Weidman, *Assassins* (libretto) (New York: Theatre Communications Group, 1991), x.

74. Stephen Sondheim in Englander, dir., *Conversation Piece*, beginning at 15:29.

75. Ibid., beginning at 5:00.

76. Ibid., beginning at 23:00.

77. Steven Swayne, "Hearing Sondheim's Voices" (PhD diss., University of California Berkeley, 1999), 118; Raymond Knapp, "*Assassins, Oklahoma!* and the 'Shifting Fringe of Dark Around the Camp-Fire,'" *Cambridge Opera Journal* 16, no. 1 (2004): 85.

78. Stephen Sondheim in Englander, dir., *Conservation Piece*, beginning at 21:40, explains the metric abnormalities as an attempt to evoke oral traditions, but I believe Knapp, "*Assassins, Oklahoma!*" 88, is correct in suggesting that the "extreme and chaotic" nature of the meter changes indicates that there is something amiss with Booth.

79. Sondheim and Weidman, *Assassins* (libretto), 59. Knapp, "*Assassins, Oklahoma!*" 93, also discusses the oddness of "Unworthy of Your Love."

80. Knapp, "*Assassins, Oklahoma!*" 89–92.

81. On the difference between alignment and allegiance, refer to Smith, *Engaging Characters*, 83–85.

82. John Weidman in Englander, dir., *Conversation Piece*, beginning at 4:40.

83. Christopher M. Culp, "Morality of the Outsider: Teaching *Assassins* and *Glee*," *Sondheim Review* 22, no. 1 (2015): 36; Scott Miller, "*Assassins* and the Concept Musical," in *Stephen Sondheim: A Casebook*, ed. Bonnie Gordon (New York: Garland, 1997), 195–96.

84. John Weidman in Englander, dir., *Conversation Piece*, beginning at 31:30.

85. I take this distinction from Murray Smith, "Gangsters, Cannibals, Aesthetes; or, Apparently Perverse Allegiances," in *Passionate Views: Thinking about Film and Emotion*, ed. Carl Plantinga and Greg Smith (Baltimore: Johns Hopkins University Press, 1999), 223.

86. Knapp, "*Assassins, Oklahoma!*" 94, 95.

87. Stephen Sondheim in Englander, dir., *Conversation Piece*, beginning at 1:03:35.

88. Richard Taruskin, "Shostakovich and the Inhuman," in *Defining Russia Musically: Historical and Hermeneutical Essays* (Princeton: Princeton University Press, 1997), 509.

89. The narrator begins: "In our parts." Nikolai Leskov, "The Lady Macbeth of Mtsensk," in *The Enchanted Wanderer*, trans. Richard Pevear and Larissa Volokhonsky (New York: Knopf, 2013), 3.

90. Caryl Emerson, "Back to the Future: Shostakovich's Revision of Leskov's *Lady Macbeth of Mtsensk District*," *Cambridge Opera Journal* 1, no. 1 (1989): 64, 67. See also Taruskin, "Shostakovich and the Inhuman," 500.

91. Leskov, "Lady Macbeth," 3–5.

92. Taruskin, "Shostakovich and the Inhuman," 500.

93. Leskov, "Lady Macbeth," 30.

94. The quotations are from Taruskin's translation in "Shostakovich and the Inhuman," 500, 501. The composer's preface was published in English as Dmitri Shostakovich, "My Opera, *Lady Macbeth of Mtzensk*," *Modern Music* 12, no. 1 (1934): 23–30.

95. On the possible influence of the feminist writer Alexandra Kollontai, refer to Elizabeth A. Wells, "'The New Woman': Lady Macbeth and Sexual Politics in the Stalinist Era," *Cambridge Opera Journal* 13, no. 2 (2001): 178–89.

96. Dmitri Shostakovich, quoted in Taruskin, "Shostakovich and the Inhuman," 502.

97. Emerson, "Back to the Future," 69–70; Robert S. Hatten, *A Theory of Virtual Agency for Western Music* (Bloomington: Indiana University Press, 2018), 208–10; Taruskin, "Shostakovich and the Inhuman," 503; Wells, "Sexual Politics," 179.

98. Taruskin, "Shostakovich and the Inhuman," 503.

99. Shostakovich, "My Opera," 28.

100. Taruskin, "Shostakovich and the Inhuman," 504.

101. A. W. Eaton, "Rough Heroes of the New Hollywood," *Revue internationale de philosophie* 64, no. 4 (2010): 516; Adriana Clavel-Vazquez, "Sugar and Spice, and Everything Nice: What Rough Heroines Tell Us about Imaginative Resistance," *Journal of Aesthetics and Art Criticism* 76, no. 2 (2018): 203. I have doubts about the extent to which spectators are invited to sustain predominantly positive attitudes toward Tony Soprano, Frank and Claire Underwood, and Walter White. *The Sopranos*, *House of Cards*, and *Breaking Bad* certainly align us with these characters, but to the extent that they aim to inspire allegiance, it is of a partial nature. For an argument to this effect about *The Sopranos*, refer to Murray Smith, "Just What Is It That Makes Tony Soprano Such an Appealing, Attractive Murderer?" in *Ethics at the Cinema*, ed. Ward E. Jones and Samantha Vice (Oxford: Oxford University Press, 201), 86.

102. Taruskin, "Shostakovich and the Inhuman," 502.

103. Although space does not permit me to delve into debates about the relationship between moral and artistic value, I have sympathy for *modest immoralism*, the view that an artwork may be artistically better in virtue of its moral flaws. Defenses of immoralism (of varying strengths) include Daniel Jacobson, "In Praise of Immoral Art," *Philosophical Topics* 25, no. 1 (1997): 155–99; Matthew Kieran, "Forbidden Knowledge: The Challenge of Immoralism," in *Art and Morality*, ed. José Bermúdez and Sebastian Gardner (New York: Routledge, 2003): 56–73; Eaton, "Robust Immoralism."

6

WORKS AND PERFORMANCES

After attending Hans Neuenfels's production of *Die Fledermaus* at the 2001 Salzburg Festival, a patron demanded his money back, claiming that he paid to see Johann Strauss II's operetta and they supplied a performance of something else. Neuenfels went well beyond the usual directorial shenanigans that patrons of the festival under Gerard Mortier had come to expect. His transgressions included rewriting the spoken dialogue and casting the decidedly nonoperatic voice of David Moss in the mezzo-soprano role of Prince Orlofsky. The case was eventually settled in court with a ruling against the plaintiff and in favor of artistic freedom.[1] Opera companies should have the freedom to put on challenging productions without the worry that they will be obliged to provide refunds to all patrons who dislike them. Yet I also have sympathy for the plaintiff's doubt that what Neuenfels delivered on this occasion is properly understood as a performance of *Die Fledermaus*.

In spite of the growing literature on opera performance and the exceptions it poses to the doctrine of *Werktreue* (fidelity to the work), opera scholars have largely failed to recognize the distinction the plaintiff was attempting to make between performances that are of preexisting works—what I will call *work-performances*—and those that are better understood in some other way.[2] In this chapter, I survey prevailing accounts of performance in opera studies (the *two-text model*) and philosophy (the *classical paradigm*), finding both to be inadequate to explain the motivations behind performances that intentionally deviate from the score or libretto. Although most opera scholars and critics assume that all opera performances are work-performances, I argue that some, such as Neuenfels's *Fledermaus*, are better understood according to the *ingredients model*, an account of spoken theater performance put forth by the philosopher James Hamilton.

The Two-Text Model

Scholars of spoken theater and dance recognize that not all performances in their respective art forms are work-performances. One of the reasons why this idea has not caught on among opera scholars stems from prevailing assumptions about the nature of operatic works. Most opera scholars understand the relationship between an opera and its performances in terms of the two-text model. This account was put forth by theater semioticians in the 1970s and entered discourse on opera with David Levin's *Unsettling Opera* (2007), the first monograph devoted to contemporary opera staging.

According to the two-text model, both the work being performed and its performance are regarded as texts. Levin refers to these as the *opera text* and the *performance text*.[3] Recall from chapter 1 that a text is merely the product the artist produced, whereas a work is more akin to a process or at the very least a contextualized product.[4] Accordingly, an opera text is merely the abstract set of sounds, words, and actions indicated in the score and libretto; a performance text is the particular sounds, vocal utterances, images, and movements the performers produce. Thus, performing an opera would seem to be a matter of playing the right notes and singing the right words. Even much so-called *Regieoper* (director's opera) meets these minimal requirements. Peter Sellars may interpret the work's score and libretto in an anachronistic way, using them to make different artistic statements from the ones they were intended to convey. Nevertheless, most of his productions display a high degree of compliance to the "letter" of their directives (the stage directions excepted).

Supporters of the two-text model explain productions that involve deviations from the score or libretto by observing that the opera text and performance text are encoded in different languages or media. Thus, they compare the act of performance to acts of translation or adaptation.[5] Due to the differences between the texts' languages or media, concerns of fidelity are regarded as irrelevant if not impossible to achieve.

Since the 1990s, the two-text model has been subject to heavy criticism by theater scholars, such as David Z. Saltz, and philosophers, such as James Hamilton. Saltz remarks that "we do not go to the theatre merely to see 'performance texts.' We go to see *plays*."[6] The two-text model cannot explain how seeing a production of *Hamlet* at the Stratford Festival amounts to seeing Shakespeare's play. "On this model," Hamilton observes, "one never sees the play, only a translation, transformation, or reconstitution of the play." He also notes that the two-text model does not evade the "fidelity standard. If a performance is a translation or even a reconstitution of a written text, it is still the written text that is responsible—at some level—for the performance."[7] Furthermore, attributing lapses in fidelity to differences in language or medium suggests that departures from the opera text result only from practical considerations, which is not always the case. Neuenfels's reasons for altering Carl Haffner and Richard Genée's libretto and going against Strauss's intentions with regard to the performance of the score stem not from an inability to realize their directives but from a desire for his production to tell a different story and make a different artistic point.

For scholars and performers interested in understanding works in light of the historical circumstances of their creation, another problem with the two-text model is its assumption that operatic works and performances are best understood as texts. The question of whether an opera is a text or a work is no mere philosophers' game. One's decisions have consequences for interpretation, both for scholars and for performers. Levin's decision to reduce operatic works to mere texts leads him to the paradoxical conclusion that Sellars was being faithful to Mozart and Da Ponte in his famous productions from the 1980s, not in spite of but through his anachronistic interpretation of their texts.[8]

In creating these productions, Sellars also seems to have been guided by the assumption that Mozart and Da Ponte's works are mere sequences of sounds and words. He pursued a high degree of fidelity to these components, even eschewing standard cuts and employing a period-instrument ensemble. Sellars's interpretation of these texts was, however, less informed by the actual influences on their creation (e.g., the conventions of late-eighteenth-century *opera buffa*) than on postmodern ideas about gender, sexuality, and human relationships. A case in point is his staging of the *lieto fine* (happy ending) of *Così fan tutte* (Pepsico Summerfare Festival, 1986). What Sellars supplies is neither happy nor anything an eighteenth-century audience would recognize as an ending. He turns a moment of reconciliation and reflection on the lessons learned at the "school for lovers" into one of social disharmony, ending in the psychological breakdown of the dramatis personae. With his staging choices, Sellars repudiates the function of the lieto fine in opera buffa, replacing it with a cynical and decidedly modern interpretation of the characters and their predicaments.[9] Both Sellars, in his staging, and Levin, in his discussion of Sellars's production, regard *Così fan tutte* not as a work but as a decontextualized text, a decision that leads them both to anachronistic interpretations.

Sellars's greater interest in the question of what *Così fan tutte* as a text could mean, as opposed to what its authors intended it to mean or what it actually meant to its original audiences, is understandable, given that his primary aim was to produce a performance that addressed present-day concerns. However, the music historian or performer who is more interested in the latter questions ought to reject the two-text model's recommendation to regard *Così fan tutte* as a text. For similar reasons, those with an interest in understanding opera *productions* as the products of human endeavor ought to regard them as works as opposed to mere texts.[10]

The Classical Paradigm

Philosophical discussions of musical performance have focused on Western instrumental music from the Classical era to the early twentieth century. For this reason, David Davies has christened the prevailing account the classical paradigm.[11] According to this account, performances are always performances of a preexisting work. Producing a work-performance involves intending to follow the score, interpreting its directives in light of the performing practices for which it was written, and achieving at least a moderate degree of success in doing so.

The musical components of most contemporary opera productions do fit this description. A director's decision to update an opera's setting often extends only to the mise-en-scène. As Richard Taruskin has observed, there have been "no techno Traviatas or R&B Götterdämmerungs."[12] Even productions that revise or add to the score typically do so in ways that would have been expected by the composer.

Before the middle of the nineteenth century, composers routinely wrote new arias for revivals of their works to better showcase the voices of the singers at hand or to adapt the work to changing tastes or social or political circumstances. Singers also had the power to make similar substitutions, without the approval of the work's authors (though usually pending the approval of the impresario).[13] Although many of these substitutions were made on an ad hoc basis, some dramatic situations attracted more substitutions than others.

One particularly favored moment was the "lesson scene" from the second act of Rossini and Cesare Sterbini's *Il barbiere di Siviglia* (1816). Count Almaviva (disguised as an impoverished student, Lindoro) has succeeded in wooing Rosina. All that remains to block their happy union is Rosina's guardian, Dr. Bartolo, who plans to marry her himself. To plan Rosina's escape, the Count gains admittance to their home in the guise of a substitute for Rosina's ailing singing teacher. At the beginning of her lesson, he asks her what she would like to sing. As Hilary Poriss has remarked, "No other question in the operatic repertory has ever received a greater variety of responses."[14] Substitutions to Rossini's original aria "Contro un cor che accende amore" began with the first Rosina, Geltrude Righetti-Giorgi, in the opera's second run in Bologna, the summer after its premiere in Rome.[15] By the 1860s, most singers were following Adelina Patti in inserting multiple arias, transforming the scene into a mini concert.[16] Given the work's comic tone and the scene's dramatic scenario, singers' choices were unfettered by the usual concerns of stylistic continuity with the rest of the work. One of Patti's favorite insertions was Henry Bishop's "Home, Sweet Home."

Barber's lesson scene is one of the few occasions where one is still apt to hear substitutions today. Most contemporary singers stick to music by Rossini, however.[17] In a move more closely mirroring nineteenth-century approaches, the director Aria Umezawa interpolated a popular tune from the 1980s in *The Barber of Cowtown* (Cowtown Opera, Calgary, 2014). As was commonplace prior to the twentieth century, the opera was performed in the language of its audience. Umezawa employed the English translation of the Schirmer edition with minor substitutions (e.g., "Cal'gry" for "Seville") and replaced the recitatives with new spoken dialogue filled with local color, including references to the Calgary Stampede and the Royal Canadian Mounted Police. When the Count asks Rosina what she would like to sing, she responds with "an aria from that new opera in town" and sings Rossini's "Contro un cor."[18] Lamenting the decline of musical taste, Bartolo decides to show the youngsters what "real music" sounds like. Instead of singing Rossini's own attempt at "bad music," Umezawa's Bartolo performs "Hello Calgary." This song by Frank Gari was commissioned by the city of Calgary in a bid to increase civic pride and played on local television in the 1980s.[19] Like many commercial musical offerings from this decade, the song has not aged well, though many middle-aged Calgarians still remember it with fondness. Umezawa's decision to perform *Il barbiere di Siviglia* in English and substitute music that was not even composed by Rossini may seem to violate the requirements of the classical paradigm. However, since such changes were commonplace in Rossini's time, *The Barber of Cowtown* does qualify as a work-performance of *Il barbiere di Siviglia*.

Where genuine exceptions arise is in productions that revise or add to scores of works composed after about the middle of the nineteenth century, when a greater concern for fidelity took hold in the opera world.[20] The Neuköllner Oper in Berlin billed *Iris Butterfly* (2016) as a production of Pietro Mascagni and Luigi Illica's *Iris* (1898), the now-forgotten work that sparked the fad of *japonaiserie* on the operatic stage (Illica also wrote the libretto to

Madama Butterfly [1904]). The plot concerns a naive girl named Iris who inspires the desire of the young lord Osaka. With the help of brothel-owner Kyoto, Osaka kidnaps Iris while she is attending a puppet show with her blind father. When Iris fails to understand what he wants from her and merely cries to return to her father and her garden, Osaka leaves her with Kyoto to use in his brothel. One day, her father recognizes Iris from the sound of her voice. Believing her to have left home of her own free will, he curses her, and she, overwhelmed with shame, commits suicide.

Illica and Mascagni's eroticization of this young girl and romanticization of her suicide would seem to have little to offer a modern audience. The director Fabian Gerhardt and his dramaturg Bernhard Glocksin found a way to present a modern spin on this sordid Orientalist tale through the phenomenon of *kawaii*, the cult of the cute or childlike in contemporary Japanese culture.[21] What set their work apart from other modernizations, such as those by Sellars, was that their updating extended to the production's aural components. While Mascagni's score was written for a typical late-Romantic orchestra, the Neuköllner Oper performed an arrangement by Alexandra Barkovskaya and Derik Listemann for only seven players: keyboard, synthesizer, horn, flute, violin, bass, and percussion. Just as Mascagni evoked the sound of Japanese music in the embedded puppet show through the use of shamisen and Japanese percussion instruments, Barkovskaya and Listemann incorporated elements of the musical sound-world of their setting—namely, J-pop. Since these additions to the score were not part of the performing practices for which Mascagni was writing, *Iris Butterfly* would not qualify as a work-performance under the classical paradigm.

Revisions or additions to an opera's libretto are even more common. Libretti are often abridged for length or to remove passages that are no longer politically correct. Most productions of *Die Zauberflöte* (1791), for example, omit some of the more sexist and racist passages of Emanuel Schikaneder's spoken dialogue. Although opera in translation is not as commonplace as it once was, there are still opera houses—most notably, the English National Opera and the Komische Oper Berlin—that perform all works in the local language.

If such textual changes were standard practice in the tradition to which the work belongs, they do not pose obstacles to a classical-paradigm description. Thus, works composed prior to about the middle of the nineteenth century tend to admit more leeway in this regard. Nevertheless, there is reason to doubt the accuracy of Sellars's advertising of his production of "Henry Purcell's *The Indian Queen*." Although Sellars used all of the extant music for this quasi-operatic fragment (as well as many other nonoperatic compositions by Purcell), the story, Susan McClary remarks, "has virtually nothing in common with the play [of the same title by John Dryden] for which the composer wrote his music."[22] The story Sellars's production tells is borrowed from Rosario Aguilar's novel *La niña blanca y los pájaros sin pies* (1992), a fictional recuperation of women's perspectives on the Spanish colonization of Central America. Like a jeweler providing old gems with a modern setting, Sellars used Purcell's airs and choruses to ornament and amplify spoken narration from an English translation of Aguilar's novel. Even though musical and textual revisions were commonplace in operatic revivals during Purcell's time, Sellars's decision to discard Dryden's plot and substitute a new one that articulates artistic and political statements in opposition to those of Purcell and Dryden's work prevents a classical-paradigm understanding of Sellars's production.

Textual revisions or additions to works composed after the middle of the nineteenth century are less common but not unheard of. Peter Konwitschny inserted new spoken text to Hans Sachs's infamous final speech in his production of Wagner's *Die Meistersinger von Nürnberg* (Hamburg, 2002). When Sachs speaks of "foreign mist" obscuring what is "German and genuine," the other singers break character and interrupt him (the relevant portion of Sachs's speech is quoted in chap. 8). For the first time in the work, the music comes to a halt and the singers launch into a spoken debate about the morality of expressing such sentiments today.[23] Even though Konwitschny's additions were much less extensive than Sellars's, they also disqualify his production from being a production of Wagner's work, according to the classical paradigm, due to the higher level of fidelity expected of work-performances in Wagner's time.

Regarding the dramatic and visual components of opera performances, few contemporary opera directors pay much heed to the stage directions detailed in the libretto or, for some nineteenth-century operas, staging manuals (*livrets de mise en scène* or *disposizioni sceniche*).[24] Still fewer ground their work in current research into historical practices of scenic design, acting, or gesture. Attempts to subject the visual dimensions of opera to the same level of authenticity expected of the musical components have largely been confined to quasi-scholarly organizations, such as the Cambridge Handel Opera Group, founded in 1985 by the Handel scholar Andrew Jones.[25] One of the rare examples at a major opera house is Benjamin Lazar's production of Lully and Quinault's *Cadmus et Hermione* (Opéra comique, 2008), which not only was based on Baroque principles of design, costuming, acting, and gesture but also was lit solely by candles.[26]

Even when historical research enters into the working processes of directors and their production teams, considerations of practicality and accessibility trump those of authenticity. Toronto's Opera Atelier specializes in productions of pre-nineteenth-century repertoire, in which the qualifier "historically informed" extends to what one sees onstage. On their website, the company's artistic directors Marshall Pynkoski (stage director) and Jeannette Zingg (choreographer) describe their work as motivated by a "desire to explore the original intention of composers, librettists and choreographers and to try to understand their creations in the context in which they were first created. This does not mean that we are a museum company or are slavishly copying something that has been created in the past, rather this interest in 'original intention' becomes the catalyst that allows us to create something brand new. . . . Opera Atelier strives to create productions that would have been recognized and respected in their own time while providing a thrilling experience for modern audiences."[27] In other words, the impetus is historical, but the abiding concern is one of providing present-day audiences with a satisfying experience.

Opera Atelier's production of Lully and Quinault's *Persée* (2000) exemplifies how Pynkoski and Zingg balance concerns of accessibility and authenticity.[28] Although prologues played important political and dramaturgical functions in Lully's operas (see the discussion of authorial narrators in chap. 3), they decided to begin with Act I. While Zingg's choreography was based on the conventions of French Baroque dance, she also incorporated gestures from more modern idioms, such as classical ballet. Pynkoski eschewed the superfluous stage business many modern directors assume to be necessary to entertain audiences today. The singers were largely stationary while they sang and addressed their utterances to the audience, not to one another. However, he also incorporated some deliberately anachronistic elements. Most notably, he and the baritone Michael Chioldi decided to model the character of Méduse on a modern drag queen. In the words of the French literature scholar Benoît Bolduc, the beginning of Act III bore a closer resemblance to a "Las Vegas night-club act than that of a noble entertainment at the Académie Royale de Musique."[29]

In sum, the classical paradigm has some applicability to the musical performances of contemporary opera productions. However, looking to directors' attitudes toward the libretto, particularly the stage directions, many exceptions arise.

In response to a similar incongruity between the classical paradigm and the norms of spoken theater performance, David Davies has put forth an alternative account that describes the practices of spoken theater. Since few theater companies aim to satisfy all of the directions contained within the script, he proposes understanding the relevant intention as one of aiming to be true to the work's "emplotted point."[30] In other words, producing a work-performance of a play involves not merely conveying a similar point to that intended by the playwright but doing so through a performance of the intended plot or event sequence, broadly conceived.

Applied to opera, Davies's looser version of the classical paradigm would recognize as work-performances the performances of late-Romantic and modern repertoire that contain revisions to the score or libretto (provided that they did not substantially alter the work's point or plot), performances in languages other than the one(s) employed by the librettist, and performances with alternative settings (provided that the chosen setting was conducive to conveying the work's point). However, requiring that the production be faithful to both the work's plot and point still excludes Sellars's *Indian Queen* and Konwitschny's *Meistersinger*. Wagner intended audiences to adopt Sachs's xenophobic views as their own, not to think critically about the dangers of this kind of nationalistic rhetoric, as Konwitschny's revisions encourage his audiences to do.

Even productions containing faithful performances of an opera's score may not qualify as work-performances under Davies's account. Katharina Thoma's *Ariadne auf Naxos* (Glyndebourne, 2013) contains an unadulterated performance of the opera's music and sung text but nevertheless conveys a substantially different plot from the one intended by Strauss and Hofmannsthal. As discussed in chapter 3, they intended Act I to represent an act of internal, theatrical storytelling. The prologue dramatizes the preparations for an embedded operatic performance, and Act I represents either the performance of "Ariadne auf Naxos" and "The Faithless Zerbinetta and Her Four Lovers" or the hypothetical result of such a mash-up.

Act I of Thoma's production represents neither of these possibilities. She decided to set her production in Glyndebourne in World War II, in recognition of the country house's role as a home for evacuee children from London. An air raid prevents the fictional performance from occurring. Act I opens not with Ariadne on Naxos but in a makeshift infirmary at Glyndebourne where the Composer and Prima Donna are convalescing. The latter has suffered a blow to the head and believes herself to be her character, Ariadne. Although the libretto does not prescribe the Composer to appear at all in Act I, he plays an important role in Thoma's revised plot, most notably by preventing the Prima Donna from committing suicide. Zerbinetta and her comedian colleagues are transformed into members of the Entertainments National Service Association (who entertained British troops during the war), the nymphs are nurses, and Bacchus is an RAF pilot who has been shot down near the estate.

In spite of the many deviations from Strauss and Hofmannsthal's plot, Thoma's production makes surprisingly good sense of the work's music and sung text. Vladimir Jurowski, who conducted the production's initial run, even suggested that Thoma's new scenario improved the work by increasing the dramatic unity between its two parts and presenting characters that were "human, three-dimensional." In so doing, she "made the drama, which evolves between all of them an absolutely plausible . . . chain of events, which you can follow and which you can feel for. . . . There is a clear dramatic narrative" to Thoma's production, something he admits "never [to have] detected in *Ariadne* before."[31]

Thoma and her team not only remained true to many of the work's points but perhaps even made those points more effectively for the modern spectator with little knowledge of or interest in Greek mythology. The critic and opera blogger Charlotte Valori remarked that "Thoma brings the major preoccupation of Strauss's work, the relationship between art and real life, to the fore: how art can distract us, in a selfish way, from grim reality (fiddling while Rome burns), but also how art can heal us, and help us to understand or make sense of life's (sometimes senseless) chain of events."[32] Matthew Rye, writing for bachtrack, noted how "her staging illuminates the serious themes of Strauss and Hofmannsthal's concoction . . . : high art versus low art; art itself transcending catastrophe; love overcoming death."[33]

Despite these merits, the majority of the press surrounding this production was decidedly less positive. Critics who expected to see a performance of *Ariadne auf Naxos* were, understandably, confused and disappointed by the lack of correspondence between the events of Thoma's Act I and those Strauss and Hoffmansthal intended to be enacted. Many were so fixated on the story they were expecting to see that they were unable to follow the story it did in fact present. Sam Smith, writing for musicOMH, complained that "this extra layer of activity on top of the original plot proves very distracting, and might make those unfamiliar with the work struggle to grasp what is happening. This is because it could be hard to ascertain which parts of the action constitute the original story, and which the additional commentary."[34] Indeed, spectators without prior knowledge of Strauss and Hofmannsthal's work would have difficulty separating the portions directly arising from their work and those that were Thoma's invention. Yet as Claire Seymour admitted in her review for *Opera Today*, "taken on its own terms Thoma's concept works well."³⁵ Those who took the production on its own terms tended to find something in it to appreciate, but those who spent the evening cataloging the differences between the production and the advertised work largely did not.

The Ingredients Model

Theater theorists have explored ways of approaching productions like Thoma's "Carry on Ariadne" on their own terms, not as productions of preexisting works.³⁶ Although the term *ingredients model* was coined only recently by James Hamilton, the idea has a long history dating at least as far back as the writings of Antonin Artaud (1896–1948).³⁷ Instead of regarding theater performances as mere executions of preexisting works, the production is regarded as a work in its own right (what I will refer to as a *performance-work*), one that may or may not employ preexisting works as ingredients. Unlike the two-text model, the ingredients model recognizes the possibility of theater performances that are not work-performances. Even in the case of performances that do take inspiration from preexisting works, Hamilton denies that one ought to regard them as performances *of* those works and provides an alternative account of how audiences identify when they have seen a performance of the same performance-work again.

Although Hamilton's focus is on spoken theater, the ingredients model has considerable applicability to opera performance and not just so-called Regieoper.³⁸ Rachel Cowgill's description of operatic performance practice in England prior to the 1830s is strikingly similar to Hamilton's characterization of the ingredients model: "an opera was regarded as raw material to be cut, altered, and adapted in response to the tastes of the town and the specialties of the principal singers. Numbers from other operas were freely interpolated into a new piece and/or substituted for its existing numbers."³⁹

By the 1810s, a new, more faithful approach to opera performance emerged to rival that of pastiche. Christina Fuhrmann illustrates the differences in these approaches by comparing two productions that premiered in London in 1814, both purporting to be of François Adrien Boieldieu and Claude de Saint-Just's *Jean de Paris* (1812). "At Drury Lane, Samuel James Arnold and Charles Edward Horn continued patterns of pastiche. Horn discarded Boieldieu's score entirely in favour of a few of his own selections and Arnold significantly rewrote Saint-Just's libretto to highlight his star performers." At Covent Garden, Henry Bishop and Isaac Pocock "vaunted their preservation of Boieldieu's score, of 'the' work." Bishop and Pocock's ideas of what "preservation" entails were, however, rather different from those that prevail today. Bishop discarded half of Boieldieu's score, subjected the remainder to extensive cuts and revisions, and inserted many vocal pieces of his own composition. Pocock, in the role of librettist, "split the comic innkeeper into two roles, one spoken and one sung, embellished the spoken half of the role, rearranged several musical numbers and created new dramatic situations for interpolated numbers." Since few spectators had any way of accessing Boieldieu and Saint-Just's work, these productions were, in effect, evaluated on their own terms or in comparison with one another, rather than as productions of *Jean de Paris*.[40]

Additional evidence in favor of understanding even Bishop's "preservations" as performance-works under the ingredients model, rather than as work-performances, may be found in the reception of the 1827 revival of his version of *Le nozze di Figaro* (premiered at Covent Garden in 1819). The primary source for Bishop's libretto was not Da Ponte but Thomas Holcroft's 1784 English-language version of Beaumarchais's play. Bishop not only included the same plot changes (e.g., the excision of Marcellina) but reproduced large stretches of dialogue. He cut half of Mozart's numbers, thereby transforming the Count into a spoken role. Bishop derived the rest of the score from other Mozart operas (*Don Giovanni*, *Così fan tutte*, and *Idomeneo*), Rossini's *Tancredi* (1813), and some of his own compositions.

Bishop's version was so popular that Covent Garden was in the habit of performing it every year. In 1827, Lucia Vestris appeared as Susanna and interpolated a song for which she was known, Horn and George Darley's "I've Been Roaming" (1824). Protests from the audience were so vociferous that Vestris left the stage. Patrons who had attended in expectation of hearing her signature tune (which had been advertised on the playbill) managed to cheer her back onstage, where she finished her song. Given that "I've Been Roaming" was hardly the only foreign ingredient in this production, why was it the target of such scorn? Although it was not the only non-Mozart aria in the performance, it was the only ingredient foreign to *Bishop's Figaro*, suggesting that *Bishop's Figaro* was the work spectators—at least those displeased by "I've Been Roaming"—were paying to see, not the opera by Mozart and Da Ponte.[41]

The ingredients model can also help us understand certain trends in contemporary opera performance. Barbara Beyer's 2005 collection of interviews with leading European opera directors contains many statements that are suggestive of ingredients-model thinking. Beyer, herself a director and dramaturg active in Germany, asks Peter Konwitschny (of the interrupted

Meistersinger), "To what extent must we, may we, or should we consider opera to be mere material?" Konwitschny responds, "It is not our responsibility to stage these works as the authors originally intended; how could that even happen? Our job is to ask specific, important questions in such a way that they stimulate discussion. The operas themselves are the material; they are no end in themselves."[42]

In conversation with Jossi Wieler and Sergio Morabito, Beyer suggests that "opera today only has a chance if we can forget everything we know about historical conditions and contexts, if we commit ourselves to an irresponsible and irreverent attitude toward this medium. . . . For example, there might be a number of new ways to deal with the score beyond re-instrumentation: not just cutting or moving arias but also inserting different music and so forth. In this sense, opera can be thought of rather like a quarry, a reserve of materials." Wieler concurs, suggesting that we "approach each piece as a world premiere," which would necessitate "conductors collaborating closely with dramaturges, as well as with someone to compose the work anew, as it were."[43]

Although Neuenfels's *Fledermaus*, Konwitschny's *Meistersinger*, and Sellars's *Indian Queen* were all billed as work-performances, due to their revisions and additions to these works' scores and libretti and articulation of artistic statements that contradict those of the works ostensibly being performed, I suggest that they are more coherently understood as performance-works along the lines Hamilton suggests. One opera company that has embraced this way of thinking is Joel Ivany's Against the Grain Theatre, based in Toronto. They produced a Mozart–Da Ponte trilogy for the twenty-first century, composed of *Figaro's Wedding* (2013), *#UncleJohn* (2014), and *A Little Too Cozy* (2016). While Sellars was content merely to modernize the subtitles, Ivany accompanied his updating with newly fashioned English-language libretti, tailored to his new dramatic scenarios. For example, Alfonso's wager in *Così fan tutte* became a reality-TV dating show in *A Little Too Cozy*. To facilitate performance by an indie opera company in unconventional venues, such as the studios of the Canadian Broadcasting Company, Against the Grain's music director Topher Mokrzewski rearranged Mozart's score for string quartet plus piano. Given *A Little Too Cozy*'s new libretto and musical arrangement, Against the Grain characterized their production as "a modern adaptation and translation of *Così fan tutte* by W. A. Mozart" rather than as a production of *Così fan tutte*.[44]

The ingredients model is also able to provide a more satisfying explanation of pastiche productions, which have been making a comeback in the twenty-first century. The Metropolitan Opera's *The Enchanted Island* (dir. Phelim

McDermott, 2011) used music by Handel, Vivaldi, Rameau, Purcell, and Campra to adorn a libretto by Jeremy Sams, which centered around the lovers from *A Midsummer Night's Dream*, who had been shipwrecked on Prospero's island (from *The Tempest*) during the course of their honeymoon. Robert Lepage's *Nightingale and Other Short Fables* (Canadian Opera Company, 2009) contained not only Stravinsky and Stepan Mitusov's *Nightingale* (1914) but also various nonoperatic works by the composer including *Renard* (1922), *Ragtime* (1920), the *Pribaoutki* (1918), and Three Pieces for Clarinet Solo (1919). More eclectically, Opera Erratica's *Orlando lunaire* (dir. Patrick Eakin Young, 2010) was a mash-up of Handel's *Orlando* (1733) and Schoenberg's *Pierrot lunaire* (1912) for soprano and countertenor.

I suggest that the ingredients model also provides a better way of thinking about some productions that contain faithful performances of the score, such as Thoma's *Ariadne* and most of Sellars's updatings.[45] Sellars's *Hercules* (Chicago Lyric, 2011) recasts the titular character as an American soldier suffering from PTSD after his tour in Iraq or Afghanistan. If Handel and his librettist Thomas Broughton's point is understood at a sufficiently abstract level—as a commentary on the difficulties soldiers face reintegrating into civilian life, for example—one could argue that Sellars's production is faithful to the work's point by exploring its relevance to contemporary society. The difficulty is that Sellars treats Handel and Broughton's work as a mere text. His interpretation of the score and libretto is not informed by the conventions of Baroque *opera seria* but by an interest in convincing present-day audiences of the dramatic efficacy of Baroque opera.

In Sellars's director's notes, he provides the following explanation of coloratura and *da capo* aria form:

> A single sentence is put through 25 permutations for the first five minutes with individual words . . . having between 25 and 50 notes: the word itself is a crisis, a meltdown, a stuttering impossibility even to speak—pushed to vocal extremes which demand the highest level of virtuosity from the performer while revealing the unfathomable damage of the character. Then there is a contrasting subject [the B section] which presents an opposing idea as if to say, 'I'm fine and I'll put the previous subject behind me.' And then the previous subject [the A section] returns repeating all over again with even wilder ornaments and tests of vocal and emotional endurance. We are not just fine.
>
> Handel's purpose in his musical structure is to depict the causes, the symptoms, and the effects of trauma.[46]

Given that coloratura and da capo form were standard features of Baroque opera seria, used to express the gamut of affective and psychological states, it is doubtful that their being employed in *Hercules* was intended to represent psychological trauma, especially that understood in a quasi-Freudian manner. Sellars's production and director's notes are of dubious value as lessons in the historical influences on Handel and Broughton's work. However, from discussing Sellars's work with students new to opera, it is clear that he is successful at making Baroque opera meaningful to such spectators by showing how works even centuries old can be used to speak to present-day social and political concerns, such as the human costs of the War on Terror. This is where the value of Sellars's work lies, in my view, but these are precisely the dimensions that are obscured by the current tendency to understand his work in terms of the classical paradigm.

At this point, one might wonder whether the ingredients model may be the best way of understanding all opera performances. That is the argument Hamilton advances in connection with spoken theater. He claims that "a [theater] performance is . . . never a performance *of* some other work nor is it ever a performance *of* a text or *of* anything initiated in a text."[47] This claim can be taken in one of two ways, Sherri Irvin notes. As an *empirical* claim about the prevailing way people understand the art of theater, it is clearly false. Many theater companies aim to afford audiences perceptual experiences of preexisting works, and many spectators attend the theater with the expectation that they will be provided with such experiences. Hamilton recognizes this incongruity and argues that a large portion of the art form's practitioners and patrons are under some sort of mass delusion. This suggests that he intended the foregoing statement as a *normative* claim; in other words, he is proposing that theater performances *should* be identified and evaluated without reference to preexisting works or texts.[48]

Irvin argues that the normative claim ought to be rejected for spoken theater, and for similar reasons, I reject it for opera. Appreciating an opera production involves understanding its relation (if any) to preexisting works. Spectators approaching Opera Atelier's *Persée* along the lines Hamilton recommends may incorrectly assume that Opera Atelier was responsible for inventing the plot and composing the music. Those who regard it as a freestanding performance-work are not in a good position with which to understand the particular challenges of Opera Atelier's artistic mission, which is not only to perform pre-nineteenth-century repertory with a high degree of fidelity but also to do so in a way that is entertaining for audiences today.

On the other hand, critics who approached Thoma's *Ariadne* as a performance-work were more successful in appreciating her artistic achievement than those who regarded it as a work-performance. Critics taking an ingredients-model approach realized that it would be wrong to fault the production for its lack of fidelity to Strauss and Hofmannsthal's work since Thoma was not intending to perform that work. Charlotte Valori and Matthew Rye were receptive to the story her production presented and were able to see the benefits of her deviations from Hofmannsthal's story, such as the continuity she created between the production's two parts. Thoma undertook a different sort of endeavor in her *Ariadne auf Naxos* than Opera Atelier did in their production of *Persée*. These differences are elided in Hamilton's unitary account.

Those seeking to apply the ingredients model to opera also face a difficulty arising from the medium-specific features of this art form. Hamilton recognizes that some of the ingredients used in theatrical performances may have an independent existence as a "work of literary art"—for example, Shakespeare's *Hamlet*. Such works, he claims, have "no theatrical mode of presentation . . . they are *only* texts to be read."[49] It is possible, though arguably not ideal, to gain an experiential engagement with *Hamlet* by reading a copy of its script. Few people are even *capable* of gaining an experiential engagement with an opera by reading its score. The supporter of an ingredients-model understanding of opera is thus faced with the problem of explaining how one goes about appreciating the works of composers and librettists if not by experiencing performances of their works.

Opera Performance: Two Paradigms

Due to the diversity of operatic performance practice, both contemporary and historical, a single account is not going to describe everything that goes on in the rehearsal room or onstage. I suggest that contemporary opera performance can be divided into two distinct paradigms. Some performances are work-performances under the classical paradigm, while others are performance-works under the ingredients model.[50] In this final section, I define more specifically the conditions under which it is appropriate to regard an opera performance as a work-performance.

Work-performances are examples of what philosophers term *instances* of the works on which they are based. What makes something an instance of a work is the role it can play in appreciating that work. More specifically, an instance provides audiences with an experience of the work by making manifest if not all of the properties that have bearing on the work's appreciation then at least a good many of them. For a performance to be an instance in this sense, some degree of fidelity to the work is required.

In light of current opinion in opera and music-performance studies that such concerns trammel performers' rights to free expression, I wish to be clear that my defense of fidelity is confined to work-performances. I am not placing any limits on what performers are at liberty to do. I am merely suggesting that if they wish their performance to be a work-performance—rather than a performance-work under the ingredients model—it must bear at least some degree of fidelity to the work ostensibly being performed. The less fidelity it displays, the less the performance is able to play an experiential role in the appreciation of that work, and the more apropos an ingredients-model description will become.

What does an operatic performance need to be faithful to? As I have suggested in connection with Thoma's *Ariadne* and Sellars's *Hercules*, mere textual fidelity is insufficient. In writing an opera, composers and librettists do not wish to put forth a mere sequence of words and sounds. They intend these utterances to convey a plot or event sequence, which in turn makes an artistic statement of some sort. As such, there is reason to doubt that performances that diverge significantly from the intended plot or point are in fact performances of the work in question. Thus, David Davies's emplotted-point-based version of the classical paradigm would seem to provide a better basis for identifying operatic work-performances.

Yet the possibility of techno *Traviatas* and R&B *Götterdämmerungs* suggests that more is required in the case of opera. Imagine that an opera company, in a bid to attract a younger clientele, hired Lin-Manuel Miranda to take the libretto to *Götterdämmerung* and reset it, in German and without alteration, to hip-hop and R&B. The result would convey the plot of *Götterdämmerung*. Although it is difficult to imagine that Miranda's musical choices would have no effect on the work's point, let's suppose that he stuck as closely as possible to Wagner's intentions in this regard. Such a production would meet the requirements of Davies's revised account of the classical paradigm, despite its lack of Wagner's music. In the case of spoken theater, a performance that successfully conveys the play's point and plot will, invariably, display a suitable degree of textual fidelity. In the case of opera, I suggest that work-performances must not only be true to the work's point but must convey that point through a moderately faithful performance of the work's plot and score.

As opera historians have amply shown, what qualifies as a faithful performance of an opera at one time and place may not pass muster at another. Rossini and his audiences recognized as work-performances those that contained arias by other composers, but Wagner and his devotees would have surely rejected the possibility of a performance of *Tristan* that concluded with anything but Wagner's *Liebestod*. Mozart and the audiences of his 1789 Viennese revival of *Le nozze di Figaro*—featuring his new arias for Adriana Ferrarese (appearing as Susanna)—recognized the performances as performances of *Figaro*. Yet when Cecilia Bartoli performed these same arias in the Metropolitan Opera's 1998 production, many critics, and even the production's director, Jonathan Miller, harbored doubts. In response, several opera scholars have come to Bartoli's defense, citing the historical practice of aria substitution.[51] I add my voice to their chorus and abstract their argument concerning this particular case into a general rule. What qualifies as a faithful performance of a work can be assessed only in conjunction with the performing practices for which that work was written.[52] A few more examples will clarify my meaning.

When performing *bel canto* (early nineteenth-century Italian opera: Rossini, Bellini, Donizetti), it is not merely *permissible* to ornament repeated passages and insert cadenzas not indicated in the score. Given that the music was designed with these practices in mind, they are *necessary* to performing this repertoire with a high degree of fidelity.[53] Without these variations, the repetitions would become tedious and thus give a false impression of the composer's skill. At the risk of stating the obvious, introducing these sorts of ornaments to performances of Wagner would not be to perform his works faithfully. Part of Wagner's point in composing his works as he did was to limit the freedom granted to singers and the focus on vocal *fioratura* in opera more generally.

Since singers in nineteenth-century Italy were contracted to a house for an entire season, performing a variety of roles, not all of which were ideally suited to their voices, it was permissible to make *puntature*, minor alterations of the vocal line to make it easier to sing.[54] Unlike ornaments and cadenzas, such changes were made only if the singer was otherwise unable to sing the role to good effect. Thus, while permissible, modern singers should not go out of their way to introduce puntature. For those working in the *stagione* system and contracted on a role-by-role basis, such alterations are typically unnecessary.

Aria substitution and insertion are similarly permissible, but not required, of performances of Italian opera prior to about the middle of the nineteenth century. Especially since Bartoli performed arias Mozart himself wrote for *Figaro*, critics were wrong to cast doubt about the performance's legitimacy.

Some opera performances, such as those by Opera Atelier, are produced with the aim of allowing audiences to experience preexisting works and understand their places in history. Work-performances not only must be faithful to the work's point but also must convey that point through a moderately faithful performance of the work's plot and score, as defined by the performing practices for which it was written. Many opera performances, both historical and contemporary, do not fit this description. Such performances, I argue, are better understood according to the ingredients model. Examples include performances that contain substantial revisions to the work's score or libretto (e.g., Neuenfels's *Fledermaus, Iris Butterfly*, and *A Little Too Cozy*), combine its texts with new ingredients (e.g., Bishop's *Figaro* and *Orlando lunaire*), or use them as mere vehicles with which to present a new story (e.g., Thoma's *Ariadne*) or to comment on contemporary social or political concerns (e.g., Sellars's *Hercules*).

The tendency to understand all of the foregoing approaches under the classical paradigm has led to confusion, even outrage, on the part of spectators, who frequently bring the wrong kinds of expectations with them when they enter the theater and are predictably dissatisfied with what they find there. Opera companies ought to have the freedom to put on productions like Neuenfels's *Fledermaus*. But rather than billing them as work-performances, they might consider following the lead of Against the Grain Theatre and encouraging spectators to appreciate them on their own terms as performance-works. The final two chapters show how these two accounts of performance can help us understand the landscape of contemporary opera production in North America and Europe.

Notes

1. Ulrich Müller, "*Regietheater*/Director's Theater," in *Oxford Handbook of Opera*, ed. Helen M. Greenwald (New York: Oxford University Press, 2014), 589; Clemens Risi, "Opera in Performance: In Search of New Analytical Approaches," *Opera Quarterly* 27, no. 2–3 (2011): 286–87.

2. Exceptions include Christina Fuhrmann, *Foreign Opera at the London Playhouses: From Mozart to Bellini* (Cambridge: Cambridge University Press, 2015), who approaches early nineteenth-century productions of opera in England as adaptations; Philip Gossett, *Divas and Scholars: Performing Italian Opera* (Chicago: University of Chicago Press, 2006), 204, on Peter Brook's *La tragédie de Carmen* (1981).

3. David J. Levin, *Unsettling Opera: Staging Mozart, Verdi, Wagner, and Zemlinsky* (Chicago: University of Chicago Press, 2007), 11.

4. For an argument that artworks ought to be regarded as actions as opposed to objects, refer to David Davies, *Art as Performance* (Malden: Blackwell, 2004). Admittedly, this is a controversial position in philosophy. Even under the more mainstream view that musical works are contextualized sound structures (see, for example, Jerrold Levinson, "What a Musical Work Is," in *Music, Art, and Metaphysics: Essays in Philosophical Aesthetics* [Oxford: Oxford University Press, 2011], 63–88), they are still not reducible to the directives contained within the score, as Levin and Sellars seem to assume.

5. Levin, *Unsettling Opera*, ch. 3, explores the comparison with translation; Clemens Risi, "The Gestures of the Dutchman: Wagner's Staging Instructions, 1852 and Today," *Opera Quarterly* 28, no. 3–4 (2012): 169, employs both metaphors.

6. David Z. Saltz, "When Is the Play the Thing? Analytic Aesthetics and Dramatic Theory," *Theatre Research International* 20, no. 3 (1995): 266.

7. James R. Hamilton, *The Art of Theater* (Malden: Wiley-Blackwell, 2007), 28.

8. Levin, *Unsettling Opera*, ch. 3.

9. Mary Hunter, "Window to the Work, or Mirror of Our Preconceptions? Peter Sellars's Production of *Così fan tutte*," *Repercussions* 4, no. 2 (1995): 49, also singles out this moment when observing that Sellars often subverts the meanings the work was intended to convey. For a laudatory discussion of the ending of this production, refer to Susan McClary, *The Passions of Peter Sellars* (Ann Arbor: University of Michigan Press, 2019), 33, 35.

10. I use the term *work* to refer to the primary focus or foci of appreciation in an art form. Some philosophers have advanced more demanding accounts of what a work is. For example, Andrew Kania, "All Play and No Work: An Ontology of Jazz," *Journal of Aesthetics and Art Criticism* 69, no. 4 (2011): 397–98, admits that "performances of classical [music] are a primary focus of appreciation" yet withholds work-status from them because they are not "enduring entities." David Davies, *Philosophy of the Performing Arts* (Malden: Wiley-Blackwell, 2011), 143–48, argues that performances of classical instrumental music are rarely works in their own right because they fail to articulate sufficient artistic content beyond that which is prescribed by the work being performed. I thank Andrew Kania for helping me to clarify my stance on this issue.

11. David Davies introduced the terms *classical paradigm*, *work-performance*, and *performance-work* in *Philosophy of the Performing Arts* (2011). A more precise definition of the conditions under which a performance of Western instrumental music ought to be understood as a work-performance may be found in Stephen Davies, *Musical Works and Performances: A Philosophical Exploration* (Oxford: Oxford University Press, 2001), 182.

12. Richard Taruskin, "Setting Limits," in *The Danger of Music and Other Anti-Utopian Essays* (Berkeley: University of California Press, 2009), 459. Others who have observed the different standards of fidelity expected of operas' visual components, as compared with their aural ones (though with different recommendations about what to do about this double standard), include Nicholas Cook, *Beyond the Score: Music as Performance* (New York: Oxford University Press, 2013), 399; Andrew V. Jones, "Staging a Handel Opera," *Early Music* 34, no. 2 (2006): 285; Roger Parker, *Remaking the Song: Operatic Visions and Revisions from Handel to Berio* (Berkeley: University of California Press, 2006), 5, 12.

13. Hilary Poriss, *Changing the Score: Arias, Prima Donnas, and the Authority of Performance* (Oxford: Oxford University Press, 2009), 17–18.

14. Ibid., 135.

15. Righetti-Giorgi substituted "La mia pace, la mia calma," of unknown authorship. Ibid.

16. Patti was not the first to take such an approach. In a review from 1848, Pauline Viardot is described as performing a series of "Spanish songs" and playing Chopin mazurkas on the piano. Ibid., 145, 158.

17. Marilyn Horne and Cecilia Bartoli have performed "Tanti affetti in tal momento" from *La donna del lago* (1819), and Lesley Garret has sung "Bel raggio lusinghier" from *Semiramide* (1823). Ibid., 136.

18. Umezawa's spoken dialogue has not been published. I am grateful to her for providing me access to her script and director's notes.

19. Aria Umezawa, in an email to the author from January 26, 2018, communicated that her choice of song was inspired by Ira Glass, "No Place Like Home," episode of podcast *This American Life*, March 14, 2014, http://www.thisamericanlife.org/520/no-place-like-home.

20. Poriss, *Changing the Score*, ch. 1, identifies the late 1830s as a pivotal period for Italian operatic performance practice, in which the freedom singers previously enjoyed to insert

music of their own choosing into their roles was being curtailed. However, as her discussion of *Barber*'s "lesson scene" testifies, aria substitution persisted at certain moments of certain works well into the second half of the nineteenth century.

21. Bernhard Glocksin, "So süss, dass es schmerzt. Mascagni, *Iris*, Japan," in *Iris Butterfly* (program) (Berlin: Neuköllner Oper, 2016), 10, mentions the Japanese popstar Kyary Pamyu Pamyu as a particular influence. I thank Zoey M. Cochran for mentioning this production and for sharing her copy of the program.

22. McClary, *Passions of Peter Sellars*, 144. The sources of the added music and text are identified in the booklet to Peter Sellars, dir., *The Indian Queen* (Sony Classical, 2016), DVD.

23. Tim Ashley, "Wagner Interrupted," *Guardian*, last modified November 23, 2002, http://www.theguardian.com/music/2002/nov/23/classicalmusicandopera.artsfeatures; Robert Sollich, "Staging Wagner—and Its History: *Die Meistersinger von Nürnberg* on a Contemporary Stage," *Wagner Journal* 3, no. 1 (2009): 8–9. Konwitschny has made similar insertions in other works. Barbara Beyer, "Interviews with Contemporary Opera Directors, Selected from Barbara Beyer's *Warum Oper? Gespräche mit Opernregisseuren* (2005)," trans. Gundula Kreuzer and Paul Chaikin, *Opera Quarterly* 27, no. 2–3 (2011): 310, mentions his *Don Giovanni* (Komische Oper Berlin, 2003), in which "Don Ottavio interrupts his aria 'Il mio tesoro' to recite Mozart's final letter to his father."

24. Livrets de mise en scène and disposizioni sceniche were published guides to restaging an opera when it was revived or toured the provinces, providing information about the design of sets, costumes, lighting, and blocking. Due to the complexities of staging grand opera, it is unsurprising that the Paris Opéra was the first to produce such guides, beginning in the 1820s. Verdi introduced the practice to Italy after producing a livret for *Les vêpres siciliennes*, premiered at the Opéra in 1855. Gossett, *Divas and Scholars*, 454–61.

25. Jones, "Staging a Handel Opera." The Cambridge Handel Opera Group disbanded in 2013 but was resurrected in 2016 as the Cambridge Handel Opera Company.

26. Mary Hunter, "Historically Informed Performance," in *Oxford Handbook of Opera*, ed. Helen M. Greenwald (Oxford: Oxford University Press, 2014), 620, 611. Electric lighting was required to film the production.

27. "About Opera Atelier," OperaAtelier.com, accessed March 5, 2020, http://www.operaatelier.com/about. The Belgian director Sigrid T'Hooft describes her work at the Drottningholm Palace Theatre in Sweden in similar terms. David Wiles, "Eighteenth-Century Acting: The Search for Authenticity," in *The Theatre of Drottningholm—Then and Now: Performance between the 18th and 21st Centuries*, ed. Willmar Sauter and David Wiles (Stockholm: Taberg Media Group, 2014), 196.

28. For a detailed discussion of this production and its relationship to Baroque performance practice, refer to Antonia L. Banducci, "The Opera Atelier Performance (Toronto, 2000): The Spirit of Lully on the Modern Stage," *Journal of Seventeenth-Century Music* 10, no. 1 (2004), http://sscm-jscm.org/v10/no1/banducci.html.

29. Benoît Bolduc, "From Marvel to Camp: Medusa for the Twenty-First Century," *Journal of Seventeenth-Century Music* 10, no. 1 (2004): para. 6.2., https://sscm-jscm.org/v10/no1/bolduc.html.

30. D. Davies, *Philosophy of the Performing Arts*, 112–20.

31. Interview with Vladimir Jurowski, included in Katharina Thoma, dir., *Ariadne auf Naxos* (Opus Arte, 2014), DVD. Barry Millington made a similar observation in "*Ariadne auf Naxos*, Opera Review: Ingenious Staging Mixes Comedy with the Mythic," *Evening Standard*, last modified June 26, 2017, https://www.standard.co.uk/go/london/arts/ariadne-auf-naxos-opera-review-ingenious-staging-mixes-comedy-with-the-mythic-a3681536.html.

32. Charlotte Valori, "Method in Its Madness: Strauss' *Ariadne auf Naxos*, Glyndebourne," Operissima (blog), last modified June 4, 2013, https://operissima.org/2013/06/04/method-in-its-madness-strauss-ariadne-auf-naxos-glyndebourne/.

33. Matthew Rye, "Keep Calm and Carry on Singing: Love and Art Overcome Wartime Adversity in Glyndebourne's *Ariadne*," bachtrack, last modified June 26, 2017, http://bachtrack.com/review-ariadne-naxos-thoma-davidsen-glueckert-glyndebourne-june-2017.

34. Sam Smith, "*Ariadne auf Naxos* @ Glyndebourne Festival Opera, Lewes," musicOMH, last modified June 28, 2017, http://www.musicomh.com/classical/reviews-classical/ariadne-auf-naxos-glyndebourne-festival-opera-lewes-2. Other reviewers with similar complaints include Tim Ashley, "*Ariadne auf Naxos*—Review," *Guardian*, last modified May 19, 2013, http://www.theguardian.com/music/2013/may/19/ariadne-auf-naxos-review; Rupert Christiansen, "*Ariadne auf Naxos*, Glyndebourne, Review," *Telegraph*, last modified May 19, 2013, http://www.telegraph.co.uk/culture/music/glyndebourne/10067281/Ariadne-auf-Naxos-Glyndebourne-review.html; Rupert Christiansen, "Lise Davidsen Surpasses All Expectations Amid a Splendid Cast—*Ariadne auf Naxos*, Glyndebourne, Review," *Telegraph*, last modified June 26, 2017, http://www.telegraph.co.uk/opera/what-to-see/lise-davidsen-magnificent-ariadne-auf-naxos-glyndebourne-review/; Alexandra Coghlan, "Don't Mention the War," *New Statesman* 142, no. 5161 (2013): 52–53; Richard Morrison, "*Ariadne* on the Emergency Ward," *Times*, May 21, 2013; Claire Seymour, "Glyndebourne's Wartime *Ariadne auf Naxos*," *Opera Today*, last modified June 27, 2017, http://www.operatoday.com/content/2017/06/glyndebournes_w.php; Michael Tanner, "*Ariadne auf Naxos* at Glyndebourne—How Can an Opera Go So Wrong?" *Spectator*, last modified May 29, 2013, http://www.spectator.co.uk/2013/06/opera-review-ariadne-auf-naxos/; Mark Valencia, "Review: *Ariadne auf Naxos* (Glyndebourne)," ClassicalSource, last modified June 26, 2013, http://www.whatsonstage.com/brighton-theatre/reviews/review-ariadne-auf-naxos-glyndebourne_43962.html. John Amis, "Glyndebourne: A Mad *Ariadne*," *Musical Opinion* 137, no. 1496 (2013): 32, suggested that "anybody seeing this as their first *Ariadne* should ask for their money back."

35. Seymour, "Glyndebourne's Wartime *Ariadne auf Naxos*."

36. A nickname employed, derisively, by Mark Berry, "Poor Staging Spoils *Ariadne auf Naxos*," Seen and Heard International, last modified May 20, 2013, http://seenandheard-international.com/2013/05/poor-staging-spoils-ariadne-auf-naxos/.

37. Hamilton, *Art of Theater*, 31–33. See also Anne Ubersfeld, *Reading Theatre*, ed. Paul Perron and Patrick Debbèche, trans. Frank Collins (Toronto: University of Toronto Press, 1999), 7, who proposes that a play's text "is only one among several elements of performance—indeed maybe the least important element. The importance of T [the play's text] is minimal, indeed perhaps nil."

38. David Davies first suggested to me the possibility of understanding certain trends in contemporary opera performance in terms of the ingredients model. See also Paul Thom, "Aesthetics of Opera," *Philosophy Compass* 6, no. 9 (2011): 576.

39. Rachel Cowgill, "Mozart Productions and the Emergence of *Werktreue* at London's Italian Opera House, 1780–1830," in *Operatic Migrations: Transforming Works and Crossing Boundaries*, ed. Roberta Montemorra Marvin and Downing A. Thomas (Burlington: Ashgate, 2006), 147.

40. Fuhrmann, *Foreign Opera*, 16, 13, 22, 34–37. I am grateful to Philip Rupprecht for bringing this book to my attention.

41. Vestris exposed the hypocrisy of the audience's reaction in a public letter to the *Morning Post* and *London Times*, December 31, 1827. Ibid., 60, 117.

42. Beyer, "Interviews," 310.

43. Ibid., 312–13.

44. *A Little Too Cozy* program (Toronto: Against the Grain Theatre, 2016). The promotional video for *A Little Too Cozy* is available on YouTube: https://www.youtube.com/watch?v=HB_GQ_JPk1g&t=6s. I am grateful to Joel Ivany for providing me access to his libretto.

45. Gossett, *Divas and Scholars*, 450, also seems to recognize this possibility when he asks, "Is there a point at which it no longer is meaningful to refer to a performance of 'Verdi's *Macbeth*,' even if the words and music of the score are being respected?"

46. Peter Sellars, "Director's Notes," in *Hercules* program (Toronto: Canadian Opera Company, 2014), 2–3.

47. Hamilton, *Art of Theater*, 32.

48. Sherri Irvin, "Theatrical Performances and the Work Performed," *Journal of Aesthetic Education* 43, no. 3 (2009): 48–49.

49. Hamilton, *Art of Theater*, 32.

50. D. Davies, *Philosophy of the Performing Arts*, 112–20; Irvin, "Theatrical Performances," make similar arguments about spoken theater.

51. Gossett, *Divas and Scholars*, 239–40; Parker, *Remaking the Song*, ch. 3; Poriss, *Changing the Score*, 187–88.

52. David Davies, "Enigmatic Variations," *Monist* 95, no. 4 (2012): 653, makes a similar point.

53. Gossett, *Divas and Scholars*, 198. A composer wishing singers to perform the score as written needed to provide a special indication to that effect, such as the one Verdi included with the recitative prior to the trio in the final act of *Rigoletto* (1851): "This recitative must be declaimed without the usual appoggiaturas." Ibid., 293.

54. Ibid., 226.

7

PERFORMANCES OF WORKS

ONE OF THE PLEASURES AND PERILS OF ATTENDING the opera today is the unpredictability of what one will see when the curtain opens. Even with a work one knows well—perhaps especially in such circumstances—one may be baffled by the spectacle, unable to reconcile it with one's prior knowledge of the work's setting and story. Yet most discussions of operatic narration ignore such realities. The present and following chapter explore how the artistic choices of the director and performers affect the point of view from which an opera is told. Both chapters deal with productions that do not follow all of the directives in the score and libretto. The ones in this chapter depart in less significant ways, such as ignoring some of the stage directions, and do so in order to illuminate aspects of the work being performed, including the historical influences on its creation. As such, most of the productions discussed in this chapter can be understood as work-performances in the classical paradigm.

I begin with cases where directors have responded to composers' strategies of aligning spectators with characters' points of view (for examples, see chap. 5) by creating analogous effects in the visual realm. This approach has been especially prevalent in productions of Wagner from the theoretical treatises of the Swiss designer Adolphe Appia (1862–1928) to productions by Peter Sellars (*Tristan und Isolde*, Opéra national de Paris, 2006) and François Girard (*Siegfried*, Canadian Opera Company, 2005). Lest I give the impression that it is an exclusive preoccupation of Wagner directors, I also discuss a production of the Tchaikovsky brothers' *Queen of Spades* by Lev Dodin (Dutch National Opera, 1998). In the second half of the chapter, I return to the two central examples of frame narrators from chapter 3, Vere in *Billy Budd* (1951) and the Governess in *The Turn of the Screw* (1954), and show how Tim Albery (English National Opera, 1988) and Tom Diamond (Opera McGill, 2011) drew attention to these characters' roles in shaping the story we are seeing enacted onstage.

Enhancing Character-Focused Narration

Inspired by the exalted place music occupied in Schopenhauer's philosophy as the art form that gave direct expression to our inner desires and drives, Wagner employed his orchestra as the primary medium for expressing characters' emotions, thoughts, psychological states, and perceptual experiences. The role of the verbal and visual components was to lend particularity to that which the music expressed.[1]

Subsequent directors have negotiated other divisions of labor, devising ways in which the visual components of a performance could assist in communicating information about characters' subjectivities. Prime mover in this shift was Adolphe Appia, a devotee of Wagner's music, but one who found the composer's naturalistic staging sensibilities to be inadequate to the task of communicating the real drama—what Appia referred to as the "inner drama"—of works like *Tristan*. In a scenario for a hypothetical production of the opera, published as an appendix to his 1899 treatise *Music and Staging*, Appia described the production's "main principle" as "making the audience see the drama through the eyes of the hero and heroine."[2]

To be sure, Appia did not intend this statement to be taken literally. Rather, his proposal was that the staging, like the music, should align spectators with the lovers' point of view. Observing their indifference to the external world, he rid the mise-en-scène of all the bric-a-brac associated with that world. The stage should not be "burdened with useless maritime items," as the lovers pay no heed to them. The one exception is when objects, such as Isolde's torch, are causally linked to the lovers' ability to be together. Thus, in Appia's description of Act II, he made the radical proposal that the only prop onstage should be the torch. "When Isolde enters she sees only two things: the absence of Tristan and the torch (the last trace of act one), the reason for his absence. The mild summer night gleaming through the tall trees has lost its meaning for Isolde." Accordingly, only the "quality of light gives an impression of outdoors. One or two lines of the barely visible setting suggest trees." Once Isolde extinguishes the torch and the lovers are together, there is nothing more to represent onstage. "Like the two leading characters we see nothing and want to see nothing but their presence."[3]

Light played a key role in Appia's productions. Having witnessed the birth of electric lighting, he realized its potential to transform the lighting engineer from a technician whose primary responsibility was to make the artistry of painted backdrops visible to the audience into an artist in his own right. Appia's theory was that light had the potential to serve an analogous function to that of an opera's music: "Light is to production what music is to the score: the expressive element in opposition to literal signs; and, like music, light can express only what belongs to 'the inner essence of all vision.'"[4] In his scenario for *Tristan*, he speaks of light taking on "the significance of a leitmotif." During the course of Act II, Appia describes the level of illumination becoming steadily dimmer, representing the lovers turning their backs on Day and retreating into Night. When King Marke and his entourage enter, "daylight slowly increases, cold, colorless. The eye begins to see the entire setting in its full severity."[5]

Appia's remark that "the aesthetic sensibility of hearing is not necessarily so universal as that of sight" points to an important difference between the media of music and light.[6] Whereas the apprehension of the aforementioned lighting effect requires only functional eyesight and the prior visual experience of a sunrise, gleaning significance from Wagner's leitmotivic manipulations requires not only considerable concentration and memory (likely formed through repeat engagements) but also extensive knowledge of musical conventions and compositional procedures.

The dissemination of Appia's theoretical ideas and design concepts occurred primarily through publications, such as *Music and Staging*, rather than practical applications. His cavalier attitude toward the Meister's stage directions, and the stark modernism of his designs, prevented them from gracing the stages of Bayreuth. Appia's scenario received its premiere only in 1923, under Toscanini at La Scala. By this point, Appia's ideas had already proved influential on the work of Mahler and Alfred Roller at the Vienna Court Opera. From their first collaboration on a production of *Tristan* in 1903, Roller employed light for subjective-expressive purposes.[7]

Modernism finally began to penetrate the walls of Bayreuth when Cosima Wagner's son, Siegfried, took the helm. Siegfried's 1927 *Tristan* bore considerable similarity to Appia's scenario. His designer Kurt Söhnlein took a more minimalist approach to the mise-en-scène, which, in Patrick Carnegy's description, "played down realism in favour of concentration on the psychological, inner action." As per Appia's recommendations, "the lighting had more to do with the characters' states of mind than with anything pictorial."[8]

However, it was the subsequent generation, under the artistic direction of Wieland Wagner (codirector of Bayreuth from 1951–66), who most fully embraced Appia's design aesthetic. Despite similarities of effect, there were profound differences in intent. Appia advocated a stripped-down approach to *Tristan*'s set design to express the particular experiences of the characters Tristan and Isolde. By contrast, Wieland's *Entrümpeln* (clearing out) was an approach he pursued with all of Wagner's works as part of his attempt to distance them from history, particularly their appropriation by National Socialism. Rather than presenting particular women and men living in a particular time and place, Wieland's productions represented the characters as archetypes inspired by the work of the psychoanalyst Carl Jung (1875–1961).

Since the 1960s, there has been decreased interest in using the visual properties of performances to express characters' points of view. Beginning in East Germany, Walter Felsenstein and his protégés at the Komische Oper Berlin strove to counteract Wieland's dehistoricizing efforts by setting their productions in the nineteenth century. Patrice Chéreau's centenary Bayreuth *Ring* (1976) is the most famous example, but it was Joachim Herz (Leipzig, 1973) who first dramatized George Bernard Shaw's interpretation of the work as a parable of the evils of capitalism.[9] Although this approach was not incompatible with employing the visual elements of performances to express characters' points of view, that aim was of secondary importance to the expression of social and political ideas.

Emerging in the 1980s, under the influence of poststructuralist notions of "deconstruction" and the "free play" of signification, Ruth Berghaus (also from East Germany) and Hans Neuenfels, among others, called into question the fundamental principles on which opera staging was previously premised:

1. The primary purpose of the visual elements of an opera performance is to tell the story prescribed by the opera's authors.
2. They do this by generating facts about the opera's fictional world and its inhabitants.

Appia and Roller cultivated an aesthetic more expressionistic than naturalistic, but they did not waver from these principles. Neither did Herz and Chéreau, even though they also used their productions as vehicles to express their own attitudes on various topics. Berghaus and Neuenfels, by contrast, abandoned a commitment to principle 1, but that is not to say that their productions are nonnarrative. Many do tell a story, but, more often than not, it is a rather different story from the one intended by the opera's authors. Thus, principle 2 is redirected toward telling the director's story. In other cases, both principles are abandoned, and the primary purpose of the performance's visual elements is to express the director's attitudes about the work or other topics (for an example, refer to the discussion of Martin Kušej's *Don Giovanni* in chap. 2).

Although Peter Sellars's work is often grouped together with the aforementioned "deconstructionists," his production of *Tristan und Isolde*, a collaboration with the video artist Bill Viola, evinced an Appian sensibility in its deployment of staging and lighting design.[10] Sellars and Viola's work, or rather works, have been presented in a variety of formats, including concert performances (e.g., Los Angeles, 2007; New York, 2007), fully staged performances (e.g., Opéra national de Paris, 2006; Canadian Opera Company, 2013), and exhibitions of Viola's videos, without Sellars's staging or Wagner's music, in art galleries. My discussion will focus on the performances of their production at the Canadian Opera Company. However, much of what I will have to say is applicable to other fully staged performances.

The majority of the discourse around this production has focused on the question of whether Viola's videos enhanced, detracted from, or, as some have even claimed, prevented one from appreciating Wagner's opera.[11] Seemingly the only point of agreement is that there were two artworks to appreciate. In actuality, there were three. It is this neglected third work, the production directed by Sellars and presented by the singers and musicians at the Canadian Opera Company, on which I will be shedding light.

For spectators able to resist the alleged "narcotic effect" of Viola's moving images, there was much to see and hear onstage—and in the theater—even though the set, props, and costumes were even more minimalist than those described in Appia's scenario.[12] As discussed in chapter 5, Wagner's prescriptions for the placement of singers and musicians align spectators with characters' aural perceptual experiences. Sellars took Wagner's directions a step further, both increasing the number of such moments and, for those the composer earmarked for special treatment, intensifying the verisimilitude of their effects.

An example of the latter is Sellars's realization of Isolde and Brangäne's conversation about the audibility of the horn calls of King Marke's hunting party at the beginning of Act II. To allow spectators to experience for themselves the difference between Isolde's and Brangäne's perceptions, Wagner specified that the horns representing what Brangäne hears perform from behind the scenery while those representing Isolde's perceptions remain in the pit and play with mutes. Sellars placed the former group behind the entrance doors of Ring 3 (the balcony above the Grand Ring). To represent Brangäne's perceptions of the horns getting farther and farther away from the castle, the door separating the real-life horns from the house was gradually closed throughout the course of the duet.[13] At least from where I was seated in Ring 3, the effect was astonishingly vivid.

Sellars and his lighting designer James F. Ingalls also used light to achieve analogous effects. My focus will be on the conclusion of Act I. By this point in the opera, the lovers have taken what they believe to be the death potion. Just as they are realizing that it did not have the intended effect, their ship docks at Cornwall. During the course of the first act, the music has become entirely consumed with expressing the lovers' subjective states. The sounds of King Marke's landing party thus represent sudden and, from the lovers' perspective, bewildering and unwelcome encroachments of the external world.

The contrast between the internal and external worlds is starkly rendered in Wagner's score. Example 7.1 represents one of the more jarring shifts in musical style. The men of the landing party sing King Marke's praises to a folksy fanfare characterized by forthright dotted rhythms and an unwavering commitment to C major. In the following measure, the ubiquitous half-diminished seventh chord makes a crashing appearance, ushering in an abrupt return of the lovers' music, which is highly chromatic, tonally ambiguous, and of an entirely different rhythmic character. Short-long-short rhythms dominate, and, elsewhere, the lovers' music takes on a metrically amorphous character through ties obscuring barlines and written-out *accelerandi* (ex. 7.2). Timbrally, the appearance of King Marke's court is marked by the intrusion of bombastic brass into a soundscape previously characterized by middle-register woodwinds, harp, and strings.

In Sellars's production, spotlights reverse direction and scan the balconies, causing spectators to shield their eyes or avert their gaze. At the Canadian Opera Company, King Marke and Melot processed up the aisles of the parterre while the rest of the landing party and half of the trumpets and trombones performed from Ring 5 (the highest balcony).[14] On the stage, and here I quote from Christopher Morris's account of the Paris performances, the lovers' "loss of privacy is signaled now by the loss of shadow in a blanket of revealing light. . . . Here the only projection is a screen-sized dull yellow band, like an abstract representation of light and day."[15]

Sellars's *coup de théâtre* has not gone unnoticed by commentators. The interpretation of its significance, however, warrants additional reflection. Morris describes its effect as follows: "In revealing the gazing Marke, the light also reveals the audience, whose spectatorial gaze is cast out of its darkened refuge and suddenly, subversively, aligned with Marke's. In the leveling glare of the Opéra Bastille's illuminated ceiling, we are caught in the act of watching Tristan and Isolde, exposed as complicit with Marke, exposed as complicit in the public gaze, and, in a pseudo-Brechtian act of distanciation, exposed to each other."[16]

In the production's performances in Paris, Marke was revealed to be seated among the spectators in the parterre. Even so, there is reason to doubt that most spectators experienced a strong sense of sharing Marke's point of view.

Example 7.1. Juxtaposition of Day and Night music in *Tristan*, end of Act I

Humans are good at making fine-grained distinctions between visual perspectives and, in practice, make a point of being precise in such matters. Thus, the sense of being aligned with Marke's point of view in terms of visual perception is fairly attenuated, even for spectators seated in the parterre. Seeing the production from a balcony, I was ignorant of Marke's physical location, so I experienced no sense of alignment with him, either in terms of visual perception or in any other capacity at the end of Act I.

From the claim that all spectators are aligned with King Marke, Morris leaps to the conclusion that spectators identify with him and are thus "complicit" in a wrongdoing on Marke's part, which, from his description, seems to have something to do with "the gaze." As discussed in chapter 5, knowing about a character's point of view is necessary for one to sympathize with that character, but it is not sufficient.

Morris's final claim, somewhat unrelated to the foregoing argument, is that there is something Brechtian about Sellars's dramaturgical tactics.

Example 7.2. Tristan and Isolde's metrically amorphous music

Putting a finer point on the issue, Morris appears to be asserting that Sellars's decision to turn on the houselights and have performers commingling with spectators triggered a *Verfremdungseffekt* (distancing effect). If so, Morris would be in good company. Clemens Risi has also argued that the inevitable effect of these and other devices that break through the so-called fourth wall is "to jolt the audience out of lethargy and passivity."[17] Not having seen the productions Risi discusses, I am not in a position to dispute the accuracy of his account of the directors' aims or the effects they achieved. What I will dispute is the validity of the general conclusions Risi extrapolates from the cases he discusses, using Sellars's *Tristan* as a counterexample.

To grasp what differentiates Sellars's work from the examples Risi discusses, it is necessary to clarify what the adjective *Brechtian* refers to when it is applied to an opera production. Joy Calico has outlined two ways in which an opera production could be said to be Brechtian. The first is by incorporating certain Brechtian stylistic features, such as a "sparsely appointed stage, the exposed apparatus [e.g., fictional characters moving scenery], actors who address the audience directly, and various other means of eliminating the fourth wall."[18] Another reason we may call an opera production Brechtian is that it aims at arousing a particular type of audience response, namely, *Verfremdung* or estrangement from the particular opera being performed, opera as an art form and social institution, or both.

Although Sellars's *Tristan* contains some of the Brechtian stylistic features Calico mentions, Sellars employs them toward un-Brechtian ends. A true Verfremdungseffekt discourages spectators from becoming absorbed with the characters and their predicaments. Instead, they are encouraged to regard the opera as the achievement of a historical individual or group and to critically examine what that person or persons were intending to communicate through their work and what effect the work has, or has had, on others. Sellars's primary concern, by contrast, was to bring spectators into the story rather than keeping them at a distance. In addition to Sellars's intensification of Wagner's acoustic effects, Ingalls's lighting at the end of Act I created an alignment between the audience and the lovers, an effect that could be experienced by a larger portion of the audience as compared with the alignment Morris argues was created between Marke and some spectators in the parterre.

After taking the love potion, Tristan and Isolde become consumed by their feelings for each other. When others attempt to interact with them, they are bewildered and unable to process what is happening. Representative is the following exchange (which occurs just prior to ex. 7.1):

TRISTAN:
(*in Verwirrung aufblickend*)   (bewildered, looking up)
Wer naht?   Who is approaching?

KURWENAL:
Der König!   The King!

TRISTAN:
Welcher König?   Which King?[19]

A similar state of bewilderment comes over theater spectators as various unexpected events come to pass. Depending on one's location in the theater, one may have found oneself amid a bunch of trombones or, for the majority of spectators in the balconies, with spotlights in one's eyes, making it physically uncomfortable to do what one is supposed to do at the opera: direct one's attention to what is happening onstage.

Through the act of blinding many of his spectators, Sellars not only draws attention to one of the most important metaphors of the opera, the Day-Night dichotomy, but also provides them with a sample of Tristan and Isolde's subjective experiences, blinded as they are by the Day world and all it represents. As the lovers explain in the *Tagesgespräch* (conversation about Day) of Act II, Day is hateful to them not merely because it is the time when they cannot be together or because it represents the duties and responsibilities to which their actions are necessarily in service. Wagner's Day-Night dichotomy maps directly onto Schopenhauer's division of total reality into the phenomenal and noumenal realms, or appearance and essence.[20] Thus, the lovers speak of Day as being prone to spreading falsehoods and engendering delusions. Isolde blames Day for her initial false apprehension of Tristan as a traitor and a foe. Night, Tristan professes, has granted him true sight, or rather insight, into the nature of the world, insight that brings him and Isolde to the understanding that the only way that they can truly be free from Day's deceits and miseries and achieve the oneness they desire is in death.

Sellars's staging, particularly the conclusion of Act I, accomplishes through its lighting and unconventional use of the acoustic space two effects analogous to those achieved by Wagner's music: expressing the lovers' thoughts and emotional and psychological states and allowing spectators to share similar experiences. Although Morris is overly hasty in assuming a direct causal relationship between strategies that orient spectators to the points of view of characters and audience identification, he is right to see *a* relation. Providing audiences with a sample of a character's subjective experience *may* facilitate sympathy, empathy, or identification, in which case it would achieve the very opposite of a Verfremdungseffekt. Sellars's staging, then, refutes Risi's claim that dramaturgical choices that deemphasize divisions between performers and spectators, or stage and house, invariably achieve Brechtian aims.

An example of the mise-en-scène being used to illustrate the inner workings of a character's mind is Michael Levine's designs for François Girard's *Siegfried* (Canadian Opera Company, 2005). Although each opera in the Canadian Opera Company's first complete *Ring* cycle was entrusted to a different director, Levine served as the set and costume designer for the entire cycle and the director for *Das Rheingold*. The benefits of this arrangement in terms of visual continuity were amply demonstrated in *Siegfried*.

Girard wisely deemphasized Siegfried's violent and boorish nature, presenting the story as his quest to piece together his past and find his place in the world. This unusually reflective Siegfried spends much of the opera seated on a stump, above which fragments of Levine's sets and props to the previous two operas are suspended (Levine's design for Act I graces the cover of this book). More than adding visual spectacle to Wagner's feast of fabulous horn playing and tests of vocal endurance, Levine's set offers a visual illustration of Siegfried's confused and incomplete understanding of his past. In having this frozen tornado of debris emanate from Siegfried, he and Girard also underscore Siegfried's role as the focal character for this portion of the cycle. Not only is he in virtually every scene but the orchestra is predominantly concerned with representing his perceptions and emotional and psychological states.[21]

Another way to draw attention to a focal character is to reframe some or all of the action as that character's memories, imaginings, or hallucinations. Lev Dodin's staging of the Tchaikovskys' *Queen of Spades* (Dutch National Opera, 1998) begins where Pushkin's story ends: Herman in an insane asylum. Herman is the focal character of both Pushkin's story and the Tchaikovskys' opera, and in both works, his quest to learn the Countess's secret to gambling success ends in madness. To the dismay of many Pushkin aficionados, the tone of his cynical tale of avarice shifted in its operatic adaptation to that of a melodrama of star-crossed lovers separated by social station. Whereas Pushkin's Herman uses the Countess's ward, Liza, as a mere means to gain access to the Countess, the Tchaikovskys' Herman is driven to the gambling table by genuine love for Liza, the Countess's granddaughter in their telling. Given her elevated social station and engagement to a prince, Herman regards cards as the only way he, a poor officer, could hope to earn her hand in marriage. Thus, the Tchaikovskys' story, James Parakilas observes, is as much about "the madness to which social inequity can drive someone" as it is about gambling addiction.[22]

Contemporary music critics also derided the opera, though for different reasons, largely stemming from the anachronisms created by the Tchaikovskys' seemingly arbitrary decision to set the opera in the reign of Catherine the Great (1762–96) instead of in Pushkin's time (the 1830s). To flesh out Pushkin's short story into an evening's entertainment, they stuffed the plot with a bunch of embedded performances of singing and dancing, many of which borrow from sources that postdate the opera's setting. In Act I, Scene 2, Liza and her friend Polina sing texts from the first decade of the nineteenth century (newly set to music by P. Tchaikovsky).[23] After the Countess returns from a particularly dissatisfying ball, she laments the decline of musical and dancing ability among the younger generation and performs a song she used to sing in her youth. Here Tchaikovsky quotes both the music and text of "Je crains de lui parler la nuit" from André Grétry and Michel-Jean Sedaine's opéra comique *Richard Coeur-de-lion* (1784), a work that "belongs to the old woman's dotage, not her youth," David Brown remarks.[24]

Other portions of the score do take inspiration from the music of the eighteenth century, particularly that of Mozart, one of Tchaikovsky's favorite composers. The opening of Act II is in a similar character to the Act II finale of *Don Giovanni* (1787), and the initial chorus of the pastoral play could make a credible substitution for one of Mozart's peasant choruses. The duet for Prilepa and Milovzor even contains quotations from the first movement of Mozart's C minor Wind Serenade, K. 388 (1783) and C major Piano Concerto, K. 503 (1786).[25] Other evocations of eighteenth-century style are less on point, however. The pastoral play also contains a common-time "sarabande" (a triple-meter dance) with decidedly Romantic harmonization and a polonaise marked "tempo di minuetto."[26]

Current scholarly opinion on these anachronisms and inaccuracies is that they were intentional and not the product of ignorance or carelessness. After all, the composer proved himself to be knowledgeable about the appropriate meters and tempi of eighteenth-century dances in his ballets *Swan Lake* (1877) and *Sleeping Beauty* (1890). Richard Taruskin and Simon Morrison explain Tchaikovsky's anachronistic borrowings and decisions to depart from eighteenth-century conventions as anticipations of Symbolism while Parakilas takes a cue from one of Tchaikovsky's diary entries during the time of composition in which he speaks of imagining that he were an eighteenth-century composer. According to Parakilas, such an imagining could not be sustained if "he had quoted or imitated eighteenth-century music literal-mindedly; instead, he needed to work like an eighteenth-century composer, adapting as he borrowed from his 'contemporaries.'"[27]

A more comprehensive and straightforward explanation of these and other oddities of the score is Tchaikovsky's attempt to musically express Herman's increasingly distorted perspective on the world, thus aligning spectators with his point of view.[28] Dodin's production illuminates this possibility by staging much of the action as Herman's memories and imaginings.[29] In light of his less than firm grip on reality, the inaccuracies are entirely to be expected. And if the scenes in the psychiatric ward take place a decade or two after the events Herman is remembering, even the anachronisms could be rationalized.

Given that the Tchaikovskys never intended the work to be staged in this fashion, some alterations of the libretto and score were necessary to successfully execute Dodin's plan. According to the libretto, Herman does not appear until the second scene. But as the source of what we're seeing and hearing, Dodin's Herman shuffles onstage well before the beginning of the overture. Dodin integrated him into the first scene by inserting a spoken request for some (imaginary) children to perform a song.

Dodin also changed the casting of the pastoral play. The Tchaikovskys intended the embedded performance to mirror Liza's choice between Herman and Prince Yeletsky. Prilepa is wooed by Milovzor, a shepherd who can offer her only love, and Zlatogor, who attempts to entice her with gold and jewels. Like Liza, Prilepa chooses love over riches, but unlike Liza, her story ends happily. The composer intended the roles of Milovzor (contralto) and Zlatogor (baritone) to be taken on by Polina and Tomsky.[30] Although he did not specify that Prilepa be performed by Liza, he did write the role for her voice type (soprano), making Liza-Prilepa a conventional doubling. Dodin decided to cast Herman as Prilepa, who is caught between love, represented by Liza as Milovzor, and avarice, represented by the Countess as Zlatogor. Dodin's unconventional casting choices required transposing multiple vocal parts. Due to these and other changes to the score and libretto, Dodin's production is somewhat deficient as a production of the Tchaikovskys' opera. Yet these changes also help solidify Dodin's focus on Herman and illuminate his inner conflict, thus making the production more effective as an artistic statement in its own right.

Drawing Attention to Character-Narrators

My discussion of the role of character-narrators in chapter 3 began with the disclaimer that I would be speaking about what is true in the story according to the work's score and libretto, rather than what is true of performances that depart from these texts. Recognizing how common such departures are, this section returns to two works with frame narrators, *Billy Budd* and *The Turn of the Screw*, and examines how the decisions of directors as well as singers performing the roles of Vere and the Governess affect our perception of these characters' roles in their respective operas.

Although these operas' framing scenes suggest that we ought to regard Vere and the Governess as the sources of everything we see and hear, in both cases there are obstacles to our entertaining this view. Both works contain scenes that the purported narrator did not witness. More seriously, Britten's music expresses perspectives on Vere and the Governess that are more critical than those justifiably attributable to either character. Yet for some spectators, particularly nonspecialists, staging choices are arguably a more important influence on how they interpret the narrative structure of an opera than the kind of musical-thematic relationships discussed in chapter 3. I focus on productions that are particularly successful at suggesting not only that our access to the fictional world is mediated by Vere and the Governess but also that these characters may not be as sane as they initially appear.

In the case of *Billy Budd*, the tendency to draw attention to Vere's role as narrator began with the original production of 1951, directed by Basil Coleman and designed by John Piper. In an interview with Coleman and Piper, published just before the premiere, the latter's first remark was "we must never lose sight of the fact that the whole thing is taking place in Vere's mind, and is being recalled by him." Coleman and Piper proceed to describe various strategies they employed to ensure that their audience did not forget it either. Instead of "realistic [back]cloths" representing the sea and sky (which would have still been the norm for opera production in mid-twentieth-century Britain), Piper opted for a completely black backdrop and floor. Coleman employed "lighting in an unrealistic way... with scenes fading in and out to help the illusion of their having been called up by Vere."[31]

In the BBC TV *Billy Budd* (1966, also directed by Coleman), Peter Pears's decision to look directly into the camera when he sang "Who has blessed me? Who saved me?" in the prologue and "for I could have saved him" in the epilogue helped to establish Vere as an external narrator.[32] Furthermore, shots of old-Vere were intercut with shots of young-Vere listening to the singing of his crew between Scenes 2 and 3 of Act I. To make it clear that old-Vere is imagining being on the *Indomitable*, a shot of him looking up is followed by an over-the-shoulder shot of young-Vere performing similar movements.

The idea of reminding spectators that what they are seeing onstage represents Vere's recollections as an old man was taken further by subsequent directors. Tim Albery (English National Opera, 1988) placed old-Vere onstage for much of Act II. Because of its commercial availability, Albery's production will be the focus of my discussion. However, it should be noted that Graham Vick pursued a similar approach a year earlier in his production for the Scottish Opera.[33] That Philip Langridge performed Vere on both occasions makes the transference of interpretive approaches between the productions probable.

In Albery's production, the timing of old-Vere's appearances is such that they cannot be understood solely as reminders of the opera's frame. His initial appearance, during Billy's final aria, highlights rather than alleviates problems with the idea of regarding Vere as the opera's fictional source. Vere has no way of knowing what Billy was thinking when he was alone in the brig before his execution. Albery's staging decisions prompt spectators to contemplate the source of what they are viewing and its reliability. If Vere is the source of this scene, it represents his speculation about what he thinks or hopes took place. Taking a closer look at the content of Billy's final aria, one may well question whether these are the probable thoughts of a man facing death by hanging: "But I've sighted a sail in the storm, the far-shining sail that's not Fate, and I'm contented. I've seen where she's bound for. She has a land of her own where she'll anchor for ever. Oh, I'm contented. Don't matter now being hanged, or being forgotten and caught in the weeds. Don't matter now. I'm strong, and I know it, and I'll stay strong, and that's all, and that's enough."[34]

By having old-Vere on stage for Billy's aria, Albery proposes an answer to the question of why portions of Billy's speech, both linguistic and musical, return in Vere's epilogue. At the end of the opera, Vere repeats his questions from the prologue ("what have I done?") but replaces his earlier talk of "confusion" with quotations from Billy's aria that answer the questions "who has blessed me? Who saved me?": "But he has saved me, and blessed me, and the love that passes understanding has come to me. I was lost on the infinite sea, but I've sighted a sail in the storm, the far-shining sail, and I'm content. I've seen where she's bound for. There's a land where she'll anchor for ever."[35]

Billy's aria and Vere's epilogue are also connected by virtue of containing partial reprises of the Interview Chords, which represent the final conversation between Vere and Billy. By viewing Vere as the narrator, the reappearance of the Interview Chords can be understood as expressing Vere's hope that Billy would recall their conversation in his final moments, finding in it the strength and comfort of which Vere imagines him singing.

The music of Billy's aria lends additional support to Albery's suggestion that spectators regard the aria as Vere's overly hopeful imaginings about Billy's state of mind prior to his execution. In light of Britten's penchant for undercutting the verbal sentiments of his characters through his musical settings, his decision to compose music worthy of the glowing optimism of Forster's text is significant. A detailed comparison of Billy's aria with Vere's quotation will be useful not only in bringing out the uncharacteristically affirmative nature of the music to the former but also in illustrating some of the ways in which the music of the latter supports Albery and Langridge's portrayal of old-Vere as a man haunted by the past.

One of the most striking contrasts between Billy's farewell and Vere's epilogue is the relation between the vocal line and its harmonic accompaniment in each case (cf. exx. 7.3 and 7.4). Almost as consistently as Billy's harmonies form consonant relations with his vocal lines, Vere's harmonies fail to do so, even at the ends of phrases. Vere's statement "I'm content" is rendered decidedly unconvincing by Vere singing a G to an A-major chord, a chord foreign to the ostensible key of this section, B♭ major. Billy's "I'm contented," by contrast, coincides with a modulation to A major with Billy singing the tonic.

Billy's aria represents a clearer tonal progression than Vere's. It begins in B♭. The modulation to A at "I'm content" is reaffirmed several times with cadences at "anchor for ever" and between "don't matter now" and "I'm strong." Britten's choice of key is not insignificant, given his consistent association of A major with beauty and innocence, not merely within this work but in various others composed throughout his career.[36] At "I'm strong," the Interview Chords take over the accompaniment, and the oscillation between F-major and C-major triads becomes the tonal anchor.

The tonal trajectory of Vere's epilogue remains a topic of debate among Britten scholars. While Arnold Whittall and J. P. E. Harper-Scott have argued that the prologue's conflict between B♭ major and B minor is left unresolved at the opera's conclusion, Philip Brett and Mervyn Cooke hear the opera as concluding triumphantly in B♭.[37] Among the evidence cited by the latter group is Britten's decision to include a B♭-major key signature when Vere begins quoting from Billy's aria. Although Vere's quotation begins in a promising manner, it does not take long for doubts about the stability of B♭ to arise from the uncertain relations between both the Interview Chords and the ostensible key of this section and between Vere's vocal line and its accompaniment.

The best piece of evidence the supporters of a B♭-major ending have is that the lines "she'll anchor for ever" are accompanied by a massive—some might say overblown—arrival on B♭. Just prior, the trumpets and trombones play the preface to Vere and Claggart's motive (ex. 3.12), but instead of leading to the familiar sequence of descending fourths, the gesture culminates in an upwardly mobile fanfare. A promising sign, one might think, except that the fanfare is in the wrong key, B major, the same key as the first appearance of Claggart's motive (ex. 3.13). Furthermore, the supposedly triumphant arrival on B♭ is weakened by the equivocal nature of Vere's vocal line. While Billy sings the tonic at important harmonic arrival

Example 7.3. Billy's final aria

Example 7.3. *(Continued)*

Example 7.3. *(Continued)*

Example 7.4. Vere's epilogue, beginning at the quotation from Billy's final aria

Example 7.4. *(Continued)*

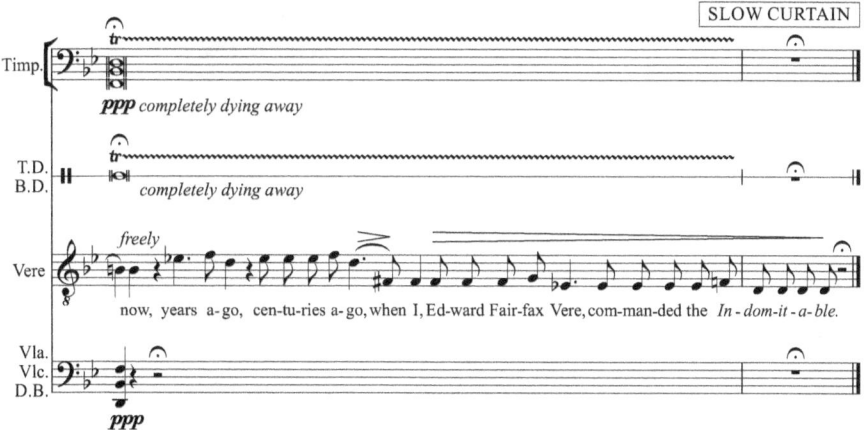

Example 7.4. *(Continued)*

points, Vere sings the fifth and, even at that, wavers between the fifth and sixth scale degrees.

The most compromising evidence is what happens after the end of Vere's quotation of Billy's aria. Although Cooke is correct that the B♭-major chord "remains unsullied at the bottom of the texture," Vere's vocal line fails to remain within the confines of that key and instead wanders back to the no-man's-land in between B♭ major and B minor. Cooke attempts to explain the problematic features of the opera's final moments through a comparison to a "cinematic fade-out."[38] Certainly the gradual dropping out of musicians lends itself to such a comparison, but Cooke provides no explanation for why the vagaries of Vere's vocal line are evocative of a fade-out. In fact, Britten's thinning out of the texture serves only to intensify the unease caused by Vere's tonal wandering. By the time Vere gets to the lines "years ago, centuries ago," the B♭-major chord is practically nonexistent, since the only pitched instrument remaining is the timpani (a somewhat dubious member of that category). Vere's final Ds thus lack any form of harmonic support (the final two measures of ex. 7.4 provide the full scoring). The implied harmony is ambiguous, as the Ds could function as the third of either a B♭-major or a B-minor triad.[39]

Closer attention to differences in orchestration offers additional insights into how Britten achieved the overwhelmingly optimistic tone of Billy's aria and, conversely, the uneasy, uncertain tenor of Vere's. Billy's aria contains a fuller texture, most noticeably through the ebullient bass clarinet arpeggios representing the motion of the sea. Whereas a full complement of strings provides melodic and harmonic support in Billy's aria, in the epilogue, Britten stripped down the strings to only violins doubling the vocal line (except at the Interview Chords). The gentler timbral character of Billy's aria comes from the fact that the rocking figures are played by flutes rather than the piccolos Britten employs in the epilogue.

Most significantly, Vere is dogged by an aggressive tattoo in the timpani and bass and tenor drums. Cooke refers to the "thumpingly militaristic timpani rhythms" as part of his argument about the "triumphant" nature of Vere's final utterance.[40] Consideration of the derivation of these rhythms points to different conclusions. The quintuplet patterns indicate that they are not related to the more verisimilar "get to work" military music heard at various points in the opera, especially the first scene. The only other time quintuplets are featured so prominently is Act II, Scene 4, Billy's execution.[41] Thus, I propose that the tattoo in the epilogue is better understood as an expression of Vere's pangs of guilt over the wrongs he committed in the name of military discipline or as Britten's accusations of guilt.

Although Britten composed music appropriate to the optimism of Forster's lyrics for Billy's aria, he preempted Forster's attempt to write a redemptive ending for Vere. Thus, Vere's psychological state at the end of the opera is indeterminate. If one privileges Forster's authorial voice, Vere is redeemed by Billy's forgiveness, but privileging Britten's, Vere is, in Whittall's words, an "archetypal Ancient Mariner, or even like the Flying Dutchman, unable to die and forced to relive the experiences he recounts in a hellish kind of endless present."[42]

The disjuncture in the expressive aims of the libretto and score places the performers in the position of having to make a choice of which to follow. Albery and Langridge decided to listen to Britten's music. Old-Vere's appearances on stage during Billy's execution suggest that he is reliving this harrowing event in his imagination. Both Billy, during his blessing, and the crew, during their revolt that ensues after Billy's execution, address old-Vere directly. At the sounds of the crew's mutinous grumblings, old-Vere covers his ears, bending over in agony. In the epilogue, Vere's tortured mental and emotional state gains expression through Langridge's hunched posture and clenched hands (to which the video recording draws special attention). Also significant is Langridge's decision to employ a more liberal, even uncontrolled vibrato *after* the allegedly exultant conclusion at "anchor for ever," thus lending a hollow character to Vere's affirmations. Finally, that Langridge returns to the same position he occupied at the beginning of the production gives the impression of a Sisyphus-like existence for the old man.

Albery's and Langridge's artistic decisions do not merely remind spectators of the opera's frame but also point to one of its consequences: the possibility of unreliable narration. Old-Vere's appearance during Billy's farewell aria encourages spectators to ask questions not normally contemplated at the opera, even performances of this opera, concerning the source of what they are seeing and hearing and whether that source is reliable.

There is one more aspect of old-Vere's appearance deserving of commentary. The costuming would appear to take literally the character's assertion that the events on the *Indomitable* occurred "centuries ago." Old-Vere bears a striking resemblance to Forster at the time of his collaboration with Britten, drawing attention to the writer's influence over the shaping of the opera, particularly its central character.[43] As Hanna Rochlitz has demonstrated, the opera was modeled not merely on Melville's novella but also on some of the themes of Forster's prose works. A narrative archetype that may be observed in many of Forster's novels and short stories is the "salvation narrative," in which a repressed middle-class Englishman with an overdeveloped intellect and an underdeveloped heart gains salvation through a man from the lower classes, or a cultural Other, who is everything he is not: beautiful, strong, and, most importantly, free of inhibitions and guilt. A crucial component of this narrative is a "forcible breaking of the [middle-class] character's self-assured emotional detachment" through a catastrophe that forces him to "recognise his personal involvement in the lives and sufferings of his fellow human beings. Only after he has been completely 'broken' does [he] become eligible for Forsterian salvation through the personal connection with the [lower-class] character."[44]

Surely one of the reasons Forster was attracted to this story was the ease with which it could be molded to the foregoing narrative archetype.[45] The chief obstacle was that Melville's Vere is never "broken" and thus does not regard himself as needing to be "saved." In order for Billy to be his savior, Vere had to be cast, perversely, in the role of a victim by downplaying his role in the verdict of Billy's trial. Despite his officers' pleas for guidance, the operatic Vere refuses to express any opinion on the matter.[46] After they predictably rule in accordance with the Articles of War, Vere is wracked with guilt and remorse (as he states in the epilogue, he "could have saved him"), feelings that plague him into old age.

The stage directions of *The Turn of the Screw* are also not especially conducive to sustaining the prologue's suggestion that we regard the rest of the opera as a dramatization of the Governess's written account. As an eleventh-hour addition, the prologue is also, unsurprisingly, not entirely consistent with the rest of the score. Much of the opera's music is more coherently understood as Britten's commentary on the Governess than as a sustained effort to align spectators with her point of view or to suggest to them that they ought to regard her as the opera's fictional source. Yet many directors have been keen to raise the salience of the "second story" (the Governess is insane and the ghosts are hallucinations) by making just such a suggestion. As with *Billy Budd*, television adaptations played a prominent role in the history of such directorial approaches. Peter Morley's Associated Rediffusion production for ITV (1959) framed the shots representing the ghosts as point-of-view shots from the Governess's perspective.[47]

The first stage production to give precedence to the second story was Geoffrey Connor's for Morley College (1966) and the Royal Theatre in Copenhagen (1967). Employing strategies similar to those used by Albery and Vick in their productions of *Billy Budd*, Connor focused the audience's attention on the Governess by having her appear onstage during scenes that otherwise pose difficulties from a second-story perspective, such as the ghosts' colloquy at the beginning of Act II. With reference to Connor's production for Danish Television (1968), Patricia Howard describes the director as using the musical interludes "to probe and illustrate the governess's alternating moods of insecurity, over-confidence and frustration. In particular, he exploited Variation VIII, which opens Act II with a sequence of instrumental cadenzas recalling music from Act I scene 8, *At Night*. During this variation Connor showed the governess reliving in her own mind the events of the earlier scene."[48] In other words, Connor oriented spectators to the Governess's point of view in terms of her emotional and psychological states and, in variation 8, her imaginative activities.

Connor's idea to place the Governess onstage for the colloquy, as well as his use of pantomime, influenced subsequent directors such as Anthony Besch (Scottish Opera, 1970), who used the prologue to enact the meeting between the Governess and the Guardian. Besch also decided to have the same singer perform the roles of the Guardian and Quint, suggesting that the Governess's infatuation with the former caused her hallucinations of the latter.

Tom Diamond's production for Opera McGill (2011) did not merely allow for the possibility of a second-story interpretation but made it more salient than a ghost-story interpretation. Due to a labor dispute, the production could not be fully staged. Although the singers acted out their parts with full force, there was no set, aside from a few pieces of furniture, and singers were responsible for outfitting themselves with costumes and props. My discussion will be directed toward what was actually achieved rather than what Diamond and his team might have done if circumstances were different. Nevertheless, in understanding Diamond's approach, it is worth noting that he intended to set the production in the fin de siècle, "with screens as a backdrop with ever-changing inkblot/Rorschach images."[49] Inspired by the probable influence of the emergent discipline of psychoanalysis on Henry James through his psychologist brother William, Diamond decided to present the events at Bly as a dramatization of the Governess's sessions of the "talking cure."

According to Piper and Britten's stage directions, the Narrator is to deliver his speech in front of the drop curtain. At the conclusion, he exits the stage and, in most productions, prepares to perform the role of Quint.[50] The curtain rises to a dark stage for the performance of the Screw theme and the first variation. At the beginning of Scene 1, the lights go up on the Governess for her first vocal entry. In Diamond's production, the Narrator begins his speech as usual, but at the first premonitions of the Screw theme during the prologue, the Governess steps forward. This staging decision not only drew attention to the nascent musical theme but also afforded Diamond the opportunity to have the Governess mime her marriage-like vow, highlighting the romantic nature of her feelings toward the Guardian.

At the conclusion of the prologue, the Narrator unexpectedly turns to greet the Governess, taking her coat and bidding her to recline on a divan. The Narrator (henceforth to be referred to as the Analyst) takes a seat in a wingback chair and, at the first variation, begins to converse with the Governess silently. When she begins to sing in Scene 1, her utterances are directed toward the Analyst, who listens intently and takes notes. Remarks the Governess makes that indicate the romantic nature of her feelings toward the Guardian appear to be of particular interest to the Analyst, as he leans in closer when she makes her confession: "Only one thing I wish, that I could see him—and that he could see how well I do his bidding."[51]

When the Bly characters appear onstage, spectators are initially invited to imagine that they represent the Governess's memories. But precisely how one ought to interpret what one sees and hears during the course of the production is a complicated matter, especially with respect to the actions of the singer performing the role of the Governess (Jessica Scarlato in the cast I saw). In the first scene and in other soliloquies and passages of orchestral music, Scarlato's appearance and actions represented those of the woman undergoing psychiatric counselling (henceforth the Analysand). At other occasions, the Analysand got so swept up in her act of storytelling that she began to imagine herself back at Bly, and Scarlato's actions represented memories of actions performed as the governess of Miles and Flora (only in such cases will I refer to Scarlato as portraying the Governess).

To further complicate matters, on several occasions Diamond called into question the neat division just outlined. Sometimes, as in the letter-writing scene (Act II, Scene 3), Scarlato's actions represented both the actions of the Governess and the Analysand. Toward the end of Act I, the Analyst becomes concerned about the vividness of the Analysand's imagination. Her recounting of the first scene by the lake causes her so much anxiety that the Analyst offers her a sedative, which puts her to sleep. Act 1, Scene 8 and Act II, Scene 1 thus represent the Analysand's dreams. When she awakens, the Analyst decides to take a different approach to her treatment, recommending that she undertake a "writing cure" instead. Scarlato's act of writing represented not only the Analysand's act of producing the account to which the Narrator refers in the prologue but also the Governess's act of writing to the Guardian.

Sometimes the stage action represented neither the occurrences at the therapist's office nor the Governess's memories. In Act I, Scene 3, when the Governess and Mrs. Grose decide what to do about Miles's dismissal from school, the children perform "Lavender's Blue," after which the Governess and Mrs. Grose remark, "See how sweetly he plays, and with how gentle a look he turns to his sister."[52] In Diamond's production, as soon as the women look away, Miles begins to sexually abuse his sister. In light of the premise of Diamond's production, one is uncertain how to interpret what one is seeing. The Governess's composure makes it clear that she did not witness this event. Thus, Diamond appears to be presenting us with an objective representation of some of the more disturbing goings-on at Bly.

In framing the story as the recollections of a woman undergoing psychiatric counseling, Diamond's production is more suggestive of a second-story interpretation than one in which Bly is actually haunted by ghosts. However, he reintroduces ambiguity in terms of how one ought to interpret what one is seeing onstage: the Analysand's memories, dreams, or hallucinations; reenactments of events at Bly (as the Analysand understands them); or objective representations of what happened at Bly.

The outcome of the Analysand's therapy sessions is also ambiguous. Describing the first scene by the lake, the Analysand recalls Flora seeing Miss Jessel. By the second lake scene, she appears to have come to the realization that she has hallucinated the ghosts. Diamond has Mrs. Grose and Flora look directly at the ghosts but fail to perceive them. If he wanted to suggest that the Analysand is headed down the road to recovery, he could have had Miles sing his final line—"Peter Quint, you devil!"—to the Governess or, more obliquely, to the audience, as Britten intended.⁵³ Instead, Miles directs his cry toward Quint, after which he runs into the Governess's arms. It would seem that the Analysand has not yet reached firm conclusions about whether there were ghosts at Bly.

When the plot of an opera is so drastically reframed, disjunctures between the staging, music, and libretto are bound to arise. Piper did not compose the Governess's utterances as a latter-day account delivered to a psychologist. The difficulty is not merely a matter of tense but also one of the Analysand viewing the events at Bly from a different perspective than the one she held while she was living them. Take, for example, the following passage representing the Governess's reaction to seeing a man, first assumed to be the Guardian, on the tower:

> Ha! 'Tis he!
> *He looks steadily at her, then turns and disappears*
> No! No! Who is it? Who?
> Who can it be?
> Some servant—no! I know them all.
> Who is it, who?
> Who can it be?
> Some curious stranger? But how did he get in?
> Who is it, who?
> Some fearful madman locked away there?
> Adventurer? Intruder?
> Who is it, who?
> Who can it be?⁵⁴

When the Analysand delivers these lines to the Analyst, she knows, or at least thinks she knows, who she saw. The disconcerting effect of such disjunctures may be lessened when considering that, in seeking psychiatric counselling, the Analysand may doubt the conclusions she had previously reached about what happened at Bly. Even the fact that the Analysand is speaking in the present tense has some basis in psychoanalytic practice. Nonetheless, the emotional state expressed by the music and her obsessive repetitions of "who is it?" remain incongruous in the context of a retrospective account.

Furthermore, since Diamond and his team did not make any alterations to the score, the musical similarities between the Governess and Quint (discussed in chap. 3) remain additional obstacles toward understanding the Governess as the source of everything spectators see and hear. The convergence of Vere's and Claggart's music is also an obstacle to Albery's proposal that we understand Vere as the source of the interior portion of *Billy Budd*. Despite a degree of incongruence with the scores to these works, both productions draw attention to one of the consequences of these operas' frames: the possibility of unreliable narration.

Albery's and Diamond's productions also illuminate aspects of how these works were made. Albery's staging of *Billy Budd* highlights the divergence of expressive effect created by the music and libretto as well as Forster's formative role in the shaping of the opera's story. Diamond's *Turn of the Screw* draws attention to aspects of the historical context in which James wrote his novella, specifically the emerging discipline of psychoanalysis. Diamond also addresses a possible flaw of the opera: the ineffectuality of its stage directions at supporting second-story interpretations for spectators approaching the opera without prior knowledge of the critical debates surrounding its source.

In the final chapter, I discuss productions that employ some of the same devices—setting the action in a psychiatric ward, reframing some of the events as a character's dream or hallucination—but do so for reasons unrelated to the work ostensibly being performed.

Notes

1. Bryan Magee, *The Tristan Chord: Wagner and Philosophy* (New York: Metropolitan Books, 2000), 211; Roger Scruton, *Death-Devoted Heart: Sex and the Sacred in Wagner's Tristan and Isolde* (Oxford: Oxford University Press, 2004), 75.

2. *Music and Staging* was written in French in 1898 but first published in German a year later as *Die Musik und die Inscenierung*. The quotation is from the following English translation: Adolphe Appia, *Music and the Art of Theatre*, ed. Barnard Hewitt, trans. Robert W. Corrigan and Mary Douglas Dirks (Coral Cables: University of Miami Press, 1962), 199.

3. Ibid., 207, 199–200.

4. Ibid., 72. Note that Appia uses "score" to refer not merely to the music but also to the libretto.

5. Ibid., 208, 201.

6. Ibid., 72.

7. Extracts from *Die Musik und die Inscenierung* were published in the *Wiener Rundschau* on December 15, 1900. Letters from Appia as well as his staging notes for *Tristan* were among Roller's effects. Patrick Carnegy, *Wagner and the Art of the Theatre* (New Haven: Yale University Press, 2006), 164–67; Evan Baker, *From the Score to the Stage: An Illustrated History of Continental Opera Production and Staging* (Chicago: University of Chicago Press, 2013), 276n49.

8. Carnegy, *Wagner and the Art of the Theatre*, 154. Appia's theoretical treatises made their way into the library at Wahnfried, the Wagner family home. Marc Roth, "Staging 'The Master's' Works: Wagner, Appia, and Theatrical Abuse," *Theatre Research International* 5, no. 2 (1980): 152.

9. Joachim Herz mentions the influence of Shaw's *The Perfect Wagnerite* (1898) in "Wagner and Theatrical Realism, 1960–1976," *Wagner* 19, no. 1 (1998): 3.

10. Wikipedia, "Regietheater," accessed March 5, 2020, https://en.wikipedia.org/wiki/Regietheater, lists Sellars among the "prominent American deconstructionists."

11. See, for example, Christopher Morris, "Wagnervideo," *Opera Quarterly* 27, no. 2–3 (2011): 237.

12. Anna Picard, "*Tristan und Isolde*, Opera Bastille, Paris – Maggini Quartet, Purcell Room, London: Big Themes, Big Voices, Enormous Videos," *Independent*, last modified May 1, 2005, https://www.independent.co.uk/arts-entertainment/music/reviews/tristan-und-isolde-opeacutera-bastille-paris-maggini-quartet-purcell-room-london-490619.html.

13. I am grateful to the horn players Joan Watson and Bardhyl Gjevori for revealing how this effect was created at the Canadian Opera Company. Email to author, November 21, 2014.

14. Wagner indicates that half the trumpets and trombones should be in the theater but does not recommend that the singers join them. Richard Wagner, *Richard Wagner Sämtliche Werke*, ed. Isolde Vetter and Egon Voss (Mainz: Schott, 1992), vol. 8, pt. 1, 180.

15. Morris, "Wagnervideo," 244.

16. Ibid.

17. Clemens Risi, "Shedding Light on the Audience: Hans Neuenfels and Peter Konwitschny Stage Verdi (and Verdians)," *Cambridge Opera Journal* 14, no. 1–2 (2001): 207.

18. Joy H. Calico, *Brecht at the Opera* (Berkeley: University of California Press, 2008), 144.

19. Translation from http://www.murashev.com/opera/Tristan_und_Isolde_libretto_German_English.

20. Magee, *Wagner and Philosophy*, 218–21; Scruton, *Death-Devoted Heart*, 55–57, 130. Sellars spoke about the influence of Schopenhauer in Alain Perroux, "La réalité pour métaphore: Entretien avec Peter Sellars," in *Tristan et Isolde à l'aube du XXIe siècle: Trois visions pour une oeuvre mythique*, ed. Alain Perroux (Genève: Labor et Fides, 2005), 70.

21. Daniel H. Foster, *Wagner's Ring Cycle and the Greeks* (Cambridge: Cambridge University Press, 2010), 136–39. Foster overstates the exclusivity of the orchestra's alignment with Siegfried. There are still moments when the orchestra expresses facts Siegfried does not know. For instance, when Siegfried contemplates how different he looks from his supposed father, Mime, the orchestra reminds the audience of his true parentage through a reprise of the Wälsungs' motive.

22. James Parakilas, "Musical Historicism in *The Queen of Spades*," in *Tchaikovsky and His Contemporaries: A Centennial Symposium*, ed. Alexander Mihailovic (Westport: Greenwood Press, 1999), 182.

23. Richard Taruskin, "*The Queen of Spades*," Grove Music Online, last modified 2002, https://www.oxfordmusiconline.com/grovemusic/view/10.1093/gmo/9781561592630.001.0001/omo-9781561592630-e-5000004733, identifies the texts as Vasily Zhukovsky's "Uzh vecher, oblakov pomerknuli kraya" ('Tis evening, the edges of the clouds have darkened, 1806) and Konstantin Batyushkov's "Podrugi milïye" (Dear girls, 1810).

24. David Brown, *Tchaikovsky: A Biographical and Critical Study*, vol. 4 (New York: Norton, 1991), 246.

25. Ibid., 244–46; Richard Taruskin, "The Great Symbolist Opera," in *On Russian Music* (Berkeley: University of California Press, 2009), 122.

26. The metrical "mistake" in the sarabande was noted by contemporary critics such as Nikolai Kashkin (1839–1920). Simon Morrison, *Russian Opera and the Symbolist Movement* (Berkeley: University of California Press, 2002), 72.

27. Taruskin, "Symbolist Opera"; Morrison, *Russian Opera and the Symbolist Movement*, ch. 1; Parakilas, "Musical Historicism," 181.

28. This argument was first suggested to me by an unpublished paper by Margaret Frainier entitled "Point-of-View Narration in Tchaikovsky's *The Queen of Spades*." Other scholars have gestured in this direction but have not pursued the idea as thoroughly. For example, Taruskin,

"Symbolist Opera," 119, 121, likens Tchaikovsky's unbalanced orchestrations to Herman's unbalanced perspective and suggests that the score's mysterious motivic connections invite spectators to "hear with paranoiac ears—Hermann's ears." Morrison, *Russian Opera and the Symbolist Movement*, 91, also remarks on Tchaikovsky's multivalent musical motives. One explanation he offers is that they reflect "discontinuities in Herman's psyche."

29. Some of what happens onstage does represent day-to-day life in the psychiatric ward. The chorus at the beginning of Act II represents patients getting some fresh air. The way the patients respond to Liza's and Polina's performances in Act I, Scene 2 suggests that these are not Herman's memories or hallucinations but representations of the women performing for Herman and the other patients (in this production, neither Liza nor Herman dies).

30. Brown, *Tchaikovsky*, 235. Dodin redistributed other sung lines as well. In Tomsky's telling of the legend of the three cards, his quotations of the Countess were sung by the Countess herself. And in Act III, Scene 1, Liza recites her letter rather than Herman. Dodin also substituted a different text for the children's song in the first scene. I am unsure about its origin. Maria Shevtsova, *Dodin and the Maly Drama Theatre: Process to Performance* (London: Routledge, 2004), 184–85, mentions other changes to the score.

31. Basil Coleman and John Piper, "*Billy Budd* on the Stage: An Early Discussion between Producer and Designer," *Tempo* 21 (Autumn 1951): 21, 25.

32. External narrators address the real-life audience of the work or performance whereas internal narrators tell their stories to other fictional characters. Refer to chapter 3 for a more thorough discussion of these categories.

33. Mervyn Cooke, "Stage History and Critical Reception," in *Benjamin Britten: Billy Budd*, ed. Mervyn Cooke and Philip Reed (Cambridge: Cambridge University Press, 1993), 146.

34. E. M. Forster and Eric Crozier, *Billy Budd* (libretto), in *The Operas of Benjamin Britten: The Complete Librettos*, ed. David Herbert (New York: Columbia University Press, 1979), 204.

35. Ibid., 205.

36. Claggart calls Billy a "beauty" and sings "beauty, handsomeness, goodness" in A major. On the significance of A major in other works, see Mervyn Cooke, "Britten's 'Prophetic Song': Tonal Symbolism in *Billy Budd*," in *Benjamin Britten: Billy Budd*, ed. Mervyn Cooke and Philip Reed (Cambridge: Cambridge University Press, 1993), 165n5.

37. Arnold Whittall, "'Twisted Relations': Method and Meaning in Britten's *Billy Budd*," *Cambridge Opera Journal* 2, no. 2 (1990): 166–69; J. P. E. Harper-Scott, *Ideology in Britten's Operas* (Cambridge: Cambridge University Press, 2018), 134–37; Philip Brett, "Salvation at Sea: Britten's *Billy Budd*," in *Music and Sexuality in Britten: Selected Essays*, ed. George E. Haggerty (Berkeley: University of California Press, 2006), 76–78; Mervyn Cooke, "Be Flat or Be Natural? Pitch Symbolism in Britten's Operas," in *Rethinking Britten*, ed. Philip Rupprecht (Oxford: Oxford University Press, 2013), 113; Cooke, "Tonal Symbolism in *Billy Budd*," 90. For more on the opera's tonal conflict, refer to Philip Rupprecht, "Tonal Stratification and Uncertainty in Britten's Music," *Journal of Music Theory* 40, no. 2 (1996): 311–32.

38. Cooke, "Pitch Symbolism in Britten's Operas," 113.

39. Others who have noted the ambiguous nature of Vere's vocal line include Shannon McKellar, "Re-Visioning the 'Missing' Scene: Critical and Tonal Trajectories in Britten's *Billy Budd*," *Journal of the Royal Musical Association* 122, no. 2 (1997): 264; Harper-Scott, *Ideology in Britten's Operas*, 136–37.

40. Cooke, "Pitch Symbolism in Britten's Operas," 113.

41. Harper-Scott, *Ideology in Britten's Operas*, 134, also notes that these rhythms derive from the music to Billy's execution.

42. Whittall, "Method and Meaning in Britten's *Billy Budd*" 168.

43. Also noted by Cooke, "Stage History," 146.

44. Hanna Rochlitz, "'I *Have* Read *Billy Budd*': The Forster–Britten Reading(s) of Melville," in *Literary Britten: Words and Music in Benjamin Britten's Vocal Works*, ed. Kate Kennedy (Woodbridge: Boydell, 2018), 298. This narrative archetype gains clearest expression in Forster's *Maurice* (published posthumously in 1971). For other examples, refer to Hanna Rochlitz, *Sea-Changes: Melville—Forster—Britten* (Göttingen: Universitätsverlag Göttingen, 2012), sec. II.2.3. Rochlitz prefers the labels *dark* and *light* to describe these archetypes, but in *Billy Budd* I find the class distinction to be more salient.

45. Forster's interpretation of Melville's novella was already along salvation-narrative lines before Britten proposed that they collaborate on an operatic adaptation. Rochlitz, "Forster–Britten Reading(s)," 300–3. For a more detailed examination of the changes to Vere's character, refer to Rochlitz, *Sea-Changes*, sec. III.2.3. Previous scholars have incorrectly attributed such changes to Britten (e.g., Clifford Hindley, "Love and Salvation in Britten's *Billy Budd*," *Music & Letters* 70, no. 3 [1989]: 374; Allen J. Frantzen, "The Handsome Sailor and the Man of Sorrows: *Billy Budd* and the Modernism of Benjamin Britten," *Modern Cultures* 3, no. 2 [2007]: 63–64). Rochlitz's book is the first study to take into consideration all extant working materials for the opera and to couple her examination of these documents with study of Forster's oeuvre, ultimately revealing Forster to be a key player, if not a prime mover, in the changes to Vere's character.

46. Harper-Scott, *Ideology in Britten's Operas*, 117–28, explores the political consequences of Vere's inaction.

47. Jennifer Barnes, *Television Opera: The Fall of Opera Commissioned for Television* (Woodbridge: Boydell, 2003), 50.

48. Patricia Howard, "*The Turn of the Screw* in the Theatre," in *Benjamin Britten: The Turn of the Screw*, ed. Patricia Howard (Cambridge: Cambridge University Press, 1985), 142.

49. Tom Diamond, "Director's Note: Necessity is the Mother of Invention," in *The Turn of the Screw* program (Montréal: Opera McGill, 2011).

50. Although not explicitly prescribed by the score, Pears performed the roles of the Narrator and Quint in the original production, directed by Basil Coleman (La Fenice, 1954), a doubling that is now standard.

51. Myfanwy Piper, *The Turn of the Screw* (libretto), in *The Operas of Benjamin Britten: The Complete Librettos*, ed. David Herbert (New York: Columbia University Press, 1979), 234.

52. Ibid. Philip Rupprecht, *Britten's Musical Language* (New York: Cambridge University Press, 2001), 160–61, discusses the musical contrasts between the children's performance and the adults' conversation in this scene.

53. Piper, *Turn of the Screw* (libretto), 248. In a letter to Neil Saunders from June 28, 1955, Britten wrote: "Myfanwy Piper and I have left the same ambiguities as Henry James did, and in the particular case you mention the boy's final cry is addressed to no one on the stage at all. . . . David Hemmings [as Miles] says the word directly to the *audience*." Mervyn Cooke, Donald Mitchell, and Philip Reed, eds., *Letters from a Life: The Selected Letters of Benjamin Britten, 1913–1976*, 6 vols. (Woodbridge: Boydell, 1991–2012), 4:301.

54. Piper, *Turn of the Screw* (libretto), 234, 239.

8

PERFORMANCES AS WORKS

In the previous chapter, I began investigating what happens to an opera's narrative when the performers depart from the score or libretto. Lev Dodin's *Queen of Spades* (Dutch National Opera, 1998) reframed most of the opera's action as memories and delusions that plague Herman, a resident of a psychiatric ward. In a similar vein, Tom Diamond's *Turn of the Screw* (Opera McGill, 2011) presented the events at Bly as dramatizations of the Governess's psychotherapy sessions. These artistic choices, while in contradiction to the stage directions, were nevertheless motivated by features of the works being performed, in particular the degree to which Herman and the Governess orient the narrative perspectives of their respective operas. The productions discussed in this chapter employ similar means but do so toward ends unrelated to any preexisting works, such as adapting the story to a new medium or meeting the needs of new audiences. As such, most of these productions are more readily understood as performance-works under the ingredients model.

I begin with productions that alter the means by which the story is presented. When Harold Prince directed the 1977 film adaptation of *A Little Night Music*, he decided to remove the Liebeslieders, who functioned as choral narrators in his original stage production. Neil Armfield took the opposite approach in his staging of *Peter Grimes* (Canadian Opera Company, 2003), elevating the status of the nonsinging character Dr. Crabbe to that of an authorial narrator. I then examine some ways directors have attempted to rectify aspects of the work that would be offensive to their audiences. Producing a film of *Der fliegende Holländer* in communist Germany, Joachim Herz reframed the opera's supernatural content as Senta's imaginings in order to reconcile the story with the principles of socialist realism. Aria Umezawa employed a similar strategy toward feminist ends in her staging of Jean-Philippe Rameau and Ballot de Sauvot's *Pygmalion* (Opera McGill, 2014). Katharina Wagner ameliorated the anti-Semitism of *Die Meistersinger* by flipping

Wagner's intended lines of allegiance from Walther and Sachs to Beckmesser in her production for the 2007 Bayreuth Festival. I conclude with a meditation on what is possibly the most pressing issue facing the opera and musical theater communities today: how to retain and even build the audience for these art forms in the twenty-first century. I explore how Deaf West Theatre has succeeded at bringing musicals, such as *Spring Awakening*, to the deaf community and highlight some other accessibility success stories from the previous two chapters.

Character-Narrators: Additions and Subtractions

Sondheim and Hugh Wheeler's *A Little Night Music* (1973) contains a quintet that functions like a Greek chorus. Ironically, given that they are commonly referred to as the Liebeslieder singers, the quintet expresses a cynical stance toward love and monogamy.[1] Although Harold Prince directed the original stage production, he decided not to include the Liebesliedrs in his 1977 film adaptation, presumably regarding them as too theatrical a device.[2] Some of their interjections were cut entirely. Others, such as their contributions to the vocal overture and "The Glamorous Life," Sondheim rewrote for the principal characters.[3] Since the principals, unlike the Liebesliedrs, are in search of the "right" partner and are relatively sanguine about their ability to find him or her, the film is decidedly less cynical than productions that contain the Liebesliedrs.

Some directors have imposed new narrators or framing devices. Noticing that Montagu Slater's libretto to *Peter Grimes* (1945) contains a silent character called Dr. Crabbe, Neil Armfield speculated that he intended this character to be a fictional version of George Crabbe, author of *The Borough* (1810), the collection of poems on which the opera is based.[4] Neither Britten nor Slater appears to have made any mention of the character of Dr. Crabbe or their reasons for including him. Joe Law is one of the only scholars to mention Dr. Crabbe, noting that he appears in "scenes in which Grimes is presented at odds with the rest of the community. In the scenes that indicate Grimes' innocence, Crabbe is absent. Since it is he who will later write the account of Grimes we have come to know, Crabbe's very limited role here may parallel his limitations as a writer of that account. To the extent that he is part of the mob that misunderstands and condemns Grimes, he shares those values and assumptions that must now be questioned as we re-read *The Borough*."[5]

Law's suggestion that Britten and Slater included a fictional surrogate of George Crabbe in order to critique his unsympathetic portrayal of Grimes is an interesting one but unfortunately fails to mesh with the facts about the work. The opera, unlike Crabbe's poem, is ambiguous with respect to Grimes's role in the wrongdoings of which he is accused at the beginning of the story. No scenes unequivocally "indicate Grimes' innocence."

Law's claim that Dr. Crabbe is "part of the mob that misunderstands and condemns Grimes" is also incorrect. The following is a summary of Dr. Crabbe's appearances:

Act I, Scene 1   A fisherman greets Dr. Crabbe and Boles remarks, "He drinks 'Good Health' to all diseases." Later in the scene, the stage directions read, "Dr Crabbe's hat blows away, is rescued for him by Ned Keene who bows him into the pub." Thus, it would seem that Dr. Crabbe remains in the pub for Act I, Scene 2.

Act II, Scene 1   Dr. Crabbe is the first to exit the church after the service. Auntie attempts to tell him what she has observed from spying on the conversation between Ellen, Peter, and the boy, but Keene tells her to "leave him out of it."

Act III, Scene 1   Dr. Crabbe exits the pub midscene and is present for the "goodnight" chorus, after which he retires for the evening.

Act III, Scene 2   The stage directions describe Dr. Crabbe going about his day with the other villagers, equally indifferent to the fate of Peter Grimes.

Given that there is no mention of the doctor being part of the mob who comes to Grimes's hut in the second scene of Act II, one must assume that Slater and Britten did not intend him to be present. Furthermore, in Act III, Scene 1, they explicitly indicate that Dr. Crabbe retires before the rest of the villagers sing the chorus condemning Grimes. Although it is likely that Britten and Slater inserted the character of Dr. Crabbe as a nod to George Crabbe, there is no evidence that they did so with critical intent.

Armfield's aim in drawing attention to this nonsinging character in his production for the Canadian Opera Company (2003) is also not evidently critical of the character's historical counterpart. The production begins with Dr. Crabbe sitting silently at a writing desk facing the stage. Curiously, he does little actual writing during the course of the performance. As Armfield explains in his director's notes, he wanted to draw attention to "the parental act of creating the story: Dr. Crabbe has conceived these characters, this story, and sits back as their father and watches as these creations of his mind come to life and act."[6] Armfield's Crabbe plays a more active role in the narrative than this description suggests. For instance, he cues the conductor to begin and, at times, exerts control over the characters as well as the set.

Armfield's promotion of Dr. Crabbe into the role of an authorial narrator draws attention to the opera's source and its author but offers little insight into the many differences between *The Borough* and *Peter Grimes*. There are also some logical inconsistencies attending Armfield's execution of his concept. The moments when characters refer to Dr. Crabbe and even interact with him physically (for example, during the dancing in Act III, Scene 1) are difficult to reconcile with the premise that we ought to regard most of what is happening onstage as products of Dr. Crabbe's imagination or as representations of the story he is working on. Additionally, if Armfield wanted Dr. Crabbe to be a fictional version of the poet George Crabbe, surely an early nineteenth-century setting would have been more apropos than the one he chose: Aldeburgh during Britten's time.

More Dreamers and Mad Men

Some productions reframe the action of the story in other ways, taking what was intended to be an objective representation of fictional events and presenting them as a character's dream, imaginative episode, or hallucination. This would seem to be the fallback option for directors confounded by a scene or even an entire character that cannot be reconciled with their directorial concept. However, the fact that some, perhaps even most, examples are the product of directorial ennui should not lead one to dismiss the approach entirely. As seen with Dodin's *Queen of Spades*, setting one's production in an asylum need not be a superfluous imposition but may in fact bring audiences to a deeper appreciation of the work, in this case suggesting an explanation of Tchaikovsky's off-kilter rococo dances. In this section, I discuss productions that reframe an opera's narrative structure as a means of tailoring the work to an audience with substantially different values and beliefs than the one for which the work was conceived.

Wagner's *Der fliegende Holländer* (1843) has received more than its fair share of "psychological" treatments, beginning with Joachim Herz's productions at the Komische Oper Berlin (1962), Leipzig Opera (1962), and Bolshoi Theatre (1963) as well as his 1964 film adaptation, produced by DEFA, East Germany's state-owned film studio. My discussion will focus on the film because it, unlike the stage productions, is viewable today, and it was the film that sparked the "veritable epidemic" of similarly premised productions.[7]

Herz's decision to reframe much of the opera's action as products of Senta's imagination was motivated by the difficult place Wagner occupied in East Germany. The supernatural elements of his plots and their reliance on hierarchical social structures and frequent indulgence in nihilism and eroticism were anathema to the state-mandated aesthetic of socialist realism. Although parts of certain works can support anticapitalist interpretations, taken as a whole, Wagner's oeuvre is not easily reconciled with the principles of socialism. Concerns that Wagner's works might have a less than salubrious effect on the populace were not confined to their plots and political content but also extended to their scores. The musical language of *Tristan* (1865) was perceived as too difficult for the everyman and more apt to promote "intoxication" than the kind of "rational reflection" true socialist art ought to inspire.[8] In the late 1950s, the critics Heinz Bär and Erika Wilde even advocated removing some of the more objectionable pieces, such as *Tristan* and *Parsifal* (1882), from the repertory.[9] However, given the centrality of these works within the German opera canon, such solutions failed to gain widespread acceptance.

In 1961, on orders from the Ministry of Culture, the Central Institute for Musicological Research established a committee to create a socialist reinterpretation of Wagner's life and works, which would be disseminated as part of his 150th birthday celebrations. Members of this committee included not only musicologists such as Georg Knepler but also practitioners such as Hanns Eisler and Joachim Herz.[10] In confecting a socialist Wagner, the committee naturally focused on Wagner's brief period as a revolutionary, culminating in his participation in the 1849 uprising in Dresden (in favor of German unification), and his early works, such as *Der fliegende Holländer*.

Holländer contains much of which a socialist would approve. Its heroine, Senta, is the only one of her society who is able to see meaning in life beyond the accumulation of wealth and the upholding of bourgeois moral strictures. Wagner, furthermore, encourages allegiance with the outsiders, Senta and the Dutchman, by associating them with his most progressive music. By contrast, the music of the other characters—Senta's materialistic father, Daland; her rival suitor, Erik; and the other townsfolk—looks backward to Wagner's German predecessors, Spohr and Marschner, French grand opera, and Bellini.

Harder to reconcile with socialist realism were the Dutchman's zombie-like existence and the opera's conclusion with Senta's suicide leading to a quasi-religious apotheosis for her and the Dutchman. To make matters worse, Wagner's glorification of Senta's suicide is not confined to the work's text and stage directions but is also expressed in its score. At the Komische Oper, Herz dealt with these problems by employing Wagner's original ending (composed in 1841) instead of his post-*Tristan* revision of 1860, which was, and still is, the standard ending of the opera.[11] What was originally just a series of D-major

Example 8.1. *Der fliegende Holländer*, original ending (1841)

chords became, in Wagner's revision, a reprise of the Dutchman's theme followed by the theme associated with his hope of redemption (cf. exx. 8.1 and 8.2). Similarly to Isolde's *Liebestod*, Wagner scored the reprise of the Redemption theme for a choir of woodwinds, accompanied by heavenly harp arpeggios.[12] He even reused a similar harmonic progression, concluding the work with a major-to-minor cadence with *religioso* suspension. Wagner further underscored these musical changes with his revised stage directions that emphasized Senta's role in the Dutchman's redemption and further glorified her suicide.

In his film, Herz naturalized the supernatural elements of the plot by presenting the sequences involving the Dutchman and his crew as products of Senta's imagination. In contrast to subsequent copycat productions, there is no suggestion of abnormal psychology. Senta merely uses her imagination to

A dazzling radiance illuminates the group in the background. Senta raises the Dutchman up, presses him to her breast, and points upwards with her eyes raised to heaven. The reef is gradually raised higher and higher and imperceptibly assumes the form of a cloud. With the last three measures, the curtain falls quickly.

Example 8.2. *Der fliegende Holländer*, revised ending (1860)

Example 8.2. *(Continued)*

expand her life beyond the confines of her narrow existence. The film begins with Senta reading about the legend of the Dutchman. When her imagination takes flight, the image format widens, and a slow dissolve connects a close-up of her listening to the wind through the shutters of her cell-like room to a shot of the violent seascape she imagines the Dutchman traversing.

At the point in the opera when Wagner prescribes that Senta hurl herself into the sea, Herz's Senta wakes up after having fallen asleep by the fire. The music of the final portion of the film is not taken from the ending of the opera but from the coda of the 1860 version of the overture. The revised overture's longer modulatory passage before the reprise of the Dutchman's theme allowed Herz the time required to present his new ending of the story. Senta takes the Dutchman's portrait off the wall and leaves her father's house, reveling in her newfound freedom and the beauty of the natural world. Herz thus neutralized the problems with Wagner's revised version of the score by changing the object of veneration. Instead of Senta and the Dutchman's mystical ascent to heaven, the music now celebrates an ordinary woman breaking free from captivity and embarking on a new life. At the entrance of the Redemption theme, the image format widens once more, suggesting that Senta will have no further need of her fantasies about the Dutchman, as her real life is now sufficiently full of possibility.

Harry Kupfer pursued a superficially similar approach in his Bayreuth production of 1978. The difference is that Kupfer's Senta is insane.[13] Lisbeth Balslev's neurotic acting realizes Wagner's fears that singers would "construe [Senta's] dreamy character in terms of a modern, sickly sentimentality."[14] She is onstage for the entire opera, including the overture, during which the Dutchman's portrait falls off the wall and she clutches it to her breast, where it remains for the rest of the evening. The Dutchman and his crew are put forth as Senta's delusions. Comparable to Herz's deployment of changes in image format to differentiate reality from fantasy, Kupfer varies the style of the mise-en-scène. His generally naturalistic approach takes on expressionist and surrealist touches when representing Senta's hallucinations.[15] Kupfer's representation of the Dutchman's arrival roots Senta's psychological problems in sexual repression. The hull of the Dutchman's ship parts in the middle, folding open to reveal a blood-red interior. In the middle of this vagina-like structure is the Dutchman, chained up as in a sadomasochist's fantasy.[16] At the production's conclusion, Senta commits suicide by defenestration. Given the absence of an apotheosis, Kupfer opted for the less glamorous 1841 ending to accompany the townspeople gaping at the body and swiftly retreating into their homes.

Both Herz and Kupfer depart significantly from Wagner's intentions with respect to the staging of this work. Even so, there is much in both the score and libretto that supports their decision to place Senta at the center of the story. Wagner described Senta's ballad, the first time we hear of the legend of the Dutchman, as the "thematic seed of all the music in the opera" and "the poetically condensed image of the whole drama."[17] Accounting for a degree of exaggeration on Wagner's part, intended to emphasize the continuity of his earlier "Romantic operas" with his later "music dramas," there is much truth to this statement. In terms of its plot, Senta's ballad is a microcosm of the opera. Although it was not the first music Wagner composed, it does *appear* to be the source of most of the opera's musical thematic material, including the themes representing the Dutchman and his redemption.[18] And despite Senta's claim that she learned the ballad from her nurse, she is the fictional author of the version she performs. Her spontaneous decision to cast herself in the part of the Dutchman's redeemer ("Ich sei's, die dich durch ihre Treu' erlöset!") was surely not a course of action recommended by her nurse.[19]

Due to the ways in which Herz's and Kupfer's productions mesh with the properties of the work's score and libretto, they are more effective as productions of Wagner's work than others that have employed the "dream" approach but have chosen different dreamers, such as the Helmsman (e.g., Jean-Pierre Ponnelle, San Francisco, 1975).[20] However, unlike the productions discussed in the previous chapter, many of Herz's creative decisions cannot be explained by an intention to be faithful to Wagner's work. Herz's primary aim was not to convey what Wagner intended *Der fliegende Holländer* to mean but, in a similar spirit to his work on the Wagner rehabilitation committee, to put forth a meaning that would be appropriate to a socialist and increasingly feminist Germany. Herz not only naturalized the supernatural elements of the opera but also endowed its heroine with more agency than Wagner intended. As Joy Calico observes, Herz's Senta "escapes both the dream world and reality by walking away from all the men who would control her: the Dutchman, her father, and Erik."[21]

Herz's success in presenting this revised story in his *Holländer* film not only hinged on clever staging choices and cinematic framing but also involved substantial changes to the score. Herz and his conductor, Rolf Reuter, cut half an hour of music, not through the expedient method of dropping a scene or two but through many short incisions, which remarkably did not sacrifice musical or narrative logic. Their revisions also involved reordering the music and plot, particularly in the first act (Herz's arrangement is given in table 8.1). According to Wagner's stage directions, Senta does not appear until Act II.

Table 8.1. Herz's arrangement of *Der fliegende Holländer*, Act I, Scenes 1–2

Number	Measures*	Description
Overture	1–150	to the middle of the storm music after the Redemption theme
2	84–135, 152–228, 259–end	from the second statement of "Wie oft Meeres tiefsten Grund" to the end of the aria, omitting some repetition and "Wann alle Toten auferstehn, dann werde ich in Nichts vergehn"
1	1–64 (48–51 repeated as a vamp), 171–82	from the beginning, omitting the conversation between the Helmsman and Daland, and resuming at the bassoon-horn duet before the Helmsman's song
Overture	175–98	music to the spinning chorus
1	147–93 (voices omitted until 162), 234–88	beginning "Nun, Steuermann," and omitting the middle of the Helmsman's song

* Measure numbers correspond to the 1860 version of the score, published in Richard Wagner, *Richard Wagner Sämtliche Werke*, ed. Egon Voss (Mainz: Schott, 2000), vol. 4, pt. 3. The numbering resets at the beginning of each number.

Herz's reordered first act helped orient viewers toward Senta's experience in ways that Kupfer's more faithful production did not.[22]

By containing an uncut performance of the 1841 version of Wagner's score, Kupfer's production is superior in its capacity to provide audiences access to Wagner's work in terms of its textual and musical content as well as the overall point it was intended to convey. However, due to the many social and political differences between Wagner's context and that of postwar Germany, Kupfer's production is less effective than Herz's at catering to the concerns of its audience. Kupfer's decision to portray Senta as suffering from hysteria brought on by sexual repression uncritically espouses nineteenth-century ideas about gender and sexuality. Given the decision to cast the African American bass-baritone Simon Estes as the Dutchman, his production also perpetuates essentialist attitudes toward race. Estes's appearance at the Bayreuth Festival was a milestone in the history of racial equality on the operatic stage as he became the first man of color to appear at the festival in a leading role. But rather than using this occasion to defy the racial stereotypes that prevented singers of color from expanding their repertoire, Kupfer merely reinscribed them by casting him in the role of the repressed white girl's sexual fantasy.

Another novel and effective revision of an opera's narrative structure for the purpose of updating a work's gender politics is Aria Umezawa's production of *Pygmalion* for Opera McGill (2014). In her director's notes, Umezawa summarizes the problems this work poses for the twenty-first-century feminist: "Not only does Pygmalion craft his ideal of what a woman should look like, but he eschews his real, living partner Cephise in favour of an inanimate object with no autonomy. When finally brought to life, The Statue declares that she was crafted by him for him, and she will always obey. To say she is not exactly the ideal portrayal of an empowered female character is an understatement." Having considered "declaring Pygmalion insane and setting the opera in a mental ward," Umezawa concluded that such an approach would "send the wrong message about gender equality—it is not a zero-sum game."[23]

In keeping with the theme of the 2014/15 McGill Opera season, Umezawa set her production in the First World War. Pygmalion is a soldier who has been wounded in battle. Contemplating the realities of his situation—"the friends that gave their lives, his physical condition at the end of the war, and the idea that the partner he left may be a stranger to him upon his return"—proves too difficult. He imagines a woman, the Statue, who understands what he has seen and done and who loves him all the same. Like Herz's Senta, Umezawa's Pygmalion is not insane. Rather, her production shows some of the roles the imagination can play in contending with difficult circumstances. "As the goddess of Love enters and calls upon the muses to declare her virtues, she summons the images of the people who bring these soldiers the most comfort. These people were women. Not only the friends, or wives, or ideals of femininity, but the nurses who served during the war, risking their lives right beside the men."[24] By means of a most unlikely vehicle, Umezawa manages to make a feminist statement after all.

Umezawa's *Pygmalion* also differs from the other productions discussed in this section as the subjective inflection of what audiences are seeing is not revealed forthwith. Only gradually do the trappings of a war hospital make an appearance, triggering a retrospective reinterpretation of the previous interactions between Pygmalion and the Statue. By leaving the epistemic structure of her production unspecified until midway through, Umezawa exposes an assumption underlying opera spectatorship—namely, that what one sees onstage is an objective representation of the fictional world.[25]

Altering Allegiances

One of the more compelling arguments in favor of revising a work's text and/or music is to rectify problematic social or political content.[26] This impulse to bring performances of works of theater in line with contemporary views on gender and race is rarely seen in other art forms, and when it is seen it is often the source of controversy. Whereas Alan Gribben's decision to replace all instances of the word *nigger* with *slave* in his 2011 edition of *The Adventures of Tom Sawyer and Huckleberry Finn* has faced fierce criticism, no musical theater company today would dream of beginning a performance of *Show Boat* with the first word of Oscar Hammerstein's original libretto: "niggers."[27] Speaking or singing racial slurs in a live performance seems to assert their continued validity.

A work whose statements about politics and race have become unutterable for many people in light of the atrocities committed by the Nazi party is Wagner's *Die Meistersinger von Nürnberg* (1868). What makes this work particularly repugnant is not only its past use in Nazi propaganda but also its aesthetic and political content that rendered it apt for such purposes. Wagner encourages audiences to applaud Walther's rather conservative performance at the singing contest, nod with approval at the aggressive nationalism of Sachs's final speech, and laugh at Beckmesser's artistic failures. To the extent that Beckmesser was intended to be regarded as a Jew, the work expresses anti-Semitic sentiments about the abilities of Jewish artists and calls into question the place of Jews in German society.

As Adorno remarked in *In Search of Wagner* (1952), and Barry Millington and Marc Weiner have elaborated, there is a remarkable similarity between Wagner's portrayal of Beckmesser and his description of Jews in his 1850 essay "Judaism in Music."[28] Beckmesser's blind commitment to the Mastersingers' rules is redolent of the "backward-looking poet," capable only of imitating the utterances of others, "just as parrots imitate human words and phrases, but without any expression or real emotion." After having failed in his attempt to perform his own composition (his serenade to Eva in Act II), Beckmesser steals Walther's Prize Song. However, his attempt to perform it on the Festival Meadow results in merely a "confused babble of sounds."[29]

Wagner's anti-Semitism is indisputable. The point on which Wagner scholars disagree is the relevance of these views to the interpretation of his art.[30] For those who reject a cordoning off of the artist from his or her works, the foregoing parallels strongly point to an intent to portray Beckmesser as a Jew and, through the character's artistic and moral failings, encourage anti-Semitic attitudes. What is less clear is the extent to which Wagner's audiences viewed Beckmesser in light of the composer's "Judaism" essay.[31] Surprisingly, it is not even clear that the Nazis regarded Beckmesser as a caricature of a Jew. David B. Dennis's thorough examination of Nazi writings on *Die Meistersinger* uncovered no evidence that the Nazis "referred in public discourse to the character of Sixtus Beckmesser as Jewish, or to his fate in *Die Meistersinger* as foreshadowing National Socialist policies against Jews." They did not "openly discuss Beckmesser as an Outsider, but rather as a highly influential Insider whose main sin was that of artistic pedantry. With regard to Beckmesser's singing, Nazi interpreters tended to explain his 'difficulties' on the basis of increasing anger and confusion as his plans go awry."[32]

Rather, what drew the Nazis to *Die Meistersinger* was the nationalist, even xenophobic sentiments expressed in Sachs's final speech, the latter portion of which is reproduced below.[33]

Habt Acht! Uns dräuen üble Streich':	Beware! Evil tricks threaten us:
zerfällt erst deutsches Volk und Reich,	if the German people and kingdom should one day decay,
in falscher wälscher Majestät	under a false, foreign rule
kein Fürst bald mehr sein Volk versteht,	soon no prince would understand his people;
und wälschen Dunst mit wälschem Tand	and foreign mists with foreign vanities
sie pflanzen uns in deutsches Land;	they would plant in our German land;
was deutsch und echt, wüsst' keiner mehr,	what is German and true none would know,
lebt's nicht in deutscher Meister Ehr'.	if it did not live in the honor of German Masters.
Drum sag' ich euch:	Therefore I say to you:
ehrt eure deutschen Meister!	honor your German Masters,
Dann bannt ihr gute Geister;	then you will conjure up good spirits!
und gebt ihr ihrem Wirken Gunst,	And if you favor their endeavors,
zerging' in Dunst	even if the Holy Roman Empire
das heil'ge röm'sche Reich,	should dissolve in mist,
uns bliebe gleich	for us there would yet remain
die heil'ge deutsche Kunst!	holy German art!

Regardless of whether Wagner intended this indictment of "foreign rule" to refer to the ascendancy of the "enemy within" or the crowd's rejection of Beckmesser to advocate something like Hitler's "final solution," that is what many spectators think of when they witness the final scene enacted according to Wagner's performance directions. Even Adorno, not generally supportive of revisionist stagings, advocated that directors intervene in Sachs's final address and liberate Wagner's works from Jewish caricatures such as Beckmesser.[34] Today, this stance is shared by directors pursuing both classical-paradigm and ingredients-model approaches. In the words of David McVicar (whose work falls mostly in the former category), "taking a critical stance is the only moral way to present [Wagner]."[35]

Of the two problems, the aggressive nationalism of Sachs's final speech is the easier one to solve. Since the offensive sentiments are confined to the sung text, the relevant lines could simply be cut.[36] And given that a complete performance lasts at least four and a half hours, cuts are likely advisable in any case. Yet appreciating the work being performed involves knowing what political messages it was intended to convey, as deplorable as they may be. Excising offensive passages or (more egregiously) retaining them and providing a more politically correct translation in the surtitles may mislead audiences into assuming that the work's politics are unobjectionable.[37] Another solution to this problem would be to retain the offensive lines but indicate that the production does not support them. An example of this approach arose in chapter 6: Peter Konwitschny's Hamburg production (2002). When Sachs gets to the offensive portion of his speech, the other singers interrupt him and engage in a spoken debate about the ethics of what he is suggesting.

Resisting the anti-Semitism of Wagner's portrayal of Beckmesser is more challenging. One might initially think that a singer could simply refuse to play into Wagner's Jewish stereotypes. Those that are confined to physical characteristics, such as limping, can easily be avoided, but as many have noted, Beckmesser's Jewishness also extends to his music, including his inept serenade in Act II, his garbled performance of Walther's song, and the unusually high tessitura of the role as well as its melismatic character.[38] Rectifying these elements would involve rewriting the work's libretto and score. In other words, one cannot remove the Jewish stereotypes from Beckmesser's role while still performing *Wagner's* work.

Another solution to the Beckmesser problem would be to stage different fictional reactions to the character's performances and a different ending to his story. Herz's production that reopened the Leipzig Opera after the Second World War presented a more sympathetic portrayal of Beckmesser than had possibly ever been seen before. As Patrick Carnegy notes, Beckmesser "did not lack for supporters in the crowd. In keeping with the conciliatory mood of the production, Beckmesser did not flee after his humiliation but stayed on to hear Walther sing the Prize Song; Sachs offered him his hand, and Beckmesser brought himself to grasp it."[39] Herz's approach was imitated by many other directors, including Götz Friedrich (Stockholm, 1977; Deutsche Oper Berlin, 1979), Wolfgang Wagner (Bayreuth, 1984, 1996), Michael Hampe (Australian Opera, 1985), and François Rochaix (Seattle, 1989).[40]

Katharina Wagner took this approach even further in her production for the 2007 Bayreuth Festival. She reversed her great-grandfather's recommended allegiances, upholding Beckmesser as the true artist of the future and inculcating Walther's and Sachs's increasing artistic conservatism with the rise of fascism. To understand Katharina Wagner's artistic decisions, it will be necessary to place her production within the history of the festival. In 2007, its director, Wolfgang Wagner, was eighty-eight, and the festival was actively seeking out a successor. With several other members of the Wagner family interested in the position, Katharina Wagner's production functioned as something of a job application, one in which the festival's board and patrons were eager to see her take a stand on the relative merits of Werktreue versus Regieoper or, in the terminology introduced in chapter 6, the classical paradigm versus the ingredients model.[41] For this reason, Katharina Wagner decided to shift the artistic medium in which the work's aesthetic debates take place from singing to visual art and opera direction.

Mirroring Walther's musical trajectory from his *Tristan*-esque Trial Song (Act I) to the relative blandness of his Prize Song (Act III), Walther begins as an avant-garde performance artist and provocateur but concludes as a popstar sellout. Sachs's portrayal traces a similar trajectory. He enters the initial meeting of the Mastersingers late, sans regalia and footwear, with his shirt gaping open and a cigarette never far from his mouth. Sachs mirrors many spectators' feelings of annoyance at the parochial concerns of the other masters and dismay at Pogner's offering of his daughter's hand in marriage as the prize of the contest. Yet after his Wahn Monologue in Act III, Sachs gradually transforms from hippie to Hitler-esque leader of a totalitarian state.[42] Beckmesser undergoes the opposite transformation in this production. He starts out as the most pedantic of all the masters, his commitment to tradition represented by his prodigious stack of Reclam editions of German literary classics. However, taking a cue from Ernst Bloch's interpretation of Beckmesser's performance on the Festival Meadow as an anticipation of literary Dadaism and the Second Viennese School, he becomes the true representative of the avant-garde in Act III.[43]

The event that brings about these transformations is the riot provoked by Beckmesser's serenade in Act II. In this production, the chorus (dressed as students) expresses their displeasure at Beckmesser's performance by throwing books at him, an act of defiance that concludes with the students hoisting Moore- and Picasso-esque sculptures above their heads and flinging paint from Campbell's soup cans (a nod to Andy Warhol). During the riot, the busts of the German masters lining the walls come to life and join the fray. Walther and Sachs react to this loss of order by retreating into the traditions of the Mastersingers. As the masters discuss the rules of the contest in Act I, Walther defaces a traditional model opera set. By Act III, when he brings this set to Sachs for advice, the master removes the graffiti, and Walther proceeds to paint a new, more conventional backdrop during his composition of the Prize Song. In the quintet, Walther's and Sachs's newfound traditionalism is revealed to extend to the social realm as well. The flower-child version of Eva that Walther liberated in Act II now appears in the guise of a 1950s housewife who poses for a family portrait with Walther (now equally well-groomed), their three children, and her father.

In lieu of the procession of the guilds prescribed during the long orchestral prelude to Act III, Scene 5, the animated busts of the German masters—now sporting carnivalesque bobbleheads—tie Sachs up and force him to watch a series of Regieoper tropes, such as the debasement of venerated historical figures, the entire cast inexplicably clothed in only their undergarments, giant phalluses, and parodies of more popular forms of musical theater.[44] Similarly to the conclusion of Peter Sellars's Trump Tower *Figaro* (Pepsico Summerfare Festival, 1988), the bobbleheads form a chorus line, concluding their performance with "jazz hands." A fictional production team comes out for a bow, after which a cleanup crew expresses their thoughts on the "Eurotrash versus Eurotreasure" debate by depositing the fictional production team in the trash. Clemens Risi relates that this act was met with spontaneous and enthusiastic applause at the production's premiere. The merriment quickly subsided, however, when Sachs set this vessel on fire, singing "Wach' auf," the phrase, Millington notes, "the Nazis used to exhort the German people, resulting in acts of barbaric inhumanity."[45]

The riot has the opposite effect on Beckmesser. As Walther and Sachs join the cleanup effort, Beckmesser tentatively smears paint on his shirt, recalling Walther's earlier tendency to use his interlocutors' bodies as canvases for his artistic experiments. By Act III, Beckmesser has fully assumed Walther's former role. When he enters Sachs's house to take a peek at his rival's model set, he sneers and uses Walther's discards as the basis for his own set design.

The Festival Meadow scene becomes a contest between "traditional" and Regieoper stagings of the story of Adam and Eve, performed for a fictional Bayreuth audience.[46] Beckmesser continues with the parade of Regieoper devices begun by the bobbleheads. Assuming the role of God, he animates a naked man from a table topped with mud. In a gesture to opera's tentative explorations of interactive theater, he selects his Eve from the fictional audience. After being divested of her clothing, she and Adam proceed to throw balls of paint at the fictional Bayreuth patrons. Mirroring the reactions of many of the actual patrons, they respond with a mixture of laughs and boos. Beckmesser, seeming to revel in the shock and outrage he has provoked, stays to watch his rival's contribution with smug satisfaction.

Walther enters the Festival Meadow in the guise of a host of *Musikantenstadl*, a German folk music television show. While he performs in the park-and-bark manner typical of the previous generation of Wagner singers, his narration is enacted by actors in nineteenth-century imitations of Renaissance costumes, employing the stilted gestural language even Richard Wagner had railed against but which still persists in some corners of the opera world. Before Walther is even finished, the audience erupts into rapturous applause. Walther receives a giant check, and Sachs attempts to award him the golden Bambi (reminiscent of a German media prize) he excavated from the production team's remains.[47]

The staging and filming of Sachs's final address is modeled on Hitler's appearances in Nazi propaganda films. He is lit from below and filmed from a low angle. Sachs emphasizes his words with the sort of rigid, militaristic gestures Hitler employed to exhort his people to action. At Sachs's mention of the threat of the "foreign mists," larger-than-life statues of Goethe and Schiller in the style of Nazi sculptor Arno Breker emerge to tower over the scene while Beckmesser's indifference turns to horror.[48]

Contrary to Wagner's intentions, the production's most musically outstanding performance was Michael Volle's Beckmesser. Millington remarked that "there is something seriously wrong [with a performance of *Die Meistersinger*] when the one character sung well is that of Beckmesser."[49] In light of Katharina Wagner's intent that audiences regard Beckmesser as the winner of the singing contest, I suspect that Volle's fine singing was not an accident, and if it was, then it was a happy one.

Katharina Wagner's production begins by encouraging Richard Wagner's allegiances with Walther and Sachs but departs from those allegiances in Act III to take a critical stance toward the work's anti-Semitic content as well as the aggressive nationalism of Sachs's final speech. With Walther's trajectory from punk to pop star, she also acknowledges and attempts to alleviate the disappointment many feel with respect to Walther's Prize Song. Given its more conservative harmonic language, in comparison with Wagner's previous work, *Tristan*, and even other portions of this work (e.g., Sachs's Wahn Monologue), the Prize Song fails to represent what it was intended to represent: the injection of new aesthetic ideas into the traditions of the Mastersingers.[50] By pointing out Walther's inadequacies, Katharina Wagner encourages her audiences to ally themselves with the underdog, Beckmesser, and the artistic program he represents in this production: an ingredients-model approach

234 | Storytelling in Opera and Musical Theater

to opera direction. Even audience members who are opposed to directorial interventions are likely to question their allegiance with the side of "tradition," given that its chief spokesperson is modeled on Hitler.

Reaching New Audiences

Another reason to reconceptualize what a work has to say is to reach new audiences. Without altering a note or sung word of Duncan Sheik and Steven Sater's *Spring Awakening* (2006), Deaf West Theatre brought their musical to the deaf community in 2014 by using it to tell a new story about the history of the education of the deaf.

Sater and Sheik's musical is an adaptation of Frank Wedekind's play *Frühlings Erwachen* (1891), an indictment of Victorian attitudes toward sex and the treatment of young people. At first blush, there seems to be little in Wedekind's work that would speak to Americans at the turn of the following century. Although the struggle for equality for all genders and sexualities is still ongoing, young people in America hardly need to be awakened about sexual matters. Yet with the return to a Republican government under George W. Bush (2001–2009), Wendla's narrative—lack of sexual education leading to unprotected sex and death from a botched abortion—became topical as questions of the place of sexual education in public schools and a woman's right to choose were reopened. Additionally, Moritz's suicide after flunking out of school and being rejected by his father spoke to the rise in rates of teen suicides and school shootings.[51]

Sater and Sheik further emphasized the contemporary relevance of the story's themes through their novel approach to their show's songs. *Spring Awakening* was by no means the first musical to employ a predominantly rock-based score. Its use of alternative rock to tell a story set in the nineteenth century was, however, novel for its time. Furthermore, rather than using the songs as a means of communication between the characters, they functioned predominantly as interior monologues and authorial commentary (an example of the latter is the ensemble's singing of "I Believe" while Wendla and Melchior have sex).[52] At the transitions from book to musical number, the singers suddenly begin to act like contemporary teens, singing directly to the audience. The rock-concert aesthetic also influenced the choreography and lighting of the songs.

Sater and Sheik's *Spring Awakening* is about the failure of an education system and the tragic consequences of miscommunication between parents and their children. It was not intended to describe the position of deaf people in the latter part of the nineteenth century. Even so, Michael Arden, director of Deaf West's production, observes some striking parallels.[53] Ten years before Wedekind wrote *Frühlings Erwachen*, the Second International Congress on Education of the Deaf (1880, also commonly referred to as the Milan Conference) decided on the superiority of oralism (speaking and lip-reading) over manualism (signing) and passed a resolution that banned sign language from schools in Europe and the United States. Deaf West's *Spring Awakening* explores the consequences of these decisions.

In pursuit of their aim to be an "artistic bridge between the deaf and hearing worlds," Deaf West typically employs mixed casts.[54] What is unusual about their production of *Spring Awakening* is their invitation to map the actor's identity as deaf or hearing onto the character.[55] To represent the historical power relations between the deaf and hearing communities, they cast deaf actors in the roles of the story's victims: Moritz, Wendla, Martha, and Ernst.

Hearing actors largely employ sim-com (simultaneous speaking and signing in ASL) while deaf actors are paired with a hearing double who performs most of their speaking and singing.[56] Some scenes involve sign language only (e.g., Moritz's rejection by his father and final monologue before his suicide), with English projections for those not conversant in ASL. The deaf actors also occasionally use their voices when forced by their teacher and in moments of extreme emotion. Examples include Moritz's father's "why?" after learning of his son's "failure" and Wendla's accusatory question to her mother: "why didn't you tell me everything [about sex]?"

The ASL in Deaf West's *Spring Awakening* is not, however, a mere translation of Sater's libretto to make the production accessible to the deaf community (though it did also accomplish this task). The signing is often more figurative than literal. During the musical numbers, it becomes more like dance or sign poetry, indicating to deaf viewers the moments when speech gives way to song.[57]

Similarly, the character doubles are not mere communication aids, hidden from view, but are integrated into the plot, particularly in the case of Wendla and Moritz, whose doubles are onstage for most of the show. While the signing actors are dressed in period costumes, their singer counterparts are in modern dress, reflecting their closer association with Sheik's modern score. In the cases of Wendla and Moritz, the signing and singing actors represent different facets of their characters. After Wendla's mother refuses to answer her questions about where babies come from, the more assertive singing-Wendla convinces her signing counterpart to insist on an explanation. Singing-Moritz supplies signing-Moritz with the gun he uses to commit suicide, after which signing-Moritz dismisses his singer. The separation of singer and signer is associated with death in Wendla's story as well. When she is taken to the doctor who will perform the abortion that will terminate her life, she is separated from her singer by force.

The clearest illustration of the tragic consequences of the Milan Conference occurs in the scene at the boys' school (Scene 2). The teacher employs oralist methods of instruction, striking the boys with his pointer when he catches them signing, and forcing them to speak. In Deaf West's production, Moritz's problems at school stem not from his preoccupation with sex but from the fact that he has trouble understanding the language of instruction and is forbidden to sign. His friend, Melchior, is hearing but knows ASL and translates the lesson for the other students when the teacher's back is turned.

Similarly, Wendla's lack of understanding of what is happening to her body stems not only from her mother's prudishness but also from a language barrier between herself and her mother as well as her doctor. The doctor doesn't sign at all but merely speaks more loudly and slowly and with exaggerated mouth movements. Deaf West's production not only teaches audiences about the ramifications of the Milan Conference but also draws attention to problems with the way some members of the hearing community interact with deaf people today.[58]

Opera and Accessibility

This chapter has examined reasons for departing from the performing directions that cannot be explained by an intent to be faithful to the work ostensibly being performed: adapting it to a new medium (e.g., Prince's *A Little Night Music* film) or to a new social or political context (e.g., Herz's *Holländer* and Umezawa's *Pygmalion*), critiquing the work's problematic politics (e.g., Katharina Wagner's *Meistersinger*), and making new artistic and political points in order to reach new audiences (e.g., Deaf West's *Spring Awakening*). Katharina Wagner's *Meistersinger* does more than merely defend such directorial interventions but asserts that the ingredients model is the only way forward for opera direction and implicates the classical paradigm with fascism.

There are several problems with her representation of this debate. Her production's many references to the Third Reich sit uncomfortably with its commentary on contemporary performance practice. Regieoper is hardly an "endangered cultural asset" in twenty-first-century Germany.[59] Katharina Wagner's production did garner a fair share of boos (audible even on the video of its 2008 revival). Yet given the many glowing reviews, ample attention in the scholarly press, and the fact that she did get the directorship (alongside

Eva Wagner-Pasquier), it is hard to see her as a victim or even as a Beckmesserish underdog.

Furthermore, given the performance history of *Die Meistersinger*, it is ill-suited as a case study from which to extrapolate general conclusions about the superiority of an ingredients-model approach over one grounded in the classical paradigm. Because of its anti-Semitic content and the association of Sachs's final speech with Hitler's "final solution," producing an uncritical *Meistersinger* today is certainly inadvisable, possibly even immoral. *Die Meistersinger* is by no means the only opera with content that contemporary audiences are likely to find objectionable. Orientalist works such as *Madama Butterfly* (1904) and *The King and I* (1951) pose similar problems. Yet not all works contain problematic content that ought to be omitted or critiqued. And given the degree to which an appreciation of Katharina Wagner's production relies on knowledge of how Wagner's work was intended to be performed, her approach is inadvisable for new or comparatively unknown works.

The extensive prior knowledge required to appreciate Katharina Wagner's production—knowledge not only of Richard Wagner's work but also of its performance history, the history of the Bayreuth Festival, and other opera productions—points to another aspect of the debate that she does not acknowledge: the obstacles many so-called Regieoper productions pose to comprehension for audiences lacking such background knowledge. One of the more common justifications of directorial innovation is its putative ability to bring new audiences to opera, a central concern of those invested in the longevity of this art form. As Deaf West's *Spring Awakening* demonstrates, it is not always necessary to change the score or to set the work in the present day in order to make it accessible to new audiences. What matters is the production's ability to provide its audience with the means with which to understand and appreciate both the production as an artistic statement as well as any preexisting work(s) being performed.

Sometimes this goal is best met by placing the work being performed in context and highlighting the historical influences on its creation. By eschewing the mythical and supernatural trappings of Wagner's works and setting them in the late nineteenth century, Joachim Herz showed how Wagner used his works as vehicles with which to critique the society in which he lived. Tom Diamond's reframing of *The Turn of the Screw* as the Governess's psychotherapy sessions alerted even spectators unaware of the critical discourses surrounding Henry James's novella to the possibility that the Governess may be an unreliable narrator and invited them to consider the influence of psychoanalysis on the story. Tim Albery's decision to costume Vere as E. M. Forster in his production of *Billy Budd* (English National Opera, 1988) drew attention to the writer's guiding role in the reshaping of the opera's central character.

In other situations, accessibility may be best pursued by taking the work out of context and showing the continued relevance of its themes to contemporary society. Peter Sellars is the best known proponent of this approach, at least in North America. In casting Handel's Hercules as an American soldier returning from a tour in the Middle East, Sellars drew attention to the difficulties soldiers still face when reentering civilian society.

Given the decline of musical literacy and knowledge of operatic conventions, another way directors can help new audiences appreciate the work being performed is by using their staging to illuminate features of the music that newcomers may not otherwise notice or know how to interpret. Sellars used lighting to draw attention to the musical contrasts between the lovers and the landing party at the end of the first act of *Tristan* as well as to Wagner's Schopenhauerian thematization of Day and Night. Philip Langridge's tortured performance of the epilogue to Albery's *Billy Budd* exposed Britten's less than affirmative setting of Forster's words.

For performance-works under the ingredients model, accessibility involves tailoring the work's content to one's audience. With some works, such as *Die Meistersinger*, that may entail omitting some objectionable lines or, as Katharina Wagner did, presenting them in a critical light. It may also involve replacing outdated references with those one's audience is more likely to recognize. Mozart and Da Ponte could rely on their audience comparing *Così fan tutte*'s Alfonso to other philosopher parodies in comedies of the late eighteenth century.[60] Producing an updated version in twenty-first-century Toronto, Joel Ivany wisely sought out contemporary reference points in *A Little Too Cozy* (Against the Grain Theatre, 2016), modeling Donald L. Fonzo's appearance on the Canadian hockey commentator Don Cherry and hosts of reality TV shows.

Against the Grain Theatre has been particularly successful at attracting and retaining a younger, more diverse audience base. One of the keys to their success is marketing campaigns that align with their artistic aims. While acknowledging the inspiration they took from Mozart and Da Ponte's works, Against the Grain billed *Figaro's Wedding*, *#UncleJohn*, and *A Little Too Cozy* as "transladaptations" rather than as work-performances. They are also sensitive to their target audience's interests, tastes, and knowledge base. Unlike many productions commonly classified as Regieoper, no prior experience with *Così fan tutte* is required to get something out of *A Little Too Cozy*. The production supplies even newbie audiences with the information required for appreciation.

Notes

1. Joseph P. Swain, "*A Little Night Music*: The Cynical Operetta," in *Oxford Handbook of Sondheim Studies*, ed. Robert Gordon (New York: Oxford University Press, 2014), 312.

2. Stephen Sondheim, *Finishing the Hat: Collected Lyrics (1954–1981)* (New York: Knopf, 2010), 280, commented that while they "served both narrative and commentary functions in the show [they] would have been a clumsily abstract presence in the movie." For more on the role of the Liebeslieders in the original stage production, refer to Barbara Means Fraser, "Revisiting Greece: The Sondheim Chorus," in *Stephen Sondheim: A Casebook*, ed. Joanne Gordon (New York: Garland, 1997), 230–34.

3. Both versions of these numbers are provided in Stephen Sondheim et al., *Four by Sondheim, Wheeler, Lapine, Shevelove and Gelbart* (New York: Applause, 2000).

4. Neil Armfield, "Director's Notes," *Peter Grimes* program (Toronto: Canadian Opera Company, 2013), 2.

5. Joe K. Law, "The Dialogics of Operatic Adaptation: Reading Benjamin Britten," *A Yearbook of Interdisciplinary Studies in the Fine Arts* 1 (1989): 416.

6. Armfield, "Director's Notes," 2.

7. Joachim Herz, "Wagner and Theatrical Realism, 1960–1976," *Wagner* 19, no. 1 (1998): 20.

8. Paul Dessau, "Musik der Gründerjahre: Ein Interview," *Theater der Zeit* (1958), quoted in Elaine Kelly, "Imagining Richard Wagner: The Janus Head of a Divided Nation," *Kritika* 9, no. 4 (2008): 818.

9. These statements were published in *Theater der Zeit*. Kelly, "Imagining Richard Wagner," 817.

10. Ibid., 823.

11. The first production to return to the original ending was Jürgen Fehling's, conducted by Otto Klemperer (Krolloper, Berlin, 1929). The decision was so controversial that the dramaturg had to justify it to the Prussian parliament! Herz, "Wagner and Theatrical Realism," 29. The preface to Richard Wagner, *Richard Wagner Sämtliche Werke*, ed. Egon Voss (Mainz: Schott, 2000), vol. 4, pt. 3, vii–xii, details the history of Wagner's revisions. For a comparison of the two versions, refer to Paul S. Machlin, "Wagner, Durand and *The Flying Dutchman*: The 1852 Revisions of the Overture," *Music & Letters* 55, no. 4 (1974): 410–28.

12. Wagner pointed out the influence of the Liebestod on his revision in a letter to Mathilde Wesendonck from March 3, 1860, quoted in Machlin, "Wagner, Durand and *The Flying Dutchman*," 416.

13. Kupfer was fond of using a character's insanity to naturalize an opera's supernatural elements. See also his production of Gluck's *Orfeo ed Euridice* (Komische Oper Berlin, 1987).

14. Richard Wagner, "Remarks on the Performance of the Opera *Der fliegende Holländer*," trans. Thomas S. Grey, in *Richard Wagner: Der fliegende Holländer*, ed. Thomas S. Grey (Cambridge: Cambridge University Press, 2000), 200. Wagner wrote this essay in 1852 for Franz Liszt who was mounting the opera in Weimar.

15. Patrick Carnegy, *Wagner and the Art of the Theatre* (New Haven: Yale University Press, 2006), 329.

16. Mike Ashman, "Wagner on Stage: Aesthetic, Dramaturgical, and Social Considerations," in *Cambridge Companion to Richard Wagner*, ed. Thomas S. Grey (Cambridge: Cambridge University Press, 2008), 265.

17. Richard Wagner, *A Communication to My Friends* (1851); translation from Carl Dahlhaus, *Richard Wagner's Music Dramas*, trans. Mary Whittall (London: Cambridge University Press, 1979), 18.

18. Stephen McClatchie, "Canonizing the Dutchman: Bayreuth, Wagnerism, and *Der fliegende Holländer*," in *Richard Wagner: Der fliegende Holländer*, ed. Thomas S. Grey (Cambridge: Cambridge University Press, 2000), 153, notes that Wagner's sketches reveal that the ballad was composed after the themes representing the Dutchman's and Daland's crews.

19. Thomas S. Grey, "Romantic Opera as 'Dramatic Ballad': *Der fliegende Holländer* and Its Generic Contexts," in *Richard Wagner: Der fliegende Holländer*, ed. Thomas S. Grey (Cambridge: Cambridge University Press, 2000), 78–79.

20. For more on Ponnelle's production, refer to Patrick Carnegy, "Landfall on the Stage: A Brief Production History," in *Richard Wagner: Der fliegende Holländer*, ed. Thomas S. Grey (Cambridge: Cambridge University Press, 2000), 117–18.

21. Joy H. Calico, "The Legacy of GDR Directors on the post-*Wende* Opera Stage," in *Art Outside the Lines: New Perspectives on GDR Art Culture*, ed. Elaine Kelly and Amy Wlodarski (Amsterdam: Rodopi, 2011), 136.

22. Joy H. Calico, "Wagner in East Germany: Joachim Herz's *Der fliegende Holländer* (1964)," in *Wagner & Cinema*, ed. Jeongwon Joe and Sander L. Gilman (Bloomington: Indiana University Press, 2010), 301, makes a similar observation about the effect of Herz's changes to Act I but does not detail what those changes were.

23. Aria Umezawa, "Director's Notes," in *Venus & Adonis* and *Pygmalion* (program) (Montréal: Opera McGill, 2014).

24. Ibid.

25. This assumption is analogous to George Wilson's *transparency thesis* for classical narrative films. Umezawa's production is comparable to what Wilson calls an *epistemological twist film*. *Fight Club* (1999) is an example I discuss in chapter 5. George M. Wilson, *Seeing Fictions in Film: The Epistemology of Movies* (Oxford: Oxford University Press, 2011), ch. 7.

26. I am grateful to Aria Umezawa for encouraging me to say more on this topic.

27. For reactions to Gribben's edition, see Julie Bosman, "Publisher Tinkers with Twain," *New York Times*, January 5, 2011, https://www.nytimes.com/2011/01/05/books/05huck.html. I thank Andrew Kania for mentioning this example. The original libretto for *Show Boat* may be found in Laurence Maslon, ed., *American Musicals, 1927–1949: The Complete Books & Lyrics of Eight Broadway Classics* (New York: Library of America, 2014), 5.

28. Theodor W. Adorno, *In Search of Wagner*, trans. Rodney Livingstone (London: Verso, 1991 [1952]), 23–24; Barry Millington, "Nuremburg Trial: Is There Anti-Semitism in *Die Meistersinger*?" *Cambridge Opera Journal* 3, no. 3 (1991): 247–60; Marc A. Weiner, *Richard Wagner and the Anti-Semitic Imagination* (Lincoln: University of Nebraska Press, 1995). Thomas S. Grey, "Masters and Their Critics: Wagner, Hanslick, Beckmesser, and *Die Meistersinger*," in *Wagner's Meistersinger: Performance, History, Representation*, ed. Nicholas Vazsonyi (Rochester: University of Rochester Press, 2003), 180–81, provides a summary of evidence that Beckmesser is a Jewish caricature.

29. Richard Wagner, "Judaism in Music," *Wagner* 9, no. 1 (1988): 26, 24. Wagner's essay was initially published anonymously in 1850. He revised and republished it under his own name in 1869, less than a year after the premiere of *Die Meistersinger*.

30. For example, Dieter Borchmeyer, *Richard Wagner: Theory and Theatre*, trans. Stewart Spencer (Oxford: Clarendon Press, 1991), 408, argues that "there are no Jewish characters in his

music dramas, still less any anti-Semitic tendencies. His hatred of the Jews was excluded from the inner sanctum of his artistic personality."

31. Grey, "Masters and Their Critics," 184–88, argues that Wagner's contemporaries did not interpret *Die Meistersinger* in light of his "Judaism" essay. He suggests that Wagner may have regarded Beckmesser as a Jew but "was satisfied for [this interpretation] to remain a kind of private subtext." Ibid., 188.

32. David B. Dennis, "'The Most German of All German Operas': *Die Meistersinger* through the Lens of the Third Reich," in *Wagner's Meistersinger: Performance, History, Representation*, ed. Nicholas Vazsonyi (Rochester: University of Rochester Press, 2003), 103, 105.

33. Translation from http://www.murashev.com/opera/Die_Meistersinger_von_N%C3%BCrnberg_libretto_German_English. On the use of *Die Meistersinger* in Nazi propaganda, see Dennis, "Third Reich," 106–13.

34. Theodor W. Adorno, "Des Meisters Worte und der Enkel Sinn," *Die Zeit* 30 (1964), accessed March 5, 2020, http://www.zeit.de/1964/30/des-meisters-worte-und-der-enkel-sinn.

35. David McVicar, quoted in Christopher Alden et al., "Which Direction Now? Leading Directors Speak Out," *Opera* 53, no. 8 (2002): 913.

36. Recordings of radio broadcasts from the Metropolitan Opera during and immediately after World War II indicate that the passage beginning "Habt Acht" and ending "lebt's nicht in deutscher Meister Ehr'" was routinely cut. Edward A. Bortnichak, "Bayreuth Masterclass in the Dynamics of Change: An Appreciation of Katharina Wagner's Production of *Die Meistersinger*," *Wagner Journal* 31, no. 1 (2009): 49n15.

37. The surtitles of most productions of *Die Zauberflöte* obscure its racist content (e.g., Diane Paulus's 2011 production for the Canadian Opera Company).

38. Weiner, *Anti-Semitic Imagination*, 299–300 (limp), 66–72 (inept performance of Walther's song), 117–24 (vocal tessitura, melismas, and other musical features).

39. Patrick Carnegy, "Stage History," in *Richard Wagner: Die Meistersinger von Nürnberg*, ed. John Warrack (Cambridge: Cambridge University Press, 1994), 147.

40. Hans Rudolf Vaget, "'Du warst mein Freund von je': The Beckmesser Controversy Revisited," in *Wagner's Meistersinger: Performance, History, Representation*, ed. Nicholas Vazsonyi (Rochester: University of Rochester Press, 2003), 204.

41. Lufan Xu, "Why *Regieoper*? Katharina Wagner's *Die Meistersinger von Nürnberg* as a Meta-Production," in *Music on Stage*, ed. Fiona Jane Schopf (Newcastle upon Tyne: Cambridge Scholars, 2015), 31.

42. Nazi critics did in fact see Hitler in the character of Sachs. Dennis, "Third Reich," 117–18.

43. Ernst Bloch, "On the Text of Beckmesser's Prize Song," in *Literary Essays*, trans. Andrew Joron (Stanford: Stanford University Press, 1998), 178–84. This essay was originally published in the program to the 1961 Bayreuth Festival. Katharina Wagner's dramaturg, Robert Sollich, "Staging Wagner—and Its History: *Die Meistersinger von Nürnberg* on a Contemporary Stage," *Wagner Journal* 3, no. 1 (2009): 12, discusses the influence of Bloch's essay, which was reprinted in the program to the 2007 festival.

44. Martin Kušej is particularly fond of the underwear trope, employing it in his productions of *Don Giovanni* (Salzburg, 2002) and *Lady Macbeth* (Dutch National Opera, 2006). Clemens Risi, "Performing Wagner for the Twenty-First Century," *New Theatre Quarterly* 29, no. 4 (2013): 351, discusses Katharina Wagner's references to the work of other directors, such as Claus Guth's use of bobbleheads in *Zaide/Adama* (Salzburg, 2006).

45. Ibid., 354. Quotation from Barry Millington, "Bayreuth Festival," *Wagner Journal* 1, no. 3 (2007): 78.

46. Barry Millington, "Taking Wagner Seriously," *Wagner Journal* 2, no. 3 (2008): 69, 72, notes that this scene was "rethought" for the 2008 festival, the version released on DVD. My discussion concerns the 2008 staging.

47. I owe the identification of these references to German popular culture to Risi, "Performing Wagner," 352, 354.

48. Sollich, "Staging Wagner," 11, mentions the influence of Arno Breker.

49. Millington, "Bayreuth Festival," 79.

50. Lydia Goehr, "The Dangers of Satisfaction: On Songs, Rehearsals, and Repetition in *Die Meistersinger*," in *Wagner's Meistersinger: Performance, History, Representation*, ed. Nicholas Vazsonyi (Rochester: University of Rochester Press, 2003), 68, also comments on the conventionalism of *Die Meistersinger* in comparison with *Tristan* but suggests that it was a "deliberate failure" on Wagner's part, carefully orchestrated to bolster the reception of *Tristan*.

51. In his preface to the libretto, Sater mentions the school shootings at Columbine (1999) and Virginia Tech (2007) and alludes to the continued opposition to contraceptives by some members of the Department of Health and Human Services. Steven Sater, *Spring Awakening* (libretto) (New York: Theatre Communications Group, 2007), vii, xiv.

52. Sater speaks about the function of the songs in ibid, viii.

53. Michael Arden, "Director's Note," in *Spring Awakening* program (Los Angeles: Deaf West Theatre, 2014).

54. DeafWest.org, accessed June 14, 2020, https://www.deafwest.org/about.

55. Linda Buchwald, "Signs of the Times: 'Spring Awakening' at Deaf West," *American Theatre*, last modified October 19, 2014, http://www.americantheatre.org/2014/10/19/signs-of-the-times-spring-awakening-at-deaf-west.

56. Many deaf viewers criticized the use of sim-com. See, for example, Max Graham-Putter, Craig Fogel, and James Guido in Kayla Epstein and Alex Needham, "*Spring Awakening* on Broadway: Deaf Viewers Give Their Verdict," *Guardian*, last modified October 29, 2015, http://www.theguardian.com/stage/2015/oct/29/spring-awakening-broadway-deaf-viewers-give-verdict.

57. Craig Fogel, an ASL-English interpreter, comments on this aspect of the production in ibid.

58. I owe this observation to a paper by Alexus Wells, written for Adaptation and Musical Theatre (Duke University, 2018). I also thank her for bringing this production to my attention and for our illuminating conversations about it.

59. The quotation is from Risi, "Performing Wagner," 354. Katharina Wagner, "The Destruction of All That Is Good and Sublime?" *Wagner News* 182 (October 2007): 17–20, casts directors such as herself as victims.

60. For a discussion of the ways in which Alfonso overturns the mold of the "vecchio filosofo," refer to Edmund J. Goehring, *Three Modes of Perception in Mozart: The Philosophical, Pastoral, and Comic in Così fan tutte* (Cambridge: Cambridge University Press, 2004), ch. 2.

FINALE

THE TYPICAL WAY OF UNDERSTANDING THE LANDSCAPE OF contemporary opera performance is to differentiate "traditional" productions from Regieoper based on their visual appearance: breeches and bodices or black tie and biker gear. I suggest that there is a more fundamental difference separating Opera Atelier's productions of Mozart from those by Peter Sellars, a difference grounded in the performers' overarching aims and the attitudes those aims lead them to take toward preexisting works.

The central aim of companies producing work-performances in the classical paradigm is to make the composer and librettist's work perceptually accessible to their audience. Accordingly, they pursue a moderate to high degree of fidelity to the score and libretto. They also aim to understand what their authors intended their work to convey and to craft a performance that makes an analogous artistic statement. Performing works from the distant past or from other cultures often involves finding analogues for references one's audience is not likely to grasp. The contemporary relevance of the work's themes may also be enhanced by updating its setting—for example, by presenting Valhalla as a boardroom and the gods as modern-day executives.

Other directors, such as Sellars in his Mozart–Da Ponte trilogy, are less concerned with conveying the meanings intended by the composer and librettist than in using the score and libretto as vehicles with which to make their own artistic and political points. Although many performance-works under the ingredients model involve updated settings, Deaf West's *Spring Awakening* demonstrates that this need not be the case. An ingredients-model approach may involve a high degree of fidelity to the score and libretto, as in both of the previous examples, or it may involve revising or rewriting these texts (e.g., Against the Grain Theatre's *A Little Too Cozy* and the Neuköllner Oper's *Iris Butterfly*) or inserting new ingredients (e.g., Sellars's *Indian Queen*).

Bringing philosophical debates about the nature of musical works and musical performance to opera studies not only helped clarify the divergent impulses underwriting contemporary operatic performance practice but also contributed to philosophical discussions of performance. In the past two decades, philosophers have expanded this line of inquiry beyond Western art music, observing how jazz, rock, and musics of other cultures constitute exceptions to the classical paradigm.[1] My consideration of the norms of operatic performance practice has revealed that the classical paradigm does not even describe all Western classical music. Few opera productions are undertaken with the same concern for fidelity that classical instrumentalists bring to their performances. Even work by historically informed companies is more easily accommodated by the point-based version of the classical paradigm David Davies has put forth to describe work-performances of spoken theater than by the text-based version that governs much classical instrumental music. And like spoken theater, not all opera performances are work-performances.

It was outside of the scope of this study to consider whether the ingredients model has any purchase in Western instrumental music, but there are signs that it does.[2] Observing that the classical paradigm assumed dominance only in the twentieth century, Nicholas Cook and Daniel Leech-Wilkinson advocate that performers reassume greater creative agency and suggest that this may be a way of renewing interest in Western art music.[3] In a collaborative lecture-recital by Leech-Wilkinson and the pianist Mine Doğantan-Dack, the latter performed a selection of canonical repertoire (e.g., Beethoven, Chopin, and Bach), treating "at least one performance parameter in a highly unconventional manner." These performances were "not constrained by any sense of the composer's intentions or sanctity of the score." Instead, they wished to "test how far notes can be taken, in various directions, while still producing persuasive musical-dramatic results: the success of the performance is to be measured solely by whether it sounds like persuasive music." Doğantan-Dack's performances were no mere academic experiments. The abstract to their paper proclaims their "political agenda: to effect a change in classical performance practice so that it need no longer be driven by slavish obedience to convention."[4] If Leech-Wilkinson and Doğantan-Dack are successful in effecting such a paradigm shift, we may expect more exceptions to the classical paradigm, even within the hallowed sphere of instrumental music of the common-practice period.

Philosophical discussions of narrative have also largely overlooked forms of sung drama. Asking of opera and musical theater questions similar to those philosophers have asked about literary and cinematic narratives has illuminated the medium-specific features of storytelling in these art forms. Operas and musicals are audiovisual fictions in which singers enact characters. Contrary to prevailing assumptions in both musicology and philosophy, characters in musicals and operas live in a world filled with music they not only create but, typically, hear.

Many works of sung drama involve characters telling stories of their lives or staging musical-theatrical performances to entertain their friends. Inspired by the role of the chorus in ancient Greek tragedy or the work's literary origins, some librettists have included narrators whose utterances are intended solely for the benefit of the work's actual audience. Comparing Britten and Piper's *The Turn of the Screw* to James's novella has revealed a key contrast between the roles narrators play in sung drama as compared with works of literature. In few cases is it coherent to imagine that narrators in operas or musicals are responsible for putting on the performance we are watching.

The orchestra's perspective on the narrative often exceeds the understanding of the characters therein. For this reason, it is often regarded as performing a narrator-like role. Since poststructuralism penetrated musicological thought in the 1990s, most scholars of opera and musical theater have resisted the tendency to understand orchestral commentary as issuing from the historical composer, preferring to invoke fictional entities (e.g., the orchestral narrator) or author-constructs (e.g., the implied author). Yet in some cases, such as Wagner's self-quotations in *Die Meistersinger*, imagining that the music is coming from a resident of the fictional world is illogical.

Regarding artworks as the artistic statements of real persons need not entail regarding every work as an autobiography or accepting composers' statements about their works at face value. Another area in which analytic philosophers have expended a considerable amount of energy in the past few decades is in developing accounts of interpretation that mediate between the extremes of E. D. Hirsch and Roland Barthes. The stance known as moderate actual intentionalism is more consistent with current practices of historical musicologists than lingering lip service to the "death of the author" or the intentional or poietic fallacies. This is the approach that has guided my interpretations throughout this study. I have taken into consideration composers' statements about their works, when they exist, but I have accepted their validity only if they mesh with the features of the finished work and evidence about how it was made. For example, Stravinsky's claim that music is incapable of expression is proven false by the manifold expressive properties of his Octet. Yet this statement is relevant to interpreting the Octet, as it provides evidence that Stravinsky did not intend it to tell a story (which is not to say that one cannot imagine narratives while listening to the Octet).

Another role the orchestra plays in opera and musical theater is to express characters' points of view, allowing us to hear what they hear or musically representing their thoughts, desires, or emotions. Just as a literary narrator may tell the story according to the point of view of a character without that character thereby assuming the role of its narrator, the orchestral music may express a character's point of view without that character being its author. In *Owen Wingrave* and *Lady Macbeth*, Britten and Shostakovich employ character-focused narration in order to arouse sympathy or empathy for their protagonists. In other works, such as *Assassins*, these processes come apart. Sondheim and Weidman align spectators with aspects of the assassins' points of view but do not encourage spectators to share in their belief that they were justified in their actions. Even in cases where the audience is encouraged to sympathize with murderers, such as *Lady Macbeth*'s Katerina, individual spectators may resist such invitations. Whether we revile or admire such characters also depends on how they are realized in performance.

For most of the history of musicology the discipline has focused on composers' works to the neglect of those of performers. In the past decade, studies of historical performers, analyses of recordings, and ethnographies of rehearsal processes and the inner workings of opera companies have begun to rectify this imbalance. Cook and Leech-Wilkinson have even argued that performers and performances are the true subjects of musicological study, not composers and scores.[5] With a deep appreciation for their pioneering work in music performance studies, I suggest that their proposed reorientation of the discipline would be just as incomplete a view of the art of music as musicology's former focus on composers and scores. Unlike literature and cinema, the study of music may be directed toward two kinds of works: those produced by composers (and their collaborators) and those produced by performers. By exploring how composers, librettists, and performers contribute to storytelling in the musical theater, I hope to have shown what may be gained by integrating the "score" and "performance" branches of musicology.

Notes

1. See, for example, Lee B. Brown, David Goldblatt, and Theodore Gracyk, *Jazz and the Philosophy of Art* (New York: Routledge, 2018), pt. III; John Andrew Fisher, "Jazz and Musical Works," *Journal of Aesthetics and Art Criticism* 76, no. 2 (2018): 151–62; Andrew Kania, "All Play and No Work: An Ontology of Jazz," *Journal of Aesthetics and Art Criticism* 69, no. 4 (2011): 391–403; Andrew Kania, "Making Tracks: The Ontology of Rock Music," *Journal of Aesthetics and Art Criticism* 64, no. 4 (2006): 401–14; Theodore Gracyk, *Rhythm and Noise: An Aesthetics of Rock* (Durham: Duke University Press, 1996), ch. 1; Stephen Davies, *Musical Works and Performances: A Philosophical Exploration* (Oxford: Oxford University Press, 2001), 30–36 (on rock), ch. 6 (on Balinese gamelan music).

2. David Davies, "Locating the Performable Musical Work in Practice: A Non-Platonist Interpretation of the 'Classical Paradigm,'" in *Virtual Works—Actual Things: Essays in Music Ontology*, ed. Paulo de Assis (Leuven: Leuven University Press, 2018), 55–56,

discusses the relevance of the ingredients model to the work of the performance collective MusicExperiment21, based at the Orpheus Institute Ghent.

3. Daniel Leech-Wilkinson, *The Changing Sound of Music: Approaches to Studying Recorded Musical Performance* (London: CHARM, 2009), last modified February 14, 2010, https://www.charm.kcl.ac.uk/studies/chapters/intro.html; Nicholas Cook, *Beyond the Score: Music as Performance* (New York: Oxford University Press, 2013), 3–4.

4. Daniel Leech-Wilkinson and Mine Doğantan-Dack, "Ontology and Aesthetics of Musical Performance: Towards a Paradigm Shift or Radical Practice," abstract to a paper presented at the 3rd Annual Conference of the Royal Musical Association Music and Philosophy Study Group, King's College, London, July 19–20, 2013. I thank Tomas McAuley for sending me a copy of the program.

5. Cook, *Beyond the Score*, 1; Daniel Leech-Wilkinson, "Compositions, Scores, Performances, Meanings," *Music Theory Online* 18, no. 1 (2012), https://www.mtosmt.org/issues/mto.12.18.1/mto.12.18.1.leech-wilkinson.php. See also Carolyn Abbate, "Music—Drastic or Gnostic?" *Critical Inquiry* 30, no. 3 (2004): 505–36.

BIBLIOGRAPHY

Abbate, Carolyn. "Music—Drastic or Gnostic?" *Critical Inquiry* 30, no. 3 (2004): 505–36.
——. *Unsung Voices: Opera and Musical Narrative in the Nineteenth Century.* Princeton: Princeton University Press, 1991.
"About Opera Atelier." Opera Atelier.com. Accessed March 5, 2020. http://www.operaatelier.com/about.
Adams, Hazard. "Titles, Titling, and Entitlement To." *Journal of Aesthetics and Art Criticism* 46, no. 1 (1987): 7–21.
Adorno, Theodor W. "Des Meisters Worte und der Enkel Sinn." *Die Zeit* 30 (1964). Accessed March 5, 2020. http://www.zeit.de/1964/30/des-meisters-worte-und-der-enkel-sinn.
——. *In Search of Wagner.* Translated by Rodney Livingstone. London: Verso, 1991. Originally published as *Versuch über Wagner* (1952).
Aguilar, Rosario. *La niña blanca y los pájaros sin pies.* Managua: Editorial Nueva Nicaragua, 1992. Published in an English translation by Edward Waters Hood as *The Lost Chronicles of Terra Firma* (1997).
Alden, Christopher, Robert Carsen, Patrice Caurier, Colin Graham, Lillian Groag, Peter Hall, Kaspar Holten, Lindy Hume, Ian Judge, Harry Kupfer, Mark Lamos, Nikolaus Lehnhoff, Moshe Leiser, Baz Luhrmann, David McVicar, Stephen Medcalf, Nicholas Muni, David Pountney, Graham Vick, Stephen Wadsworth, and Francesca Zambello. "Which Direction Now? Leading Directors Speak Out." *Opera* 53, no. 8 (2002): 906–37.
Allen, Stephen Arthur. "*Billy Budd*: Temporary Salvation and the Faustian Pact." *Journal of Musicological Research* 25, no. 1 (2006): 43–73.
Almén, Byron. *A Theory of Musical Narrative.* Bloomington: Indiana University Press, 2008.
Altman, Rick. *The American Film Musical.* Bloomington: Indiana University Press, 1987.
Amis, John. "Glyndebourne: A Mad *Ariadne*." *Musical Opinion* 137, no. 1496 (2013): 32.
Appia, Adolphe. *Music and the Art of the Theatre.* Edited by Barnard Hewitt. Translated by Robert W. Corrigan and Mary Douglas Dirks. Coral Cables: University of Miami Press, 1962. Originally published as *Die Musik und die Inscenierung* (1899).
Arden, Michael. "Director's Note." In *Spring Awakening* Program. Los Angeles: Deaf West Theatre, 2014.
Aristotle. *Poetics.* Edited and translated by Stephen Halliwell. Cambridge, MA: Harvard University Press, 1995.
Armfield, Neil. "Director's Notes." In *Peter Grimes* Program, 2. Toronto: Canadian Opera Company, 2013.
Ashley, Tim. "*Ariadne auf Naxos*—Review." *Guardian.* Last modified May 19, 2013. http://www.theguardian.com/music/2013/may/19/ariadne-auf-naxos-review.
——. "Wagner Interrupted." Review of Peter Konwitschny's *Meistersinger* (Hamburg). *Guardian.* Last modified November 23, 2002. http://www.theguardian.com/music/2002/nov/23/classicalmusicandopera.artsfeatures.
Ashman, Mike. "Wagner on Stage: Aesthetic, Dramaturgical, and Social Considerations." In *Cambridge Companion to Richard Wagner*, edited by Thomas S. Grey, 246–75. Cambridge: Cambridge University Press, 2008.

Aspden, Suzanne. *The Rival Sirens: Performance and Identity on Handel's Operatic Stage.* Cambridge: Cambridge University Press, 2013.
Bacharach, Sondra, and Deborah Tollefsen. "We Did It Again: A Reply to Livingston." *Journal of Aesthetics and Art Criticism* 69, no. 2 (2011): 225–30.
———. "We Did It: From Mere Contributors to Coauthors." *Journal of Aesthetics and Art Criticism* 68, no. 1 (2010): 23–32.
Badiou, Alain. *Five Lessons on Wagner.* Translated by Susan Spitzer. London: Verso, 2010.
Baker, Evan. *From the Score to the Stage: An Illustrated History of Continental Opera Production and Staging.* Chicago: University of Chicago Press, 2013.
Banducci, Antonia L. "The Opera Atelier Performance (Toronto, 2000): The Spirit of Lully on the Modern Stage." *Journal of Seventeenth-Century Music* 10, no. 1 (2004). http://sscm-jscm.org/v10/no1/banducci.html.
Banfield, Stephen. *Sondheim's Broadway Musicals.* Ann Arbor: University of Michigan Press, 1993.
Barnes, Jennifer. *Television Opera: The Fall of Opera Commissioned for Television.* Woodbridge: Boydell, 2003.
Barthes, Roland. "The Death of the Author." In *Image—Music—Text*, edited and translated by Stephen Heath, 142–48. New York: Hill and Wang, 1977. Originally published as "La mort de l'auteur" (1968).
———. "From Work to Text." In *Image—Music—Text*, edited and translated by Stephen Heath, 155–64. New York: Hill and Wang, 1977. Originally published as "De l'oeuvre au texte" (1971).
———. "Introduction to the Structural Analysis of Narratives." In *Image—Music—Text*, edited and translated by Stephen Heath, 79–124. New York: Hill and Wang, 1977. Originally published as "Introduction à l'analyse structurale des récits" (1966).
Beckett, Lucy. "Sachs and Schopenhauer." In *Richard Wagner: Die Meistersinger von Nürnberg*, edited by John Warrack, 66–82. Cambridge: Cambridge University Press, 1994.
Benson, Alan, dir. *Sweeney Todd: Scenes from the Making of a Musical.* Broadcast by the South Bank Show. London Weekend Television, July 11, 1980. Accessed March 5, 2020. https://www.youtube.com/watch?v=o3OAf45IaUk.
Berger, Karol. "*Der Dichter spricht*: Self-Representation in *Parsifal*." In *Representation in Western Music*, edited by Joshua S. Walden, 182–202. New York: Cambridge University Press, 2013.
Bergeron, Vincent, and Dominic McIver Lopes. "Hearing and Seeing Musical Expression." *Philosophy and Phenomenological Research* 78, no. 1 (2009): 1–16.
Bernstein, Leonard. *Trouble in Tahiti: An Opera in Seven Scenes* (Vocal Score). New York: Boosey & Hawkes, 2000.
Berry, Mark. "Poor Staging Spoils *Ariadne auf Naxos*." Seen and Heard International. Last modified May 20, 2013. http://seenandheard-international.com/2013/05/poor-staging-spoils-ariadne-auf-naxos.
Bettelheim, Bruno. *The Uses of Enchantment: The Meaning and Importance of Fairy Tales.* New York: Knopf, 1976.
Beyer, Barbara. "Interviews with Contemporary Opera Directors, Selected from Barbara Beyer's *Warum Oper? Gespräche mit Opernregisseuren* (2005)." Translated by Gundula Kreuzer and Paul Chaikin. *Opera Quarterly* 27, no. 2–3 (2011): 307–17.
Bloch, Ernst. "On the Text of Beckmesser's Prize Song." Translated by Andrew Joron. In *Literary Essays*, 178–84. Stanford: Stanford University Press, 1998. Originally published in the program to the 1961 Bayreuth Festival.

Block, Geoffrey. *Enchanted Evenings: The Broadway Musical from Show Boat to Sondheim*. 2nd ed. New York: Oxford University Press, 2009.
Bolduc, Benoît. "From Marvel to Camp: Medusa for the Twenty-First Century." *Journal of Seventeenth-Century Music* 10, no. 1 (2004). https://sscm-jscm.org/v10/no1/bolduc.html.
Bond, Christopher G. *Sweeney Todd: The Demon Barber of Fleet Street*. New York: Samuel French, 1974.
Booth, Wayne C. *The Company We Keep: An Ethics of Fiction*. Berkeley: University of California Press, 1988.
———. *The Rhetoric of Fiction*. 2nd ed. Chicago: University of Chicago Press, 1983.
Borchmeyer, Dieter. *Richard Wagner: Theory and Theatre*. Translated by Stewart Spencer. Oxford: Clarendon Press, 1991.
Bordwell, David. *Narration in the Fiction Film*. Madison: University of Wisconsin Press, 1985.
Bortnichak, Edward A. "Bayreuth Masterclass in the Dynamics of Change: An Appreciation of Katharina Wagner's Production of *Die Meistersinger*." *Wagner Journal* 31, no. 1 (2009): 45–60.
Bosman, Julie. "Publisher Tinkers with Twain." *New York Times*. Last modified January 4, 2011. https://www.nytimes.com/2011/01/05/books/05huck.html.
Bowles, Hugo. *Storytelling and Drama: Exploring Narrative Episodes in Plays*. Amsterdam: John Benjamins, 2010.
Boyd, Brian. *On the Origin of Stories: Evolution, Cognition, and Fiction*. Cambridge, MA: Belknap Press, 2009.
Brett, Philip. "Eros and Orientalism in Britten's Operas." In *Music and Sexuality in Britten: Selected Essays*, edited by George E. Haggerty, 129–53. Berkeley: University of California Press, 2006.
———. "'Fiery Visions' (and Revisions): *Peter Grimes* in Process." In *Benjamin Britten: Peter Grimes*, edited by Philip Brett, 47–87. Cambridge: Cambridge University Press, 1983.
———. *Owen Wingrave* Liner Notes, 7–12. English Chamber Orchestra conducted by Benjamin Britten. London: Decca, 1993. CD.
———. "Pacifism, Political Action, and Artistic Endeavor." In *Music and Sexuality in Britten: Selected Essays*, edited by George E. Haggerty, 172–85. Berkeley: University of California Press, 2006.
———. "*Peter Grimes*: The Growth of the Libretto." In *The Making of Peter Grimes*, edited by Paul Banks, 53–78. Woodbridge: Boydell, 2000.
———. "Salvation at Sea: Britten's *Billy Budd*." In *Music and Sexuality in Britten: Selected Essays*, edited by George E. Haggerty, 70–80. Berkeley: University of California Press, 2006.
Britten, Benjamin. *Owen Wingrave* (Study Score). London: Faber Music, 1995.
Brown, David. *Tchaikovsky: A Biographical and Critical Study*. 4 vols. New York: Norton, 1991.
Brown, Lee B., David Goldblatt, and Theodore Gracyk. *Jazz and the Philosophy of Art*. New York: Routledge, 2018.
Buchwald, Linda. "Signs of the Times: 'Spring Awakening' at Deaf West." *American Theatre*. Last modified October 19, 2014. http://www.americantheatre.org/2014/10/19/signs-of-the-times-spring-awakening-at-deaf-west.
Burgess, Geoffrey. "Revisiting *Atys*: Reflections on Les Arts Florissants' Production." *Early Music* 34, no. 3 (2006): 465–78.
Cairns, David. *Berlioz*. 2 vols. London: Deutsch, 1989.

Calcagno, Mauro. *From Madrigal to Opera: Monteverdi's Staging of the Self.* Berkeley: University of California Press, 2012.

Calico, Joy H. *Brecht at the Opera.* Berkeley: University of California Press, 2008.

———. "The Legacy of GDR Directors on the post-*Wende* Opera Stage." In *Art Outside the Lines: New Perspectives on GDR Art Culture*, edited by Elaine Kelly and Amy Wlodarski, 131–54. Amsterdam: Rodopi, 2011.

———. "Wagner in East Germany: Joachim Herz's *Der fliegende Holländer* (1964)." In *Wagner & Cinema*, edited by Jeongwon Joe and Sander L. Gilman, 294–311. Bloomington: Indiana University Press, 2010.

Campana, Alessandra. *Opera and Modern Spectatorship in Late Nineteenth-Century Italy.* Cambridge: Cambridge University Press, 2014.

Carnegy, Patrick. "Landfall on the Stage: A Brief Production History." In *Richard Wagner: Der fliegende Holländer*, edited by Thomas S. Grey, 92–128. Cambridge: Cambridge University Press, 2000.

———. "Stage History." In *Richard Wagner: Die Meistersinger von Nürnberg*, edited by John Warrack, 135–54. Cambridge: Cambridge University Press, 1994.

———. *Wagner and the Art of the Theatre.* New Haven: Yale University Press, 2006.

Carroll, Noël. "Art and the Moral Realm." In *Blackwell Guide to Aesthetics*, edited by Peter Kivy, 126–51. Malden: Blackwell, 2004.

———. "Forget the Medium!" In *Engaging the Moving Image*, 1–9. New Haven: Yale University Press, 2003.

———. "On the Narrative Connection." In *Beyond Aesthetics*, 118–33. New York: Cambridge University Press, 2001.

Chafe, Eric. *The Tragic and the Ecstatic: The Musical Revolution of Wagner's Tristan und Isolde.* New York: Oxford University Press, 2005.

Chatman, Seymour. *Coming to Terms: The Rhetoric of Narrative in Fiction and Film.* Ithaca: Cornell University Press, 1990.

———. *Story and Discourse: Narrative Structure in Fiction and Film.* Ithaca: Cornell University Press, 1978.

Chion, Michel. *Audio-Vision: Sound on Screen.* Translated by Claudia Gorbman. New York: Columbia University Press, 1994. Originally published as *L'Audio-Vision* (1990).

Chrissochoidis, Ilias. "An Emblem of Modern Music." *Early Music* 39, no. 4 (2011): 519–30.

Christiansen, Rupert. "*Ariadne auf Naxos*, Glyndebourne, Review." *Telegraph*. Last modified May 19, 2013. http://www.telegraph.co.uk/culture/music/glyndebourne/10067281/Ariadne-auf-Naxos-Glyndebourne-review.html.

———. "Lise Davidsen Surpasses All Expectations Amid a Splendid Cast – *Ariadne auf Naxos*, Glyndebourne, Review." *Telegraph*. Last modified June 26, 2017. https://www.telegraph.co.uk/opera/what-to-see/lise-davidsen-magnificent-ariadne-auf-naxos-glyndebourne-review.

Clavel-Vazquez, Adriana. "Sugar and Spice, and Everything Nice: What Rough Heroines Tell Us about Imaginative Resistance." *Journal of Aesthetics and Art Criticism* 76, no. 2 (2018): 201–12.

Clippinger, David. "The Hidden Life: Benjamin Britten's Homoerotic Reading of Henry James's *The Turn of the Screw*." In *Literature and Musical Adaptation*, edited by Michael J. Meyer, 137–51. Amsterdam: Rodopi, 2002.

Cluck, Nancy Anne. "Showing or Telling: Narrators in the Drama of Tennessee Williams." *American Literature* 51, no. 1 (1979): 84–93.

Coghlan, Alexandra. "Don't Mention the War." Review of Katharina Thoma's *Ariadne auf Naxos* (Glyndebourne). *New Statesman* 142, no. 5161 (2013): 52–53.

Cohn, Dorrit. *The Distinction of Fiction*. Baltimore: Johns Hopkins University Press, 1999.
Coleman, Basil, and John Piper. "*Billy Budd* on the Stage: An Early Discussion between Producer and Designer." *Tempo* 21 (Autumn 1951): 13–14, 21–25.
Cone, Edward T. *The Composer's Voice*. Berkeley: University of California Press, 1974.
———. "The Old Man's Toys: Verdi's Last Operas." In *Music, a View from Delft: Selected Essays*, edited by Robert P. Morgan, 159–75. Chicago: University of Chicago Press, 1989.
———. "The World of Opera and Its Inhabitants." In *Music, a View from Delft: Selected Essays*, edited by Robert P. Morgan, 125–37. Chicago: University of Chicago Press, 1989.
Cook, Nicholas. *Beyond the Score: Music as Performance*. New York: Oxford University Press, 2013.
Cook, Susan C. "*Der Zar lässt sich photographieren*: Weill and Comic Opera." In *A New Orpheus: Essays on Kurt Weill*, edited by Kim H. Kowalke, 83–101. New Haven: Yale University Press, 1986.
Cooke, Mervyn. "Be Flat or Be Natural? Pitch Symbolism in Britten's Operas." In *Rethinking Britten*, edited by Philip Rupprecht, 102–27. Oxford: Oxford University Press, 2013.
———. *Britten and the Far East: Asian Influences in the Music of Benjamin Britten*. Woodbridge: Boydell, 1998.
———. "Britten's 'Prophetic Song': Tonal Symbolism in *Billy Budd*." In *Benjamin Britten: Billy Budd*, edited by Mervyn Cooke and Philip Reed, 85–110. Cambridge: Cambridge University Press, 1993.
———. "Stage History and Critical Reception." In *Benjamin Britten: Billy Budd*, edited by Mervyn Cooke and Philip Reed, 135–49. Cambridge: Cambridge University Press, 1993.
Cooke, Mervyn, Donald Mitchell, and Philip Reed, eds. *Letters from a Life: The Selected Letters of Benjamin Britten, 1913–1976*. 6 vols. Woodbridge: Boydell, 1991–2012.
Cowgill, Rachel. "Mozart Productions and the Emergence of *Werktreue* at London's Italian Opera House, 1780–1830." In *Operatic Migrations: Transforming Works and Crossing Boundaries*, edited by Roberta Montemorra Marvin and Downing A. Thomas, 145–86. Burlington: Ashgate, 2006.
Crozier, Eric. "The Writing of *Billy Budd*." *Opera Quarterly* 4, no. 3 (1986): 11–27.
Culp, Christopher M. "Morality of the Outsider: Teaching *Assassins* and *Glee*." *Sondheim Review* 22, no. 1 (2015): 35–37.
Currie, Gregory. *Image and Mind: Film, Philosophy, and Cognitive Science*. Cambridge: Cambridge University Press, 1995.
———. *Narratives and Narrators: A Philosophy of Stories*. Oxford: Oxford University Press, 2010.
———. "Visual Fictions." *Philosophical Quarterly* 41, no. 163 (1991): 129–43.
Dahlhaus, Carl. *Richard Wagner's Music Dramas*. Translated by Mary Whittall. London: Cambridge University Press, 1979.
Darion, Joe, and Dale Wasserman. *Man of La Mancha: A Musical Play* (Libretto). New York: Random House, 1966.
Davies, David. "Analytic Philosophy of Music." In *Oxford Handbook of Western Music and Philosophy*, edited by Tomas McAuley, Jerrold Levinson, and Nanette Nielsen. Oxford: Oxford University Press, forthcoming.
———. *Art as Performance*. Malden: Blackwell, 2004.
———. "Eluding Wilson's 'Elusive Narrators.'" *Philosophical Studies* 147, no. 3 (2010): 387–94.
———. "Enigmatic Variations." *Monist* 95, no. 4 (2012): 643–62.
———. "Locating the Performable Musical Work in Practice: A Non-Platonist Interpretation of the 'Classical Paradigm.'" In *Virtual Works—Actual Things: Essays in Music Ontology*, edited by Paulo de Assis, 45–64. Leuven: Leuven University Press, 2018.

———. "Medium." In *Routledge Companion to Philosophy and Music*, edited by Theodore Gracyk and Andrew Kania, 48–58. London: Routledge, 2011.
———. *Philosophy of the Performing Arts*. Malden: Wiley-Blackwell, 2011.
Davies, Stephen. "Analytic Philosophy and Music." In *Routledge Companion to Philosophy and Music*, edited by Theodore Gracyk and Andrew Kania, 294–304. London: Routledge, 2011.
———. *Musical Works and Performances: A Philosophical Exploration*. Oxford: Oxford University Press, 2001.
DeafWest.org. Accessed June 14, 2020. https://www.deafwest.org/about.
Dean, Winton. Review of *Owen Wingrave* (Covent Garden Premiere). *Musical Times* 114, no. 1565 (1973): 719–26.
Deathridge, John, and Carl Dahlhaus. *The New Grove Wagner*. New York: Norton, 1984.
Dennis, David B. "'The Most German of All German Operas': *Die Meistersinger* through the Lens of the Third Reich." In *Wagner's Meistersinger: Performance, History, Representation*, edited by Nicholas Vazsonyi, 98–119. Rochester: University of Rochester Press, 2003.
Deutsch, Michelle. "Ceremonies of Innocence: Men, Boys and Women in *The Turn of the Screw*." In *Henry James on Stage and Screen*, edited by John R. Bradley, 72–83. New York: Palgrave, 2000.
Devereaux, Mary. "Moral Judgments and Works of Art: The Case of Narrative Literature." *Journal of Aesthetics and Art Criticism* 62, no. 1 (2004): 3–11.
Diamond, Tom. "Director's Note: Necessity Is the Mother of Invention." In *The Turn of the Screw* Program. Montréal: Opera McGill, 2011.
Duncan, Ronald. *The Rape of Lucretia* (Libretto). In *The Operas of Benjamin Britten: The Complete Librettos*, edited by David Herbert, 115–34. New York: Columbia University Press, 1979.
Dunnett, Roderic. "A Collaboration Recalled." Interview with Myfanwy Piper. *Opera* 46, no. 10 (1995): 1158–64.
Eaton, A. W. "Robust Immoralism." *Journal of Aesthetics and Art Criticism* 70, no. 3 (2012): 281–92.
———. "Rough Heroes of the New Hollywood." *Revue internationale de philosophie* 64, no. 4 (2010): 511–24.
Eggers, Walter F., Jr. "Shakespeare's Gower and the Role of the Authorial Presenter." *Philological Quarterly* 54, no. 2 (1975): 434–43.
Emerson, Caryl. "Back to the Future: Shostakovich's Revision of Leskov's *Lady Macbeth of Mtsensk District*." *Cambridge Opera Journal* 1, no. 1 (1989): 59–78.
Englander, Roger, dir. *Assassins: A Conversation Piece*. New York: Music Theatre International, 1991. Accessed March 5, 2020. https://www.youtube.com/watch?v=29P7x4z6NXU.
Epstein, Kayla, and Alex Needham. "*Spring Awakening* on Broadway: Deaf Viewers Give Their Verdict." *Guardian*. Last modified October 29, 2015. http://www.theguardian.com/stage/2015/oct/29/spring-awakening-broadway-deaf-viewers-give-verdict.
Esse, Melina. "Encountering the *improvvisatrice* in Italian Opera." *Journal of the American Musicological Society* 66, no. 3 (2013): 709–70.
Evans, John. "*Owen Wingrave*: A Case for Pacifism." In *The Britten Companion*, edited by Christopher Palmer, 227–37. London: Faber, 1984.
Evans, Peter. "Britten's Television Opera." *Musical Times* 112, no. 1539 (1971): 425–28.
———. *The Music of Benjamin Britten*. London: J. M. Dent & Sons, 1979.
Everett, Yayoi Uno. *Reconfiguring Myth and Narrative in Contemporary Opera: Osvaldo Golijov, Kaija Saariaho, John Adams, and Tan Dun*. Bloomington: Indiana University Press, 2015.

Feldman, Martha. *The Castrato: Reflections on Natures and Kinds*. Berkeley: University of California Press, 2015.
Fillion, Michelle. *Difficult Rhythm: Music and the Word in E. M. Forster*. Urbana: University of Illinois Press, 2010.
Fisher, John Andrew. "Jazz and Musical Works." *Journal of Aesthetics and Art Criticism* 76, no. 2 (2018): 151–62.
Fleischman, Avrom. *Narrated Films: Storytelling Situations in Cinema History*. Baltimore: Johns Hopkins University Press, 1992.
Fludernik, Monika. *Towards a 'Natural' Narratology*. London: Routledge, 1996.
Forster, E. M. *Howard's End*. Abinger Edition, edited by Oliver Stallybrass, vol. 4. London: Edward Arnold, 1973. Originally published in 1910.
———. "Not Listening to Music." In *Two Cheers for Democracy*. Abinger Edition, edited by Oliver Stallybrass, 11:122–25. London: Edward Arnold, 1972. Originally published in 1939.
Forster, E. M., and Eric Crozier. *Billy Budd* (Libretto). In *The Operas of Benjamin Britten: The Complete Librettos*, edited by David Herbert, 181–206. New York: Columbia University Press, 1979.
Foster, Daniel H. *Wagner's Ring Cycle and the Greeks*. Cambridge: Cambridge University Press, 2010.
Frainier, Margaret. "Point-of-View Narration in Tchaikovsky's *The Queen of Spades*." Unpublished paper.
Frantzen, Allen J. "The Handsome Sailor and the Man of Sorrows: *Billy Budd* and the Modernism of Benjamin Britten." *Modern Cultures* 3, no. 2 (2007): 57–70.
Fraser, Barbara Means. "Revisiting Greece: The Sondheim Chorus." In *Stephen Sondheim: A Casebook*, edited by Joanne Gordon, 223–49. New York: Garland, 1997.
Freitas, Roger. *Portrait of a Castrato: Politics, Patronage, and Music in the Life of Atto Melani*. Cambridge: Cambridge University Press, 2009.
Fry, Katherine. "Nietzsche, *Tristan und Isolde*, and the Analysis of Wagnerian Rhythm." *Opera Quarterly* 29, no. 3–4 (2014): 253–76.
Frye, Northrop. *Anatomy of Criticism: Four Essays*. Princeton: Princeton University Press, 1957.
Fuhrmann, Christina. *Foreign Opera at the London Playhouses: From Mozart to Bellini*. Cambridge: Cambridge University Press, 2015.
Gaut, Berys. *Art, Emotion and Ethics*. Oxford: Oxford University Press, 2007.
———. *A Philosophy of Cinematic Art*. Cambridge: Cambridge University Press, 2010.
Gendler, Tamar Szabó. "Imaginative Resistance Revisited." In *The Architecture of the Imagination: New Essays on Pretence, Possibility, and Fiction*, edited by Shaun Nichols, 149–74. Oxford: Clarendon Press, 2006.
———. "The Puzzle of Imaginative Resistance." *Journal of Philosophy* 97, no. 2 (2000): 55–81.
Genette, Gérard. *Narrative Discourse: An Essay in Method*. Translated by Jane E. Lewin. Ithaca: Cornell University Press, 1983. Originally published as *Discours du récit: Essai de méthode* (1972).
———. *Narrative Discourse Revisited*. Translated by Jane E. Lewin. Ithaca: Cornell University Press, 1988. Originally published as *Nouveau discours du récit* (1983).
Glass, Ira. "No Place Like Home." Episode of podcast *This American Life*. Last modified March 14, 2014. https://www.thisamericanlife.org/520/no-place-like-home.
Glocksin, Bernhard. "So süss, dass es schmerzt. Mascagni, Iris, Japan." In *Iris Butterfly* Program, 5–10. Berlin: Neuköllner Oper, 2016.

Goehr, Lydia. "The Dangers of Satisfaction: On Songs, Rehearsals, and Repetition in *Die Meistersinger*." In *Wagner's Meistersinger: Performance, History, Representation*, edited by Nicholas Vazsonyi, 56–70. Rochester: University of Rochester Press, 2003.

Goehring, Edmund J. *Coming to Terms with Our Musical Past: An Essay on Mozart and Modernist Aesthetics*. Rochester: University of Rochester Press, 2018.

———. *Three Modes of Perception in Mozart: The Philosophical, Pastoral, and Comic in Così fan tutte*. Cambridge: Cambridge University Press, 2004.

Gossett, Philip. *Divas and Scholars: Performing Italian Opera*. Chicago: University of Chicago Press, 2006.

Grabarchuk, Alexandra. "'The Finality of Stories Such as These': Exploring Narrative and Concept in Stephen Sondheim's *Into the Woods*." In *From Stage to Screen: Musical Films in Europe and United States (1927–1961)*, edited by Massimiliano Sala, 113–24. Turnhout: Brepols, 2012.

Gracyk, Theodore. *Rhythm and Noise: An Aesthetics of Rock*. Durham: Duke University Press, 1996.

Grey, Thomas S. "Masters and Their Critics: Wagner, Hanslick, Beckmesser, and *Die Meistersinger*." In *Wagner's Meistersinger: Performance, History, Representation*, edited by Nicholas Vazsonyi, 165–89. Rochester: University of Rochester Press, 2003.

———. "Romantic Opera as 'Dramatic Ballad': *Der fliegende Holländer* and Its Generic Contexts." In *Richard Wagner: Der fliegende Holländer*, edited by Thomas S. Grey, 65–91. Cambridge: Cambridge University Press, 2000.

Gribben, Alan, ed. *Mark Twain's Adventures of Tom Sawyer and Huckleberry Finn*. Montgomery, AL: NewSouth Books, 2011.

Guck, Marion A. "Rehabilitating the Incorrigible." In *Theory, Analysis and Meaning in Music*, edited by Anthony Pople, 57–73. Cambridge: Cambridge University Press, 1994.

Gunn, Daniel P. "Free Indirect Discourse and Narrative Authority in *Emma*." *Narrative* 12, no. 1 (2004): 35–54.

Halliwell, Michael. "Narrative Elements in Opera." In *Word and Music Studies: Defining the Field*, edited by Walter Bernhart, Steven Paul Scher, and Werner Wolf, 135–53. Amsterdam: Rodopi, 1999.

———. *Opera and the Novel: The Case of Henry James*. Amsterdam: Rodopi, 2005.

Hamilton, James R. *The Art of Theater*. Malden: Wiley-Blackwell, 2007.

———. "Mimesis and Showing." In *Mimesis: Metaphysics, Cognition, Pragmatics*, edited by Gregory Currie, Petr Kotatko, and Martin Pokorny, 343–82. London: College Publications, 2012.

Hanning, Barbara Russano. "Apologia pro Ottavio Rinuccini." *Journal of the American Musicological Society* 26, no. 2 (1973): 240–62.

Hansen, Jette Barnholdt. "From Invention to Interpretation: The Prologues of the First Court Operas Where Oral and Written Cultures Meet." *Journal of Musicology* 20, no. 4 (2003): 556–96.

Harper-Scott, J. P. E. *Ideology in Britten's Operas*. Cambridge: Cambridge University Press, 2018.

———. "Made You Look! Children in *Salome* and *Death in Venice*." In *Benjamin Britten: New Perspectives on His Life and Work*, edited by Lucy Walker, 116–37. Woodbridge: Boydell, 2009.

Harris-Warrick, Rebecca. *Dance and Drama in French Baroque Opera: A History*. Cambridge: Cambridge University Press, 2016.

Hatten, Robert S. *A Theory of Virtual Agency for Western Music*. Bloomington: Indiana University Press, 2018.

Headington, Christopher. *Peter Pears: A Biography*. London: Faber, 1992.
Hefling, Stephen E. "Mahler's *Todtenfeier* and the Problem of Program Music." *19th-Century Music* 12, no. 1 (1988): 27–53.
Hennemann, Monika. "Operatorio?" In *Oxford Handbook of Opera*, edited by Helen M. Greenwald, 73–91. New York: Oxford University Press, 2014.
Henson, Karen. *Opera Acts: Singers and Performance in the Late Nineteenth Century*. Cambridge: Cambridge University Press, 2015.
Hepokoski, James. Review of *Die Tondichtungen von Richard Strauss* by Walter Werbeck. *Journal of the American Musicological Society* 51, no. 3 (1998): 603–25.
Herman, David, James Phelan, Peter J. Rabinowitz, Brian Richardson, and Robyn Warhol. "Authors, Narrators, Narration." In *Narrative Theory: Core Concepts and Critical Debates*, edited by David Herman, James Phelan, Peter J. Rabinowitz, Brian Richardson, and Robyn Warhol, 29–56. Columbus: Ohio State University Press, 2012.
Herz, Joachim. "Wagner and Theatrical Realism, 1960–1976." *Wagner* 19, no. 1 (1998): 3–33. Originally delivered as a lecture, "Die realistisch-komödiantische Wagnerinterpretation 1960–1976" (1983).
Heyworth, Peter. "Britten Tackles the Great Divide." Review of *Owen Wingrave* (Television Broadcast). *Observer*, May 16, 1971. Reprinted in Cooke, Mitchell, and Reed, eds., *Letters from a Life*, 6:433.
Hick, Darren Hudson. "Authorship, Co-Authorship, and Multiple Authorship." *Journal of Aesthetics and Art Criticism* 72, no. 2 (2014): 147–56.
Hindley, Clifford. "Love and Salvation in Britten's *Billy Budd*." *Music & Letters* 70, no. 3 (1989): 363–81.
Hirsch, E. D. *Validity in Interpretation*. New Haven: Yale University Press, 1967.
Hirsch, Foster. *Harold Prince and the American Musical Theatre*. New York: Applause, 2005.
Hobbs, Jerry R. *Literature and Cognition*. Stanford: Centre for the Study of Language and Information, 1990.
Holmes, Jessica A. "Singing beyond Hearing." *Journal of the American Musicological Society* 69, no. 2 (2016): 542–48.
Horowitz, Mark Eden, ed. *Sondheim on Music: Minor Details and Major Decisions*. Lanham: Scarecrow, 2003.
Howard, Patricia. *Gluck: An Eighteenth-Century Portrait in Letters and Documents*. Oxford: Clarendon Press, 1995.
———. *The Modern Castrato: Gaetano Guadagni and the Coming of a New Operatic Age*. New York: Oxford University Press, 2014.
———. "Myfanwy Piper's *The Turn of the Screw*: Libretto and Synopsis." In *Benjamin Britten: The Turn of the Screw*, edited by Patricia Howard, 23–62. Cambridge: Cambridge University Press, 1985.
———. "Structures: An Overall View." In *Benjamin Britten: The Turn of the Screw*, edited by Patricia Howard, 71–90. Cambridge: Cambridge University Press, 1985.
———. "*The Turn of the Screw* in the Theatre." In *Benjamin Britten: The Turn of the Screw*, edited by Patricia Howard, 126–49. Cambridge: Cambridge University Press, 1985.
Huebner, Steven. "*Tristan*'s Traces." In *Richard Wagner: Tristan und Isolde*, edited by Arthur Groos, 142–66. Cambridge: Cambridge University Press, 2011.
Hume, David. "Of the Standard of Taste." In *Four Dissertations*, 203–40. London: A. Millar, 1757.
Hunter, Mary. "Historically Informed Performance." In *Oxford Handbook of Opera*, edited by Helen M. Greenwald, 606–26. Oxford: Oxford University Press, 2014.

———. "Window to the Work, or Mirror of Our Preconceptions? Peter Sellars's Production of *Così fan tutte*." *Repercussions* 4, no. 2 (1995): 42–58.
Hutcheon, Linda. *A Theory of Adaptation*. New York: Routledge, 2006.
Hutcheon, Linda, and Michael Hutcheon. *Opera: Desire, Disease, Death*. Lincoln: University of Nebraska Press, 1996.
Irvin, Sherri. "Theatrical Performances and the Work Performed." *Journal of Aesthetic Education* 43, no. 3, Special Issue on *The Art of Theater* by James Hamilton (2009): 37–50.
Irwin, William. "Authorial Declaration and Extreme Actual Intentionalism: Is Dumbledore Gay?" *Journal of Aesthetics and Art Criticism* 73, no. 2 (2015): 141–47.
———. *Intentionalist Interpretation: A Philosophical Explanation and Defense*. Westport: Greenwood Press, 1999.
Jacobson, Daniel. "In Praise of Immoral Art." *Philosophical Topics* 25, no. 1 (1997): 155–99.
Jahn, Manfred. "Narrative Voice and Agency in Drama: Aspects of a Narratology of Drama." *New Literary History* 32, no. 3 (2001): 659–79.
James, Henry. *The Art of the Novel: Critical Prefaces*. New York: Scribner's, 1934.
———. "Owen Wingrave." In *The Complete Tales of Henry James*, edited by Leon Edel, 9:13–51. London: Rupert Hart-Davis, 1963.
———. *The Turn of the Screw: Authoritative Text, Contexts, Criticism*, edited by Deborah Esch and Jonathan Warren. New York: Norton, 1999.
———. *What Maisie Knew*. London: Penguin, 1985.
Janese, Branden. "*Hamilton* Roles Are This Rapper's Delight." *Wall Street Journal*. Last modified July 7, 2015. https://www.wsj.com/articles/hamilton-roles-are-this-rappers-delight-1436303922.
Jones, Andrew V. "Staging a Handel Opera." *Early Music* 34, no. 2 (2006): 277–88.
Juhl, P. D. *Interpretation: An Essay in the Philosophy of Literary Criticism*. Princeton: Princeton University Press, 1980.
Kania, Andrew. "Against the Ubiquity of Fictional Narrators." *Journal of Aesthetics and Art Criticism* 63, no. 1 (2005): 47–54.
———. "All Play and No Work: An Ontology of Jazz." *Journal of Aesthetics and Art Criticism* 69, no. 4 (2011): 391–403.
———. "Making Tracks: The Ontology of Rock Music." *Journal of Aesthetics and Art Criticism* 64, no. 4 (2006): 401–14.
———. Review of *Art as Performance* by David Davies. *Mind* 114, no. 453 (2005): 137–41.
Karl, Gregory. "Structuralism and the Musical Plot." *Music Theory Spectrum* 19, no. 1 (1997): 13–34.
Kelly, Elaine. "Imagining Richard Wagner: The Janus Head of a Divided Nation." *Kritika* 9, no. 4 (2008): 799–829.
Kennedy, Michael. *Britten*. Rev. ed. Oxford: Oxford University Press, 2001.
Kenton, Edna. "Henry James to the Ruminant Reader: *The Turn of the Screw*." In *A Casebook on Henry James's The Turn of the Screw*, edited by Gerald Willen, 102–14. New York: Thomas Y. Crowell Company, 1960. Originally published in *The Arts* (1924).
Kerman, Joseph. *Opera as Drama*. Rev. ed. Berkeley: University of California Press, 1988. Originally published in 1956.
Kieran, Matthew. "Forbidden Knowledge: The Challenge of Immoralism." In *Art and Morality*, edited by José Bermúdez and Sebastian Gardner, 56–73. New York: Routledge, 2003.
Kinderman, William. "Hans Sachs's 'Cobbler's Song,' and the 'Bitter Cry of the Resigned Man.'" *Journal of Musicological Research* 13, no. 3–4 (1993): 161–84.

Kitcher, Philip. *Deaths in Venice: The Cases of Gustav von Aschenbach*. New York: Columbia University Press, 2013.
Kivy, Peter. "Action and Agency." In *Antithetical Arts: On the Ancient Quarrel between Literature and Music*, 119–56. Oxford: Clarendon Press, 2009.
———. "How Did Mozart Do It? Living Conditions in the World of Opera." In *The Fine Art of Repetition: Essays in the Philosophy of Music*, 160–77. Cambridge: Cambridge University Press, 1993.
———. "Opera Talk: A Philosophical 'Phantasie.'" *Cambridge Opera Journal* 3, no. 1 (1991): 63–77.
———. "Realistic Song in the Movies." *Journal of Aesthetics and Art Criticism* 71, no. 1 (2013): 75–80.
Klaiber, Isabell. "Multiple Implied Authors: How Many Can a Single Text Have?" *Style* 45, no. 1 (2011): 138–52.
Knapp, Raymond. *The American Musical and the Performance of Personal Identity*. Princeton: Princeton University Press, 2006.
———. "*Assassins, Oklahoma!* and the 'Shifting Fringe of Dark Around the Camp-Fire.'" *Cambridge Opera Journal* 16, no. 1 (2004): 77–101.
Knapp, Raymond, and Mitchell Morris. "The Filmed Musical." In *The Oxford Handbook of the American Musical*, edited by Raymond Knapp, Mitchell Morris, and Stacy Wolf, 136–51. Oxford: Oxford University Press, 2011.
Knapp, Steven, and Walter Benn Michaels. "Against Theory." *Critical Inquiry* 8, no. 4 (1982): 723–42.
———. "Against Theory 2: Hermeneutics and Deconstruction." *Critical Inquiry* 14, no. 1 (1987): 49–68.
Köppe, Tilmann, and Jan Stühring. "Against Pan-Narrator Theories." *Journal of Literary Semantics* 40, no. 1 (2011): 59–80.
Kozloff, Sarah. *Invisible Storytellers: Voice-Over Narration in American Fiction Film*. Berkeley: University of California Press, 1988.
Kreuzer, Gundula. *Curtain, Gong, Steam: Wagnerian Technologies of Nineteenth-Century Opera*. Berkeley: University of California Press, 2018.
Lanser, Susan S. "The 'I' of the Beholder: Equivocal Attachments and the Limits of Structuralist Narratology." In *A Companion to Narrative Theory*, edited by James Phelan and Peter J. Rabinowitz, 206–19. Malden: Blackwell, 2005.
Larson, Jonathan. *Rent* (Libretto). In *The New American Musical: An Anthology from the End of the Century*, edited by Wiley Hausam, 99–228. New York: Theatre Communications Group, 2003.
Law, Joe K. "The Dialogics of Operatic Adaptation: Reading Benjamin Britten." *A Yearbook of Interdisciplinary Studies in the Fine Arts* 1 (1989): 407–27.
———. "'We Have Ventured to Tidy Up Vere': The Adapters' Dialogue in *Billy Budd*." *Twentieth-Century Literature* 31, no. 2–3 (1985): 297–314.
Lebrecht, Norman. "Singers in Uproar over Critical Body Insults at Glyndebourne." Slipped Disc. Last modified May 19, 2014. https://slippedisc.com/2014/05/singers-in-uproar-at-critical-body-insults-at-glyndebourne.
Leech-Wilkinson, Daniel. *The Changing Sound of Music: Approaches to Studying Recorded Musical Performance*. London: CHARM, 2009. Last modified February 14, 2010. https://www.charm.kcl.ac.uk/studies/chapters/intro.html.
———. "Compositions, Scores, Performances, Meanings." *Music Theory Online* 18, no. 1 (2012). https://www.mtosmt.org/issues/mto.12.18.1/mto.12.18.1.leech-wilkinson.php.

Leech-Wilkinson, Daniel, and Mine Doğantan-Dack. "Ontology and Aesthetics of Musical Performance: Towards a Paradigm Shift or Radical Practice." Abstract to a paper presented at the 3rd Annual Conference of the Royal Musical Association Music and Philosophy Study Group. King's College, London, July 19–20, 2013.

Leskov, Nikolai. "The Lady Macbeth of Mtsensk." Translated by Richard Pevear and Larissa Volokhonsky. In *The Enchanted Wanderer*, 3–46. New York: Knopf, 2013. Originally published in Russian in 1865.

Leve, James. *Kander and Ebb*. New Haven: Yale University Press, 2009.

Levin, David J. *Richard Wagner, Fritz Lang, and the Nibelungen: The Dramaturgy of Disavowal*. Princeton: Princeton University Press, 1998.

———. *Unsettling Opera: Staging Mozart, Verdi, Wagner, and Zemlinsky*. Chicago: University of Chicago Press, 2007.

Levinson, Jerrold. "Film Music and Narrative Agency." In *Contemplating Art: Essays in Aesthetics*, 143–83. Oxford: Oxford University Press, 2006.

———. "Intention and Interpretation in Literature." In *The Pleasures of Aesthetics: Philosophical Essays*, 175–213. Ithaca: Cornell University Press, 1996.

———. "Music as Narrative and Music as Drama." In *Contemplating Art: Essays in Aesthetics*, 129–42. Oxford: Oxford University Press, 2006.

———. "Song and Music Drama." In *The Pleasures of Aesthetics: Philosophical Essays*, 42–59. Ithaca: Cornell University Press, 1996.

———. "Titles." In *Music, Art, and Metaphysics: Essays in Philosophical Aesthetics*, 159–78. Oxford: Oxford University Press, 2011.

———. "What a Musical Work Is." In *Music, Art, and Metaphysics: Essays in Philosophical Aesthetics*, 63–88. Oxford: Oxford University Press, 2011. Originally published in 1980.

Liszka, James Jakób. *The Semiotic of Myth: A Critical Study of the Symbol*. Bloomington: Indiana University Press, 1989.

A Little Too Cozy Program. Toronto: Against the Grain Theatre, 2016.

Livingston, Paisley. *Art and Intention: A Philosophical Study*. Oxford: Clarendon Press, 2005.

———. *Cinema, Philosophy, Bergman: On Film as Philosophy*. Oxford: Oxford University Press, 2009.

———. "Cinematic Authorship." In *Film Theory and Philosophy*, edited by Richard Allen and Murray Smith, 132–48. Oxford: Clarendon Press, 1997.

———. "Nested Art." *Journal of Aesthetics and Art Criticism* 61, no. 3 (2003): 233–45.

Loppert, Max. "Tim Albery." *Opera* (November 1993): 1286–93.

Lovensheimer, Jim. "Stephen Sondheim and the Musical of the Outsider." In *Cambridge Companion to the Musical*, edited by William A. Everett, 181–96. Cambridge: Cambridge University Press, 2002.

———. "Texts and Authors." In *Oxford History of the American Musical*, edited by Raymond Knapp, Mitchell Morris, and Stacy Wolf, 20–32. New York: Oxford University Press, 2011.

Lurie, Kathryn. "Playing the Man Who Shot Hamilton." *Wall Street Journal*. Last modified August 6, 2015. https://www.wsj.com/articles/playing-the-man-who-shot-hamilton-1438896589.

Machlin, Paul S. "Wagner, Durand and *The Flying Dutchman*: The 1852 Revisions of the Overture." *Music & Letters* 55, no. 4 (1974): 410–28.

Magee, Bryan. *The Tristan Chord: Wagner and Philosophy*. New York: Metropolitan Books, 2000.

Malloy-Chirgwin, Antonia. "*Gloriana*: Britten's 'Slighted Child.'" In *Cambridge Companion to Benjamin Britten*, edited by Mervyn Cooke, 113–34. Cambridge: Cambridge University Press, 1999.

Mankin, Nina. "The *PAJ* Casebook #2: *Into the Woods*." *Performing Arts Journal* 11, no. 1 (1988): 46–66.
Mann, Thomas. *Death in Venice*. In *Death in Venice and Seven Other Stories*, 3–73. Translated by H. T. Lowe-Porter. New York: Vintage, 1989. Originally published as *Der Tod in Venedig* (1912).
———. *Letters of Thomas Mann, 1889–1955*. Translated by Richard Winston and Clara Winston. New York: Knopf, 1971.
March, Kevin. *Les feluettes* (Full Score). Unpublished score, 2016.
Marissen, Michael. *The Social and Religious Designs of J. S. Bach's Brandenburg Concertos*. Princeton: Princeton University Press, 1995.
Martin, Robert K. "Saving Captain Vere: *Billy Budd* from Melville's Novella to Britten's Opera." *Studies in Short Fiction* 23, no. 1 (1986): 49–56.
Martínez Bonati, Félix. *Fictive Discourse and the Structures of Literature: A Phenomenological Approach*. Ithaca: Cornell University press, 1981.
Maslon, Laurence, ed. *American Musicals, 1927–1949: The Complete Books & Lyrics of Eight Broadway Classics*. New York: Library of America, 2014.
Matravers, Derek. *Fiction and Narrative*. Oxford: Oxford University Press, 2014.
———. "Fictional Assent and the (So-Called) 'Puzzle of Imaginative Resistance.'" In *Imagination, Philosophy, and the Arts*, edited by Matthew Kieran and Dominic McIver Lopes, 91–106. London: Routledge, 2003.
Maus, Fred E. "Music as Drama." In *Music and Meaning*, edited by Jenefer Robinson, 105–30. Ithaca: Cornell University Press, 1998.
———. "Music as Narrative." *Indiana Theory Review* 12 (1991): 1–41.
Maus, Fred E., Marion A. Guck, Charles Fisk, James Webster, Alicyn Warren, and Edward T. Cone. "Edward T. Cone's *The Composer's Voice*: Elaborations and Departures." *College Music Symposium* 29 (1989): 1–80.
McClary, Susan. "The Blasphemy of Talking Politics during a Bach Year." In *Music and Society: The Politics of Composition, Performance, and Reception*, edited by Susan McClary and Richard Leppert, 13–62. Cambridge: Cambridge University Press, 1987.
———. *The Passions of Peter Sellars*. Ann Arbor: University of Michigan Press, 2019.
McClatchie, Stephen. "Benjamin Britten, *Owen Wingrave* and the Politics of the Closet; Or, 'He Shall Be Straightened out at Paramore.'" *Cambridge Opera Journal* 8, no. 1 (1996): 59–75.
———. "Canonizing the Dutchman: Bayreuth, Wagnerism, and *Der fliegende Holländer*." In *Richard Wagner: Der fliegende Holländer*, edited by Thomas S. Grey, 151–65. Cambridge: Cambridge University Press, 2000.
McGill, Craig M. "'It Might Have Been Sophisticated Film Music': The Role of the Orchestra in Stage and Screen Versions of *Sweeney Todd, the Demon Barber of Fleet Street*." *Studies in Musical Theatre* 8, no. 1 (2014): 5–26.
McHugh, Dominic. "'I'll Never Know Exactly Who Did What': Broadway Composers as Musical Collaborators." *Journal of the American Musicological Society* 68, no. 3 (2015): 605–52.
McKellar, Shannon. "Re-Visioning the 'Missing' Scene: Critical and Tonal Trajectories in Britten's *Billy Budd*." *Journal of the Royal Musical Association* 122, no. 2 (1997): 258–80.
McLaughlin, Robert L. *Stephen Sondheim and the Reinvention of the American Musical*. Jackson: University Press of Mississippi, 2016.
McMillin, Scott. *The Musical as Drama*. Princeton: Princeton University Press, 2006.
Mele, Alfred R. "Deciding to Act." *Philosophical Studies* 100, no. 1 (2000): 81–108.
———. *Springs of Action: Understanding Intentional Behaviour*. Oxford: Oxford University Press, 1992.

Melville, Herman. *Billy Budd, Sailor: An Inside Narrative*. Chicago: Chicago University Press, 1962.
Miller, Robin A. "The Prologue in the Seventeenth-Century Venetian Operatic Libretto: Its Dramatic Purpose and the Function of Its Characters." PhD diss., University of North Texas, 1998.
Miller, Scott. "*Assassins* and the Concept Musical." In *Stephen Sondheim: A Casebook*, edited by Bonnie Gordon, 187–204. New York: Garland, 1997.
Millington, Barry. "*Ariadne auf Naxos*, Opera Review: Ingenious Staging Mixes Comedy with the Mythic." *Evening Standard*. Last modified June 26, 2017. https://www.standard.co.uk/go/london/arts/ariadne-auf-naxos-opera-review-ingenious-staging-mixes-comedy-with-the-mythic-a3681536.html.
———. "Bayreuth Festival." Review of Katharina Wagner's *Meistersinger* and Tankred Dorst's *Ring*. *Wagner Journal* 1, no. 3 (2007): 74–84.
———. "Nuremburg Trial: Is There Anti-Semitism in *Die Meistersinger*?" *Cambridge Opera Journal* 3, no. 3 (1991): 247–60.
———. "Taking Wagner Seriously." Review of Katharina Wagner's *Meistersinger* and Stefan Herheim's *Parsifal*. *Wagner Journal* 2, no. 3 (2008): 63–72.
———. "'A Theatre of Generosity.'" Interview with Keith Warner. *Wagner Journal* 1, no. 3 (2007): 64–73.
Miranda, Lin-Manuel, and Jeremy McCarter. *Hamilton: The Revolution*. New York: Grand Central Publishing, 2016.
Mitchell, Donald. "A *Billy Budd* Notebook (1979–1991)." In *Benjamin Britten: Billy Budd*, edited by Mervyn Cooke and Philip Reed, 111–34. Cambridge: Cambridge University Press, 1993.
———. "*Owen Wingrave* and the Sense of the Past." In *Cradles of the New: Writings on Music, 1951–1991*, edited by Mervyn Cooke, 419–38. London: Faber, 1995.
———. "Violent Climates." In *Cambridge Companion to Benjamin Britten*, edited by Mervyn Cooke, 188–216. Cambridge: Cambridge University Press, 1999.
Monahan, Seth. "Action and Agency Revisited." *Journal of Music Theory* 57, no. 2 (2013): 321–71.
Monteverdi, Claudio. *Claudio Monteverdi Madrigals*. Book 8: Madrigali Guerrieri et Amorosi. Edited by Francesco Malipiero. Translation by Stanley Appelbaum. New York: Dover, 1991.
Moran, Richard. "The Expression of Feeling in Imagination." *Philosophical Review* 103, no. 1 (1994): 75–106.
Morris, Christopher. "Wagnervideo." *Opera Quarterly* 27, no. 2–3 (2011): 235–55.
Morrison, Richard. "*Ariadne* on the Emergency Ward." *Times*. May 21, 2013.
Morrison, Simon. *Russian Opera and the Symbolist Movement*. Berkeley: University of California Press, 2002.
Mueller, John. "Fred Astaire and the Integrated Musical." *Cinema Journal* 24, no. 1 (1984): 28–40.
Müller, Ulrich. "Regietheater/Director's Theater." In *Oxford Handbook of Opera*, edited by Helen M. Greenwald, 582–605. New York: Oxford University Press, 2014.
Muus, Arne. "'The Minstrel Boy to the War Is Gone': Father Figures and Fighting Sons in Britten's *Owen Wingrave*." In *Benjamin Britten: New Perspectives on His Life and Work*, edited by Lucy Walker, 97–115. Woodbridge: Boydell, 2009.
Nattiez, Jean-Jacques. "Can One Speak of Narrative Music?" *Journal of the Royal Musical Association* 115, no. 2 (1990): 240–57.

———. *Music and Discourse: Toward a Semiology of Music.* Translated by Carolyn Abbate. Princeton: Princeton University Press, 1990. Originally published as *Musicologie générale et sémiologie* (1987).

———. *Wagner Androgyne: A Study in Interpretation.* Translated by Stewart Spencer. Princeton: Princeton University Press, 1993. Originally published in French as *Wagner androgyne* (1990).

———. "Y a-t-il une diégèse musicale?" In *Musik und Verstehen*, edited by Peter Faltin and Hans-Peter Reinecke, 247–57. Cologne: Arno Volk Verlag, 1973.

Neville, Don J. "*La clemenza di Tito*: Metastasio, Mazzolà, and Mozart." *Studies in Music from the University of Western Ontario* 1 (1976): 124–48.

Newcomb, Anthony. "Action and Agency in Mahler's Ninth Symphony, Second Movement." In *Music and Meaning*, edited by Jenefer Robinson, 131–53. Ithaca: Cornell University Press, 1997.

———. "Narrative Archetypes and Mahler's Ninth Symphony." In *Music and Text: Critical Inquiries*, edited by Steven Paul Scher, 118–36. Cambridge: Cambridge University Press, 1992.

Nisbet, Ian. "Transposition in Jonathan Larson's *Rent*." *Studies in Musical Theatre* 5, no. 3 (2011): 225–44.

Noble, Jeremy. "Old Haunts." Review of *Owen Wingrave* (Covent Garden Premiere). *Sunday Telegraph*, May 13, 1973. Reprinted in Cooke, Mitchell, and Reed, eds., *Letters from a Life*, 6:547.

Nouvel, Walter. *Igor Stravinsky: An Autobiography*. New York: Simon and Schuster, 1936.

Obey, André. *Le viol de Lucrèce*. Paris: Nouvelles éditions latines, 1931.

Parakilas, James. "Musical Historicism in *The Queen of Spades*." In *Tchaikovsky and His Contemporaries: A Centennial Symposium*, edited by Alexander Mihailovic, 177–85. Westport: Greenwood Press, 1999.

Parker, Roger. *Remaking the Song: Operatic Visions and Revisions from Handel to Berio*. Berkeley: University of California Press, 2006.

———. "Verdi and *La traviata*: Two Routes to Realism." In *La traviata*, edited by Gary Kahn, 25–37. London: Overture Publishing, 2013.

Penner, Nina. "Intentions in Theory and Practice." *Music & Letters* 99, no. 3 (2018): 448–70.

———. "Opera Singing and Fictional Truth." *Journal of Aesthetics and Art Criticism* 71, no. 1 (2013): 81–90.

———. "Rethinking the Diegetic/Nondiegetic Distinction in the Film Musical." *Music and the Moving Image* 10, no. 3 (2017): 3–20.

Perroux, Alain. "La réalité pour métaphore: Entretien avec Peter Sellars." In *Tristan et Isolde à l'aube du XXIe siècle: Trois visions pour une oeuvre mythique*, edited by Alain Perroux, 68–73. Genève: Labor et Fides, 2005.

Pfister, Manfred. *The Theory and Analysis of Drama*. Translated by John Halliday. Cambridge: Cambridge University Press, 1988. Originally published as *Das Drama* (1977).

Picard, Anna. "*Tristan und Isolde*, Opera Bastille, Paris – Maggini Quartet, Purcell Room, London: Big Themes, Big Voices, Enormous Videos." Review of Peter Sellars's *Tristan* (Opéra national de Paris). *Independent*. Last modified May 1, 2005. https://www.independent.co.uk/arts-entertainment/music/reviews/tristan-und-isolde-opeacutera-bastille-paris-maggini-quartet-purcell-room-london-490619.html.

Piper, Myfanwy. *Owen Wingrave* (Libretto). In *The Operas of Benjamin Britten: The Complete Librettos*, edited by David Herbert, 329–50. New York: Columbia University Press, 1979.

———. *The Turn of the Screw* (Libretto). In *The Operas of Benjamin Britten: The Complete Librettos*, edited by David Herbert, 231–48. New York: Columbia University Press, 1979.

———. "Writing for Britten." In *The Operas of Benjamin Britten: The Complete Librettos*, edited by David Herbert, 8–21. New York: Columbia University Press, 1979.

Plato. *The Republic*. Edited by G. R. F. Ferrari. Translated by Tom Griffith. Cambridge: Cambridge University Press, 2000.

Plomer, William. *Curlew River* (Libretto). In *The Operas of Benjamin Britten: The Complete Librettos*, edited by David Herbert, 281–94. New York: Columbia University Press, 1979.

———. *Gloriana* (Libretto). In *The Operas of Benjamin Britten: The Complete Librettos*, edited by David Herbert, 207–30. New York: Columbia University Press, 1979.

Ponech, Trevor. "Moral Agency, Artistic Immorality, and Critical Appreciation: Lars von Trier's *The Idiots*." In *Cine-Ethics: Ethical Dimensions of Film Theory, Practice, and Spectatorship*, edited by Jinhee Choi and Mattias Frey, 163–77. New York: Routledge, 2013.

———. *What Is Non-Fiction Cinema? On the Very Idea of Motion Picture Communication*. Boulder: Westview Press, 1999.

Poriss, Hilary. *Changing the Score: Arias, Prima Donnas, and the Authority of Performance*. Oxford: Oxford University Press, 2009.

Porter, Andrew. "Britten's *Billy Budd*." *Music & Letters* 33, no. 2 (1952): 111–18.

Rabinowitz, Peter J. "'The Absence of Her Voice from That Concord': The Value of the Implied Author." *Style* 45, no. 1 (2011): 99–108.

Reed, Philip. "From First Thoughts to First Night: A *Billy Budd* Chronology." In *Benjamin Britten: Billy Budd*, edited by Mervyn Cooke and Philip Reed, 42–73. Cambridge: Cambridge University Press, 1993.

Rice, John A. "Mazzolà's Revision." In *W. A. Mozart: La clemenza di Tito*, 31–44. Cambridge: Cambridge University Press, 1991.

———. *Mozart on the Stage*. Cambridge: Cambridge University Press, 2009.

Richardson, Brian. "Introduction." *Style* 45, no. 1, Special Issue: Implied Author: Back from the Grave or Simply Dead Again (2011): 1–10.

———. "Point of View in Drama: Diegetic Monologue, Unreliable Narrators, and the Author's Voice on Stage." *Comparative Drama* 22, no. 3 (1988): 193–214.

———. "Voice and Narration in Postmodern Drama." *New Literary History* 32, no. 3 (2001): 681–94.

Rieger, Eva. "'I Married Eva': Gender Construction and *Die Meistersinger*." Translated by Nicholas Vazsonyi. In *Wagner's Meistersinger: Performance, History, Representation*, edited by Nicholas Vazsonyi, 209–25. Rochester: University of Rochester Press, 2003.

Risi, Clemens. "The Gestures of the Dutchman: Wagner's Staging Instructions, 1852 and Today." Translated by Jake Fraser. *Opera Quarterly* 28, no. 3–4 (2012): 159–71.

———. "Opera in Performance: In Search of New Analytical Approaches." *Opera Quarterly* 27, no. 2–3 (2011): 283–95.

———. "Performing Wagner for the Twenty-First Century." *New Theatre Quarterly* 29, no. 4 (2013): 349–59.

———. "Shedding Light on the Audience: Hans Neuenfels and Peter Konwitschny Stage Verdi (and Verdians)." *Cambridge Opera Journal* 14, no. 1–2 (2001): 201–10.

Rochlitz, Hanna. "'I *Have* Read *Billy Budd*': The Forster–Britten Reading(s) of Melville." In *Literary Britten: Words and Music in Benjamin Britten's Vocal Works*, edited by Kate Kennedy, 296–317. Woodbridge: Boydell, 2018.

———. *Sea-Changes: Melville—Forster—Britten*. Göttingen: Universitätsverlag Göttingen, 2012.

Romberg, Bertil. *Studies in the Narrative Technique of the First-Person Novel.* Translated by Michael Taylor and Harold H. Borland. Stockholm: Almqvist and Wiksell, 1962.

Roth, Marc. "Staging 'The Master's' Works: Wagner, Appia, and Theatrical Abuse." *Theatre Research International* 5, no. 2 (1980): 138–57.

Rupprecht, Philip. "Agency Effects in the Instrumental Drama of Musgrave and Birtwistle." In *Music and Narrative since 1900*, edited by Michael L. Klein and Nicholas Reyland, 189–215. Bloomington: Indiana University Press, 2012.

———. *Britten's Musical Language.* New York: Cambridge University Press, 2001.

———. "Tonal Stratification and Uncertainty in Britten's Music." *Journal of Music Theory* 40, no. 2 (1996): 311–46.

Rutherford, Susan. *The Prima Donna and Opera, 1815–1930.* Cambridge: Cambridge University Press, 2006.

———. *Verdi, Opera, Women.* Cambridge: Cambridge University Press, 2013.

Ryan, Marie-Laure. "Meaning, Intent, and the Implied Author." *Style* 45, no. 1 (2011): 29–47.

Rye, Matthew. "Keep Calm and Carry on Singing: Love and Art Overcome Wartime Adversity in Glyndebourne's *Ariadne*." bachtrack. Last modified June 26, 2017. https://bachtrack.com/review-ariadne-naxos-thoma-davidsen-glueckert-glyndebourne-june-2017.

Sadie, Stanley. "Owen Wingrave." Review of Television Broadcast. *Musical Times* 112, no. 1541 (1971): 663, 665–66.

Saltz, David Z. "When Is the Play the Thing? Analytic Aesthetics and Dramatic Theory." *Theatre Research International* 20, no. 3 (1995): 266–76.

———. "Why Performance Theory Needs Philosophy." *Journal of Dramatic Theory and Criticism* 16, no. 1 (2001): 149–54.

Sater, Steven. *Spring Awakening* (Libretto). New York: Theatre Communications Group, 2007.

Schafer, Murray. "British Composers in Interview: Benjamin Britten." In *Britten on Music*, edited by Paul Kildea, 223–32. Oxford: Oxford University Press, 2008. Originally published in *British Composers in Interview* (1963).

Scott, Derek B. "Musical Theater(s)." In *Oxford Handbook of Opera*, edited by Helen M. Greenwald, 53–72. New York: Oxford University Press, 2014.

Scruton, Roger. *Death-Devoted Heart: Sex and the Sacred in Wagner's Tristan and Isolde.* Oxford: Oxford University Press, 2004.

Sebesta, Judith. "Of Fire, Death, and Desire: Transgression and Carnival in Jonathan Larson's *Rent*." *Contemporary Theatre Review* 16, no. 4 (2006): 419–38.

Sellars, Peter. "Director's Notes." In *Hercules* Program, 2–3. Toronto: Canadian Opera Company, 2014.

Sellors, C. Paul. "Collective Authorship in Film." *Journal of Aesthetics and Art Criticism* 65, no. 3 (2007): 263–71.

Seymour, Claire. "Glyndebourne's Wartime *Ariadne auf Naxos*." *Opera Today*. Last modified June 27, 2017. http://www.operatoday.com/content/2017/06/glyndebournes_w.php.

———. *The Operas of Benjamin Britten: Expression and Evasion.* Woodbridge: Boydell, 2004.

Shaw, George Bernard. *The Perfect Wagnerite: A Commentary on the Niblung's Ring.* New York: Dover, 1967. Originally published in 1898.

Shawe-Taylor, Desmond. "Haunted House." Review of *Owen Wingrave* (Covent Garden Premiere). *Sunday Times*, May 13, 1973. Reprinted in Cooke, Mitchell, and Reed, eds., *Letters from a Life*, 6:549.

Sheppard, W. Anthony. *Revealing Masks: Exotic Influences and Ritualized Performance in Modernist Music Theater.* Berkeley: University of California Press, 2001.

Shevtsova, Maria. *Dodin and the Maly Drama Theatre: Process to Performance*. London: Routledge, 2004.
Shostakovich, Dmitri. "My Opera, *Lady Macbeth of Mtzensk*." *Modern Music* 12, no. 1 (1934): 23–30.
Slugan, Mario. "Some Thoughts on Controlling Fictional Narrators in Fiction Film." *American Society for Aesthetics Graduate E-Journal* 6, no. 2 (2014): 1–7.
Smart, Mary Ann. *Mimomania: Music and Gesture in Nineteenth-Century Opera*. Berkeley: University of California Press, 2004.
Smith, Murray. *Engaging Characters: Fiction, Emotion, and the Cinema*. Oxford: Clarendon Press, 1995.
———. *Film, Art, and the Third Culture: A Naturalized Aesthetics of Film*. Oxford: Oxford University Press, 2017.
———. "Gangsters, Cannibals, Aesthetes; or, Apparently Perverse Allegiances." In *Passionate Views: Thinking about Film and Emotion*, edited by Carl Plantinga and Greg Smith, 217–38. Baltimore: Johns Hopkins University Press, 1999.
———. "Just What Is It That Makes Tony Soprano Such an Appealing, Attractive Murderer?" In *Ethics at the Cinema*, edited by Ward E. Jones and Samantha Vice, 66–90. Oxford: Oxford University Press, 2011.
Smith, Sam. "*Ariadne auf Naxos* @ Glyndebourne Festival Opera, Lewes." musicOMH. Last modified June 28, 2017. http://www.musicomh.com/classical/reviews-classical/ariadne-auf-naxos-glyndebourne-festival-opera-lewes-2.
Smither, Howard E. "Oratorio." *Grove Music Online*. Last modified 2001. https://www.oxfordmusiconline.com/subscriber/article/grove/music/20397.
Sollich, Robert. "Staging Wagner—and Its History: *Die Meistersinger von Nürnberg* on a Contemporary Stage." *Wagner Journal* 3, no. 1 (2009): 5–13.
Sondheim, Stephen. *Finishing the Hat: Collected Lyrics (1954–1981)*. New York: Knopf, 2010.
Sondheim, Stephen, and James Lapine. *Into the Woods* (Libretto). New York: Theatre Communications Group, 1987.
Sondheim, Stephen, and John Weidman. *Assassins* (Libretto). New York: Theatre Communications Group, 1991.
Sondheim, Stephen, and Hugh Wheeler. *Sweeney Todd: The Demon Barber of Fleet Street* (Libretto). New York: Dodd, Mead, & Co., 1979.
Sondheim, Stephen, Hugh Wheeler, James Lapine, Burt Shevelove, and Larry Gelbart. *Four by Sondheim, Wheeler, Lapine, Shevelove and Gelbart*. New York: Applause, 2000.
Spalding, Frances. "Dramatic Invention in Myfanwy Piper's Libretto for *Owen Wingrave*." In *Benjamin Britten: New Perspectives on His Life and Work*, edited by Lucy Walker, 86–96. Woodbridge: Boydell, 2009.
Staël, Madame de. *De l'Allemagne*. 5 vols. Paris: Hachette, 1959. Originally published in 1813.
Stecker, Robert. "Film Narration, Imaginative Seeing, and Seeing-In." *Projections* 7, no. 1 (2013): 147–54.
Stein, Erwin. "*Billy Budd*." In *Benjamin Britten: A Commentary on His Work from a Group of Specialists*, edited by Donald Mitchell and Hans Keller, 198–210. London: Rockliff, 1952.
Stock, Kathleen. "Free Indirect Style and Imagining from the Inside." In *Art, Mind, and Narrative: Themes from the Work of Peter Goldie*, edited by Julian Dodd, 103–20. Oxford: Oxford University Press, 2016.
———. *Only Imagine: Fiction, Interpretation, and Imagination*. Oxford: Oxford University Press, 2017.
Strachey, Lytton. *Elizabeth and Essex: A Tragic History*. New York: Harcourt, 1928.

Stravinsky, Igor. *Oedipus Rex* (Full Score). London: Boosey & Hawkes, 1949.
———. "Some Ideas about My Octuor." In *Stravinsky: The Composer and His Works* by Eric Walter White, 2nd ed., 574–77. Berkeley: University of California Press, 1979. Originally published in English in 1924.
Swain, Joseph P. "*A Little Night Music*: The Cynical Operetta." In *Oxford Handbook of Sondheim Studies*, edited by Robert Gordon, 309–18. New York: Oxford University Press, 2014.
Swayne, Steven. "Hearing Sondheim's Voices." PhD diss., University of California Berkeley, 1999.
———. *How Sondheim Found His Sound*. Ann Arbor: University of Michigan Press, 2005.
Talbot, Michael. "Introduction." In *The Musical Work: Reality or Invention?* edited by Michael Talbot, 1–13. Liverpool: Liverpool University Press, 2000.
Tanner, Michael. "*Ariadne auf Naxos* at Glyndebourne – How Can an Opera Go So Wrong?" *Spectator*. Last modified May 29, 2013. https://www.spectator.co.uk/2013/06/opera-review-ariadne-auf-naxos.
———. "Richard Wagner and Hans Sachs." In *Richard Wagner: Die Meistersinger von Nürnberg*, edited by John Warrack, 83–97. Cambridge: Cambridge University Press, 1994.
Taruskin, Richard. "From Fairy Tale to Opera in Four Moves." In *On Russian Music*, 214–22. Berkeley: University of California Press, 2009.
———. "The Great Symbolist Opera." In *On Russian Music*, 114–24. Berkeley: University of California Press, 2009.
———. "*The Queen of Spades*." *Grove Music Online*. Last modified 2002. https://www.oxfordmusiconline.com/grovemusic/view/10.1093/gmo/9781561592630.001.0001/omo-9781561592630-e-5000004733.
———. "Setting Limits." In *The Danger of Music and Other Anti-Utopian Essays*, 447–65. Berkeley: University of California Press, 2009.
———. "Shostakovich and the Inhuman." In *Defining Russia Musically: Historical and Hermeneutical Essays*, 468–543. Princeton: Princeton University Press, 1997.
———. *Stravinsky and the Russian Traditions: A Biography of the Works through Mavra*. 2 vols. Berkeley: University of California Press, 1996.
Terasti, Eero. *Signs of Music: A Guide to Musical Semiotics*. Berlin: Mouton, 2002.
Tessing Schneider, M. "From Metastasio to Mazzolà: Clemency and Pity in *La clemenza di Tito*." In *Mozart's La clemenza di Tito: A Reappraisal*, edited by M. Tessing Schneider and Ruth Tatlow, 56–96. Stockholm: Stockholm University Press, 2018.
Thelwell, Chinua. "Who Tells Your Story? *Hamilton*, Future Aesthetics, and Haiti." In *Theater and Cultural Politics for a New World*, edited by Chinua Thelwell, 109–21. London: Routledge, 2017.
Thom, Paul. "Aesthetics of Opera." *Philosophy Compass* 6, no. 9 (2011): 575–84.
Thompson, Kirsten Moana. "Falling in (to) Color." *Moving Image* 15, no. 1 (2015): 62–84.
Thomson-Jones, Katherine. "The Literary Origins of the Cinematic Narrator." *British Journal of Aesthetics* 47, no. 1 (2007): 76–94.
Tomlinson, Gary. *Metaphysical Song: An Essay on Opera*. Princeton: Princeton University Press, 1999.
Treadwell, James. "Reading and Staging Again." *Cambridge Opera Journal* 10, no. 2 (1998): 205–20.
———. "The *Ring* and the Conditions of Interpretation: Wagner's Writing, 1848 to 1852." *Cambridge Opera Journal* 7, no. 3 (1995): 207–31.
Ubersfeld, Anne. *Reading Theatre*. Edited by Paul Perron and Patrick Debbèche. Translated by Frank Collins. Toronto: University of Toronto Press, 1999. Originally published as *Lire le théâtre 1* (1996).

Umezawa, Aria. "Director's Notes." In *Venus & Adonis* and *Pygmalion* Program. Montréal: Opera McGill, 2014.

———. "Met's *Otello* Casting Begs the Question: Is Whitewash Better than Blackface?" *Globe and Mail*. Published August 7, 2015. Last modified March 25, 2018. https://www.theglobeandmail.com/opinion/mets-otello-casting-begs-the-question-is-whitewash-better-than-blackface/article25879634/?arc404=true.

Vaget, Hans Rudolf. "'Du warst mein Freund von je': The Beckmesser Controversy Revisited." In *Wagner's Meistersinger: Performance, History, Representation*, edited by Nicholas Vazsonyi, 190–208. Rochester: University of Rochester Press, 2003.

Valencia, Mark. "Review: *Ariadne auf Naxos* (Glyndebourne)." ClassicalSource. Last modified June 26, 2013. http://www.whatsonstage.com/brighton-theatre/reviews/review-ariadne-auf-naxos-glyndebourne_43962.html.

Valori, Charlotte. "Method in Its Madness: Strauss' *Ariadne auf Naxos*, Glyndebourne." Operissima (blog). Last modified June 4, 2013. https://operissima.org/2013/06/04/method-in-its-madness-strauss-ariadne-auf-naxos-glyndebourne/.

Wagner, Katharina. "The Destruction of All That Is Good and Sublime?" *Wagner News* 182 (October 2007): 17–20.

Wagner, Richard. *Gesammelte Schriften*. 2nd ed. 10 vols. Hildesheim: Olms, 1976.

———. "Judaism in Music." *Wagner* 9, no. 1 (1988): 20–33. Originally published as "Das Judenthum in der Musik" (1850).

———. *Opera and Drama*. Translated by William Ashton Ellis. Lincoln: University of Nebraska Press, 1995. Originally published as *Oper und Drama* (1851).

Wagner, Richard. "Remarks on the Performance of the Opera *Der fliegende Holländer*." Translated by Thomas S. Grey. In *Richard Wagner: Der fliegende Holländer*, edited by Thomas S. Grey, 193–200. Cambridge: Cambridge University Press, 2000.

———. *Richard Wagner Sämtliche Werke*. Volume 4: *Der fliegende Holländer*. Edited by Egon Voss. Mainz: Schott, 2000.

———. *Richard Wagner Sämtliche Werke*. Volume 8: *Tristan und Isolde*. Edited by Isolde Vetter and Egon Voss. Mainz: Schott, 1992.

———. *Richard Wagner to Mathilde Wesendonck*. Translated by William Ashton Ellis. New York: Scribner's, 1905.

Walsh, Stephen. *Stravinsky: Oedipus Rex*. Cambridge: Cambridge University Press, 1993.

Walton, Kendall L. "Categories of Art." *Philosophical Review* 79, no. 3 (1970): 334–67.

———. *Mimesis as Make-Believe: On the Foundations of the Representational Arts*. Cambridge, MA: Harvard University Press, 1990.

———. "On the (So-Called) Puzzle of Imaginative Resistance." In *The Architecture of the Imagination: New Essays on Pretence, Possibility, and Fiction*, edited by Shaun Nichols, 137–48. Oxford: Clarendon Press, 2006.

Walton, Kendall L., and Michael Tanner. "Morals in Fiction and Fictional Morality." *Proceedings of the Aristotelian Society* 68 (1994): 27–66.

Warrack, John. "Box for the Opera." Review of *Owen Wingrave* (Television Broadcast). *Sunday Telegraph*, May 16, 1971. Reprinted in Cooke, Mitchell, and Reed, eds., *Letters from a Life*, 6:432–33.

———. "The Sources and Genesis of the Text." In *Richard Wagner: Die Meistersinger von Nürnberg*, edited by John Warrack, 1–37. Cambridge: Cambridge University Press, 1994.

Weiner, Marc A. *Richard Wagner and the Anti-Semitic Imagination*. Lincoln: University of Nebraska Press, 1995.

Wells, Elizabeth A. "'The New Woman': Lady Macbeth and Sexual Politics in the Stalinist Era." *Cambridge Opera Journal* 13, no. 2 (2001): 163–89.

Werbeck, Walter. *Die Tondichtungen von Richard Strauss*. Tutzing: Hans Schneider, 1996.
White, Eric Walter. *Stravinsky: The Composer and His Works*, 2nd ed. Berkeley: University of California Press, 1979.
White, Kimberly. *Female Singers on the French Stage, 1830–1848*. Cambridge: Cambridge University Press, 2018.
Whitesell, Lloyd. "Britten's Dubious Trysts." *Journal of the American Musicological Society* 56, no. 3 (2003): 637–94.
Whittall, Arnold. "Billy Budd." *Grove Music Online*. Last modified 2002. https://www.oxfordmusiconline.com/subscriber/article/grove/music/O009276.
———. "Breaking the Balance." *Musical Times* 137, no. 1843 (1996): 4–7.
———. "Britten's Lament: The World of *Owen Wingrave*." *Music Analysis* 19, no. 2 (2000): 145–66.
———. *The Music of Britten and Tippett: Studies in Themes and Techniques*. Cambridge: Cambridge University Press, 1982.
———. "'Twisted Relations': Method and Meaning in Britten's *Billy Budd*." *Cambridge Opera Journal* 2, no. 2 (1990): 145–71.
Widdicombe, Gilliam. Review of *Owen Wingrave* (Covent Garden Premiere). *Financial Times*, May 11, 1973. Reprinted in Cooke, Mitchell, and Reed, eds., *Letters from a Life*, 6:544–47.
Wiebe, Heather. *Britten's Unquiet Pasts: Sound and Memory in Postwar Reconstruction*. Cambridge: Cambridge University Press, 2012.
Wikipedia. "Regietheater." Accessed March 5, 2020. https://en.wikipedia.org/wiki/Regietheater.
Wiles, David. "Eighteenth-Century Acting: The Search for Authenticity." In *The Theatre of Drottningholm—Then and Now: Performance between the 18th and 21st Centuries*, edited by Willmar Sauter and David Wiles, 185–213. Stockholm: Taberg Media Group, 2014.
Wilson, Edmund. "The Ambiguity of Henry James." In *A Casebook on Henry James's The Turn of the Screw*, edited by Gerald Willen, 115–53. New York: Thomas Y. Crowell Company, 1960. Originally published in 1934.
Wilson, George M. *Narration in Light: Studies in Cinematic Point of View*. Baltimore: Johns Hopkins University Press, 1986.
———. *Seeing Fictions in Film: The Epistemology of Movies*. Oxford: Oxford University Press, 2011.
Wimsatt, William K., and Monroe C. Beardsley. "The Intentional Fallacy." *Sewanee Review* 54, no. 3 (1946): 468–88.
Woodruff, Paul. *The Necessity of Theater: The Art of Watching and Being Watched*. Oxford: Oxford University Press, 2008.
Xu, Lufan. "Why *Regieoper*? Katharina Wagner's *Die Meistersinger von Nürnberg* as a Meta-Production." In *Music on Stage*, edited by Fiona Jane Schopf, 28–45. Newcastle upon Tyne: Cambridge Scholars, 2015.
Yacobi, Tamar. "Narrative Structure and Fictional Mediation." *Poetics Today* 8, no. 2 (2007): 335–72.
Zadan, Craig, ed. *Sondheim & Co*. New York: Harper & Row, 1986.

Productions (listed by director)

Albery, Tim. *Billy Budd*. Conducted by David Atherton. Featuring Philip Langridge (Vere), Sir Thomas Allen (Billy), and Richard van Allan (Claggart). English National Opera, 1988. Recorded by BBC Television. Released on DVD by Image Entertainment, 2001.

Arden, Michael. *Spring Awakening*. Conducted by Jared Stein. Featuring Sandra Mae Frank (Wendla), Katie Boeck (Voice of Wendla), Austin McKenzie (Melchior), Daniel N. Durant (Moritz), and Rustin Cole Sailors (Voice of Moritz). ASL Translation: Elizabeth Greene, Anthony Natale, and Shoshannah Stern. Deaf West Theatre, Los Angeles, 2014. Remounted on Broadway, 2015.

Armfield, Neil. *Peter Grimes*. Conducted by Johannes Debus. Featuring Anthony Dean Griffey (Grimes) and Ileana Montalbetti (Ellen). Canadian Opera Company, 2013. Production premiere: 2003.

Baumgarten, Sebastian. Mozart's Requiem and Armin Petras and Jan Kauenhowen's play *In der Schlangengrube*. Komische Oper Berlin, 2008.

Chéreau, Patrice. *Der Ring des Nibelungen*. Conducted by Pierre Boulez. Featuring Donald McIntyre (Wotan) and Gwyneth Jones (Brünnhilde). Bayreuth, 1976. Recorded for TV in 1979–80. Video direction by Brian Large. Released on DVD by Deutsche Grammophon, 2005.

Coleman, Basil. *Billy Budd*. London Symphony Orchestra and Ambrosian Opera Chorus conducted by Charles Mackerras. Featuring Peter Pears (Vere), Peter Glossop (Billy), and Michael Langdon (Claggart). Produced by BBC Television. Video direction by Cedric Messina. Broadcast on December 11, 1966. Released on DVD by Decca, 2008.

Denoncourt, Serge. *Les feluettes* by Kevin March and Michel Marc Bouchard. Conducted by Timothy Vernon. Featuring Étienne Dupuis (Simon), Jean-Michel Richer (Vallier), and James McLennan (Bilodeau). Opéra de Montréal, 2016.

Diamond, Tom. *The Turn of the Screw*. Conducted by Andrew Bisantz. Featuring Jessica Scarlato (Governess), Aaron Sheppard (Narrator), and Frank Mutya (Quint). Opera McGill, Montréal, 2011.

Dodin, Lev. *The Queen of Spades*. Conducted by Gennadi Rozhdestvensky. Featuring Vladimir Galouzine (Herman), Hasmik Papian (Liza), Irina Bogatcheva (Countess), and Nikolai Putilin (Tomsky). Opéra national de Paris, 2005. Video direction by François Roussillon. Released on DVD by Arthaus Musik, 2011. Production premiere: Dutch National Opera, 1998.

Gerhardt, Fabian. *Iris Butterfly*. Based on Pietro Mascagni and Luigi Illica's *Iris*. Textual adaptation by dramaturg Bernhard Glocksin. Musical arrangement by Alexandra Barkovskaya and Derik Listemann. Conducted by Hans-Peter Kirchberg. Featuring SuJin Bae in the title role. Neuköllner Oper, Berlin, 2016.

Girard, François. *Siegfried*. Conducted by Johannes Debus. Featuring Stefan Vinke (Siegfried). Canadian Opera Company, 2016. Production premiere: 2005.

Graham, Colin. *Owen Wingrave*. English Chamber Orchestra conducted by Benjamin Britten. Featuring Benjamin Luxon (Owen). Produced by BBC Television. Video direction by Brian Large. Broadcast on May 16, 1971. Released on DVD by Decca, 2009.

Guth, Claus. *Le nozze di Figaro*. Vienna Philharmonic conducted by Nikolaus Harnoncourt. Featuring Ildebrando D'Arcangelo (Figaro) and Anna Netrebko (Susanna). Salzburg Festival, 2006. Video direction by Brian Large. Attended revival at the Canadian Opera Company, 2016, conducted by Johannes Debus.

Herz, Joachim. *Der fliegende Holländer*. Gewandhaus Orchestra and Leipzig Opera Chorus conducted by Rolf Reuter. Featuring Anna Prucnal (Senta, visual), Gerda Hannemann (Senta, voice), Fred Düren (Dutchman, visual), and Rainer Lüdecke (Dutchman, voice). Opera film produced by DEFA, 1964.

Ivany, Joel. *A Little Too Cozy*. Based on Mozart and Da Ponte's *Così fan tutte*. Libretto by Joel Ivany. Musical arrangement by conductor Topher Mokrzewski. Featuring Cairan Ryan (Donald L. Fonzo). Against the Grain Theatre, Toronto, 2016.

Kail, Thomas. *Hamilton*. Conducted by Alex Lacamoire. Featuring Lin-Manuel Miranda (Hamilton), Leslie Odom Jr. (Burr), Phillipa Soo (Eliza), Renée Elise Goldsberry (Angelica), Christopher Jackson (Washington), and Daveed Diggs (Lafayette and Jefferson). Public Theater, New York City, 2015.

Konwitschny, Peter. *Die Meistersinger von Nürnberg*. Textual adaptation by Peter Konwitschny. Conducted by Ingo Metzmacher. Featuring Wolfgang Schöne (Sachs), John Treleaven (Walther), and Anja Harteros (Eva). Hamburg Staatsoper, 2002.

Kupfer, Harry. *Der fliegende Holländer*. Conducted by Woldemar Nelsson. Featuring Lisbeth Balslev (Senta) and Simon Estes (Dutchman). Bayreuth Festival, 1985. Video direction by Brian Large. Released on DVD by Deutsche Grammophon, 2005. Production premiere: 1978.

———. *Orfeo ed Euridice*. Conducted by Hartmut Haenchen. Featuring Jochen Kowalski (Orfeo) and Gillian Webster (Euridice). Covent Garden, 1991. Video direction by Hans Hulscher. Released on DVD by Kultur, 2001. Production premiere: Komische Oper Berlin, 1987.

Kušej, Martin. *Don Giovanni*. Vienna Philharmonic conducted by Daniel Harding. Featuring Thomas Hampson (Don Giovanni). Salzburg Festival, 2006. Video direction by Karina Fibich. Released on DVD by Decca, 2006. Production premiere: 2002.

———. *Lady Macbeth of the Mtsensk District*. Conducted by Mariss Jansons. Featuring Eva-Maria Westbroek (Katerina), Christopher Ventris (Sergei), and Vladimir Vaneev (Boris). Dutch National Opera, 2006. Video direction by Thomas Grimm. Released on DVD by Opus Arte, 2006.

Lazar, Benjamin. *Cadmus et Hermione*. Conducted by Vincent Dumestre. Featuring André Morsch (Cadmus) and Claire Lefilliâtre (Hermione). Opéra comique, Paris, 2008. Video direction by Martin Fraudreau. Released on DVD by Alpha, 2009.

Lepage, Robert. *Nightingale and Other Short Fables*. Conducted by Jonathan Darlington. Featuring Olga Peretyatko (Nightingale). Canadian Opera Company, 2009.

McDermott, Phelim. *The Enchanted Island*. Music by Handel, Vivaldi, Rameau, Purcell, and Campra. Libretto by Jeremy Sams, inspired by *The Tempest* and *A Midsummer Night's Dream*. Conducted by William Christie. Featuring David Daniels (Prospero), Joyce DiDonato (Sycorax), Danielle de Niese (Ariel), and Luca Pisaroni (Caliban). Metropolitan Opera, 2011. Video direction by Barbara Willis Sweete. Released on DVD by Virgin Classics, 2012.

Mendes, Sam. *Cabaret*. Textual adaptation by Sam Mendes. Musical adaptation by Michael Gibson. Featuring Alan Cumming (Emcee). Donmar Warehouse, London, 1993. Reworked for Broadway, 1998.

Miller, Jonathan. *Le nozze di Figaro*. Conducted by James Levine. Featuring Cecilia Bartoli (Susanna). Metropolitan Opera, 1998. Live broadcast from November 11 available for streaming from Met Opera on Demand.

Neuenfels, Hans. *Die Fledermaus*. Textual adaptation by Hans Neuenfels. Mozarteum Orchestra Salzburg conducted by Marc Minkowski. Featuring David Moss (Orlofsky). Salzburg Festival, 2001. Video direction by Don Kent. Released on DVD by Arthaus Musik, 2003.

Paulus, Diane. *The Gershwins' Porgy and Bess*. Textual adaptation by Suzan-Lori Parks. Musical arrangement by Diedre L. Murray. Featuring Audra McDonald (Bess) and Norm Lewis (Porgy). American Repertory Theater, 2011.

———. *Die Zauberflöte*. Conducted by Johannes Debus. Featuring Michael Schade (Tamino) and Isabel Bayrakdarian (Pamina). Canadian Opera Company, 2011.

Prince, Harold. *A Little Night Music*. Conducted by Jonathan Tunick. Featuring Len Cariou (Fredrik) and Elizabeth Taylor (Desirée). Film musical, 1977. Released on DVD by New World, 2007.

Pynkoski, Marshall. *Persée*. Choreography by Jeannette Zingg. Tafelmusik Baroque Orchestra and Chamber Choir conducted by Hervé Niquet. Featuring Rufus Müller (Persée), Monica Whicher (Mérope), Nathalie Paulin (Andromède), and Michael Chioldi (Méduse). Opera Atelier, Toronto, 2000.

Schenk, Otto. *Die Walküre*. Conducted by James Levine. Featuring Jessye Norman (Sieglinde) and Gary Lakes (Siegmund). Metropolitan Opera, 1989. Video direction by Brian Large. Released on DVD by Deutsche Grammophon, 2002. Production premiere: 1986.

Sellars, Peter. *Così fan tutte*. Vienna Philharmonic conducted by Craig Smith. Featuring Sanford Sylvan (Alfonso). Recorded in 1990. Released on DVD by Decca, 2005. Production premiere: Pepsico Summerfare Festival, Purchase, NY, 1986.

———. *Hercules*. Conducted by Harry Bicket. Featuring Eric Owens (Hercules), Alice Coote (Dejanira), David Daniels (Lichas), Richard Croft (Hyllus), and Lucy Crow (Iole). Canadian Opera Company, 2014. Production premiere: Chicago Lyric, 2011.

———. *The Indian Queen*. With other music by Purcell and additional text by Rosario Aguilar. Conducted by Teodor Currentzis. Featuring Julia Bullock in the title role. Teatro Real de Madrid, 2013. Released on DVD by Sony Classical, 2016. Production premiere: Perm Opera, 2013.

———. *Le nozze di Figaro*. Vienna Philharmonic. Conducted by Craig Smith. Featuring Sanford Sylvan (Figaro) and Jeanne Ommerlé (Susanna). Recorded in 1990. Released on DVD by Decca, 2005. Production premiere: Pepsico Summerfare Festival, Purchase, NY, 1988.

———. *Tristan und Isolde*. Conducted by Johannes Debus. Featuring Ben Heppner (Tristan), Melanie Diener (Isolde), and Franz-Josef Selig (King Marke). Canadian Opera Company, 2013. Production premiere: Opéra national de Paris, 2006.

Syberberg, Hans-Jürgen. *Parsifal*. Conducted by Armin Jordan. Featuring Michael Kutter and Karin Krick (Parsifal, image) and Reiner Goldberg (Parsifal, voice). Opera film, 1982. Released on DVD by Image Entertainment, 1999.

Tcherniakov, Dmitri. *Don Giovanni*. Conducted by Louis Langrée. Featuring Bo Skovhus (Don Giovanni) and Kristine Opolais (Elvira). Aix-en-Provence, 2010. Video direction by Andy Sommer. Released on DVD by Bel Air Classiques, 2013. Attended revival at the Canadian Opera Company, 2015.

Thoma, Katharina. *Ariadne auf Naxos*. Conducted by Vladimir Jurowski. Featuring Kate Lindsey (Composer) and Soile Isokoski (Prima Donna). Glyndebourne, 2013. Video direction by François Roussillon. Released on DVD by Opus Arte, 2014. Production premiere: 2007.

Umezawa, Aria. *The Barber of Cowtown*. Based on Rossini and Cesare Sterbini's *Il barbiere di Siviglia*. Textual adaptation by Aria Umezawa. Conducted by Trevor Chartrand. Cowtown Opera, Calgary, 2014.

———. *Pygmalion*. Conducted by Hank Knox. Featuring John Cook (Pygmalion), Juliana Urban (Statue), and Anna Bond (Céphise). Opera McGill, Montréal, 2014.

Wagner, Katharina. *Die Meistersinger von Nürnberg*. Dramaturg: Robert Sollich. Conducted by Sebastian Weigle. Featuring Franz Hawlata (Sachs), Klaus Florian Vogt (Walther), and Michael Volle (Beckmesser). Bayreuth Festival, 2008. Video direction by Andreas Morell. Released on DVD by Opus Arte, 2010. Production premiere: 2007.

Young, Patrick Eakin. *Orlando lunaire*. Mash-up of Handel's *Orlando* and Schoenberg's *Pierrot lunaire*. Classical Music Consort conducted by Ashiq Aziz. Featuring Carla Huhtanen and Scott Belluz. Opera Erratica, Toronto, 2010.

INDEX

Abbate, Carolyn: on communication in opera, xxi, 32–33, 35–36; on fictional authorship of orchestral music, 48, 84n27, 110–11; on *mise-en-abyme* songs, 47, 83n17; on narrative, xvi, 1–2, 4, 7; on Wagner's narration scenes, 45
Adamo, Mark, 47
Adorno, Theodor W., 228, 229
Against the Grain Theatre, 173, 179, 238–39
agents: and narratives, 3, 13, 15, 18, 34–35
Albery, Tim, xxiii, 108n28, 184, 197–98, 206–7, 211–12, 238
alignment. *See* character-focused narration
All About Eve, 42, 49, 82n6
allegiance, 142, 160n101; in *Assassins*, 149–50, 154, 246; and ethics, 149–53, 154; in *Der fliegende Holländer*, 220; in *Lady Macbeth*, 151, 152–53, 154, 246; in *Die Meistersinger*, 228, 230–31, 233–34; in *Owen Wingrave*, 142–44
Almén, Byron, xvi, 1, 2–4, 13, 17, 19n5
Amadis, 78, 87n77
American Idiot, 77
L'amour des trois oranges, 78, 81, 88n78
analytic philosophy. *See* philosophy, analytic
Appia, Adolphe, 184, 185–86, 212nn7–8
L'apprenti sorcier, 2, 12
Arden, Michael, 234–35
Ariadne auf Naxos, 61–62, 81; production by Katharina Thoma, 169–71, 175–76, 179
aria substitution/insertion, 164–65, 171–72, 177–78, 181n20
Armfield, Neil, 216, 217, 218–19
Arnold, Samuel James, 171–72
Artaud, Antonin, 171
Assassins: and allegiance, 149–50, 154, 246; assassins' twisted perspective in, 79, 148–49, 159n78; Balladeer in, 78–80, 150; and ethics, 80, 81, 145–46, 148, 149–50; quotations and allusions in, 147–49
Atys, 75
audience expansion, xxiii–xxiv, 217, 234–39

audio dissolve, 84n34
audiovisual fictions, 28, 29–30, 36, 244
aural fictions, 28
author figures (authorial narrators), 42, 74–76, 80, 81, 82n5, 216, 218–19
authors: as narrators, xvi, 7, 43, 82n3, 99–101. *See also* authorship; implied author; orchestral narration: as authorial commentary
authorship, 102–6, 108n33

Bach, Johann Sebastian, 3
Barber of Cowtown, The, 165, 180n19
Il barbiere di Siviglia, 164–65, 181n20
Barthes, Roland, 4, 5, 6, 245
Bartoli, Cecilia, 178, 180n17
Baumgarten, Sebastian, 23, 37n1
Bayreuth Festival, 91, 186–87, 224, 226, 230–34, 236–37, 241n43
Beardsley, Monroe C., 5
Beethoven, Ludwig van, 17
bel canto, 178
Bellérophon, 75
Berghaus, Ruth, 187
Berlioz, Hector, 97–98
Bernstein, Leonard, 63, 81, 85n42, 93
Besch, Anthony, 208
Beyer, Barbara, 172–73
Billy Budd: Billy's final aria in, 197–99, 200–202, 205–6; Forster's contributions to, 71, 102, 104, 206, 207, 215nn44–45; and Melville's novel, 69–70, 71, 207, 215n45; music-text conflicts in, 102, 198–99, 203–6; Peter Pears in, 66, 70–71, 197; production by Tim Albery, xxiii, 184, 197–98, 206–7, 211–12, 238; productions by Basil Coleman, 197; Vere as frame narrator in, 66, 69–71, 86n57, 196–98, 206–7; Vere-Claggart convergence in, 71–74, 86n62, 91, 211
Bishop, Henry, 165, 171–72
Bloch, Ernst, xxiii, 231
Booth, Wayne C., 5–6, 101

273

Boris Godunov, 45
Bouchard, Michel Marc, 50, 51
Brecht, Bertolt, 62, 81, 189, 190–92
Brett, Philip, 143, 145, 199
Britten, Benjamin, 62, 66, 158n58. *See also specific operas*

Cabaret, 49, 77; production by Sam Mendes, xxvin16
Cadmus et Hermione: production by Benjamin Lazar, 167
Calcagno, Mauro, 80
Calico, Joy, 192, 225
Cambridge Handel Opera Group, 167, 181n25
Campana, Alessandra, 112, 141
Canadian Opera Company, 105–6, 174, 187–89, 192–93, 217, 218–19, 241n37
Carnegy, Patrick, 186, 230
Carroll, Noël, 23–24
Casablanca, 31, 32, 38n23
casting, 27, 161, 235; and race, 30–31, 38n18, 226
Castor et Pollux, 75, 80
character-focused narration, xxi, 114; and artistic value, 143–44, 145; and audience response, 112, 115, 141–42, 149–50, 154, 190, 193, 246; aural perceptions, 110–11, 116–17, 131–33, 136, 188; emotional alignment, 117–19, 121–22, 126, 129, 131, 152; epistemic alignment, 47, 133, 136; in film, 115–16; and lighting, 185–86, 188–89, 192–93; in literature, 111–12, 113, 114–15; and staging, 112, 184, 185, 193–94, 206, 208; visual perceptions, 112, 116, 189–90
characters, 33–35, 36; psychological depth of, 117–19, 121–22, 126, 156n29. *See also* character-focused narration
character-to-character storytelling, 44–47, 80, 83n17, 94
Chatman, Seymour, 1, 42–43
Chéreau, Patrice, 187
Chicago Lyric Opera, 174–75
choral narrators, 62–65, 81, 85n42, 216, 217
cinematic narrator, 42, 43–44, 89, 99
classical paradigm, xxiii, xxvin17, 184, 243; and accessibility, 237–38; operatic exceptions to, xxii, 161, 165–68, 169–70, 244; point-based version, 168–69, 177, 244; text-based version, 164, 244
Clavel-Vazquez, Adriana, 153

La clemenza di Tito, 104–5
Coleman, Basil, 197
Il combattimento di Tancredi e Clorinda, 62, 63, 84n38
conductors, 105–6. *See also specific conductors*
Cone, Edward T., xvi, 20n19, 23, 26, 84n27
Connor, Geoffrey, 208
Les contes d'Hoffmann, 48–49, 66, 85n46
Cook, Nicholas, xxvin13, 244, 246
Cooke, Mervyn, 143, 199, 205, 206
L'coq d'or, 37n12, 76
Così fan tutte: production by Peter Sellars, 163–64. See also *Little Too Cozy, A*
Cowgill, Rachel, 171
Cowtown Opera, 165
Crozier, Eric, 69, 70, 104
Curlew River, 76, 81, 87n72
Currie, Gregory, 28, 33; *Narratives and Narrators*, xix, 82nn3–5, 114–15, 141, 142, 155n11, 155n14

Dafne, 74–75, 80
dance, xx, 38n25, 168
Davies, David, xvii, xviii, 23, 180n11, 246n2; on the classical paradigm, xxvin17, 164, 168–69, 177, 244; on work ontology, 19n15, 179n4, 180n10
Davies, Stephen, xvii, xviii
Deaf West Theatre, xxiv, 27, 217, 234–36, 237, 243
Dean, Winton, 144
Death in Venice, 24, 116, 141, 143, 144, 158n57
Debus, Johannes, 105–6
Delibes, Léo, 27, 47
Dennis, David B., 228–29
Denoncourt, Serge, 50–51
Der Tod in Venedig, 24, 101–2
Diamond, Tom, xv–xvi, xxiii, 184, 208–12, 216, 237–38
Dichterliebe, 29
diegesis (Plato's use), 26
diegetic music, 35–36. *See also* nested musical performances
Diggs, Daveed, 30
directors, xvi, 103, 105–6, 167. *See also specific directors*
disposizione scenica, 112, 167, 181n24
Dodin, Lev, 184, 194, 195–96, 214nn29–30, 216, 219

Doğantan-Dack, Mine, 244
Don Giovanni: production by Dmitri Tcherniakov, 29; production by Martin Kušej, 31, 38n22, 241n44
Don Quixote (tone poem), 8–13, 15, 16
Drottningholm Palace Theatre, 181n27
Dukas, Paul, 2, 12
Duncan, Ronald, 63, 64, 103, 104
Dutch National Opera, 152, 194, 195–96

Eaton, A. W., 153
Einstein on the Beach, 25, 105
embedded performances. See nested musical performances; nested theatrical performances
Emerson, Caryl, 151
empathy, 112, 115, 141–42, 149–50, 154, 193, 246
enacting character, 26, 27
Enchanted Island, The, 173–74
English National Opera, 166, 197–98, 206–7
Die Entführung aus dem Serail, 47
"Der Erlkönig," 26
Estes, Simon, 226
Esther, 37n13
ethics: and allegiance, 149–53, 154; and artistic value, 153, 160n103; and authorial intentions, 145–46, 149–50, 152–53, 154, 159n70; and casting 30–31, 38n18, 226; and performing racist works, 229–30, 237
Eugene Onegin, 47
Euridice, 74

Face Opera II, 25, 37n8
Falstaff, 47
Felsenstein, Walter, 187
Les feluettes, 50–61, 81, 84nn31–32; nested theatrical performances in, 50–51, 56, 61, 62; production by Serge Denoncourt, 50–51; quotations of Le Martyre in, 51–56, 84n33; quotations of other works in, 56–61
Ferrarese, Adriana, 177–78
Festival d'Aix-en-Provence, 29
fidelity: and work-performances, 176–78. See also classical paradigm
Fight Club, 115, 240n25
film musicals, xx, 84n34; A Little Night Music, 216, 217, 236, 239n2; My Fair Lady, 25, 34
Die Fledermaus: production by Hans Neuenfels, 161, 163, 173, 179

Der fliegende Holländer: endings of, 220–21, 222–23, 224, 239n11; film adaptation by Joachim Herz, xxiii, 216, 219–21, 224, 225–26, 236; production by Harry Kupfer, 224–26
focalization, 114, 155n4, 155n14. See also character-focused narration
Forster, E. M.: as librettist for Billy Budd, 71, 102, 104, 206, 207, 215nn44–45; on narrative listening, 17, 22n41
Foster, Daniel H., 213n21
frame narrators, xv, 65–71, 80–81, 184, 196–98, 206–12
framework. See allegiance
free indirect discourse, 114–15, 133, 151, 155n16
Frye, Northrop, 2–3
Fuhrmann, Christina, 171–72
Fun Home, 26–27

Gaut, Berys, 23, 24, 103
Genette, Gérard, xvi; on narrative, 1, 7; on point of view, 111, 113–14, 115, 154, 155n14
Gerhardt, Fabian, 165–66
Girard, François, 184, 193–94
Glass, Philip, 25, 105
Gloriana, 121–26
Gluck, Christoph Willibald, 96–98
Glyndebourne, 38n21, 169–71
Goehr, Lydia, 242n50
Gossett, Philip, 183n45
Götterdämmerung, 45, 47, 92–93
Graham, Colin, 126, 127, 131, 157n43
Greek drama, xxi, 62, 90–91, 245
Grey, Thomas S., 241n31
Guth, Claus, 105–6, 241n44

Halliwell, Michael, 91, 99
Hamburg Staatsoper, 167
Hamilton, xx, 30, 47–48
Hamilton, James: on the ingredients model, xxii, 161, 171, 175–76; on the two-text model, 162–63
Hammerstein, Oscar, II, 228
Hampson, Thomas, 38n22
Handel, George Frideric, 25, 37n13
Harnoncourt, Nikolaus, 105
Harper-Scott, J. P. E., xviii, 141, 158n57, 199, 214n41
Harrison, Rex, 25, 34

Háry János, 66
Hennemann, Monika, 23, 37n1
Hercules: production by Peter Sellars, 174–75, 179, 238
Herz, Joachim, 220, 237; *Der fliegende Holländer* film, xxiii, 216, 219–21, 224, 225–26, 236; *Ring* cycle production, 187, 212n9
Hirsch, E. D., 20n18, 245
Hoffmansthal, Hugo von, 61–62
Horn, Charles Edward, 171–72
Howard, Patricia, 68, 208
Howard's End, 17, 22n41
Les Huguenots, 116–17
Hutcheon, Linda, 85n52, 108n31

Illica, Luigi, 112, 165–66
imaginative resistance, 141–42, 153, 154, 157n53, 246
immoralism, 160n103
implied author, 5–6, 20nn19–20, 83n11, 101–2, 108n29
L'incoronazione di Poppea, 80
Indian Queen, The: production by Peter Sellars, 166–67, 169, 173, 243
Ingalls, James F., 188–89, 192–93
ingredients model, xxii–xxiii, 171, 243; and accessibility, 238–39; and contemporary opera performances, 161, 172–76, 179, 216; and instrumental music, 244, 247n2; and pre-1850 opera performances, 171–72
instrumental music: and narrative, xvi, 2–4, 8, 12–13, 15–18; and representation, 12, 18
intentionalism, 5–6, 20n16, 20n21–22, 101–2, 245
interior monologues, 47–48
Into the Woods, 40–41, 77–78, 80
Iphigénie en Tauride, 96–98
Iris, 165–66. See also *Iris Butterfly*
Iris Butterfly, 165–66, 179, 181n21, 243
Irvin, Sherri, 175
Ivany, Joel, 173, 238–39

James, Henry, 111; "Owen Wingrave," 126–27, 129, 133, 143–44, 158n66; *The Turn of the Screw*, xv, 66–67, 85n48; *What Maisie Knew*, 111–12, 113, 114, 154
Jean de Paris, 171–72
Jurowski, Vladimir, 170

Kabuki, 62, 65
Kail, Thomas, 30
Kania, Andrew, 19n15, 43, 83n12, 180n10
King and I, The, 237
Kitcher, Philip, 101
Kivy, Peter, xviii, 4, 17, 38n23, 84n27, 156n29
Knapp, Raymond, 34, 106n8–9, 148, 150, 159n78
Kodály, Zoltán, 66
Komische Oper Berlin, 23, 37n1, 166, 187, 219, 220–21
Konwitschny, Peter, 172–73, 181n23; *Die Meistersinger* production, 167, 169, 173, 230
Kron, Lisa, 26–27
Kupfer, Harry, 224–26
Kušej, Martin, 31, 38n22, 152, 241n44

Lady Macbeth of the Mtsensk District: and allegiance, 152–53, 154, 246; and ethics, 146, 151, 153, 154; and Leskov's short story, 151–52; production by Martin Kušej, 152, 241n44
Lakmé, 27, 47
Langridge, Philip, 197, 198, 206, 207, 238
Larson, Jonathan, 76–77
Law, Joe K., 217–18
Lazar, Benjamin, 167
Leech-Wilkinson, Daniel, 244, 246
Leipzig Opera, 187, 219, 230
leitmotivs: and orchestral narration, 89, 92–94, 96, 99, 213n21
Leoncavallo, Ruggero, 76, 88n85
Lepage, Robert, 174
Levin, David, xxvin17, 45–46, 162, 163
Levine, Michael, 193–94
Levinson, Jerrold, xviii, 6, 19n15, 24, 43
libretto revision, 166–67, 171–72, 173, 196, 214n30. See also ingredients model
lighting design, 185–86, 188–89, 192–93, 197, 238
Little Night Music, A: film adaptation by Harold Prince, 216, 217, 236, 239n2
Little Too Cozy, A, 173, 179, 183n44, 238–39, 243
Little Women, 47
Livingston, Paisley, 84n28; on authorship, 61, 103–4, 105; on intentionalism, 5, 6
livrets de mise en scène, 167, 181n24
Loewe, Frederick, 34
Lully, Jean-Baptiste, 75, 78, 87n65, 87n77, 168

Madama Butterfly, 237
Mahler, Gustav, 16, 22n37, 186
Les mamelles de Tirésias, 75
Mann, Thomas, 24, 101–2, 108n23
Man of La Mancha, 48, 49–50, 62, 84n30
Manon Lescaut, 112
March, Kevin. See *Les feluettes*
marketing, 161, 173, 179, 238–39
Mascagni, Pietro, 165–66
Mauerschau, 47, 63
Mazzolà, Caterino, 104–5
McClary, Susan, 3, 5, 167
McClatchie, Stephen, 143, 240n18
McLaughlin, Robert K., 62
McMillin, Scott, 38n26
McVicar, David, 229
medium specificity, 23–24. See also instrumental music; opera
megamusicals, xx
Die Meistersinger von Nürnberg: and allegiance, 228, 230–31, 233–34; and anti-Semitism, 167, 216–17, 228–30, 241n31; production by Joachim Herz, 230; production by Katharina Wagner, xxiii, 216–17, 230–34, 236–37, 241n43; production by Peter Konwitschny, 167, 169, 173, 230; *Tristan* quotations and allusions in, 99–100, 107n16, 245
Mélange à trois, 24, 37n7
Melville, Herman, 69–70, 71, 207, 215n45
Mendes, Sam, xxviin16
La mer, 18
Messiah, 25
Metastasio, Pietro, 104
Metropolitan Opera, 30, 173–74, 178, 241n36
Meyerbeer, Giacomo, 116–17
Miller, Jonathan, 178
Millington, Barry, 228, 232, 233
mimesis (Plato's use), 26
Miranda, Lin-Manuel, 30, 47–48, 177
mise-en-abyme songs, 47, 83n17
mise-en-scène, 185, 193–94, 224
Mitchell, Donald, 71, 86n62, 158n61
moderate actual intentionalism, 6, 20n21, 101, 245
Mokrzewski, Topher, 173
Monteverdi, Claudio, 62, 63, 74, 80, 84n38
morality. See ethics
Morris, Christopher, 189–91, 193
Morris, Mitchell, 34
Morrison, Simon, 195, 214n28

Mortier, Gerard, 161
Moses und Aron, 142
Moss, David, 161
Mozart, Wolfgang Amadeus, 29; *La clemenza di Tito*, 104–5; *Le nozze di Figaro*, 35, 48, 67–68, 177–78
musical theater, xxvin16; and authorship, 102–6, 108n33; vs. opera, xix–xx, xxii, xx-vnn11–12, 38n25. See also specific musicals
Music Man, The, 148
musicology: and analytic philosophy, xvii, xviii; performative turn in, xvii, 246; and literary theory, xvi, xx, 1–2, 4; New Musicology, xvi, 4–5; and intentionalism, 4–6, 20n21
Musorgsky, Modest, 45
My Fair Lady, 25, 34

narratives: Abbate on, xvi, 1–2, 7; and agents, 3, 13, 15, 18, 34–35; Almén on, 1, 2–4, 17, 19n5; Genette on, 1, 7; and instrumental music, xvi, 2–4, 8, 12–13, 15–18; internal vs. external perspectives on, 34–35, 39n32, 141, 157n50; moderate intentionalist definition of, 18; necessity of fictional narrators to, xv, xx, 1–2, 7, 42–44, 81; and particularity, 13, 16–17, 18, 22n38
narrative theory and musicology, xvi, xx, 1–2
narrators, 8, 41; ambiguous cases of, 76–80, 81; authorial (author figures), 42, 74–76, 80, 81, 82n5, 216, 218–19; and authors, xvi, xxi, 7, 82n3, 99–101; choral, 62–65, 81, 85n42, 216, 217; and direct addresses, 42, 48, 74–75, 76–77; effaced or elusive, 41, 111–12, 127; in film, 42, 43–44, 82n6; vs. focal characters, 111–12, 154, 245–46; frame, xv, 65–71, 80–81, 184, 196–98, 206–12; internal vs. external, 41–42, 82n4, 214n32; in literature, 7, 42, 71, 82n7; as necessary to narratives, xv, xx, 1–2, 7, 42–44, 81; oral storytelling, 44–49, 80, 83n17, 94; types in opera, 77. See also nested theatrical performances; orchestral narrator; unreliable narration
Nattiez, Jean-Jacques, 12, 19n4, 19n15
nested musical performances, 36, 48–49, 84n28; in *Il barbiere di Siviglia*, 164–65; in *Der fliegende Holländer*, 225; in *Gloriana*, 121; in *Les Huguenots*, 116–17; in *Die Meistersinger*, 228, 231; in *The Queen of Spades*, 194–95

nested theatrical performances, 36, 84n28; in *Ariadne auf Naxos*, 61–62, 169; in *Les feluettes*, 50–51, 56, 61, 62; in *Iris*, 166; in *Man of La Mancha*, 49–50, 62, 84n30; in *The Queen of Spades*, 196
Neuenfels, Hans, 161, 163, 173, 179, 187
Neuköllner Oper, 165–66
New Musicology, xvi, 4–5
Nietzsche, Friedrich, xviii, 106n4
Nightingale and Other Short Fables, 174
Noh, 62, 76, 87n72
Norman, Jessye, 30
noumenal music, 35–36. *See also* orchestral narration
Le nozze di Figaro, 35, 48, 67–68, 177–78; production by Claus Guth, 105–6; production by Henry Bishop, 172, 179, 182n41; production by Jonathan Miller, 178

Oedipus Rex, 75, 81, 87n66
Offenbach, Jacques, 48–49, 66, 85n46
ontology of works. *See* works
opera: communication in, xxi, 24–25, 32–35, 36, 38n25, 136, 244; vs. musical theater, xix–xx, xxii, xxvnn11–12, 38n25; vs. oratorio, 27–31, 36; vs. song, 25–27, 28–29, 36; vs. spoken theater and film, xxi, 31–32, 36
Opera Atelier, 168, 175, 176, 178
opéra comique (genre), xix, 38n25
Opéra comique (opera house), 167
Opéra de Montréal, 50–51
Opera Erratica, 174
opera films, xx; *Billy Budd* by Basil Coleman, 197; *Der fliegende Holländer* by Joachim Herz, xxiii, 216, 219–21, 224, 225–26; *Owen Wingrave* by Colin Graham, 126, 127, 131, 157n43; *Parsifal* by Hans-Jürgen Syberberg, 27; *The Turn of the Screw* by Peter Morley, 208
Opera McGill, 208–12, 226–27
Opéra national de Paris, 187–90, 192–93
opera staging, xxvnn4–5; dream or hallucination scenes, 194, 195–96, 216, 219, 221, 224–25, 226–27, 239n13; historically informed, 167–68, 175, 181n27; as vehicle for composers' and librettists' stories, 187 (*see also* work-performances); as vehicle for directors' statements, 31, 187 (*see also* performance-works). *See also specific directors and designers*

operatic performances, 27–28; marketing of, 161, 173, 179, 238–39; of offensive works, xxii, xxiii, xxvin16, 167, 216–17, 226–34, 237, 241nn36–37; of preexisting works, *see* work-performances; revisionist, *see* performance-works
orchestral music: fictional authorship of, 48–49, 61, 84n27, 110–11. *See also* orchestral narration; orchestral narrator
orchestral narration, xv; as authorial commentary, xxi, 99–101, 126, 206; and leitmotivs, 89, 92–94, 96, 99, 213n21; and music-text conflicts, 89, 96–98, 99
orchestral narrator, xxi, 89, 90–91, 99. *See also* orchestral narration
Orfeo, 74
Orientalist operas, 165–66, 237. *See also* racism
Orlando lunaire, 174, 179
ornamentation, 178, 183n53
Owen Wingrave: alignment with Owen in, 127, 129, 131–33, 134–35, 154; alignment with Owen's family in, 133, 135, 136; framework of, 142–44, 145; and James's short story, 126–27, 129, 133, 143–44, 158n66, 212; musical parodies and caricatures in, 136–41, 142, 144, 157n47, 157n49; music of military traditions in, 128, 129, 130, 142, 143, 158n57; original television production of, 126, 127, 131, 157n43; Owen's theme in, 128–29, 131; peace aria from, 127, 142–43, 158n61; Piper's contributions to, 127, 128, 136, 144–45

Pacific 231, 18, 22n43
Pacific Overtures, 62, 65, 81, 85n45
Pagliacci, 76, 88n85
Parakilas, James, 194, 195
Parsifal: film by Hans-Jürgen Syberberg, 27
pastiche productions, 171–72, 173–74
Patti, Adelina, 165, 180n16
Paulus, Diane, xxvin16, 241n37
Pears, Peter, 66, 70–71, 105, 197, 215n50
performance-works, 171–72, 173–76, 179, 216, 230–36, 238–39, 243. *See also* ingredients model
Persée: production by Opera Atelier, 168, 175, 176
Peter Grimes, 105, 217–18; production by Neil Armfield, 216, 217, 218–19
Phelan, James, 102

phenomenal music, 35–36. *See also* nested musical performances
philosophy, analytic, xvii–xix, xxvn7, 5–6, 243–44, 245. *See also specific philosophers*
Pilgrim's Progress, 66
Piper, John, 197
Piper, Myfanwy: *Owen Wingrave*, 127, 128, 136, 144–45; *The Turn of the Screw*, 68, 85n48, 86n57, 209, 211
Plato, 26
Pocock, Isaac, 171–72
point of view, 114, 155n14. *See also* character-focused narration
Ponech, Trevor, 159n70
Porgy and Bess: production by Diane Paulus, xxvin16
Poriss, Hilary, 164–65, 180n20
Poulenc, Francis, 75
Prince, Harold, 216, 217, 239n2
program music, 18; *L'apprenti sorcier*, 2, 12; *Don Quixote*, 8–13, 15, 16; *Todtenfeier*, 16, 22n37
Puccini, Giacomo, 47, 112
puntature, 178
Purcell, Henry, 121, 166–67
Pygmalion: production by Aria Umezawa, 216, 226–27, 236, 240n25
Pynkoski, Marshall, 168

Queen of Spades, The, 46–47, 194–95, 213n23, 213n26, 213n28; production by Lev Dodin, 184, 194, 195–96, 214nn29–30, 216, 219
Quinault, Philippe, 75, 78, 87n65, 87n77

Rabinowitz, Peter J., 102
racism, xxii, xxvin16, 216–17, 226, 228–30, 237, 241n37
Rameau, Jean-Philippe, 75, 87n77
Rape of Lucretia, The, 85n51; authorship of, 103, 104; choral narrators in, 41–42, 62, 63, 64–65; and Obey's play, 63–64
Rebel without a Cause, 115–16
Regieoper, xxiii, 162, 231, 232, 236–37, 238–39, 243. *See also* ingredients model
Renard, 26
Rent, 76–77
Reuter, Rolf, 225–26
Das Rheingold, 92, 94, 96, 97
Righetti-Giorgi, Geltrude, 165, 180n15

Rimsky-Korsakov, Nikolai, 37n12, 76
Ring cycle, the: narration scenes in, 44–46, 47; orchestral narration in, 92–93, 93–94, 96, 99; production by Joachim Herz, 187, 212n9; production by Patrice Chéreau, 187; production by the Canadian Opera Company, 193–94
Rinuccini, Ottavio, 74–75
Risi, Clemens, 191, 193, 232, 241n44
Rochlitz, Hanna, 86n61, 104, 207, 215nn44–45
rock opera, xx
Roller, Alfred, 186, 187, 212n7
Rossini, Gioachino, 164–65, 177
rough hero/heroine, 153, 160n101
Rupprecht, Philip, xvi, 37n7, 85n52, 86nn61–62, 116, 214n37, 215n52
Rye, Matthew, 170, 175–76

Saltz, David Z., 162
Salzburg Festival, 31, 105–6, 161
Sater, Steven, 234, 242n51
Scarlato, Jessica, 209–10
Schenk, Otto, 30
score revision, 166–67, 171–72, 173, 177, 196, 225–26. *See also* ingredients model
Sellars, Peter: anachronistic interpretations by, 162, 163–64, 174–75; *Hercules* production, 174–75, 179, 238; *The Indian Queen* production, 166–67, 169, 173, 243; Mozart–Da Ponte trilogy, 163–64, 232; *Tristan und Isolde* production, xxiii, 184, 187–93, 238
set design, 185, 193–94, 224
sexism, xxii, 226–27
Seymour, Claire, 170–71
Shaw, George Bernard, 45, 187, 212n9
Sheik, Duncan, 234
Show Boat, 228
Siegfried, 194, 213n21; production by François Girard, 184, 193–94
sign language, 25, 235–36
singers, xxvn4, 38n21; agency of, 164–65, 178, 180n20; and authorship, 103, 105; opera vs. musical theater, xix, xxvn11. *See also* casting; *and specific singers*
singing, defined, 25
Single Man, A, 116
Singspiel, xix, 38n25, 166
Slater, Montagu, 105, 217–18
Smith, Murray, 115, 142, 154, 160n101

Smith, Sam, 170
Söhnlein, Kurt, 186
Sondheim, Stephen: narrators in, 40–41, 62, 78–80, 81, 88n79; and orchestral narration, 94, 95, 106n8. *See also specific musicals*
Spring Awakening, 234, 242n51; production by Deaf West Theatre, 27, 234–36, 237, 243
stagione system, 178
Stock, Kathleen, 20n18, 115
story-discourse distinction, 1–2
Strauss, Johann, II, 161, 163
Strauss, Richard: *Ariadne auf Naxos*, 61–62, 81; *Don Quixote*, 8–13, 15, 16
Stravinsky, Igor, 26, 62, 81, 245; Octet, 13–16, 245; *Oedipus Rex*, 75, 87n66
subjective access. *See* character-focused narration
Sun Kim, Christine, 25
surtitles, 230, 241n37
Swayne, Steven, 88n79, 148
Sweeney Todd, xxvn11, 156n27; and Bond's play, 117; orchestral narration in, 94, 95, 106nn8–9; Todd's "Epiphany" in, 117–21
Syberberg, Hans-Jürgen, 27
sympathy, 112, 141–42, 149–50, 154, 193, 246

Taruskin, Richard, 26, 88n78, 164; on *Lady Macbeth*, 151, 153; on *The Queen of Spades*, 195, 213n23, 213n28
Tchaikovsky, Pyotr Il'yich, 46–47, 194–95, 213n28
Tcherniakov, Dmitri, 29
telling about character, 26, 27, 44–47, 94
Tesori, Jeanine, 26–27
texts: vs. works, 4–5, 162, 163. *See also* two-text model
Thessaly trilogy, 42, 43
Thoma, Katharina, 169–71, 175–76
Thomson-Jones, Katherine, 42–43
T'Hooft, Sigrid, 181n27
Todtenfeier, 16, 22n37
Tosca, 47
transladaptations, 238; *The Barber of Cowtown*, 165; *A Little Too Cozy*, 173, 179, 238–39
La traviata, 33–34, 36, 47
Treadwell, James, 45
Tristan und Isolde: Appia's staging notes for, 185–86, 212n7; character-focused narration in, 110–11, 188–89; production by Peter Sellars, xxiii, 184, 187–93, 238; production by Siegfried Wagner, 186
Trouble in Tahiti, 63, 81, 85n42
Il trovatore, 46
Turn of the Screw, The, 86n57, 143, 158n57, 209, 215n50; and ambiguity, 68, 85n52, 210–11, 215n53; Governess as frame narrator in, xv, 66, 67–69, 184, 196–97, 207–8; and James's novella, xv, 66–67, 85n48, 209, 212, 245; production by Tom Diamond, xv–xvi, xxiii, 184, 208–12, 216, 237–38; productions foregrounding the "second story," 208–12
two-text model, xxii, xxvin17, 161, 162–4

Ubersfeld, Anne, 182n37
Umezawa, Aria, 38n18; *The Barber of Cowtown*, 165, 180n19; *Pygmalion* production, 216, 226–27, 236, 240n25
unreliable narration, xxiii, 46, 66–69, 198, 207, 211–12, 237–38

Valori, Charlotte, 170, 175–76
Vaughan Williams, Ralph, 66
Verdi, Giuseppe, 33–34, 36, 46, 47, 181n24, 183n53
Verfremdungseffekt, 191, 192, 193
Vestris, Lucia, 172, 182n41
Vick, Graham, 197
Le viol de Lucrèce, 63–64
visual fictions, 28
Volle, Michael, 233

Wagner, Katharina, xxiii, 216–17, 230–34, 236–37, 238, 241n43, 242n59
Wagner, Richard, 36, 107n20, 178; and anti-Semitism, 216–17, 228, 230, 240n30; and character-focused narration, 110–11, 189, 194; in East Germany, 219–21, 224–26; influence of Schopenhauer on, xviii, 185, 193; and narration scenes, 44–46, 83n18; in Nazi Germany, 187, 228–29, 232, 233, 241n42; and orchestral narration, 89, 90–91, 92–93, 93–94, 96, 99–100. *See also specific operas*
Wagner, Siegfried, 186
Wagner, Wieland, 186–87
Die Walküre, 48, 49, 93–94; production by Otto Schenk, 30
Walsh, Stephen, 75, 87n66

Walton, Kendall, 20n22, 33, 107n14
Weidman, John: *Assassins*, 78, 145–46, 149–50, 154, 246; *Pacific Overtures*, 62, 81, 85n45
Weill, Kurt, 87n69
Weiner, Marc, 228
Werktreue, xxii, xxiii, 161, 231. *See also* classical paradigm
Westbroek, Eva-Maria, 152
West Side Story, 93
What Maisie Knew, 111–12, 113, 114, 154
Whittall, Arnold, 158n61, 199, 206
Wiebe, Heather, 121
Wieler, Jossi, 173
Wilson, George, 43–44, 83n14, 115–16, 240n25
Wilson, Robert, 105
Wimsatt, William K., 5

Woolf, Luna Pearl, 24
work-performances, 161, 168, 176–78, 184, 237–38, 243. See also *Billy Budd*: production by Tim Albery; classical paradigm; *Siegfried*: production by François Girard; *Tristan und Isolde*: production by Peter Sellars; *The Turn of the Screw*: production by Tom Diamond
works, 180n10; and performances, 44 (*see also* classical paradigm); as processes vs. as products, 1, 4–5, 19n15, 162, 163, 179n4

Der Zar lässt sich photographieren, 87n69
Die Zauberflöte, 166, 241n37; production by Diane Paulus, 241n37
Zingg, Jeannette, 168

NINA PENNER is Assistant Professor of Music at Brock University in St. Catharines, Ontario.

www.ingramcontent.com/pod-product-compliance
Lightning Source LLC
Chambersburg PA
CBHW020639230426
43665CB00008B/235